CW00538375

CRIMINAL LAW REFORM AND TRANSITIONAL JUSTICE

INTERNATIONAL AND COMPARATIVE CRIMINAL JUSTICE

Series Editors:

Mark Findlay, *Institute of Criminology, University of Sydney, Australia*
Ralph Henham, *Nottingham Law School, Nottingham Trent University, UK*

This series explores the new and rapidly developing field of international and comparative criminal justice and engages with its most important emerging themes and debates. It focuses on three interrelated aspects of scholarship which go to the root of understanding the nature and significance of international criminal justice in the broader context of globalization and global governance. These include: the theoretical and methodological problems posed by the development of international and comparative criminal justice; comparative contextual analysis; the reciprocal relationship between comparative and international criminal justice and contributions which endeavor to build understandings of global justice on foundations of comparative contextual analysis.

Other titles in the series:

Codification, Macaulay and the Indian Penal Code
The Legacies and Modern Challenges of Criminal Law Reform
Edited by Wing-Cheong Chan, Barry Wright and Stanley Yeo
ISBN 978 1 4094 2442 0

Exploring the Boundaries of International Criminal Justice
Edited by Ralph Henham and Mark Findlay
ISBN 978 0 7546 4979 3

The International Criminal Court and National Courts
A Contentious Relationship
Nidal Nabil Jurdi
ISBN 978 1 4094 0916 8

The Limits of Criminal Law
A Comparative Analysis of Approaches to Legal Theorizing
Carl Constantin Lauterwein
ISBN 978 0 7546 7946 2

Criminal Law Reform and Transitional Justice
Human Rights Perspectives for Sudan

Edited by

LUTZ OETTE
School of Law, SOAS, University of London, UK;
REDRESS, London, UK

ASHGATE

Published by
Ashgate Publishing Limited
Wey Court East
Union Road
Farnham
Surrey, GU9 7PT
England

Ashgate Publishing Company
Suite 420
101 Cherry Street
Burlington
VT 05401-4405
USA

www.ashgate.com

British Library Cataloguing in Publication Data
Criminal law reform and transitional justice : human rights perspectives for Sudan. – (International and comparative criminal justice)
  1. Criminal law – Sudan. 2. Law reform – Sudan. 3. Human rights – Sudan.
  I. Series II. Oette, Lutz.
  345.6'24–dc22

Library of Congress Cataloging-in-Publication Data
Criminal law reform and transitional justice : human rights perspectives for sudan / edited by Lutz Oette.
    p. cm. – (International and comparative criminal justice)
    Includes bibliographical references and index.
    ISBN 978-1-4094-3100-8 (hardback : alk. paper) – ISBN 978-1-4094-3101-5 (ebook)
    1. Criminal justice, Administration of–Sudan. 2. Law reform – Sudan. 3. Transitional justice. 4. Human rights. I. Oette, Lutz.
    KTQ3409.C75 2011
    345.624'05–dc22

2011017230

ISBN 9781409431008 (hbk)
ISBN 9781409431015 (ebk)

Printed and bound in Great Britain by the
MPG Books Group, UK

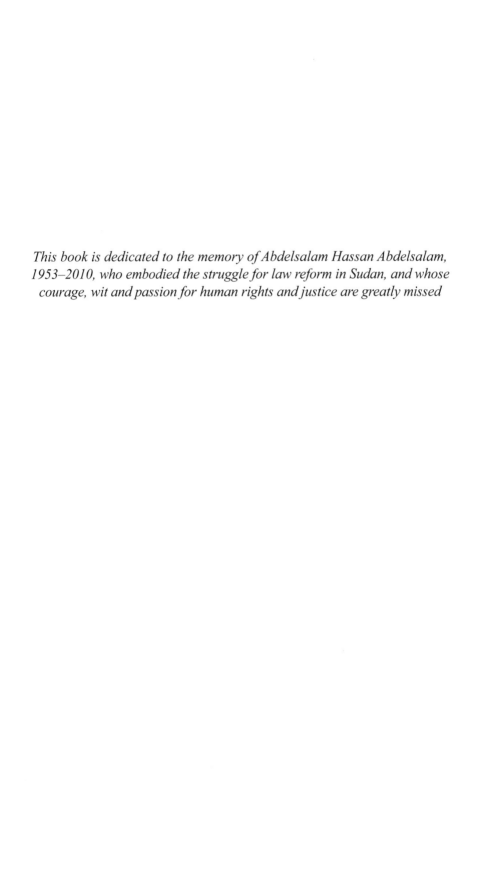

This book is dedicated to the memory of Abdelsalam Hassan Abdelsalam, 1953–2010, who embodied the struggle for law reform in Sudan, and whose courage, wit and passion for human rights and justice are greatly missed

Contents

Abbreviations

ACHPR	African Commission on Human and Peoples' Rights
ACHR	American Convention on Human Rights
AfrCHPR	African Charter on Human and Peoples' Rights
AIDS	Acquired Immune Deficiency Syndrome
AU	African Union
AUPD	African Union High-Level Panel on Darfur
CAR	Central African Republic
CAT	Committee against Torture
CEDAW	Committee on the Elimination of all Forms of Discrimination against Women
CNDP	Congrès National Pour la Défence du Peuple
CPA	Comprehensive Peace Agreement
CrPC	Criminal Procedure Code
DEVAW	Declaration on the Elimination of Violence against Women
DRC	Democratic Republic of Congo
ECHR	European Convention on Human Rights
ECtHR	European Court of Human Rights
EU	European Union
FC	Female Circumcision
FSC	Federal Shariat Court
GOS	Government of Sudan
GOSS	Government of Southern Sudan
HIV	Human Immunodeficiency Virus
HRC	Human Rights Committee
ICC	International Criminal Court
ICCPR	International Covenant on Civil and Political Rights
ICD	Independent Complaints Directorate
ICGLR	International Conference on the Great Lakes Region
ICTR	International Criminal Tribunal for Rwanda
ICTY	International Criminal Tribunal for the former Yugoslavia
IHL	International Humanitarian Law
INC	Interim National Constitution
Inter-Am. CtHR	Inter-American Court of Human Rights
JEM	Justice and Equality Movement
MMA	Muthida Majlis e Amal
NCP	National Congress Party
NCRC	National Constitutional Review Commission
NCSW	National Commission on the Status of Women

NGO	Non-Governmental Organization
NISS	National Intelligence and Security Services
NSA	National Security Act
NSS	National Security Service
PEP	Post-Exposure Prophylaxis
PPC	Pakistan's Penal Code
PSMA	Personal Status for Muslims Act
RoC	Republic of Congo
SADC	Southern African Development Community
SCPA	Sudan Criminal Procedure Act
SGBV	Sexual and gender-based violence
SPLM	Sudan Peoples' Liberation Movement
SPLM/SPLA	Sudan Peoples' Liberation Movement/Army
UHRC	Uganda Human Rights Commission
UK	United Kingdom of Great Britain and Northern Ireland
UN	United Nations
UNCAT	United Nations Convention against Torture and other Cruel, Inhuman or Degrading Treatment or Punishment
UNHCHR	United Nations High Commissioner for Human Rights
USA	United States of America
WHO	World Health Organization
WPA	Women's Protection Act

Contributors

Abdelsalam Hassan Abdelsalam was a human rights lawyer and political analyst. He worked for a number of Sudanese and international human rights organizations, including at REDRESS (from 2007 until his tragic death in 2010) where he was the Sudan legal advisor on the project for criminal law reform in Sudan. Abdesalam Hassan had played a pivotal role in advocating for law reform in Sudan since the 1980s, and was instrumental in organizing the 1999 Kampala conference that resulted in the seminal book *The Phoenix State: Civil Project in Sudan*, co-edited by Abdelsalam Hassan and Alex de Waal and published by the Red Sea Press in 2001.

Nabil Adib is a senior lawyer based in Khartoum. He has been the legal representative in a number of leading human rights cases, including before the Sudanese Constitutional Court. Nabil Adib has worked as an expert in an advisory capacity on questions of law reform in Sudan and is a member of the Advisory Committee on Criminal Law Reform in Sudan.

Ibrahim Aljazy is Associate Professor of the Faculty of Law, University of Jordan, and partner of the law firm Aljazy & Co. He is also a member of the Jordanian National Committee on the International Criminal Court in his capacity as an expert on the implementation of the ICC Rome Statute in the Middle East. Dr Aljazy has published widely on human rights and criminal law in the Middle East, including *Civil and Political Rights in the Arab Constitutions: A Comparative Analysis with Special Reference to Egypt* (University of London, 2001).

Mohamed Abdelsalam Babiker is Assistant Professor at the Faculty of Law at Khartoum University and expert on international criminal law. He has worked with several UN and AU agencies in Sudan with a particular focus on law reform and is a member of the Advisory Committee on Criminal Law Reform in Sudan. Dr Babiker is the author of *Application of International Humanitarian and Human Rights Law to the Armed Conflicts of Sudan: Complementary or Mutually Exclusive Regimes* (Intersentia, Antwerp Oxford, 2007).

Deirdre Clancy is the Co-director of the International Refugee Rights Initiative (IRRI) where she directs programmes dealing with international criminal justice and international refugee law, including engagement with African regional standards and mechanisms. She has lectured on international humanitarian law and human rights law in Ireland, Uganda and the United States and has been instrumental in the publication of a number of major reports, including IRRI's

In the Interest of Justice? Prospects and challenges for international justice in Africa, published in 2008.

Asma Abdel Halim is a graduate of the Faculty of Law, University of Khartoum, currently Assistant Professor at the department of Women and Gender Studies at the University of Toledo, Ohio. She has published widely on the protection of women's rights, including her book on *Sudanese Women in the United States: The Double Problem of Gender and Culture* (Edwin Mellen Press, New York, 2006). Dr Abdel Halim is the founder of the Sudanese Women's Rights NGO Mutawinat.

Rashida Manjoo is an advocate of the High Court of South Africa and Professor in the Department of Public Law, University of Cape Town. In recognition of her contribution to the field of combating gender discrimination and gender-based violence, Rashida Manjoo was appointed as UN Special Rapporteur on Violence against Women, Its Causes and Consequences, in 2009. Her co-authors, **Gift Kweka** and **Suzzie Onyeka Ofuani**, were LLM students in the class of 2009, University of Cape Town, South Africa. Gift Kweka is currently an assistant lecturer at the Institute of Judicial Administration – Lushoto, Tanzania, and an executive secretary to the IJA-Legal Aid and Education Trust, Lushoto. Suzzie Ofuani is currently a research fellow at the Nigerian Institute of Advanced Legal Studies, Lagos, Nigeria.

Amin M. Medani is a senior lawyer who held a number of official posts, including that of Cabinet Minister (portfolio for peace, reconciliation and elections) in the Democratic Transitional Government of Sudan, and as representative of the Regional Office of the UN High Commissioner for Human Rights of the Arab Region, Beirut. He has also played a leading role in several Sudanese, regional and international human rights organizations, and is a member of the Advisory Committee on Criminal Law Reform in Sudan. Dr Medani is the author of a number of publications, including *Crimes against International Humanitarian Law in Sudan: 1989–2000* (Dar El Mostaqbal El Arabi, Cairo 2001).

Jamil Ddamulira Mujuzi is a Ugandan lawyer and a post-doctoral fellow, Faculty of Law, University of the Western Cape 2010–2011. He has published over forty articles on human rights, international law, international humanitarian law and criminal justice, and his publications have been cited by, *inter alia*, the South African Supreme Court of Appeal, the South African High Court, and in the 2010 UN Secretary General's Report on the death penalty.

Lutz Oette is counsel at REDRESS and a lecturer in international human rights law at the School of Oriental and African Studies (SOAS), London. He has worked extensively on human rights protection, justice and the role of law in the context of repression, conflict and transition. Dr Oette leads the project for criminal law reform in Sudan at REDRESS and has published widely on human rights and justice in Sudan from an international human rights law perspective.

P.J. Schwikkard is currently the Dean of Law of the Faculty of Law, University of Cape Town. Over the past twenty years she has taught courses in gender and the law, criminal law, criminal procedure, evidence, youth justice, conflict resolution, civil procedure, legal interpretation, legal skills and special contracts, and has published widely in the fields of criminal procedure and evidence. Professor Schwikkard is one of seven legal professionals to have been appointed to the South African Law Reform Commission.

Sohail Akbar Warraich is a human rights defender with a specific focus on violence against women and laws of personal status, especially in the Muslim contexts. He has worked for various national and international human rights organizations, particularly as law coordinator for Shirkat Gah Women's Resource Centre in Pakistan, and brings to the field of law a strong interest in the interrelationship between the principles of law and the realities of people's lives.

Preface

This book is the outcome, and forms part of the ongoing work, of a number of Sudanese and international actors to promote and protect human rights in Sudan. Legislative reforms, particularly in the field of criminal law where violations are most acute, have become an important part of this endeavour. REDRESS, an international human rights organization seeking justice for torture survivors (www.redress.org), together with its Sudanese partners, has been implementing a project on criminal law reform in Sudan (www.pclrs.org) for the last five years. The book was developed in the course of this work and benefited from an expert seminar in Kampala in March 2009 attended by most of the contributing authors, as well as other Sudanese stakeholders and Ugandan experts. The seminar brought together national, regional and international experts and practitioners to share experiences and reflect on the nature of the challenges facing law reform in the context of uncertain transitions such as in Sudan. The rich discussions informed this book, which includes a chapter reflecting on the seminar proceedings.

This book is dedicated to Abdelsalam Hassan Abdelsalam, a Sudanese human rights lawyer, colleague and friend who tragically died in March 2010. He had been a pivotal figure in law reform efforts in Sudan since the 1980s, and had, together with the editor, initiated the project on criminal law reform in Sudan at REDRESS. Indeed, Abdelsalam was the designated co-editor of this book and had almost finished the chapter on the history of criminal law reform at the time of his premature death. His intellectual contribution provided the inspiration and foundation for this book, which he had hoped would constitute an important milestone and reference point in the struggle for greater human rights protection in the country he cared about passionately.

A great many individuals and organizations have contributed to the book throughout the project. I am particularly grateful to the contributing authors, who have provided a rich tapestry of analysis and practical insights from many parts of the world, providing national, regional and international perspectives. Special acknowledgment is also due to the Advisory Committee on criminal law reform in Sudan, some of whose members contributed to this book, Najlaa Ahmed, the project coordinator for the law reform project, as well as Hala Al-Karib from the Strategic Initiative for Women in the Horn of Africa (SIHA) for co-hosting the Kampala seminar. The contribution of the Sudan Human Rights Monitor (SHRM) as well as other human rights organizations and individuals that have taken a leading role or have otherwise engaged in the campaign for law reform is also greatly appreciated.

I would like to thank a number of individuals for their support in writing this book, particularly Jehangir Jelani for his valuable research assistance, Jo Baker for her editing and proofreading skills, Elham Saudi for her timely assistance, and Alison Kirk from Ashgate Publishers for her professional support. On behalf of REDRESS, I would also like to acknowledge the financial support of the UK Foreign and Commonwealth Office and the Department for International Development, without which this book would not have been possible.

Dr Lutz Oette

Introduction

Lutz Oette

The context of criminal law reform and human rights in times of transitions: Challenges for Sudan

How best to respond to major human rights violations and address their underlying structural causes is one of the main challenges in transitional periods. The term 'transitional justice' was initially conceived to refer to periods of political transition following the end of conflict or dictatorship, but is now increasingly applied to conflict- or mixed/post-conflict situations to denote the measures that ought to be taken to effectuate the intended change. In this context it may form part of a series of processes, among them peace agreements and their implementation, state-building and reconstruction. All of these processes inevitably raise the question of how they contribute to human rights protection, and of the role of law to provide the same.

The multitude of actors involved and the complexity of these processes constitute major challenges, which are often particularly acute when addressing law reform, including in the crucial area of criminal justice. Structural legacies, a lack of political commitment (which can also be due to other political priorities of various actors), institutional resistance and limited capacity are critical factors in this regard. Sudan constitutes a case that illustrates the importance of criminal law and its reform in times of uncertain transition, along with the specific substantive and political challenges that this process entails.

Since its independence in 1956, the Sudanese context has been characterized to varying degrees by political repression, violence and conflict. The political root causes for Sudan's instability have been analyzed in detail elsewhere;[1] however, there has been less focus on the role of the law in this context, which has been used both symbolically as political statement, and as an instrument of repression.[2] Laws may themselves breach human rights or may facilitate violations; they may also fail to protect those at risk or to provide for accountability and remedies in

---

1   Idris, A. 2005. *Conflict and Politics of Identity in Sudan*. New York: Palgrave MacMillan, and de Waal, A. (ed.). 2006. *War in Darfur and the Search for Peace*. Cambridge, Massachusetts: Harvard University Press.

2   A good pre-2005 analysis can be found in Abdel Salam, A.H. and de Waal, A. (eds). 2002. *The Phoenix State: Civil Society and the Future of Sudan*. Asmara: The Red Sea Press. See also Tier, A. and Badri, B. (eds). 2008. *Law Reform in Sudan: Collection of Workshop Papers*. Khartoum: Ahfad University for Women.

the case of breaches. Examples to this effect abound in Sudan. Following on from the precedent of using *Shari'a* (Islamic law) for political ends in the period from 1983–1985 during Nimeiri's dictatorship, the legislation passed since the current government came to power in 1989 has often served to entrench state control at the expense of political opposition and civil society, and to impose a societal order that reinforces gender discrimination. Efforts by Sudanese civil society and political actors in the 1990s helped to create an awareness that has contributed to the strong references to human rights and the provision for specific legislative reforms in the 2005 Comprehensive Peace Agreement (CPA) that ended the North–South conflict. The CPA was complemented by the Interim National Constitution (INC), in particular its Bill of Rights, and marked an important break: it appeared to present an enormous opportunity to bring about the legislative changes needed to foster the rule of law and to protect human rights in Sudan. Given the legacy of violence, the peace at stake, and the investment of regional and international actors in the peace process, law reform provided a litmus test for Sudan's ability to address the lack of human rights protection and justice. This process soon became intertwined with investigations by the Prosecutor of the International Criminal Court (ICC) into international crimes alleged to have been committed in Darfur, which compelled Sudan to show that it was able and willing to investigate and prosecute international crimes itself. This also prompted it to undertake some legislative reforms, particularly following the arrest warrant issued against Sudan's President al-Bashir in March 2009.

This book explores the nature, policy aspects and interrelationship of criminal law and law reform in the context of an uncertain transition from conflict to a post-conflict society. It takes an international law perspective, situating current developments in Sudan in the broader debates relating to international human rights, the rule of law and transitional justice.

Law reform forms an integral part of several interrelated processes that are simultaneously taking place in Sudan. These developments include the CPA in relation to the North–South conflict and, to a lesser degree, the Darfur peace process, as well as the Bill of Rights and the role of the Constitutional Court. The scope of processes relevant in the context of law reform also encompass the multiple efforts aimed at truth, justice and reconciliation for past and present violations in Sudan that relate to the various conflicts and the legacy of political repression. The main goals of these processes have been to secure lasting peace and to build a stable and democratic political system, of which respect for the rule of law and effective human rights protection are key indicators. The extent of reforms in the field of criminal law reflects the level of commitment of the Government of Sudan and constitutes a measurable yardstick for rights protection. A closer look at the history, nature and experiences of law reform in Sudan in their regional, cultural and political context is therefore of critical importance in informing current and future efforts.

The substantive issues and the dynamics of law reform in Sudan also hold critical lessons for other countries, particularly for societies undergoing transitions that seek to respond to serious human rights violations and systemic discrimination. These concern the type of violations that need to be addressed as a prerequisite for greater human rights protection, the challenges experienced in this regard, and the contribution of civil society in campaigning for reforms. Of particular interest from a substantive perspective are the *Shari'a* elements that have been infused in Sudan's criminal law, the legal framework governing international crimes, and the myriad laws impacting on women's rights. Conversely, the challenges experienced in other countries undergoing similar law reform efforts can serve as instructive comparative reference points for Sudanese actors in this context.

The book brings together law reform experts, advocates and academics who have worked in the field of criminal justice and human rights law, and have engaged in law reform and transitional justice efforts, largely in Sudan and its neighbouring countries, but also elsewhere, particularly in Africa and Asia. As the analysis and experiences of practitioners shared in this book make clear, the task of law reform as a means of strengthening human rights protection is particularly acute in countries that face legacies of institutionalized violations. Sudan is a primary example of a country that urgently needs to address the same if it is to avoid reinforcing its long-running cycle of conflict and violations.

Overview: Structure and contents

This book: (i) situates the Sudanese situation in broader debates about the interplay of peace processes, transitional justice and rule of law promotion; (ii) assesses law reform efforts in African states and countries with a Muslim majority, with particular reference to Sudan in its historical, political, legal and civil society context; (iii) examines to what extent reforms have addressed the main areas of violations and concerns from an international law perspective; and (iv) draws on the experiences of countries facing similar challenges with a view to identifying lessons in respect of the use of law reform as a tool to advance human rights protection. The book is divided into two main parts. Part One, entitled 'Perspectives on Law Reform, Transitional Justice and Human Rights', provides the contextual background, informed by an international law perspective. Part Two, 'Reforming Sudan's Criminal Laws: Challenges and Comparative Experiences', examines the normative framework, challenges and experiences in relation to four areas of primary human rights concern: repressive legislation; arrest, detention and fair trial; accountability for international crimes; and criminal law and gender-based violence. A brief overview introduces each theme and sets out relevant international standards and developments, and is complemented by substantive chapters that provide Sudanese, comparative and regional perspectives.

The first chapter, written by Lutz Oette, examines the various processes that come into play during times of transition, including uncertain and incomplete ones, such as in Sudan. It considers the nature and interrelationship of the implementation of peace agreements, 'transitional justice' measures, constitutional changes and rule of law initiatives with a view to better understanding how they interact and facilitate or hinder the goal of enhanced human rights protection and justice. Law reform, particularly in the field of criminal justice, is a critical aspect of transitions as it is called upon both to address legacies of violations and provide a framework for better rights protection. Against this background, the chapter analyzes criminal law reform as an integral part of processes that have sought to address the crisis in Sudan. Sudan constitutes one of the 'hard' cases that have tested the capacity of national, regional and international actors to respond to systemic human rights violations and conflict. The nature and development of the criminal law reform process has in this context been influenced by the implementation of the Comprehensive Peace Agreement (CPA), constitutional arrangements and transitional justice initiatives, especially in regard of Darfur, which have developed their own logic in Sudan. These developments hold a number of lessons. The model used to effectuate a democratic transformation resulting in greater human rights protection was flawed. It was based on a power-sharing process coupled with an in-built separation clause (for Southern Sudan), which has perpetuated existing power structures in the absence of fundamental institutional reforms and an acknowledgment of the legacy of human rights violations and impunity. Inevitably, these dynamics impacted adversely on criminal law reform, which has been marked by limited legislative changes, several of which were in response to the investigations by the ICC in the Darfur situation.

The second chapter, written by the late Abdelsalam Hassan Abdelsalam and Dr Amin M. Medani, examines the development of Sudan's criminal law and law reform efforts in their regional, historical, political and substantive legal setting. This inquiry is set in the context of developments in African states facing colonial legacies, and in countries with a Muslim majority with histories characterized by the tensions that surround the appropriate role of *Shari'a*. The chapter identifies the sources that have influenced Sudanese criminal law and criminal justice, including the relationship between formally enacted legislation and customary laws. The nature, role and use of *Shari'a* are particularly important in this context as a recurring theme of Sudanese criminal law, and the chapter examines its genesis in depth. This encompasses the influence of *Shari'a* in the Funj and Darfur sultanates; its prominent place and idiosyncratic application during the reign of the *Mahdi*; the confinement of *Shari'a* to personal laws during the Anglo-Egyptian condominium; its marginal status in the first decades following independence; its infamous rediscovery under Nimeiri; and its role as one of the defining elements of the current regime. This examination forms part of the broader analysis of the role that criminal legislation has played in Sudan's history. It shows that its use as a means to gain and maintain power has had a corrosive impact on the integrity of criminal law and a stable and peaceful society, particularly in respect of the rule of law and human rights. In parallel, the chapter charts the efforts of civil society and political actors throughout Sudan's history to reform criminal law with a view to enhancing human rights protection, and then identifies key themes that have emerged in various campaigns. Recent developments demonstrate that law reform remains an important site in the broader struggle for the recognition and protection of human rights for everyone in Sudan.

The first section of Part Two addresses the nature and role of repressive legislation. The third chapter written by Amin M. Medani identifies the aspects of Sudan's criminal laws that lend themselves to repressive use. As understood in this context, these comprise offences against the state, emergency legislation, public order legislation and certain types of punishments, particularly flogging and other forms of corporal punishment. The chapter provides a detailed exposition and analysis of relevant provisions. It examines in particular how repressive criminal legislation has been or is being used in Sudan and places it in its political context, such as with the introduction of *Shari'a* as part of criminal law under Nimeiri. The chapter finds that the law has frequently served as the handmaiden for state interests. This is evident from the panoply of broad offences and harsh punishments, combined with extraordinarily wide executive powers and an apparent lack of independence of criminal justice institutions, which has facilitated myriad violations. The CPA and the Bill of Rights have not substantially altered this assessment due to the inadequacy of reforms and the failure by the Sudanese Constitutional Court to act as a true guardian of human rights.

The fourth chapter, written by Jamil Ddamulira Mujuzi, provides a case study of the nature and use of repressive legislation in some of Sudan's neighbouring countries in East Africa, with a particular focus on Uganda. It demonstrates a number of parallels in the different types of repressive legislation. This applies particularly to those laws that constitute colonial legacies and anti-terrorism legislation. The chapter examines in detail the recent use of treason laws and military courts against political opponents. It highlights the risk inherent in vague provisions that carry severe punishments, especially if used in a politicized context and if applied by tribunals whose independence is questionable. However, unlike in the case of Sudan, the Ugandan Constitutional Court has acted as a guardian of human rights in several instances where it has declared pieces of legislation to be unconstitutional.

The right to liberty and security and the right to a fair trial are the subject of the second section of Part Two. The fifth chapter, written by Nabil Adib, provides a detailed examination of the provisions that govern arrest and detention in the Sudanese Criminal Procedure Act. It identifies a number of concerns, including overly broad grounds for arrest, the lack of adequate safeguards – in particular regarding access to a lawyer – and the absence of effective judicial oversight. The system of bail depicted here is flawed and keeps individuals in detention for longer than necessary. The recently adopted National Security Act of 2010 fails to allay existing concerns. It effectively maintains a system that provides the security services with broad powers of arrest and detention without effective safeguards, which has frequently resulted in violations. The right to a fair trial and the independence of the judiciary are recognized in the INC, but several provisions and attendant practices are not in conformity with international human rights standards and have yet to be complemented or put into effect by legislative reforms.

The sixth chapter, written by P.J. Schwikkard, provides a case study of legislative developments in South Africa that pertain to the right to liberty and fair trial. Arbitrary arrest, detention and unfair trials were an integral part of the apartheid system, and following the political changes in the early 1990s, these rights were stipulated in great detail in the new Constitution. The South African Constitutional Court has since upheld and elaborated on their scope in a number of important judgments. While the South African experience provides an example of best practice, the high rate of crime in the country has generated political pressure, under which the right to liberty risks being compromised. The developments in South Africa show again that law reform is an important site in the political struggle for the recognition of rights, which once achieved may still have to be defended and adjusted to respond to systemic or newly emerging challenges.

The third section of Part Two concerns accountability for international crimes. In the seventh chapter Mohamed Abdelsalam Babiker offers a detailed analysis of recent moves to incorporate international crimes into Sudanese legislation, namely via the Armed Forces Act of 2007 and amendments to the Criminal Act in 2009. The chapter recognizes the significance of these developments, which were mainly prompted by the ICC's investigation of the Darfur situation, but identifies several discrepancies between the legislation adopted and international standards, as well as inconsistencies between the two acts mentioned above. In addition, the changes made have not been accompanied by other amendments that are needed to make the prosecution of international crimes effective. Many obstacles remain – the lack of command responsibility, immunities, and statutes of limitations in particular. Without these steps it is unlikely that the legal recognition of international crimes in and of itself will effectively address the impunity that prevails in Sudan for perpetrators of serious human rights violations.

The eighth chapter, written by Deirdre Clancy, analyzes the extent to which the Great Lakes Pact, a sub-regional instrument that entered into force in 2008, and to which Sudan is a party, has contributed to the strengthening of accountability for international crimes in the region. The chapter examines the 'international justice' protocols of the pact, and their scope to provide for a comprehensive normative framework for criminal law reform. It also assesses the factors that have contributed to the limited application and impact of the pact to date, as well as its potential to become more effective. To this end the chapter situates the pact's genesis and development in the broader context of the international justice debate in Africa and developments at the African Union (AU) level, noting that a sub-regional approach can help to bring justice efforts closer to the regional and domestic domain. It concludes by exploring the ways in which the pact can add to greater human rights protection and accountability in Sudan, which includes the reform of laws in line with its substantive provisions.

The ninth chapter, written by Ibrahim Aljazy, examines the position of Arab states on international criminal justice, particularly the ICC, and gives an insider's account of efforts to implement the ICC Rome Statute in Jordanian law. It charts the genesis of the ICC a decade ago and identifies the objections and concerns that have been raised by Arab states. The Arab Model Code on the Rome Statute is analyzed in some detail here because it constitutes an important though partly flawed effort to develop a normative framework for its implementation in a region that faces both a legacy of conflicts as well as ongoing conflict. In this context, the chapter considers the background and drafting history of ICC implementing legislation in Jordan, the only state in the Middle East that has become a party to the Rome Statute. These developments constitute an important precedent for law reform in the area of international criminal law in Arab states, though the undertaking has faced delays that threaten to undermine the momentum towards implementation.

The fourth section of Part Two addresses the issue of gender-based violence. The tenth chapter demonstrates that the gendered justice of Sudan's legal system, in particular its criminal law, has resulted in multiple violations of women's rights. Asma Abdel Halim notes that the law on sexual violence has failed to adequately protect women's rights to physical and mental integrity, whether in the course of conflict (such as widespread sexual violence in Darfur) or in other contexts. Instead, the provision on rape defines the offence as 'involuntary adultery' and creates high evidentiary hurdles, putting women at risk of prosecutions for adultery, which constitutes a crime in its own right. Other acts of sexual violence are either subject to inadequate punishments or are not recognized at all in Sudanese law. In addition, Sudanese criminal law and public order acts provide the authorities with broad powers to arrest, detain and punish anyone perceived to have violated public order, which is a power that is frequently used against women. This was illustrated by a recent case in which several women were whipped for wearing trousers, which sparked women's protests in the country and reinforced calls by the women's rights movement for a fundamental reform of Sudan's legal system.

In the eleventh chapter Sohail Akbar Warraich provides a detailed study of the rise and fall of the *hudood* rape laws in Pakistan, a development that shows several parallels to the situation in Sudan. Legislation making rape a form of adultery was implemented in the wake of Pakistan's 'Islamization' in 1979, and was subsequently applied by Shariat courts, whose jurisprudence was widely seen as erratic and legally unsound. The chapter illustrates the ways in which human rights lawyers and the women's rights movement successfully used litigation and public campaigns to delegitimize the law, which was finally amended in 2006. The reform has not addressed all problems pertaining to protection against sexual violence in Pakistan, but can be seen as an important first step towards conceiving the law as a tool for protection rather than as a site for political symbolism at the expense of women's rights.

In the twelfth chapter Rashida Manjoo, Gift Kweka and Suzzie Onyeka Ofuani provide a detailed case study of the recent wave of legislative reforms that seek to strengthen the protection of women against sexual violence in Southern Africa. It highlights a number of best practices, such as the broadening of the definition of rape and sexual violence, a greater understanding of non-consensual acts that covers various forms of coercion, the recognition of marital rape, the criminalization of various acts of sexual violence, and a change in the scale of punishments reflecting the seriousness of sexual crimes. These developments can to a large degree be attributed to regional women's rights initiatives and efforts by regional organizations such as the Southern African Development Community (SADC). While constituting a success, several omissions and inconsistencies remain in the law, and challenges of implementation abound.

The final chapter explores future perspectives for criminal law reform and human rights in Sudan. It reflects on the key themes and challenges discussed during the proceedings of a seminar organized by REDRESS and co-hosted by the Strategic Initiative for Women in the Horn of Africa (SIHA) in Kampala in March 2010, with the financial support of the Foreign and Commonwealth Office (FCO). The seminar was attended by most of the authors contributing to this book, along with Sudanese stakeholders and several Ugandan experts and practitioners. The forum highlighted several challenges, among them the need to 'demystify' *Shari'a*. Participants also underscored the importance of international human rights standards as a yardstick for existing laws and as guide for reforms. Emphasis was placed on the task of developing a culture of accountability based on solutions that were nationally generated but that would build on regional and international efforts – such as the AU High-Level Panel on Darfur, commissions of inquiry and the ICC – without overly depending on them. Participants agreed on the need for a holistic approach to gender-based violence, which deconstructs the underlying claims that are employed to justify violence and discrimination, and which uses existing openings to influence public debates and change perceptions. The consensus at the seminar – out of which this book has been developed – advanced the understanding that law reform is an ongoing process, requiring multiple strategies to raise awareness and seize political openings. This collection is an integral part of this endeavour.

PART ONE
Perspectives on Law Reform, Transitional Justice and Human Rights

Chapter 1

Law Reform in Times of Peace Processes and Transitional Justice: The Sudanese Dimension

Lutz Oette

Introduction

The last two decades have witnessed an increasing focus on the role of law and justice in securing peace and facilitating transitions from dictatorship or conflict, a development that has led to the emergence of new fields of inquiry.[1] This endeavour has been characterized by its interdisciplinary nature, and by the interface between academics and practitioners who reacted simultaneously to major crises and conflicts – notably in former Yugoslavia and Rwanda – and influenced momentous institutional developments, such as the establishment of the International Criminal Court (ICC). These developments have raised questions about the relationship between the respective goals of peace processes, transitional justice and rule of law initiatives, particularly concerning the nature and coherence of emerging practices.[2]

Law reform is a key component of these practices. It may be among the terms of peace agreements, and constitutes a prerequisite for accountability and reparation measures. It also plays an important role in providing a framework that guarantees civil, political, social, economic and cultural rights of individuals and communities, and embodies fundamental values of governance. As such, reforms are often part of broader efforts to (re)-establish and promote the 'rule of law'.[3]

---

1   See on peace processes, transitional justice and state-building, Bell, C. 2008. *On the Law of Peace: Peace Agreements and the Lex Pacificatoria*. Oxford: Oxford University Press; Teitel, R.G. 2003. Transitional Justice Genealogy. *Harvard Human Rights Journal* 16, 69–94; and on statebuilding, Paris, R. and Sisk, T.D. 2008. Introduction: Understanding the contradictions of postwar statebuilding, in *The Dilemmas of Statebuilding*, edited by R. Paris and T.D. Sisk. Abingdon Oxon and New York: Routledge, 1–20; Samuels, K. 2008. Postwar constitution building, opportunities and challenges, in Paris and Sisk. 2008, 173–95.

2   See for the UN response, UN Secretary-General. 2004. *The rule of law and transitional justice in conflict and post-conflict societies*. UN Doc. S/2004/616.

3   See UN Secretary-General. 2004, para. 6, for a definition of the rule of law. See for a critical review of contemporary practices in the field, Carothers, T. 2006. *Promoting the Rule of Law Abroad: In Search of Knowledge*. Washington DC: Carnegie Endowment for

Since the law has often been at the heart of abuse of state power, and by definition shares its coercive nature, legislative reforms are fraught with challenges, particularly in fragile times of transition. Process is critical in this context, which includes the legitimacy of national and international actors, and the role of judicial and other bodies. The involvement of the public and civil society organizations is pivotal in these often highly politicized environments. These components are crucial in determining whether law reform can fulfil its multiple roles of securing peace, enabling justice for past violations, and leading to an order in which human rights are better protected.

This chapter examines the nature and interrelationship of the processes that come into play during times of transition,[4] with a view to better understanding how they interact, and facilitate or hinder human rights protection and justice.[5] This examination focuses on criminal law and justice, which is a specific, critical aspect of law reform in transitions. It also considers the ambivalent role of criminal law in relation to human rights and conflict, providing an analysis that is key to the understanding needed when addressing structural legacies in reform debates.

The chapter also analyzes criminal law reform as an integral part of processes that have sought to address the crisis in Sudan. Sudan is one of the 'hard' cases. It has greatly tested the capacity of national, regional and international actors to respond to systemic human rights violations and conflict, much of which is rooted in inequality, marginalization, the weakness of the rule of law, and a lack of democratic structures.[6] The intensification of the war in Darfur in 2003 triggered

---

International Peace, and Sannerholm, R. 2007. Legal, judicial and administrative reforms in post-conflict societies: beyond the rule of law template. *Journal of Conflict & Security Law*, 12(1), 65–94.

4   The term transition implies a development from one situation to another and can be broadly associated with changes from dictatorships, authoritarian rule or conflict to systems that show more respect for all sets of rights (which is by some understood to mean a liberal and democratic system) and to a peaceful society. In the context of Sudan, transition refers primarily to the North–South peace process, which identifies a number of steps to be taken by the parties in the implementation period, and to responses to the conflict to Darfur even though the latter has not entered into a clearly identifiable transition period at the time of writing. The political power structure of Sudan, and this applies particularly to the North, has not undergone fundamental change during the CPA implementation. Sudan has for these reasons not witnessed a full transition but can be said to undergo a period of change that shares at least some transitional elements.

5   The term justice is commonly used to refer to the panoply of measures taken to respond to past violations, such as truth, criminal accountability and reparation measures, and may also have forward-looking elements, such as guarantees of non-repetition that entail reforms. See for its understanding in the Darfur context, African Union High-Level Panel on Darfur (AUPD). 2009. *Darfur: The quest for peace, justice and reconciliation*. Report to the African Union. PSC/AHG/2 (CCVII), 88, at para. 317.

6   See in particular Johnson, D.H. 2003. *The Root Causes of Sudan's Civil Wars*. Oxford: The International African Institute; Hassan, S.M. and Ray, C.E. (eds). 2009. *Darfur*

a wide array of responses aimed at ending the conflict, providing protection, and ensuring justice for victims.[7] In parallel, one of the longest conflicts on the continent, between the North and South in Sudan, came to an end following regional and international mediation, resulting in the Comprehensive Peace Agreement (CPA) in 2005. The CPA envisaged power-sharing and major constitutional, legislative and institutional reforms that would bring about what was colloquially referred to as 'democratic transformation', including human rights protection and respect for the rule of law.[8] The responses to the Darfur conflict and the North–South peace process operated in different contexts but shared a number of commonalities. They raised a host of questions regarding: (a) the constitutive role of peace processes; (b) law and human rights protection, including the capacity of domestic bodies to provide such protection; (c) the role of 'transitional justice', in particular justice and reconciliation; (d) reconstruction and the rule of law; and (e) the involvement of regional and international actors. The fact that the very same actors frequently fulfilled different roles and pursued different goals in the context of the CPA implementation process and in the Darfur conflict is an important factor that merits separate consideration in view of the prominence and impact of international actors in Sudan. The chapter examines these critical factors and analyzes their impact on the nature and outcome of the reform process in Sudan's period of simultaneous transition and conflict from 2005 to 2010.

Criminal law, human rights and conflict

Criminal law and human rights

The relationship between criminal justice and human rights is deeply ambivalent. Criminal justice systems – and criminal law as one of their key components – are at the heart of the exercise of state power, engaging its legislative, executive and judicial functions. Criminal justice is integral to fulfilling the classical state function of ensuring the safety and protection of its population from harm,[9] and is meant to protect fundamental social values. It is also part of the larger notion

---

and the Crisis of Governance in Sudan. Ithaca, New York: Cornell University Press (various contributions in section 1: Origins and Evolution of the Conflict); as well as de Waal, A. 2006. Sudan: the turbulent state, in *War in Darfur and the Search for Peace*, edited by A. de Waal. Cambridge, Massachusetts: Harvard University Press, 1–38.

   7   See Flint, J. and de Waal, A. 2008. *Darfur, A New History of a Long War.* 2nd edition. London, New York: Zed Books.

   8   See Basha, S. 2006. The Comprehensive Peace Agreement – a synopsis, in *Peace in the Balance: The Crisis in Sudan*, edited by B. Raftopoulos and K. Alexander. Cape Town: Institute for Justice and Reconciliation, Cape Town, 23–38.

   9   See Beccaria, C. 1986 (originally published in 1764). *Of Crimes and Punishment.* Indianapolis, Indiana: Hackett Publishing, Chapter 1: Of the Origins of Punishment.

of human security, which includes freedom from fear and want, and seeks to ensure the well-being and dignity of individuals.[10] Indeed, international human rights law requires states to provide protection against harmful conduct, and this positive obligation involves creating a legislative framework to repress violations by state and non-state actors.[11] However, the system of criminal justice is ultimately based on the use of coercion, which flows from the state's monopoly of force and is foremost reflected in its power to punish. This power carries the inherent risk of violating both rights and the very notion of justice that it is meant to reflect and advance.

Criminal laws themselves may violate rights, for example, where they criminalize the legitimate exercise of the right to privacy and freedom of expression.[12] They may also be applied in a manner that violates rights. While purporting to protect and uphold societal values, state authorities frequently use criminal law as a tool of repression and/or for ideological ends, which invariably results in the criminalization of minorities, marginalized members of the community, or those politically opposed to the government.[13] In its most naked manifestation, criminal law becomes a handmaiden of the state, serving as a tool and a legal fig-leaf for officially sanctioned repression. This instrumental use is often equally characterized by impunity and the absence of an adequate criminal legal framework that can repress serious human rights violations, protect individuals, and hold perpetrators to account. In addition, criminal law may be applied in a highly selective fashion, reflecting a state's dual character: strong and heavy-handed in securing its interests and weak in controlling certain territories and/or groups and protecting individuals from harm where it has limited interest or its grip on power is weak.

Criminal law and conflict

The relationship between criminal law and conflict is equally ambivalent. Thinkers such as Hobbes built the very legitimacy of the use of sovereign power

---

10   See Sen, A. 2001. *Development as Freedom*. Oxford: Oxford University Press, and Edwards, A. and Ferstman, C. 2010. Humanising non-citizens: the convergence of human rights and human security, in *Human Security and Non-Citizens: Law, Policy and International Affairs*, edited by A. Edwards and C. Ferstman. Cambridge: Cambridge University Press, 3–46, in particular at 21–33.

11   Human Rights Committee (HRC). 2004. *General Comment 31: The Nature of the General Legal Obligation imposed on States Parties to the Covenant*. UN Doc. CCPR/C/21/Rev.1/Add.13, para. 8.

12   See for example HRC. 2010. *Draft General Comment 34: Article 19*. UN Doc. CCPR/C/GC/34/CRP.4, paras 31–2.

13   See Scraton, P. and Chadwick, K. 2003. The theoretical and political priorities of critical criminology, in *Criminal Perspectives*, edited by E. McLaughlin et al. 2nd Edition. Open University. London: Sage Publishing, 294–309, at 298–300.

on the state's capacity to provide for a stable and secure society.[14] The link between criminal law and a peaceful society is also evident in the goals of the former, namely deterrence, rehabilitation and restorative justice,[15] with retribution arguably being the only exception.

Deterrence is closely linked with utilitarian thinking.[16] It functions effectively where the credible threat of punishment stops a potential offender from committing a crime (general deterrence) or an offender from reoffending (specific deterrence), that is the collective and the individual dimension of deterrence. Punishment may also rehabilitate the offender where it results in a change of attitude, which in turn contributes to the prevention of crime.[17] Restorative justice focuses on reconciliation between victims and the offender.[18] Forms of sanctions other than imprisonment are favoured to achieve this end, such as reparation or community service. This notion draws heavily on forms of communitarian justice that have been revived in particular contexts, such as juvenile justice.[19] Its nexus to dispute settlement and the goal of contributing to a peaceful society is particularly evident.

The role of criminal justice as a cause or contributing factor to conflict, or the lack thereof, is less clear when firm empirical evidence is difficult to establish.[20] A number of precedents indicate that overly repressive criminal laws and/or the lack of a functioning criminal justice system can contribute to the outbreak or perpetuation of conflict. A failed state is partially defined by the limited capacity to enforce its laws and a resulting breakdown of law and order,[21] and can be both

---

14 Hobbes, T. 1968 (first published 1651). *Leviathan*. London: Penguin Books, Part II, 'Of Commonwealth', Chapter XVII.

15 Fletcher, G.P. 1998. *Basic Concepts of Criminal Law*. Oxford: Oxford University Press, 30–32. See also section 142(1) of the UK Criminal Justice Act, 2003.

16 See for example, Bentham, J. 1995. Principles of Penal Law, in *Works of Jeremy Bentham*. Volume 1. Bristol: Thoemmes Press, 396.

17 Hart, H.L.A. 1968. *Punishment and Responsibility: Essays in the Philosophy of Law*. Oxford: Oxford University Press, 24–7.

18 See Johnstone, G. 2001. *Restorative Justice: Ideas, Values, Debates*. Uffculme, Devon: Willan Publishing.

19 Johnstone. 2001, 36–61; Doak, J. 2008. *Victims' Rights, Human Rights and Criminal Justice, Reconceiving the Role of Third Parties*. Oxford: Hart, 254–65.

20 See for a debate on the causes of conflict, including human rights violations, Sannerholm. 2007, 67–70, who concludes that 'for the planning and preparation of post-conflict statebuilding interventions with a substantial rule of law component, the multifaceted anatomy of crisis situations – the mixing of justice, economic and social conflicts – requires a holistic approach.' For Sudan, see AUPD. 2009, 11, at para. 48.

21 Von Bogdandy, A. et al. 2005. State-building, nation-building, and constitutional politics in post-conflict situations: conceptual clarifications and an appraisal of different approaches, in *Max Planck Yearbook of United Nations Law*, edited by A. von Bogdandy and R. Wolfrum. Volume 9. Leiden: Brill, 579–613, at 581.

cause and consequence of conflict.[22] Such a failure often creates a vacuum that is filled by warlords and characterized by banditry. Somalia is considered a prime example of this,[23] but the latest developments in Darfur have raised concerns that it may become a local variant of a failed state.[24] Yet the precise role of a repressive criminal justice system as contributing factor to conflict is not easily ascertainable, not least because it is often but one element of a larger failure of 'governance'. However, there are prominent instances where criminal law itself was a major factor in the outbreak or resumption of conflict. The introduction of *Shari'a* (Islamic law) in Sudan's criminal law in 1983 immediately raised concerns about the state's identity and the rights of those living in it,[25] and commentators have identified this step as an important factor in the resumption of the civil war between the North and the South at the time.[26]

Criminal law and reform in conflict and post-conflict societies

Law reform in conflict and post-conflict societies

Many modern armed conflicts are characterized by serious violations of human rights and norms of international humanitarian law,[27] and where an authoritarian or dictatorial regime is in power violations are also often committed outside of the conflict. In these situations criminal law may become a tool of repression and counterinsurgency (for example where suspected members of rebel groups are prosecuted for having committed offences against the state), or can foster a climate of impunity, particularly through the use of immunities and amnesties. In these circumstances criminal laws that fall short of required international standards

---

22   UN Secretary-General. 1995. *Supplement to an agenda for peace: Position paper on the occasion of the fiftieth anniversary of the United Nations*. UN Doc. A/50/60 – S/1995/1, para. 13: 'Another feature of such conflicts is the collapse of state institutions, especially the police and judiciary, with resulting paralysis of governance, a breakdown of law and order, and general banditry and chaos.'

23   See Philipp, C.E. 2005. Somalia – A Very Special Case, in *Bogdandy and Wolfrum*. 2005, 517–54.

24   AUPD. 2009, 17–8, at paras 74–8 and UN Secretary-General. 2010. *Report on the African Union–United Nations Hybrid Operation in Darfur (UNAMID)*, UN Doc. S/2010/543, paras 20–34.

25   See for a detailed study of the history and introduction of *Shari'a* in 1983, Layish, A. and Warburg, G.R. 2002. *The Reinstatement of Islamic Law in Sudan under Numayri: An Evaluation of a Legal Experiment in the Light of its Historical Context, Methodology and Repercussions*. Leiden: Brill.

26   See Collins, R.O. 2008. *A History of Modern Sudan*. Cambridge: Cambridge University Press, 245–71.

27   See on Sudan, Babiker, M.A. 2007. *Application of International Humanitarian and Human Rights Law to the Armed Conflicts of the Sudan*. Antwerp–Oxford: Intersentia.

frequently reflect the bigger failure of the criminal justice system to secure peace, prevent human rights violations, and offer justice to victims.[28]

There is growing awareness of the need to address past violations and their systemic roots in order to effectuate transitions and to overcome dictatorship and/ or armed conflict.[29] The series of post-conflict situations and political transitions in recent years have raised a host of challenges for national and international actors. In this context the reform of criminal laws and criminal justice systems has served to hold perpetrators of serious violations to account, and to provide security while respecting human rights and making broader efforts to establish the rule of law.[30]

International policy discourse on the role of law reform in transitions – particularly criminal justice reforms – and its analysis frequently draws on a series of case studies.[31] The United Nations (UN) has administered law reform directly in situations such as in Kosovo and East Timor, and has assisted governments in Africa and elsewhere to reform laws in accordance with the mandate of the country missions.[32] In this regard, the UN and others have articulated the now received wisdom that emphasizes process, local ownership, participation and sustainability of reforms.[33] These are important principles that reflect concerns over the role of external actors,[34] but they mask a series of challenges, if not tensions, especially where there is limited political space and capacity to adequately implement reforms.

The context within which such reforms take place, and the goals pursued, are of critical importance. Reforms may: (i) be part of peace processes; (ii) be complementary to constitutional processes; (iii) form a component of transitional justice; (iv) constitute an element of statebuilding or of rule of law promotion; or (v) be a combination thereof. Peace agreements between the parties concerned must address the question of human rights protection and, where they are meant to provide a framework for a transition to lasting peace, the need for institutional

---

28   See in the Sudanese context, Medani, A.M. 2001. *Crimes against International Humanitarian Law in Sudan: 1989–2000*. Cairo: Dar El Mostaqbal El Arabi.

29   See in particular UN Secretary-General. 2004.

30   See Ratner, S.R. et al. 2009. *Accountability for Human Rights Atrocities in International Law*. 3rd Edition. Oxford: Oxford University Press; on complementarity and the need for effective national mechanisms, Akhavan, P. 2010. Whither national courts? The Rome Statute's missing half: towards an express and enforceable obligation for the national repression of international crimes. *Journal of International Criminal Justice*, 8(5), 1245–66; and, on criminal law reform in post-conflict societies more generally, Rausch, C. 2006. *Combating Serious Crimes in Postconflict Societies: A Handbook for Policymakers and Practitioners*. Washington DC: United States Institute of Peace Press.

31   See in particular various case studies in *Bogdandy and Wolfrum*. 2005, which focus on the 'management of post-conflict situations'.

32   Sannerholm. 2007, 80–81.

33   UN Secretary-General. 2004. See also the UN Rule of Law website, in particular at http://www.unrol.org/article.aspx?article_id=25 [accessed 9 December 2010].

34   Stromseth, J.E. 2006. *Can Might Make Rights? Building the Rule of Law after Military Interventions*. Cambridge: Cambridge University Press, and Sannerholm. 2007, 81.

and legislative changes to reduce the risk of recurring violations.[35] One element of this process may be the adoption of a new constitution and the setting up of a court tasked with guarding the constitution. Ideally, such steps succeed in embedding constitutionalism: that is, a system in which the constitution provides an agreed-upon framework for the exercise of powers and the protection of rights.[36]

Peace agreements and constitutional, legislative and institutional changes also constitute part of the 'transitional justice' process. This umbrella term has been defined broadly as the 'distinctive conception of law and of justice in the context of political transformation'[37] and seeks to capture both backward- and forward-looking measures taken to achieve truth, justice and ideally reconciliation for past violations, and to remove the causes for conflict and/or violations so as to ensure a lasting transition.[38] Transitional justice is also closely related to reconstruction and socio-economic development,[39] and can thus form part of the process of 'statebuilding'. This structural term can be understood to denote the goals of strengthening the 'functional capacity of the state and … enabling effective political processes',[40] which will be of particular importance where the state has failed or is failing to fulfil its functions.[41] Nationbuilding is a broader concept that reaches beyond the function of the state. It has been described as 'the most common form of a process of collective identity formation with a view to legitimizing public power within a given territory'.[42] It is evident that such an outcome can be an important goal of transitions, particularly where public power has been seriously undermined and a country divided.

---

35   According to Bell. 2008, 60, '[s]ubstantive or framework agreements aim to sustain ceasefires and provide a framework for governance that will address the root causes of conflict, thereby halting violent conflict more permanently.' See on the actual practice, Office of the UN High Commissioner for Human Rights. 2009. *Analytical study on human rights and transitional justice: inventory of human rights and transitional justice aspects of recent peace agreements*. UN Doc. A/HRC/12/18/Add.1.

36   See Cottier, T. and Hertig, M. 2003. The prospects of 21st century constitutionalism, in *Max Planck Yearbook of United Nations Law*, edited by A. von Bogdandy and R. Wolfrum. Volume 7. Leiden: Brill, 261–328, at 275–82, and, for different notions of constitutionalism, Teitel, R.G. 2000. *Transitional Justice*. Oxford: Oxford University Press, 191–201.

37   Teitel. 2000, 4.

38   Teitel. 2000, 3–6.

39   See de Greiff, P. and Duthie, R. (eds). 2009. *Transitional Justice and Development: Making Connections*. New York: Social Science Research Council. See also the link made by the AUPD in AUPD. 2009, xx, at paras 28 and 75, at para. 267.

40   Barnes, C. 2009. Renegotiating the political settlement in war-to-peace transitions. [Online: Conciliation Resources, 20 March] Available at: http://www.c-r.org/resources/occasional-papers/documents/CR_2Renegotiating_Settlement_20Mar09-2.pdf [accessed 9 December], 8.

41   Bogdandy et al. 2005, 585.

42   Bogdandy et al. 2005, 586.

The impact of transitional processes on human rights protection and law reform

Peace agreements, transitional justice, constitutionalism and rule of law promotion share a focus on human rights protection and attendant reforms. However, each of these processes, which overlap to a certain degree in Sudan, have specific objectives and follow their own logic, which may dictate certain outcomes. These may in turn result in tensions that impact on the nature of reforms, depending on the context in which they are undertaken. Human rights and law reform are means to create a framework conducive to the goals of peace processes such as the CPA, and form part of a political process that seeks to institute political, legal, institutional and other transformations that guarantee lasting peace.[43] While the creation of an order based on human rights and the rule of law is defined as an ultimate aim of this process, its overarching goal is to ensure peace. This means that human rights and the rule of law are seen as constitutive elements of peace, and of instrumental value throughout peace processes. This view can lead to the compromising, if not manipulation of human rights if they become part of political interests, rather than fundamental building blocks of a different political order.

Peace processes may in and of themselves not provide the requisite impetus for relevant reforms if they are not part of a broader transitional justice process. While both of these processes may overlap to a large degree, they may differ with regard to their primary objectives, key actors and the modalities that they employ. The process of transitional justice denotes a shared commitment to (re)-establish the rule of law and human rights protection. Its goal is to transform society through necessary reforms whereby its modalities – that is, the setting up of inclusive bodies, public debates, participatory reforms – are themselves seen as part of this transformation. Law reform may in this context reflect popular demand, constitute a governmental policy commitment, be one of the recommendations of bodies set up to inquire into causes and consequences of past violations, such as Truth and Reconciliation Commission,[44] or be largely driven by external actors. Significantly, such reform may conflict with peace agreements. This is particularly the case where law reform is part of calls for justice and accountability, especially of members of the very parties that have entered peace

---

43   See the Chapeau of the CPA: 'The Parties further acknowledge that the successful implementation of the CPA shall provide a model for good governance in the Sudan that will help create a solid basis to preserve peace and make unity attractive and therefore undertake to fully adhere to the letter and spirit of the CPA so as to guarantee lasting peace, security for all, justice and equality in the Sudan.'

44   The Truth and Reconciliation Commission of South Africa. 1998. *Report*. Volume V. Chapter 8, 304–49, for example, contains a series of recommendations relating to legislative and institutional reforms, in particular concerning the security apparatus and the police forces.

agreements. The developments surrounding the granting of amnesties in the Lomé Peace Agreement in Sierra Leone are particularly instructive in this regard.[45]

The reliance on law as a transformative agent in transitional contexts can be highly ambivalent. Legal reforms are premised on law as a neutral category or a positive agent of change, which is highly contingent on the legitimacy of the law-making process and the institutional structure within which the laws are applied. To focus on the 'supply' side of strengthening state structures when undertaking such reforms may perpetuate structural problems if neglecting the 'demand side' – that is, rights awareness, access to justice and the role of human rights defenders.[46]

Constitutionalism can be an important offspring of both peace and transitional justice processes. The concept denotes the limitation of power and adherence to fundamental rights in a system in which 'power is ultimately derived from the citizens'.[47] In transitional settings, constitutions perform the dual function of reflecting and transforming the prevailing consensus.[48] The manner in which constitutions are built in such contexts is increasingly seen as critical for their success, with a broad participatory process viewed as being particularly conducive to enhanced legitimacy.[49] Conversely, a constitution-making process based on the power-sharing of elites may not have the transformative power needed, and may perpetuate extant systemic deficiencies.[50] This is particularly acute in the context of peace agreements, which 'can be understood as a distinctive form of political constitution'.[51] In addition, the '[paradox of institutionalization] becomes an intensely practical challenge of designing innovative power-sharing arrangements that disaggregate power so as to serve both conflict resolution needs and requirements of democratic legitimacy'.[52] The nature of the transition process, the actors involved and the understanding of the goals of transition are paramount in determining whether the constitution and its designated judicial custodians are subordinate to political influence, or whether they act as catalysts for a transition

---

45 See Goldmann, M. 2005. Sierra Leone: African solutions to African problems? in *Bogdandy and Wolfrum*. 2005, 457–515.

46 See Maguire, S. 2010. Creating demand in Darfur: squaring the circle, in *Peacebuilding and Rule of Law in Africa*, edited by C.L. Sriram et al. Abingdon, Oxon and New York: Routledge, 161–78.

47 Cottier and Hertig. 2003, 280.

48 Teitel. 2000, 191.

49 See Samuels. 2008, 175–83, and Benomar, J. 2003. *Constitution-making and peace building: lessons learned from the constitution-making processes of post-conflict countries.* [Online: United Nations Development Programme] Available at: http://www.unrol.org/files/Constitution%20making%20and%20peace%20building%20Report_Jamal%20Benomar.doc [accessed 28 December 2010].

50 Samuels. 2008, 176, referring to negative experiences in South America.

51 Bell. 2008, 202.

52 Bell. 2008, 203.

driven by human rights considerations.[53] These processes may conflict where, for example, a strong emphasis on law reform to promote human rights accountability and/or an independent judiciary, particularly a strong supreme or constitutional court, is opposed by parties to a conflict, and therefore excluded from the ambit of any peace agreements, or downplayed in its subsequent implementation.

The role of international actors is an important factor in shaping peace processes, transitions and statebuilding. The approach taken by states and international organizations varies considerably. It ranges from their leading processes directly, such as in Kosovo and East Timor, to their providing largely technical advice or supporting the development of political processes to create an environment conducive to transitional justice processes and legitimate constitution-making, or a combination thereof.[54] Observers and practitioners have increasingly criticized the supposedly neo-colonial nature of international involvement and the deeply ambivalent role of various interventions, which often do not visibly contribute to a more peaceful society in which human rights are better protected, but instead perpetuate elite-based policies.[55] Equally, there is an increasing awareness of the multiple and sometimes even contradictory objectives pursued by various actors, which may undermine the overall goal of political transitions.

In relation to law reform, the UN, states and other actors have focused on building capacities, supporting domestic constituencies and providing expertise[56] while promoting the adherence to and implementation of international standards.[57] This has included the drawing up of model codes, which are effectively composite laws reflecting (what are considered) best practices.[58] These model codes may serve useful purposes for guidance, but may of themselves not ensure the requisite 'fit'; ultimately the law must also gain domestic legitimacy in terms of process and substance, and this includes systematic coherence. The latter is of particular relevance when considering the 'agents' of implementation, which include the executive and the judiciary.[59] In practice these two branches must be able to apply legislation in line with legislative intentions, which requires knowledge of the law

53   South Africa is often referred to as a particularly successful constitution-making process in times of transition. See Samuels. 2008, 178 and Von Bogdandy et al. 2005, 603–7. See for a critical perspective on the limits of rights discourse as tool for transformation in the South African context, Mutua, M. 2002. *Human Rights: A Political and Cultural Critique*. Philadelphia: University of Pennsylvania Press, 126–53.

54   See case studies of West New Guinea, Cambodia, Bosnia-Herzegovina, Kosovo, Afghanistan, Sierra Leone and Somalia in *Bogdandy and Wolfrum*. 2005.

55   See in particular Stromseth. 2006.

56   UN Secretary-General. 2004, paras 14–37.

57   Sannerholm. 2007, 79–81.

58   See O'Connor, V. and Rausch, C. (eds). 2007. *Model Codes for Post-conflict Criminal Justice*. Volume 1. Model Criminal Code. Washington DC: United States Institute of Peace Press. Positive, Sannerholm. 2007, 72. Critical, Benzing, M. 2005. Midwifing a new state: the United Nations in East Timor, in *Bogdandy and Wolfrum*. 2005, 295–372, at 359.

59   HRC. 2004, para. 4.

and underlying principles, as well as an adequate degree of consistency within the legal system so as to avoid interpretative conflicts. Beyond these considerations, laws must gain legitimacy in the public at large if the broader goal of establishing the rule of law is to be successfully enshrined.[60] The UN and other international actors inevitably play an ambivalent role in such contexts depending on the approach they take, and become political actors occupying a hybrid position of local participant and foreign entity.

The context of law reform in Sudan

The political processes and legal background for legislative reforms in Sudan

The peace agreement and normative framework: Comprehensive Peace Agreement, Interim National Constitution and Bill of Rights
Sudan's transition resulting from the North–South conflict was based on the CPA. This agreement was concluded between the two main warring factions after negotiations with regional and international political actors, but without involving other Sudanese political forces or civil society members. The CPA builds on the commitment to human rights promoted by Sudanese civil society and parties such as the Sudan People's Liberation Movement/Army (SPLM/SPLA) since the 1990s,[61] and firmly roots criminal justice within the human rights framework.[62] The Interim National Constitution (INC) adopted pursuant to the CPA in 2005 further entrenches this commitment with its reference to international human rights standards and its enunciation of specific rights.[63] The CPA and the Bill of Rights contained in the INC formed the substantive reference point for the law reform process during the interim period envisaged in the CPA (from 2005 to mid-2011). The main purpose of this period was to secure the peace settlement through a democratic system of governance and to make the unity of Sudan attractive by professing 'values of justice, democracy, good governance, respect for fundamental human rights and freedom of the individual, mutual understanding and tolerance of diversity within the realities of Sudan'.[64]

---

60   See Sannerholm. 2007.

61   See Abdel Salam, A.H. and de Waal, A. (eds). 2001. *The Phoenix State, Civil Society and the Future of Sudan*. Asmara: The Red Sea Press, Annex: Kampala Declaration on Human Rights, 291–300.

62   Article 1.6. of the Power Sharing Protocol.

63   Article 27(3) INC. See on the Bill of Rights, Medani, A.M. 2005. *Human Rights in the Interim Constitution*. Khartoum University Students Union, KUSU, in cooperation with Sudan Social Development Organisation, SUDO. Khartoum, and Ibrahim, N. 2008. The Sudanese Bill of Rights. *The International Journal of Human Rights,* 12(4), 613–35.

64   Chapeau of the Comprehensive Peace Agreement.

The Bill of Rights itself, however, is not free of ambiguity. A plain reading of its article 27(3)[65] suggests that international human rights standards that are binding on Sudan can be applied directly (that is, can be invoked before courts in so far as they are self-executing, and govern any legislative reforms as a matter of constitutional law). Indeed, article 27(4) provides that '[l]egislation shall regulate the rights and freedoms enshrined in this Bill and shall not detract from or derogate any of these rights', and the Bill of Rights guarantees a number of rights contained in the major human rights treaties. However, several rights do not mention certain aspects guaranteed by the International Covenant on Civil and Political Rights (ICCPR), such as the right to be brought promptly before a judge and the right to an independent tribunal within the rights to liberty and to a fair trial.[66] Other rights, such as freedom of expression have claw-back clauses according to which limitations can be determined by law, and these may be overly restrictive or ambiguous when judged by international standards.[67] In addition, the definition of some rights is at variance with international treaties. For example in contrast to article 7 of the ICCPR, article 33 of the Bill of Rights omits cruel, inhuman or degrading punishment. This raises the question of how to interpret the Bill of Rights, or in other words, of what constitutes Sudanese law in case of conflict. As a general principle national law should, or indeed must, be interpreted so as to avoid any discrepancies with a state's international obligations.[68] To this end international treaty provisions may be read into the Bill of Rights, either by adding them or by interpreting ambiguous provisions accordingly. However, this approach becomes difficult where the respective provisions of the relevant international treaty and the Bill of Rights are irreconcilable. This includes cases in which an element of a right has been deliberately omitted, as appears to have been the case in relation to article 33 mentioned above. The Sudanese Constitutional Court has not yet addressed this matter in its jurisprudence but the ambiguity of the Bill of Rights in this regard is clearly unsatisfactory. This is not only of theoretical interest. The lawmaker may use a particular reading of the Bill of Rights to justify the introduction or retention of laws, such as those on corporal punishments, which may be compatible with a

---

65   Article 27(3) INC: 'All rights and freedoms enshrined in international human rights treaties, covenants and instruments ratified by the Republic of the Sudan shall be an integral part of this Bill.'

66   See articles 29 and 34 of the Bill of Rights and articles 9 and 14 of the ICCPR respectively.

67   Article 39 Bill of Rights. See on claw-back clauses HRC. 2010, paras 25–7.

68   See, for example, section 233 of the 1996 Constitution, South Africa: 'When interpreting any legislation, every court must prefer any reasonable interpretation of the legislation that is consistent with international law over any alternative interpretation that is inconsistent with international law.' Section 39(1): 'When interpreting the Bill of Rights, a court, tribunal or forum – (a) must promote the values that underlie an open and democratic society based on human dignity, equality and freedom; (b) must consider international law; and (c) may consider foreign law.'

literal reading of article 33 but at variance with article 7 of the ICCPR. This would clearly run counter to Sudan's international obligations.

The confusion the Bill of Rights creates about the nature of applicable rights may be seen as coincidental, and part of a curious mix of international and domestic standards. However, it reflects a discrepancy between the higher standards of international protection and domestic interpretations, which has risked and perhaps even foreshadowed a compromising of rights. It thus undermines one of the CPA's fundamental tenets and introduces a degree of uncertainty into debates about requisite legislative reforms.

The ICC and reforms

In a process running largely parallel to the implementation of the CPA, Sudan has been prompted to change its legislation in response to investigations by the ICC into international crimes alleged to have been committed in Darfur, pursuant to the UN Security Council referral based on resolution 1593 (2005).[69] One of the central planks of the ICC's Rome Statute is complementarity; that is, the notion that the ICC should only investigate and prosecute crimes where the state concerned is unable or unwilling to do so.[70] Sudan has insisted throughout the process that it is capable of prosecuting international crimes that were committed on its territory, and it amended several of its laws to lend credibility to this claim, among them the Armed Forces Act in 2007 and the Criminal Act in 2009.[71] However, the report of the African Union (AU) High-Level Panel on Darfur (AUPD), published in October 2009, urged Sudan to undertake further legislative reforms in order to put in place the legal framework needed to ensure justice, accountability and reparations.[72] This highlights the importance of the ICC's Darfur investigation as impetus for legislative reforms, but the resulting process may rather be called 'shadow complementarity' due to the doubtful practical impact of the changes undertaken so far; there appear to have been no meaningful investigations of anyone implicated in the commission of international crimes in Darfur.

---

69   See for a brief summary with further references, Oette, L. 2010. Peace and justice, or neither? The repercussions of the al-Bashir case for international criminal justice in Africa and beyond. *Journal of International Criminal Justice*, 8(2), 345–64, at 347–50.

70   Article 17 of the ICC Rome Statute. See Pichon, J. 2008. The principle of complementarity in the cases of the Sudanese nationals Ahmad Harun and Ali Kushayb before the International Criminal Court. *International Criminal Law Review*, 8, 185–228; and Benzing, M. 2003. The Complementarity Regime of the ICC, in *Bogdandy and Wolfrum*. 2003, 591–632.

71   See chapter 7.

72   AUPD. 2009, paras 317–55.

The interplay of peace processes and transitional justice in the Sudanese context

In 2011 the situation in Sudan shared many of the tensions in the interplay between peace processes, transitional justice and broader reconstruction efforts. The underlying process had been based on the CPA as 'foundational' peace agreement with constitutional elements implemented in a transitional period. The CPA provided the impetus for the process of transition that included reforms to address structural legacies of violations (such as the reform of the national security services).[73] The constitutional framework and the legislative and institutional changes were an integral part of the CPA implementation. Having deliberately excluded the question of justice and accountability for past violations, its parties adopted a forward-looking notion, which envisioned a CPA that would provide a framework for political transition (forming a Government of National Unity, elections, and a referendum concerning the future status of South Sudan). The CPA was also meant to serve as a framework for the transformation of the legal and institutional set up, with a view to strengthening human rights protection and the rule of law.[74] These two parallel developments were envisaged to secure lasting peace between the North and the South.

The CPA provided an important framework for the peace implementation process, albeit one that was fragile, and flawed in parts.[75] The constitutional, legal and institutional reforms failed to generate the sense of constitutionalism and the fundamental change that were to remove the causes for human rights violations and provide effective remedies. The INC and its Bill of Rights did not bring about a discernable change in attitudes and practices. A number of laws remained in place, such as the laws governing the various forces, which vest the executive with substantial powers without adequate judicial review (or parliamentary control for that matter), and foster impunity, such as immunities legislation.[76] The primacy of *Shari'a* was maintained in the North with limited safeguards against abuse, despite its legacy to that effect.[77]

---

73   See chapter 2.

74   See CPA Chapeau.

75   Idris, A. 2005. *Conflict and Politics of Identity in Sudan*. New York: Palgrave MacMillan, 91, views the CPA as reproducing the colonial discourse in Sudan and, presciently in 2005, concludes that: 'the fundamental task of democratic transformation seems to be completely ignored in the current peace process. The outcome of this disjointed framework, in the long run, will be the persistence of an undemocratic racialised state in the North and the creation of a despotic/decentralised government in the South.'

76   See REDRESS. 2009. *Promoting law reform in Sudan to enhance human rights protection, strengthen the rule of law and foster democratic processes. Written Evidence submitted by the Redress Trust to the UK Associate Parliamentary Group on Sudan: Parliamentary Hearings: Sudan's Comprehensive Peace Agreement.* [Online, 15 October] Available at http://www.redress.org/documents/REDRESS%20Submission%20CPA%20 15%20October%202009.pdf [accessed 9 December 2010].

77   Idris. 2005, 91.

This situation can be attributed to the prevailing political power balance, which favoured the status quo. The composition of parliament was weighted in favour of the two main parties, the National Congress Party (NCP) in particular, which also had de facto power over key institutions, a situation that was further entrenched following the NCP's victory in the 2010 elections after the SPLM withdrew its presidential candidate.[78] Being primarily concerned with surviving and strengthening its grip on power, the Government of Sudan (GoS) showed a limited desire to embark on genuine reforms. Meanwhile the apparent focus of the SPLM on securing independence also contributed to its scant engagement in bringing about fundamental changes in the whole of Sudan. This situation was compounded by the weakness of the political opposition, of civil society and of the media, which was to a considerable degree due to their marginalization in the CPA and subsequently to repressive laws and practices that hindered their free development and the exercise of their rights.[79] However, civil society actors, such as women's groups, have used the limited political openings to highlight the nature of violations, systemic shortcomings in the system, such as gender-based discrimination, and the need for reforms.[80]

The Sudanese Constitutional Court, which was reconstituted on the basis of the INC and vested with the power of constitutional review,[81] has not acted as a counterweight in exercising its assigned role of guardian of the supreme law. Instead it has been beset with institutional weaknesses, and its jurisprudence has largely upheld existing laws, including provisions and acts whose abolishment been persistently called for by UN bodies, such as immunities laws.[82] In several instances this jurisprudence was based on rather questionable functional arguments, for example that the offences were so serious that they required maximum punishments while disregarding the defendants' claim that their confessions had been extracted under torture.[83] The jurisprudence has also been marked by its limited reference to binding international standards or relevant comparative

---

78   UN Secretary-General. 2010. *Report on Sudan*. UN Doc. S/2010/388, paras 2–12.

79   See in the context of elections UN Secretary-General. 2010, para. 8, and Independent expert on the situation of human rights in the Sudan, Mohammed Chande Othman. 2010. *Report*. UN Doc. A/HRC/14/41, para. 22.

80   See chapter 10 and the regular *Sudan Law Reform Update*, available at http://www.pclrs.org/smartweb/english/news-and-events [accessed 5 April 2011].

81   Articles 119–122 in the INC.

82   See in particular HRC. 2007. *Concluding observations: Sudan*. UN Doc. CCPR/C/SDN/CO/3/CRP.1, para. 9(e), and Group of experts mandated by Human Rights Council resolution 4/8 presided by the Special Rapporteur on the situation of human rights in the Sudan and composed of the Special Representative of the Secretary-General for children and armed conflict et al. 2007. *Report on the situation of human rights in Darfur*. UN Doc. A/HRC/5/6, 24, Recommendation 3.2.

83   See *Paul John Kaw and others v (1) Ministry of Justice; (2) Next of kin of Elreashhed Mudawee*, Case No. MD/QD/51/2008, Constitutional Court, Judgment of 13 October 2009.

experiences.[84] The Constitutional Court therefore functioned as the custodian of the existing order in the CPA interim period, even though the CPA and the INC were based on an implicit acknowledgment that this order had contributed to, if not caused conflict, and that there was a need for fundamental change.

The fact that the CPA was built on a one-sided notion of transitional justice that ignored past violations, in conjunction with the limited changes in the existing balance of power, stifled a genuine discourse on the transformations needed to guarantee better human rights protection. The elections of April 2010 were seen by many as a final, and ultimately missed, opportunity to generate the necessary momentum among civil society members and sympathetic parties to bring about the transformation promised by the CPA.

The Darfur peace process initially did not provide an opening for law reform and justice initiatives. Instead, the question of accountability was externalized through the ICC, and the structural shortcomings of the law were dealt with in an ad hoc fashion by setting up special courts, and through limited reforms that were not complemented by the requisite institutional changes.[85] Comprehensive notions of transitional justice (including changes to the legislative framework) only became more central to the debate with the work of the AUPD and the weight given to civil-society-held positions in the Doha peace process in 2010.[86] However, the focus on elections and on the referendum on the independence of the South diverted attention away from the transitional justice process mapped out by the AU Panel. Initial responses by the GoS and subsequent delays suggested little commitment to the fundamental legislative changes needed to facilitate accountability, such as the removal of immunities and statutes of limitation.[87]

The role of the UN and of other international actors in Sudan has been characterized by conflicting policy objectives and a lack of coherence. The UN, the United States US and the Intergovernmental Authority on Development (IGAD) – that is, mainly Sudan's neighbouring countries – had a vested interest in the successful implementation of the CPA. However, as became apparent during the implementation phase, the Assessment and Evaluation Commission mandated to monitor CPA implementation, as well as the UN and other international actors, were faced with a policy dilemma: where is the limit of compromising,

84   See for example *Farouq Mohamed Ibrahim Al Nour v (1) Government of Sudan; (2) Legislative Body*; Final order by Justice Abdallah Aalmin Albashir President of the Constitutional Court, 6 November 2008.

85   AUPD. 2009, 56–63, at paras 215–38.

86   See in this context Max-Planck-Institute for Comparative and Public International Law, Heidelberg, and Peace Research Institute, University of Khartoum. 2010. *Heidelberg Darfur Dialogue Document containing Draft Proposals for Consideration in a Future Peace Agreement*. [Online, May] Available at: http://www.mpil.de/shared/data/pdf/hdd_outcome_document.pdf [accessed 16 December 2010].

87   Human Rights Watch. 2010. *The Mbeki Panel Report One Year on: Continued Inaction on Justice for Darfur Crimes*. [Online, 29 October] Available at: http://www.hrw.org/en/news/2010/10/27/mbeki-panel-report-one-year [accessed 9 December 2010].

or at least downplaying the importance of substantive changes, for the sake of achieving progress in power-sharing arrangements and milestones laid down in the CPA timetable? This was particularly evident during the run-up to the April 2010 elections, when international organizations and foreign states were primarily focused on the event instead of demanding the prerequisites for a free and fair election.[88] It was also illustrated by the inability of international actors to combine efforts aimed at the organization of elections with calls for a substantive implementation of the CPA and the Bill of Rights, despite the forcible dissolution of demonstrations for legislative reforms in December 2009, and the adoption of a new Security Act in January 2010 that clearly fell short of constitutional and international law requirements. This had been a theme throughout the CPA implementation phase, though it ostensibly gave the GoS legitimacy as implementing partner, and put international actors in a position where they felt compelled to make concessions so as not to jeopardize the ultimate outcome (particularly regarding the referendum on the independence of Southern Sudan).[89] As a result of this constellation and the pull of the SPLM towards independence, the GoS has had little incentive to engage in legislative reforms that would result in the protection of rights and democratic transformation, as envisaged in the CPA. This equation was not changed by the role of the AU, the UN and other monitoring bodies urging reforms; the UN missions, and others working on law reform in Sudan, relied considerably on cooperation from the GoS.[90] Such cooperation was not forthcoming (with few exceptions such as the adoption of the Child Act in 2010), which may be attributed to the perception that law reform was not an international policy priority. As a result of these factors, the focus on the referendum on the independence of the South undermined the impetus for genuine legislative and institutional changes in the Sudanese system, at least in the North. The South, meanwhile, benefited from considerable financial and technical support for the building up of its legal infrastructure and legal system, which had been rudimentary at the time the CPA was agreed upon. While this process resulted in a number of promising initiatives, it has also witnessed the close alignment of international actors with the Government of Southern Sudan.[91] This development is to be seen in the context of building the capacity of a new state in the making,

---

88   REDRESS. 2009, 8–11 and Sudan Democracy First Group. 2010. *An Open Letter to President Carter.* [Online, 15 April] Available at: http://www.darfurconsortium.org/ Sudanese%20voices/2010/April/SDFG%20StatementII.041010.pdf [accessed 9 December 2010].

89   REDRESS. 2009, 7.

90   Some actively engaged experts viewed the UN Mission in Sudan (UNMIS) as neglecting the role of civil society in the law reform process. Remarks made during a meeting of the Advisory Committee, Project for Criminal Law Reform in Sudan. May 2010. Khartoum (notes on file with author).

91   See on the position of international actors in the context of the referendum, in particular the United States, Romita, P. 2010. The Sudan Referenda: What Role for International Actors? *International Peace Institute, Policy Papers* [Online, 27 October]

but it can lead to dependency. It may also be further questioned once Southern Sudan is independent and effectively turns into a one-party state, considering the potential for arbitrary law enforcement and violations in a fledgling state that is also facing tribal divisions. From a state-building perspective, the dominance of the SPLM in the process of law-making, in cooperation with international experts such as the UN Development Programme, may become problematic if it is not carried out in consultation with other political forces and civil society. This process, particularly where it results in legislation that does not reflect good practice, may in turn undermine the impact that law reform in the South could potentially have in the North of the country.

The role of international actors in the Darfur conflict has been characterized by a series of policy objectives: to provide protection, secure peace and hold perpetrators of international crimes to account. The UN and the AU in particular relied on GoS cooperation where ground troops were tasked with providing protection, and in the course of mediation efforts towards a peaceful settlement. These objectives were seemingly at odds with the work of the ICC following the UN Security Council referral, with major diplomatic tensions triggered by the application for an arrest warrant against Sudan's President al-Bashir in 2008.[92] This move further politicized any attempts to introduce legislative changes that would have a bearing on events in Darfur. The GoS agreed to cooperate with the AUPD as part of its effort to defer the case against al-Bashir (pursuant to article 16 of the ICC Rome Statute). This has partly shifted the debates back to the regional level and could impact on reforms, since the panel recommended significant legislative and institutional changes, such as the setting up of a hybrid tribunal.[93] Legislative changes may also form part of a peaceful settlement of the Darfur conflict, in which the AUPD has been equally engaged. The GoS has, throughout the conflict, shown itself adept at refraining from agreeing to fundamental changes, particularly those that would result in enhanced accountability and potentially undermine its power. This was in no small part due to the pull of the CPA, which paradoxically resulted in the limited opening of a human rights debate in Sudan while also seemingly shielding the GoS from strong diplomatic pressure, in addition to the broader economic interests at stake for international actors.

Available   at: http://www.ipacademy.org/media/pdf/publications/sudanreferenda.pdf [accessed 9 December 2010].

92   Oette. 2010, 348–9.

93   See Oette, L. 2010. *The African Union High-Level Panel on Darfur: A precedent for regional solutions to the challenges facing international criminal justice?* Paper presented at International Conference: Africa and the Future of International Criminal Justice. Witwatersrand University. Johannesburg. 14–16 July 2010 (on file with author, publication forthcoming).

Conclusion

Despite intense regional and international engagement, the Darfur conflict and the implementation of the CPA left an unreformed government virtually intact and in power along with its enforcement arms, whose members have been implicated in serious human rights violations. This arguably lies at the core of the limited substantive changes made. Irrespective of whether Sudan is characterized as a conflict or post-conflict society, or both, there has been a failure to realize a major transition based on the fundamental values envisaged in the CPA and called for by a multitude of national and international actors. These developments hold a number of important lessons for Sudan and beyond. Firstly, the implementation process was given a state-centric focus due to the lack of participation of broad-based domestic constituencies in peace negotiations, constitution-making and law reform. The process provided limited incentive for either party to engage in the envisaged fundamental transformation of the country. In the case of the ruling party, such an engagement would have necessitated major changes in the power structures that it found unacceptable; on the part of the SPLM, the focus on an independent South became overwhelming following the death of its then-leader John Garang in 2005. Secondly, victims of past violations were not recognized by a peace process and elite-based constitutional, legislative and institutional changes that did not acknowledge the nature, truth and causes of past violations (ideally through mechanisms that would question the way of governance and persisting inequalities and injustices). This has reinforced existing power relations and failed to provide the structural impetus to build a momentum for fundamental change, especially where democratic structures are absent. Thirdly, international engagement sent mixed messages and resulted in contradictory outcomes, combining an outwardly confrontational approach with a cooperative one; this was further compounded by rifts among international actors as to what policy to adopt vis-à-vis Sudan.

The relationship between various international actors and the GoS has been characterized by both underlying tensions and compromises. The GoS to date has seemingly succeeded in making limited concessions, including in the field of legislative and institutional reforms, while equally escaping accountability for serious human rights violations other than verbal condemnation and some narrow sanctions. The AU has emerged as an important actor in the wake of the ICC arrest warrant against President al-Bashir. However, at the time of writing there were concerns as to whether it would be capable of translating its comprehensive and participatory approach – which emphasized transitional justice and development as solutions to the Darfur crisis – into reality, so as to facilitate the more fundamental changes needed to achieve peace, justice and reconciliation. What has become clear is that in these circumstances law reform efforts have been an important indicator of progress, and a critical reference point for key civil society human rights campaigns. However, the nature of the legislative reforms that were actually undertaken has largely constituted a highly visible and unmistakable reminder of the political transition that never was.

Chapter 2

Criminal Law Reform and Human Rights in African and Muslim Countries with Particular Reference to Sudan

Abdelsalam Hassan Abdelsalam and Amin M. Medani

Introduction

The historical development of Sudan's criminal law and its reform constitute an integral part of broader histories. Being located at the interface of African and Islamic heritages, it shares the experience of colonial influences, and the tradition of – as well as experimentation with – *Shari'a* (Islamic law). The legacy of state-centric repression coupled with limited law enforcement in the periphery is one of the enduring challenges bequeathed by colonialism. *Shari'a*, which constitutes an alternative contender for the governing of criminal justice, has itself a mixed history. This history ranges from its original application on the Arab peninsula to its export to very different political and societal contexts, which have given rise to a number of persistent challenges that are particularly pronounced in the Sudanese context.

Sudan's law draws from a range of sources and rich legal traditions. Common law and other legislation inherited from colonial times, Islamic law and Egyptian laws are all reflected in its legislation to varying degrees. These sources are complemented by customary laws whose importance varies depending on the locality. The genesis of Sudan's modern criminal law is characterized by colonial legislation and its radical rejection (during the time of the *Mahdi* in the late nineteenth century), as well as attempts to reflect Sudanese experiences in a modern Criminal Act (1974) and the subsequent, politically motivated incorporation of *Shari'a* components into the 1983 and 1991 Criminal Act.

The changes of 1983 and 1991 have given the impression of an Islamization of Sudan's criminal law. A closer examination reveals that only a limited number of provisions of the Criminal Act are directly governed by *Shari'a*. However, *Shari'a* has taken on great political significance, to the point of stifling debates about particular offences, punishments, and the reform thereof. The consideration of the nature and impact of *Shari'a* must therefore be part of an examination of the protection of human rights in Sudan's criminal law. This must be done, however, without losing perspective on the problematic features of the corpus of the entire criminal law.

An informed debate about the reform of Sudan's law must not only be based on a contextualized understanding of its origins, application and political use; it must also be conscious of the history of attempted reforms over the years. This history provides rich lessons for any current efforts, in terms of the actors and factors that have been influential in shaping reform proposals and bringing about actual changes. To this end this chapter examines Sudan's legal history from its early days to identify relevant sources and assess reform experiences with a particular focus on criminal law. This is with a view to discerning recurring themes and patterns that shed light on systemic challenges experienced and to providing building blocks for any meaningful future reform efforts.

The use of criminal law in the African context: Colonial legacies, repression and conflict

In the African context, the practice of an overbearing state apparatus using criminal law and punishment to enforce its rule can be traced back to colonialism. In pre-colonial times, various systems were in place that provided sanctions for unacceptable conduct. At the risk of oversimplification, these systems were largely based on traditions, at times in combination with elements of Islamic law, and were often geared towards collective reconciliation.[1] The system of colonial rule fostered a mindset, legislation and institutions that made punishments for legally prohibited conduct (and beyond) an integral part of the exercise of state power. Colonial criminal laws were ostensibly designed to maintain and enforce colonial power relations. This applied both at the central and the delegated level of 'customary' chief powers, transforming the system of customary law in the process.[2] In the British sphere of influence, the Indian Penal Code, which also served as template for Sudan, was the paradigm for colonial laws that criminalized a range of activities viewed as threatening the (colonial) state and social order.[3] Such penal codes were often complemented by emergency legislation granting the executive extraordinary powers to criminalize and punish conduct challenging the status quo.[4] At the local level, chiefs were vested with broad discretionary

---

1   See in the context of Sudan, Bleuchot, H. 1994. *Les Cultures Contre L'Homme, Essai D'Anthropologie Historique Du Droit Penal Soudanais*. Aix-En-Provence: Presse Universitaires D'Aix-En-Provence, 212–16.

2   Mamdani, M. 1996. *Citizen and Subject: Contemporary Africa and the Legacy of Late Colonialism*. Princeton: Princeton University Press, 125–7, and in the case of Sudan, particularly Southern Sudan, Idris, A. 2005. *Conflict and Politics of Identity in Sudan*. New York: Palgrave MacMillan, 38–40.

3   Bleuchot. 1994, 294–5.

4   See Rajagopal, B. 2003. *International Law from Below: Development, Social Movements and Third World Resistance*. Cambridge: Cambridge University Press, 178–80.

powers to define and punish misconduct.[5] Taken together, the colonial subject was exposed to the panoply of punishments wielded by the state and its officials acting as agents of a repressive order, though implementation and local practices differed considerably. The criminal justice system of the time provided limited if any checks to counter the essentially arbitrary exercise of power.[6]

Independence would appear to have been an opportune moment to pose the question of the objectives and function of criminal law, punishment and the criminal justice system in a post-colonial state. In practice, most states did little to shake off the colonial legacy. Even though new constitutions were adopted, many of which recognized fundamental rights, criminal laws retained broad and vague offences that lent themselves to repressive abuse.[7] Newly introduced criminal laws, be they of a secular or religious nature, largely perpetuated this practice.[8] Governments frequently resorted to emergency legislation to broaden extant powers even further.[9] These legislative measures often contributed to conflict and facilitated a range of human rights violations. It is therefore no coincidence that, particularly in the wake of transitions from conflict and dictatorships, the reform of laws and institutions, including in the field of criminal justice, has been identified as an important means of enhancing the rule of law and human rights protection.[10]

At present many states, including Sudan, are faced with several critical challenges, some of which constitute a continuing legacy of colonialism and others that are integral to the nature of criminal law. How can criminal law seek to genuinely reflect and protect societal values without degenerating into a repressive tool for the maintenance of state power, especially where the latter is not democratically legitimated? How can an effective criminal justice system be built that respects cultural and societal preferences, and whose system of punishments

---

5   Mamdani. 1996, 125–7.

6   See on the colonial legal order in the service of the postcolonial state, Prempeh, H.K. 2005–2006. *Marbury* in Africa: Judicial Review and the Challenge of Constitutionalism in Contemporary Africa. *Tulane Law Review* 80(4), 1239–324, at 1262–5.

7   The Law and Order (Maintenance) Act [Chapter 11:07] is an instructive example. It was adopted in Southern Rhodesia in 1960 and used as an 'instrument of political oppression wielded by a white minority' during the racist Smith regime from 1965–1979. It was retained after Zimbabwe's independence and repealed in 2002 (to be replaced by the Public Order and Security Act [Chapter 11:17]). See Devittie, J.R. 1987. The Law and Order (Maintenance) Act – an anthology of horrors? *Public Prosecutor's Association of Zimbabwe, Bulletin*, 1(2) (unpaginated).

8   See in particular Keith, L.C. and Ogundele, A. 2007. Legal systems and constitutionalism in Sub-Saharan Africa: An empirical examination of colonial influences on Human Rights. *Human Rights Quarterly* 29(4), 1065–97, particularly at 1067–72.

9   See for example Special Rapporteur of the Sub-Commission, on Human Rights and States of Emergency, Mr Leandro Despouy. 1997. *Final report*. UN Doc. E/CN.4/Sub.2/1997/19 and Add.1.

10   United Nations Secretary-General. 2004. *The Rule of Law and Transitional Justice in Conflict and Post-conflict Societies*. UN Doc. S/2004/616.

is compatible with human rights? From a theoretical perspective, the question of how to ensure that criminal law is based on generally agreed upon principles, applied coherently and in accordance with constitutional precepts and rights, is of crucial importance, both for the legitimacy of the system and the state of the rule of law.

The development of criminal law in states with a Muslim majority

The development of criminal law in states with a Muslim majority has witnessed two seemingly contradictory developments. Following the lead taken by the Ottoman Empire, many states in which elements of Islamic law or customary law were applied adopted criminal codes, drawing primarily on the earlier Ottoman Penal Code (Iraq, Jordan, Lebanon and Syria), French law (Algeria, Lebanon, Morocco), Italian law (Lebanon and Libya), and the Indian Penal Code of 1860 (Bahrain, Kuwait and Pakistan).[11] Other states, in contrast, adopted criminal laws purportedly applying *Shari'a*, which were introduced by dictatorships (Pakistan, Sudan), or following the overthrow of the previous regime (Iran).[12] *Shari'a* has also been invoked and applied by de-facto regimes, such as the Taliban in Afghanistan in the 1990s and regional entities, such as federal states in Northern Nigeria and the North-Western provinces in Pakistan.[13] The use of Islamic law has in these contexts served either as a means of seeking political legitimacy or of expressing or forming a new national identity, or both. Notably, *Shari'a* has simultaneously formed part of the revolutionary armoury of movements, such as political Islamists, including in Sudan, and acted as model of justice used by orthodox forces, with Saudi Arabia arguably providing the main paradigm.[14] In many contexts, the introduction or

---

11   See Ziadeh, F.J. Criminal Law. *The Oxford Encyclopedia of the Islamic World.* [Online, Oxford Islamic Studies] Available at: http://www.oxfordislamicstudies.com/ article/opr/t236/e0170 [accessed 16 December 2010]. See also Peters, R. 2005. *Crime and Punishment in Islamic Law: Theory and Practice from the Sixteenth to the Twenty-first Century.* Cambridge: Cambridge University Press, in particular at 103–5.

12   See on the 'reintroduction of Islamic Criminal Law' in Libya, Pakistan, Iran, Sudan and Northern Nigeria, Peters. 2005, 153–73. On Iran, see also, Zubaida, S. 2003. *Law and Power in the Islamic World.* 2010 Paperback Edition. London and New York: I.B. Tauris, 208–10.

13   See on Northern Nigeria, Peters. 2005, 169–73, and Harnischfeger, J. 2008. *Democratization and Islamic Law: The Sharia Conflict in Nigeria.* Frankfurt and New York: Campus Verlag, 86–104 and 155–87. See on the North–West Frontier Province, Amnesty International. 2010. *As if hell fell on me: The Human Rights Crisis in Northwest Pakistan.* [Online, 9 June] Available at: http://www.amnesty.org/en/library/asset/ASA33/004/2010/ en/1ea0b9e0-c79d-4f0f-a43d-98f7739ea92e/asa330042010en.pdf [accessed on 16 December 2010].

14   According to article 1 of Saudi Arabia's Basic Law of 1992, 'God's Book and the Sunnah of His Prophet' are its constitution. See on Saudi law, Vogel, F.E. 2000. *Islamic Law*

demise of *Shari'a* was therefore closely linked to political developments, thus giving expression to political alignments and changes.

The application of *Shari'a* in a contemporary setting faces a central paradox: how to apply a purportedly divine law within the structures of a modern state? *Shari'a* is essentially a judge-made law that draws on divine sources. Its very codification, as undertaken in Iran, Sudan and elsewhere, compromises this notion, transforming laws based on *Shari'a* into peculiar hybrids. This development harks back to the reforms in the Ottoman period, which have been commented upon as follows:

> The content in the new form [codification] is a different and entirely profane creature. Crucially, codified law in its modern form is the law of the state, and the judge is a functionary of the state who has to arrive at a judgment from the codes and procedures determined by it, rather than by autonomous judgment through reference to sacred sources and the principles derived from them by authoritative ancestors.[15]

Where *Shari'a* had been reverted to in the field of criminal law, it has often given rise to a series of challenges and concerns. This has ranged from the lack of judicial expertise concerning the substance of the law, its selective application, and its repressive use against political and religious opponents, minorities and others.[16] Both the rigid political use of *Shari'a*, such as under Nimeiri in Sudan, and its erratic application, such as the *hudood* laws in Pakistan, have triggered domestic opposition, which contributed to the fall of Nimeiri and political changes in Sudan, and the reform of the laws in Pakistan.[17]

The chequered modern history of the application of *Shari'a* raises a number of questions. Some of these are internal to *Shari'a*, such as whether its design and application in a contemporary state can conform to its principles and serve its objectives, which include it being a reflection of a just society. Others are external, in particular whether laws based on *Shari'a* conform to international human rights standards.[18] From a broader perspective, the use of *Shari'a*-based criminal laws gives rise to concerns familiar in other contexts, including arbitrary law enforcement, overly wide judicial discretion and the repressive application

---

and Legal System: Studies of Saudi Arabia. Leiden: Brill.

15   Zubaida. 2003, 134.

16   The application of *Shari'a* law in Pakistan exhibited a number of these factors: see chapter 11. See more generally on the application of *Shari'a* law in practice, Peters. 2005, particularly at 142–8.

17   See below, *Shari'a as a Focal Point in the Legal and Constitutional Debate in Modern Sudan*, and chapter 11.

18   See Baderin, M. 2005. *International Human Rights and Islamic Law.* Oxford: Oxford University Press, and Mayer, A.E. 2006. *Islam and Human Rights: Tradition and Modernity.* 4th Edition. Boulder, Colorado: Westview Press.

of criminal law to impose a particular social order. How best to overcome these challenges within the *Shari'a* framework remains an enduring challenge for a criminal law with a strong tradition of literal application of sources dating back more than a thousand years.

The development of Sudan's legal system

Historical background: The Funj kingdom of Sinnar and the Fur Sultanate (Darfur)

The Funj kingdom of Sinnar, lasting from 1504–1821,[19] was the first Sudanese entity that drew on both customary law and Islamic law, coming in the wake of earlier Islamization from the tenth century onwards.[20] Sinnar's justice system depended highly on customary law as interpreted by the Sultan, or provincial kings in the urban centres and local chiefs in remote areas. A nucleus of Islamic justice based on the *Maliki* school began to emerge in the sixteenth century and reached its peak in the eighteenth century. Even then, its jurisdiction was limited geographically and in terms of the subject-matters dealt with. The Islamic knowledge and culture that prevailed in the kingdom differed substantially from orthodox Islam, to the extent that some observers concluded that either the Sudanese were bad Muslims or that Sudanese Islam was different from other peoples' Islam.[21] On the whole, the system relied on a plurality of sources, that is, royal, Islamic and customary law, and was characterized by a considerable degree of fluidity and flexibility.[22]

The Fur Sultanate (1650–1916) was another important political entity on the territory of what was later to become Sudan.[23] In Darfur, *Shari'a* and customary law existed side by side and were exercised by the Chiefs, the Elderly, the *Fugra* (Sudanese Arabic for jurists or holy men, singular *Fagir*) and *Qadis* (judges). Criminal matters were adjudicated by the *Shartai* (district chiefs) with the advice of the *Fugra* in accordance with customary law and as laid down in the criminal code known as the book of Dali.[24] The criminal law's primary purpose has been described as providing both power and a source of income for the chiefs and officials through fines, 'the lynchpin of fur law'.[25] *Shari'a* only governed matters

---

19   Holt, P.M. and Daily, M.W. 2000. *A History of the Sudan: From the Coming of Islam to the Present Day*. 5th Edition. Harlow, Essex: Pearson Education Limited, 22–47.

20   Fluehr-Lobban, C. 1987. *Islamic Law and Society in the Sudan*. 1st Edition. London: Frank Cass, 22–3 and 25.

21   Spaulding, J.L. 1967. The evolution of the Islamic Judiciary in the Sinnar. *The International Journal of African Historical Studies*, 3, 408–26, at 409.

22   Bleuchot. 1994, 155.

23   O'Fahey, R.S. 2008. *The Darfur Sultanate: A History*. London: Hurst.

24   See for an account of the book of Dali as reported by the nineteenth-century traveller Nachtigal, Bleuchot. 1994, 159–60.

25   Fahey. 2008, 212.

such as inheritance and marriage affairs, and its status in the Fur Sultanate appears to have been even weaker than in Sinnar.

Other parts of what today constitutes Sudan were largely ruled by customary law.[26] This applied in particular to rural areas and the South. The system of the Dinka, for example, is based on notions of 'unity, solidarity, and harmony with the members of the group' and individual and collective dignity.[27] While wrongs ('criminal offences') are known and may be subject to punishment, the primary goal of customary proceedings is to settle the conflict, provide restitution and restore harmonious relations.[28]

The pre-independence period: The Turko-Egyptian administration, the Mahdiya and the Anglo-Egyptian Condominium (1821–1956)

'Sudan' as a unified geopolitical entity, with all its social, cultural, ethnic and political diversity, took shape in 1821 with the Turko-Egyptian invasion by Khedive Mohamed Ali, the ruler of Egypt on behalf of the Ottoman Empire.[29] The invasion was a colonial enterprise driven by the ambition to exploit Sudan's mineral resources and to forcibly recruit Sudanese men as slaves to strengthen the expansionist military power and might of the Ottoman army in Egypt. Law and justice were not among the priorities of the Turko-Egyptian administration. Criminal law was secular and administered by criminal courts.[30] Customary law and the local mechanisms of justice played their traditional role outside the urban centres.[31] *Shari'a* in its orthodox form was introduced only in the sphere of personal matters related to marriage and inheritance, with a strong influence of the *Hanafi* school.[32] However, the general picture of the applicable laws was by no means clear: '[o]ne cannot say with any degree of certainty what law was applied during that period. The innumerable documents available in the Abidn Archives in Cairo show that *Shari'a* was applied in some cases whereas Egyptian military and civil codes were applied in others. Local custom was recognized and enforced in

26 Mustafa, Z. 1971. *The Common Law in the Sudan: An Account of the 'Justice, Equity, and Good Conscience' Provision.* Oxford: Clarendon Press, 34, suggests that 'the law as applied within the Funj Kingdom in Dongola and Sennar as well as the two independent Sultanates of Kordofan and Darfur was a blend of Islamic law, customary law and superstition. Away from these Kingdoms and Sultanates the rules of customary law reigned supreme'.
27 See Deng, F.M. 2010. *Customary Law in the Modern World: The Crossfire of Sudan's War of Identities.* London and New York: Routledge, 16–17.
28 Deng. 2010, 18–21.
29 Holt and Daily. 2000, 41–51.
30 Fluehr-Lobban. 1987, 30.
31 Deng. 2010, 5.
32 The *Hanafi* school was the then dominant school in Egypt whereas the Sudanese followed the *Malaki* school. See on the influence of both schools in Sudan, Fluehr-Lobban. 1987, 4–6.

civil matters especially in the outer districts where justice was dispensed by local notables'.[33] The regime was marked by heavy taxation and cruel and inhumane means of collecting it. Although complaints about the injustices of the officials were considered, the maximum punishment that would be imposed was the summoning of the official in question to Cairo or his dismissal from service. The law, where applied, thus largely served as the handmaiden of the colonial power to the detriment of the rule of law and human rights: '[w]ith very few exceptions, corruption, exploitation and injustice were the main characteristics of the rulers'.[34]

The oppressive nature and practices of the Ottoman rule provided the impetus for the *Mahdist* uprising against foreign rule and the application of the principles of *Shari'a* for the general governance of the country.[35] Support for the movement that began in 1881 soon spread all over Northern Sudan until the *Mahdi*'s army conquered Khartoum, killed the British governor General Gordon, and won independence. The *Mahdi* died soon after, but the system of rule that he had established was subsequently strictly followed by his successor, Khalifa Abdullahi (1885–1898). It was a rigorous system purporting to apply *Shari'a* in the most extreme way based on 'a unique legal methodology that provided [the Khalifa] with unlimited authority to enact positive rules without any institutional restriction on the part of orthodox *ulama* [Islamic scholars]'.[36] The *Qur'an* and *Sunna* (the prophet's sayings or deeds) were the only sources of law and were applied literally by the courts as interpreted and complemented by the directives (*Manshurat*) of the *Mahdi* and, later Khalifa Abdullahi.[37] Punishments of death, flogging amputations and perishing in prison were ordinarily inflicted, the latter also on judges or emirs who dared disagree with or show dissent to the Khalifa's authority, directives (*fatwas*) or policy decisions.[38] However, 'it is likely that custom did not disappear completely from the Sharia in its Mahdist version',[39] and was applied particularly in those areas where the hold of the *Mahdist* regime was limited.

---

33 Mustafa. 1971, 37.

34 Lutfi, G.A. 1967. The future of the English in the Sudan. *Sudan Law Journal and Reports*, 219–49, at 222.

35 Muhammad Ahmad Ibn 'Abdallah headed a liberation movement against the Egyptian occupation based on his claim to be the *Mahdi*, that is 'the divine leader chosen by God at the end of time to fill the earth with justice and equity, even as it had been filled with oppression and wrong' (Holt and Daily. 2000, 76). See on the *Mahdist* state, Holt and Daily. 2000, 75–97, and for a 'brief examination of early *Mahdist* ideology and politics', Layish, A. and Warburg, G.R. 2002. *The Reinstatement of Islamic Law in Sudan under Numayri: An Evaluation of a Legal Experiment in the Light of its Historical Context, Methodology and Repercussions.* Leiden: Brill, 2–8.

36 Layish, A. 1997. The legal methodology of the Mahdi. *Sudanic Africa*, 8, 37–66, at 39.

37 Fluehr-Lobban. 1987, 32.

38 See Omer, E.F.E. 1964. The administration of justice during the Mahdiya. *Sudan Law Journal and Reports*, 167–70.

39 Layish. 1997, 43.

The *Mahdist* rule, though short-lived, has had considerable historical significance as it was the first concerted attempt to apply *Shari'a* in Sudan. However, its claim to adhere to *Shari'a* was questionable in terms of methodology.[40] The application of *Shari'a* was characterized by the rigorous and idiosyncratic enforcement of customary moral standards and the suppression of women's rights, as well as its use against political offenders labelled as apostates.[41] Nevertheless, many viewed the *Mahdiya* as national emancipation.[42] This includes its claim to establish *Shari'a* as law of the land, which set a precedent for political groups subsequently to refer to it as the foundation for Sudanese law.[43] The *Mahdi*'s brand of Islamic law thus combined an explosive mixture of anti-colonial, nationalist, Islamic and authoritarian features that were to influence the later development of *Shari'a* in Sudan.

The *Mahdist* rule came to an end in 1898 with the conquest of the country by the Anglo-Egyptian forces led by General (later Lord) Kitchener. Although many developments and changes have occurred since the British established the legal system of the Anglo-Egyptian Sudan, in particular criminal law, the current legal system remains to a great extent an offshoot thereof.[44] The Anglo-Egyptian condominium agreement of 1899 on Sudan gave the British Governor General overall supreme military and civil command, as well as supreme legislative authority.[45] The British policy was to develop a modern legal system different from the legal system of Egypt. Article 5 of the Anglo-Egyptian agreement stipulated that '[n]o Egyptian Law, Decree, Ministerial Arrete, or other enactment hereafter to be made or promulgated shall apply to the Sudan or any part thereof, save in so far as the same shall be applied by Proclamation of the Governor-General in manner hereinbefore provided'. This allowed the British to apply the laws they knew best. Another reason for avoiding the Egyptian system was to save Sudan from the injustices of mixed courts. According to this system, citizens of European countries who were residents in the territories of the Ottoman Empire were only subject to the jurisdiction of their consuls and subsequently in front of mixed courts.[46] This system was created to exempt Europeans from the *hudud*

---

40   Bleuchot. 1994, 190–97, on the 'fundamentalist' but contradictory features of *Mahdist* law.

41   Bleuchot. 1994, 192; Mustafa. 1971, 39; Fluehr-Lobban. 1987, 32–3.

42   Fluehr-Lobban. 1987, 32.

43   Layish and Warburg. 2002, 8–69.

44   Deng. 2010, 9–10.

45   See article 3 of the Anglo-Egyptian Agreement of 1899 'relative to the future administration of the Sudan', reproduced in Al-Rahim, M.A. 1969. *Imperialism and Nationalism in the Sudan: A Study in Constitutional and Political Development 1899–1956.* Oxford: Oxford University Press, 233–5. All Governors General, from Lord Kitchener who led the re-conquest of Sudan to Sir Robert Howe who handed the country to the first national government, were British.

46   See Wilner, G.M. 1975. The mixed courts of Egypt: A study on the use of Natural Law and Equity. *Georgia Journal of International and Comparative Law.* 5(2), 407–30,

punishments of amputation, lapidation (stoning) and whipping. Mixed courts continued in Egypt even after the fall of the Ottoman Empire up until the 1930s.[47]

The penal and criminal procedure codes introduced in 1898 effectively constituted the first codification of criminal laws in modern Sudan. The penal code adapted the code drafted by Lord Macaulay for India in 1860 to the needs of Sudan.[48] Both the penal and criminal procedure codes were amended in 1925 and remained in force until the early 1970s. The British administration tried from the outset to make the laws compatible with the social and religious values of the Sudanese people. The adoption of the Indian model was based on the assumption that the then social structure and habits of India were closer to Sudan than that of England. However, the new administration did not fully cede to Sudanese customs and values in its application and interpretation of laws where this was held to be intolerable. Examples of this are the 'prohibition of slavery, which was a recognized institution in the agricultural communities of Sudan, and the prohibition of the pharaonic type of female circumcision ... which [was] not considered wrong by many Sudanese' at the time.[49]

The 1925 Penal Code developed over the years to become truly Sudanese. In some instances, this was done by allowing *dia* (blood money) in settlement of homicide cases. The judges, in their application of the law, took into consideration the social elements of Sudan's many localities and cultures. This was evident in the precedents that formed an important part of Sudanese law until 1983, which was similar to the system followed in other common law countries.

These developments were also reflected in the sphere of civil and commercial law in which the rules to be applied were stipulated in Section 9 of the Civil Justice Ordinance, 1929: '[i]n cases not provided for by this or any other enactment for the time being in force; the Court shall act according to justice, equity and good conscience'. It was this provision that seemed to have given rise to the most intense controversy in the historical development of Sudanese law. Since justice was administered by British judges, trained only in the British tradition, it was natural that they would interpret 'justice, equity and good conscience' in light of the principles of English law, that is the only jurisdiction with which they were familiar. This seemed to be rather illogical, as the standards of conduct, social

---

at 410–11, according to whom the system of mixed courts was established in Egypt in the late nineteenth century, composed of judges drawn from foreign powers who applied and substantive law derived from various legal codes.

47   Article 6 of the Anglo Egyptian Agreement of 1899 stated that, '[i]n the definition by Proclamation of the conditions under which Europeans, of whatever nationality, shall be at liberty to trade with or reside in the Sudan, or to hold property within its limits, no special privileges shall be accorded to the subjects of any one or more Power'. See Al-Rahim. 1969, 234.

48   Mustafa. 1971, 43–6, and Guttmann. 1957. The Reception of Common Law in the Sudan. *International and Comparative Law Quarterly*, 6(3), 401–17, at 405.

49   Guttmann. 1957, 405.

customs, moral and religious values prevailing in Sudan at the time were very different from those applicable in late Victorian England. Some of the leading British judges, however, were from the very beginning aware of this problem and senior judges among them endeavoured to emphasize that their role should not be just to fill the legal vacuum by transplanting English law into the new system. Rather, they sought to adapt it to the prevailing local values, needs and customs. In so doing, they managed to prevent a blind replication of English law into the Sudanese system, and contributed to what later emerged as 'Sudanese Law' by the middle of the twentieth century.[50]

In the realm of *Shari'a*, this trend was supported by the judicial circulars and memoranda of the Grand *Qadi*[51] which 'over the years have provided the major vehicle for reform and for adaptation of the principles of the *Shari'a* to local conditions in the Sudan'.[52] When the first Grand *Qadi* was tasked to establish the *Shari'a* courts for personal affairs in 1899 he faced two major challenges, namely a shortage of personnel qualified in *Shari'a* and a lack of an established court system. Sudan had been ruled by Islamic law before the re-conquest during the *Mahdi* era, and one would have expected there to be a reasonable number of people qualified in *Shari'a*. However, the problems faced by the first Grand *Qadi* were indicative of the poor quality of the then extant system of justice. To overcome the dearth of qualified personnel, courses in Islamic law were introduced in the Faculty of Law of the newly established Gordon Memorial College in the 1930s. As a result, the work of the *Shari'a* courts steadily improved and gained in respect.[53]

However, the new system had several shortcomings. The Penal Code contained the vague crime of inciting hatred against government. There were also crimes prescribed in anticipation of any communist activities laid down in the Combating Subversive Activities Act of 1953, which, judging by today's standards, may be said to have infringed upon the freedom of association and freedom of expression. These provisions remained in the statute book after independence, and have been used by national governments against the opposition notwithstanding calls for their abolition, especially from the political left.

Independence and the early phases of law reform (1956–1974)

At the time of the country's independence in 1956, Sudanese judges were in full control of the administration of justice. Nationalist feelings and the fact that an increasing number of lawyers graduated under the civil law tradition, mainly in Egypt, in other Arab countries and, later, from the Cairo University, Khartoum

---

50   Mustafa. 1971, 92–105.

51   The Grand Qadi is the president of the *Shari'a* judiciary who had the power to issue legal circulars, see on his role Layish and Warburg. 2002, 72–5.

52   Fluehr-Lobban. 1987, 37.

53   Guttmann. 1957, 407.

Branch, led to the raising of high-sounding patriotic slogans of law reform, to rid the country of 'colonial laws' and to promulgate national Sudanese laws. The late Chief Justice, G.A. Lutfi, provided some insight into the background of those calling for law reform:

> The first idea is that of a group which consisted of some of the Muslims from the Northern Sudan who asked for the application of Islamic law in all matters. Another group is formed of those who are in favour of some sort of closer relationship with the United Arab Republic and the Arab world, demanded [sic] the adoption of the Egyptian law, which is the basic law of all other Arabic countries.
>
> A third group which believed in election, advocated the ideas that the suitable system to be adopted is that which consists of what is chosen from the best laws of each country from all over the world.
>
> As opposed to the above three groups [which, except for the Islamists, were neither organised nor provided any projects or draft laws to be implemented], the majority of the population are of opinion that, since the present laws did not prove unsuitable there is no need to change them.[54]

The call for the implementation of Egyptian laws and the Egyptian legal system was driven by pan-Arab sentiments. Unifying the laws in the Arab countries was seen as a step on the road to unifying the whole Arab nation. Egypt has always been important in the Arab world and during the 1950s it was seen as the leading Arab country under the leadership of President Nasser. The advocacy for Egyptian laws was thus based on a wider nationalist rationale rather than a purely legal one. However, the supporters ignored the fact that changing to the Egyptian model would have in fact meant replacing one European model by another: civil law in place of common law or French law in place of Anglo-Saxon law. In addition, as Egon Guttmann noted, '[t]o change the basis of that law from common law to that underlying the law of Egypt would be a change for the sake of change and would have neither intrinsic merit nor popular appeal'.[55]

The Nimeiri regime (1969–1985)[56] was initially characterized by strong Arab nationalist tendencies among some of its leadership. In 1970 the regime introduced a new civil code, copied in large part from the Egyptian Civil Code of 1949. The new law was alien to Sudan's legal education and training and met with strong opposition from the legal profession. Largely as a result of this, the experiment was short-lived and the government repealed this code in 1973, returning the country's legal system to its pre-1970 common law basis.[57] In 1974,

---

54   Lutfi. 1967, 219.
55   Guttmann. 1957, 416.
56   Holt and Daily. 2000, 166–79.
57   Metz, H.C. (ed.). 1991. *Sudan: A Country Study.* [Online, Washington: GPO for the Library of Congress] Available at: http://countrystudies.us/sudan/65.htm [accessed 15 January 2010].

the Minister of Justice, Dr Zaki Mustafa, a former dean of the Faculty of Law at the University of Khartoum, made an invaluable contribution to the codification and stabilization of the laws of Sudan. Aided by some of his colleagues at the Ministry of Justice and the Faculty of Law, he embarked on a colossal process that codified all the criminal and civil laws of Sudan in eleven volumes that, except for some miscellaneous changes and additions made subsequently, can still be considered the basic reference for Sudanese law today.

Shari'a *as a focal point in the legal and constitutional debate in modern Sudan*

Shari'a encompasses the *Qur'an* and *Sunna* as well as the principles and rules developed by the Islamic *ulama* (scholars) in what is known as *fiqh* (Islamic jurisprudence). In the field of criminal law, three types of crimes were specified: *hudud, qisas* (retribution), and *ta'azir*. *Hudud* are crimes determined by the *Qur'an* or *Sunna* that carry fixed punishments, and are confined to the following: (i) *hadd al-zina* adultery or fornication; (ii) *hadd al-qadf* false accusation of adultery or fornication; (iii*) hadd al-sariqa* theft; (iv) *hadd al-haraba* robbery or rebellion; (v) *hadd al-shurb* drinking of alcohol; and (vi) *hadd al-ridda* apostasy (renunciation of Islam). The crimes of *qisas* (retribution) cover homicide and personal injuries. In respect of these crimes the plaintiff has the right to choose between retribution and *dia* (a fixed amount of compensation).

Ta'azir was originally understood to refer to ad-hoc punishments passed by the judge for acts other than those defined as *qisas* and *hudud*. Some observers refer to all crimes other than *qisas* and *hudud* in modern penal codes as *ta'azir* crimes. However, some scholars insist that *ta'azir* crimes should not be codified and have a specific punishment attached to them. For example, in 1982 the Iranian parliament enacted the penal code with four parts. The first contains *hudud*, the second *qisas*, the third *dia*, and the fourth *ta'azir*, which includes all the crimes that are not within the scope of the previous three parts. The Council of Guardians, which examines the compatibility of legislation with the *Shari'a*, refused to pass the law on the grounds that the *ta'azir* should not be fixed and that it should be left to the judge to identify the crime and set the punishment. The parliament insisted on the act because of the rule of *nullem crime sine lege* (prohibition of retroactive application). The conflict was eventually resolved by Ayatollah Khomeini's intervention and the act was passed.[58]

The supporters of *Shari'a* in Sudan and other countries use the dichotomy of divine law and manmade law (*wad'i*). They assert that Muslim believers who are the majority in Sudan should undoubtedly follow the divine law. So the question of *Shari'a* versus secular laws is a question of whether or not to apply the *hudud* and *qisas*. Supporters insist that *Shari'a* provisions should be implemented

---

58   Azadeh, N. 1999. The Islamisation of law in Iran: A time of disenchantment, in *Middle East Report*, edited by Cairo Institute of Human Rights Studies. Cairo: Roaa Mugaira.

irrespective of the consequences, including concerns over their compatibility with international human rights treaties binding on Sudan.

The status of *Shari'a* in the legal system has always been an important and sensitive subject in Sudan. There were two types of courts in Sudan: *Shari'a* courts headed by the Grand *Qadi* and civil courts headed by the Chief Justice. The first type had jurisdiction over Muslims' personal status matters concerning marriage, divorce, guardianship, inheritance, gifts, and *waqf* in accordance with Islamic law and the second over the rest of all other civil and criminal matters. However, according to the Mohammedan Law Courts Ordinance of 1902, any other civil dispute could be determined according to *Shari'a* 'provided that all the parties, whether being Mohammedan or not, make a formal demand signed by them asking the court to entertain the question and stating that they agree to be bound by the ruling of Mohammedan law'. However, by the time of independence, the only two recorded cases under the Law concerned Copts, 'whose succession laws used to be the same as the rules laid down in *Shari'a*, [and who] had their dispute over an estate determined by the Mohammedan Law Court'.[59] The second schedule of the civil procedures code of 1974 restated the same provision as that in the Mohammedan Law Courts Ordinance referred to above but there is nothing to indicate that any other exception occurred until 1983 when *Shari'a* was declared.

Notwithstanding the apparent lack of recourse to Islamic law in non-religious disputes, the collective call for the implementation of *Shari'a* has always been strong in Sudanese politics, especially after independence. In the second parliamentary period (1964–1969), *Shari'a* supporters succeeded in securing a majority to pass a draft constitution based on *Shari'a*, which was pre-empted by Nimeiri's coup of 25 May 1969. However, the same regime, having lost the allegiance of other political groups and seeking the support of the Islamists, formed a committee in the mid-1970s to review Sudanese laws in accordance with *Shari'a*. The committee did not finish its work but some of its members stated that 85 per cent of the then Sudanese laws were compatible with *Shari'a*. This led to the impression that only limited amendments were needed in order to ensure that the laws were not in violation of *Shari'a*. However, Nimeiri unexpectedly declared the rule of *Shari'a* in September 1983, in a step that had been preceded by the proclamation of a state of emergency. Within a few weeks President Nimeiri had declared the immediate applicability of Islamic criminal law based on drafts prepared by some three young lawyers in the Presidential Palace. In a most extraordinary development, the laws were adopted by Presidential Decree although Parliament was in session.[60]

What have become known as the 'September laws' introduced the whole set of *Shari'a* crimes to Sudan. The Penal Code of 1974 was amended to add the Islamic punishments of *huddud* and *qisas*. This included the amputation of a hand for theft, cross amputation or death for robbery, stoning to death for *zina* (adultery) if the person is married or 100 lashes otherwise, 100 lashes and possible imprisonment

---

59   Guttmann. 1957, 407, at note 10.
60   See on the 'policy of Islamizing the law', Layish and Warburg. 2002, 75–7.

of up to five years for sodomy, and the death penalty or life imprisonment in the case of a third conviction. Rape was subject to 100 lashes and imprisonment of up to ten years unless it also amounted to adultery or sodomy in which case it carried the death penalty. Flogging was the prescribed punishment for drinking or possession of alcohol.

The September laws were applied in the most ruthless and widespread fashion.[61] Special courts, called the 'Prompt Justice Courts', were established under the state of emergency. Police and security forces confronted men and women in their houses, clubs, cars and elsewhere and presented them before these kangaroo courts, which sought to excel each other in the passing of extremely severe punishments, ranging from amputation, cross amputation, floggings and imprisonment to death. Radio and TV broadcasters and newspapers were quick to publish the full names of persons convicted and punished. Men and women found in cars together were promptly charged and sent to trial for 'attempted adultery' unless they produced evidence of marriage or an intimate blood relationship. Terror reigned over the country.

In December 1984, Mahmoud M. Taha, a well-known leader of the Islamic Republicans, distributed a leaflet through his supporters in which he criticized the practices of the regime as an insult that undermined Islamic principles. A special court was set up before which he refused to plead or defend himself. The court convicted and sentenced him to death for committing a crime against the state under the Penal Code. Instead of sending the verdict to the High Court as required by law, a Special Court of Appeal headed by the infamous Prompt Justice Court Judge Al Mikashfi not only confirmed the sentence of death, but changed the conviction to 'apostasy' (*ridda*), even though no such offence was recognized under the Penal Code. This he did by relying on another infamous September Law called The Sources of Judicial Decision Act, 1983, which enabled judges, in the absence of a legislative provision, to apply their own opinions on Islamic jurisprudence and make decisions accordingly. Thus, in contradiction to the established and common law principle of no punishment without law, the court applied ex-post facto or pocket pistol law. Needless to say, the president confirmed the sentence and Taha was executed on 18 January 1985, a sad day for justice in Sudan, condemned the world over.[62]

Not surprisingly the 1983 September laws created a heated debate. Many opposed them on the ground of their incompatibility with basic rights and freedoms. Some considered them a deviation from the true provisions of Islam. Among those who held this opinion was Mr. Al-Sadiq Al-Mahdi, the leader of the Ummah Party and Ansar sect, who described it as not worth the ink that it was written with. Nevertheless, the September laws were not abolished during his premiership (1986–1989), which followed the overthrow of Nimeiri by a popular

---

61   See for a detailed study of the introduction of *Shari'a* in Sudan's criminal law in 1983, Layish and Warburg. 2002, 75–142.

62   See Layish and Warburg. 2002, 54–60.

uprising. The debate over *Shari'a* and the fate of the September laws marked the third democracy as civil society organizations, left-wing political forces and the political representatives of marginalized peoples called for their repeal. Abolishment of the September laws was also a precondition for the peaceful settlement to the civil war in the south of Sudan, the Nuba mountains, and the Blue Nile. Nevertheless these forces, despite support from groups in the two major parties, the Ummah Party and Democratic Unionist Party (DUP), failed to change the September laws. Conversely, the parliamentary majority of *Shari'a* supporters was insufficient to impose its application and they failed to pass a penal code based on *Shari'a* (known as Turabi's Law) due to a strong campaign led by the Bar Association and other parts of civil society. The only change of significance was the amendment of the Sources of Judicial Decisions Act of 1983, restricting its application to civil, as opposed to criminal, matters. A new Judiciary Act was also adopted in 1986 purporting to confirm the independence of the judiciary. In mid 1989 the then government adopted the blue print of an agreement made by John Garang and Mulana Muhammad Osman Almirghani to end the civil war between the North and the South that had been rekindled by the 1983 September laws; the agreement, *inter alia*, envisaged the suspension of the 1983 September laws based on *Shari'a*. However, the plan was stopped by the Islamists' coup d'etat of June 1989.[63]

After the coup the new military rulers abrogated the constitution, and dissolved all executive and legislative organs, trade unions, professional associations and non-governmental organizations (NGOs). Thousands of army and police officers, civil servants and employees of state corporations were summarily dismissed 'in the public interest', and so were hundreds of judges from the district to the high court level.[64] Large numbers of political trade union leaders, whom the regime considered 'possible' opponents, were arbitrarily detained for months or years in prisons and 'safe houses' throughout the country. Many suffered physical and psychological injuries, or were tortured to death.[65] None of the foregoing violations was justiciable as the courts were prevented from entertaining any such complaints under the state of emergency, which lasted several years. Several military and special courts were established, and tried those opposed to the regime.[66]

---

63   See for an account of these developments, Layish and Warburg. 2002, 293–302.

64   See on the long-term consequences of these dismissals, interview of Dr A.M. Medani and O. El Farouk Shoumena by F. Deng, in Deng. 2010, 294.

65   See Medani, A.M. 2001. *Crimes Against Humanity in Sudan, 1989–2000*. Cairo: Dar El Mostaqbal El Arabi, 95–132.

66   See Human Rights Watch/Africa. 1996. *Behind the Red Line: Political Repression in Sudan*. New York: Human Rights Watch, and *Amnesty International and others v Sudan*, African Commission on Human and Peoples' Rights, Communications 48/90, 50/91, 52/91 and 89/93 (1999).

The regime sought to transform Sudanese society into a model Islamic society through what it called the 'civilization project'.[67] It enacted a new Criminal Act in 1991, that is, a criminal code on an Islamic basis that was technically better drafted than the September 1983 models.[68] This act has remained in force since, though it has been opposed by many, in particular the Southern Sudanese. In 2005, an agreement was reached with the Sudan People's Liberation Movement/Army (SPLM/A), known as the Comprehensive Peace Agreement (CPA). The CPA exempted the South from *Shari'a* while it kept it in the North. This triggered a fierce debate over the status of *Shari'a* in the national capital. Many argued that the capital being the national capital of all Sudanese should be exempted from *Shari'a*. The ruling National Congress Party (NCP) insisted that *Shari'a* should be applied to Muslims in the capital and this is what was agreed upon.[69]

The NCP hoped that this would be the end of the debate over *Shari'a*. However, the CPA set the democratic transformation of Sudan as an objective. This task included the harmonization of laws with the Interim National Constitution (INC) of 2005, which includes a Bill of Rights containing fundamental rights. It also required that laws need to be harmonized with the international human rights instruments ratified by Sudan in accordance with article 27(3) of the INC, which reads, '[a]ll rights and freedoms enshrined in international human rights treaties, covenants and instruments ratified by the Republic of the Sudan shall be an integral part of this Bill'.This raised the question of whether *hudud* punishments are compatible with the International Covenant on Civil and Political Rights, the African Charter on Human and Peoples' Rights, and other treaties to which Sudan is a state party. There are no easy answers to the question of *Shari'a* and human rights, but it has to be addressed wisely and in a manner that can gain the greatest possible consensus.

Law reform initiatives in Sudan

The Sudan Bar Association's campaign for law reform

Many Sudanese lawyers share a history of knowledge and commitment to human rights and the rule of law. The Sudan Bar Association was very active throughout the 1980s in defending human rights, basic freedoms and the rule of law. In 1981,

---

67   See de Waal, A. and Abdel Salam, A.H. 2004. Islamism, state power and Jihad in Sudan, in *Islamism and its Enemies in the Horn of Africa*, edited by A. de Waal. London: Hurst, 71–113.

68   See for an insider's perspective of the 1991 Criminal Law, interview of O. Yassin, then Minister of Justice in 2005, by F. Deng, in Deng. 2010, 279–80.

69   See Medani, A.M. 2005. *Human Rights in the Interim Constitution*. Khartoum: Khartoum University Students Union in Cooperation with Sudan Social Development Organization, 16–22.

in celebration of the silver jubilee of Sudan's independence, the council of the Bar Association organized a series of seminars to discuss a range of issues related to the administration of justice, independence of the judiciary, promotion of the legal profession, human rights and basic freedoms, and the rule of law. In those seminars individual lawyers presented research findings on a number of laws and made suggestions towards reform. This was effectively the first time in which law reform was comprehensively considered in Sudan.

The Bar Association continued this line of activism, and the tradition of studying existing and newly enacted legislation in terms of their intrinsic legal quality and in relation to human rights. When Nimeiri introduced the September laws in 1983 the Bar Association organized several fora to discuss them, and by the time of the third democratic period (1985–1989) it was able to prepare alternative law proposals. The best known among these drafts is the Bar Penal Code, which was based on the 1974 code with some amendments. This rich heritage of initiating and overseeing law reform initiatives might offer a foundation for future law reform efforts, provided the requisite political will exists.

The civil project

In 1997 four organizations came together with the aim of furthering human rights in any future transition to democracy in Sudan. These were the Sudan Human Rights Organization, the South Sudan Law Society, Nuba Mountains Solidarity Abroad, and Africa Rights (which was later replaced by Justice Africa). The four organizations formed the Steering Committee for Human Rights during Transition in Sudan. It was later renamed the Committee for the Civil Project in Sudan. The committee worked for two years preparing for a conference that would bring together Sudanese democratic political forces and civil society organizations to discuss the human rights challenges in any future transition. The conference was convened in Kampala, Uganda, in February 1999; a second conference took place in July 2000. The committee prepared well-researched and well-written issue papers that helped the conference have rich and useful discussions on the issues.[70] The conferences adopted two declarations that were signed by the participating political parties and civil society organizations. The declarations confirmed the participants' commitment to a range of issues pertaining to accountability, human rights and law reform:

> The Conference examined issues of the penal code, customary law, and the structure and reform of the judicial, police and penal institutions of Sudan. The Conference agreed that:

---

70   The papers were published in two books: Abdel Salam, A.H. and De Waal, A. (eds). 2002. *The Phoenix State: Civil Society and the Future of Sudan*. Asmara: The Red Sea Press, and De Waal, A. and Ajawin, Y. (eds). 2002. *When Peace Comes: Civil Society and Development in Sudan*. Asmara: The Red Sea Press.

1. In all matters of law, commitment to international human rights law should be supreme.
2. In line with the Charter of NDA [National Democratic Alliance], the 1974 Penal Code, with suitable revisions to make it consonant with international human rights Conventions, was appropriate for Sudan and the rights and needs of Sudanese citizens.
3. Customary law, in all parts of Sudan, has both positive and negative elements. It reflects the needs and experiences of Sudan's people with their diverse cultures. There is a need to codify it and reform some aspects of customary law, especially concerning women's rights, and native administration to make them consonant with basic human rights, and to coordinate customary law and the structures to enforce it.
4. Sudan's judicial, police and penal structures are in urgent need of drastic reform including the recruitment of qualified personnel … and making justice more accessible to the people, that is cheaper, fairer, and less subject to various biases and corrupting influences.
5. Independence of the judiciary as an institution and judges as state officials should be provided with [sic] along with legal aid and a reduction in the cost of litigation.[71]

The second Kampala conference called upon the Transitional Government to do the following:

1. Cancel all laws that contradict basic rights in a way that ensures full rights for expression and association as well as women's basic rights.
2. Undertake radical transformation in the legal and judicial structures and amend laws in a way that enshrines the values of justice, equality and the rule of law and independence of the judiciary.
3. Abrogate any laws that are contrary to freedom of association, including the Voluntary Work Act 1999.
4. Establish an independent Human Rights Commission or high council for civil society issues within the structure of the government to ensure the promotion of civil society.[72]

The Kampala Forum, as the two conferences were called, derived its significance from the fact that it was representative of Sudan's political forces and geographical, social and cultural diversity. Although the signatures of political parties are not legally binding, it has great moral value and reflects the common grounds that existed between the main political players, with the exception of the government party.

---

71   Abdelsalam and de Waal. 2002, 296–7.
72   De Waal and Ajawin. 2002, 289.

Current efforts (2005–2010)

The issue of law reform gained new impetus with the adoption of the CPA in 2005. Its chapter II, 1.6., contains a commitment of the Republic of Sudan to comply fully with its international human rights treaty obligations and lists a series of human rights and fundamental freedoms. The CPA also provides for the setting up of a National Constitutional Review Commission (NCRC) tasked with preparing the INC and 'such other legal instruments as is required to give effect to the Peace Agreement (2.12.9)'.

In 2005, the INC was adopted, which contains a Bill of Rights. Its article 27(3) incorporates international human rights treaties binding on Sudan. Article 27(2) stipulates that '[t]he State shall protect, promote, guarantee and implement this Bill' and, pursuant to article 27(4), '[l]egislation shall regulate the rights and freedoms enshrined in the Bill and shall not detract from or derogate any of these rights'. The INC also makes provision for the NCRC (article 140) and the establishment of a Constitutional Court, which is vested with the power to protect human rights and rule on the constitutionality of laws (articles 119–122).

In a flurry of initial activities, several committees were tasked with law reform. In 2005, the NCRC and Ministry of Justice identified over 60 laws in need of harmonization with international human rights standards. The Legislative Standing Committee of Parliament earmarked 12 laws as priority areas, including the 1991 Criminal Act and 1991 Criminal Procedure Act. However, the effectiveness of these bodies was hampered by a series of factors, including their limited resources, capacity and composition – primarily of members selected by the two main parties. The absence of a single dedicated body such as a law reform commission has undermined law reform in the absence of a coordinated and concerted effort by the various bodies to identify priorities and concentrate on concrete reforms.[73]

Civil society has sought to use the opportunity provided by the CPA to advocate for legislative reforms and several campaigns have been undertaken. However, civil society groups initially struggled to generate a broad public debate and momentum towards law reform. This changed in 2009 when the issue of legislative reforms was taken up by the political opposition parties and was made a part of the election demands. Law reform, in particular the reform of the national security laws, became a focal point of the political debate, but the impact of these efforts was lessened by the insistence of the NCP to dominate the political scene,

---

73   See for a comprehensive study of the process of law reform in Sudan, REDRESS and SORD. 2009. *Implementing the Comprehensive Peace Agreement and the National Interim Constitution? An empirical assessment of the law reform process in Sudan: Challenges and prospects.* [Online, December] Available at: http://www.pclrs.org/downloads/Miscellaneous/Implementing%20the%20Comprehensive%20Peace%20Agreement.pdf [accessed 28 December 2010].

the weakness of political parties, political repression, and the limited attention given by international actors.[74]

Civil society initiatives, with the support of United Nations (UN) bodies, have had some effect on legislation such as the Child Act of 2010. This success was based on effective coalition building and the fact that the law was ostensibly less controversial than others. In contrast, legislation concerning core aspects of the exercise of state power, such as the Armed Forces Act of 2007, the Police Act of 2008, the amended Criminal Act of 2009 and the National Security Act of 2010, have retained if not added a number of problematic features that raise concerns over their compatibility with human rights standards.[75] The reform of other sensitive aspects of the law, such as on rape and sexual violence,[76] public order[77] and family law,[78] have stalled. This reflects the lack of support these initiatives enjoy on the part of the ruling party that holds the majority in parliament, and the limited influence that national and international actors, such as the UN Mission in Sudan (UNMIS) and other agencies have been able to exert in regard of critical areas of the law.

The CPA envisages three layers of government for Southern Sudan, comprising the GOS, the Government of Southern Sudan (GOSS) and separate governments for the ten states of the South. Each of these governments can pass laws that apply in Southern Sudan, making the applicable legal system 'cumbersome'.[79] In addition, the transitional areas of Southern Blue Nile, Southern Kordofan (Nuba mountains) and Abyei are subject to special arrangements. The GOSS relied on the laws of the new Sudan drafted by the SPLM before the adoption of the CPA and

---

74   See REDRESS. 2009. *Promoting law reform in Sudan to enhance human rights protection, strengthen the rule of law and foster democratic processes. Written Evidence submitted by the Redress Trust to the UK Associate Parliamentary Group on Sudan: Parliamentary Hearings: Sudan's Comprehensive Peace Agreement.* [Online, 15 October] Available at: http://www.redress.org/documents/REDRESS%20Submission%20CPA%20 15%20October%202009.pdf [accessed 16 December 2010].

75   See position papers and reports on the respective laws available at: http://www. pclrs.org/resources.htm [accessed 16 December 2010].

76   REDRESS and KCHRED. 2008. *Time for Change – Reforming Sudan's Legislation on Rape and Sexual Violence.* [Online, October] Available at: http://www.pclrs.org/ downloads/Miscellaneous/Position%20Paper%20Rape.pdf [accessed 16 December 2010].

77   SIHA. 2009. *Beyond Trousers: The Public Order Regime and the Human Rights of Women and Girls in Sudan.* [Online, 12 November] Available at: http://www.pclrs.org/ downloads/Miscellaneous/Public%20Order%20Submission%20Paper%20MASTER%20 FINAL.pdf [accessed 16 December 2010].

78   See in this context the study by Tønnessen, T. 2008. Gendered citizenship in Sudan: competing debates on family laws among northern and southern elites in Khartoum. *The Journal of North African Studies*, 13(4), 455–69.

79   Tier, A.M. 2008. The legal system of Southern Sudan in transition, in *Law Reform in Sudan: Collection of Workshop Papers*, edited by A.M. Tier and B. Badri. Khartoum: Ahfad University for Women, 43–54, at 43.

adopted newly drafted laws to govern state institutions and newly formed bodies, such as the National Human Rights Commission.[80] In late 2010, the GOSS set up a law reform commission against the backdrop of possible independence following the 2011 referendum to undertake a wholesale review of the laws applicable in the South. In addition, a Customary Law Steering Committee involving 'representatives from the judiciary, legal affairs, women and child welfare, local government, and the law society' was in the process of considering the reform of customary law.[81] Important laws such as the 2009 Child Act were adopted in the South and lauded by international organizations for the level of protection provided.[82] However, the law reform process in the South has been characterized by delays and legislation such as the new criminal law (Penal Code of 2008 largely following Sudan's 1974 Penal Code) has been criticized for provisions falling short of international standards.[83]

The future role of *Shari'a*

The preceding review showed that criminal Islamic law in its orthodox form did not exist in Sudan prior to 1983, except for during the brief and idiosyncratic interlude of the *Mahdiya*. Yet Islam is an important part of the culture of Northern Sudan and anything that is perceived to be hostile to Islam will not be acceptable to the majority of the population. The use of Islam by both the Nimeiri regime and the current regime has consistently been associated with attempts to impose a repressive order, crush opposition and justify violations. This raises a series of important and challenging questions, which will need to be addressed in any debate about criminal law reform in Sudan:

- Do the majority of the people in Northern Sudan agree with the claim that *Shari'a* crimes form an integral, if not non-negotiable, part of Sudan's criminal law?
- Are the severe punishments of amputation, cross amputation and death by stoning not applied as a matter of an undeclared official policy? If correct, what are the implications for the application of *Shari'a*, the rule of law and protection from crime?

80   Southern Sudan Human Rights Commission Act of 16 February 2009.
81   Deng. 2010, 45–8.
82   See UNICEF. 2009. Unicef lauds the launch of the first Child Act in Southern Sudan. [Online, 8 April] Available at: http://www.unicef.org/media/media_49248.html [accessed 16 December 2010].
83   See UN Special Rapporteur on the Situation of Human Rights in the Sudan, Sima Samar. 2009. *Report*. UN Doc. A/HRC/11/14, para. 83.

- What lessons can be gleaned from the experiences of other Islamic countries that have decided to abolish corporal punishments, including those who have used interpretations ostensibly based on Islamic law to do so?
- Can a common ground be established between those who call for secular laws and those who insist on *Shari'a* as law? Is there any way forward? If so, what would and should it entail?

The history of law reform initiatives and efforts in Sudan demonstrates the capacity of its lawyers and civil society organizations, and their commitment to the ideals of human rights. This potential and commitment are great assets for any scheme of law reform in Sudan. The current interim period seems ideal for bringing existing laws in harmony with the INC as mandated by the CPA. Furthermore, the adherence of the INC to international human rights standards means that any amendments have to be in line with such standards. Despite all these advantages, the challenges facing law reform are enormous. The limited progress made more than five years after the passing of the INC raises concerns about the political will available to expedite law reform. The controversy over the issue of *Shari'a* is bound to remain one of the biggest challenges. However, the CPA itself is living proof of what can be achieved through dialogue and strong political will. The ongoing task will be to implement its human rights provisions so that the protection of such rights becomes integral to Sudanese laws.

Lessons from Sudan

In the development of its criminal law, Sudan shares a number of features with other African states and other countries with a Muslim majority. This was characterized by the traditionally heavy-handed use of criminal law when it came to core state interests and the reliance on local and largely customary law considerations in other matters. This pattern was largely perpetuated during colonial rule, which, though adopting some repressive legislation, also introduced foundations for Sudan's criminal law that enjoyed a degree of acceptance following independence. However, the role of criminal laws as the building blocks of a functioning system of criminal justice has been undermined by the lack of political stability. The system has also been subject to political tampering. Since the 1980s successive regimes have effectively experimented with criminal law, establishing a system characterized by its eclectic reliance on *Shari'a*, repressive legislation and immunities. This is an example of criminal justice being instrumentalized as a means of state control and used for ideological ends. This applies in particular to the use of *Shari'a* to impose a particular order, justified with reference to Sudan's national identity. This very identity was defined on religious grounds, rather than the pluralistic grounds that would have better reflected its diversity. Civil society has resisted changes throughout this period and sought to provide alternative visions, but it has encountered a series of obstacles in difficult political conditions.

In these circumstances criminal law reform constitutes an important site of contestation that forms a critical part of the broader struggle over the exercise of power and governance.

PART TWO
Reforming Sudan's Criminal Laws:
Challenges and Comparative
Experiences

I. Repressive Criminal Legislation

The use of repressive laws: Nature, practice and concerns

Criminal law is coercive by definition. It prescribes punishment for conduct deemed worthy of sanction, and the system of criminal justice in which it applies vests the state with the power to establish criminal liability and enforce such sanctions. Legal systems frequently stipulate a series of safeguards to limit the inherent scope for abuse, and these concern both the conditions under which sanctions can be imposed as well as the administrative and in particular judicial control of their use.

The use of repressive legislation (such as offences against the state in cases of treason) and the employment of special or military courts is a recurring feature in many countries, as the Ugandan experience illustrates.[1] In addition, the criminal laws of authoritarian or dictatorial states are often characterized by harsh punishments. A particularly drastic example was the range of broad offences carrying severe punishments in Iraq under Saddam Hussein's reign.[2]

Criminal laws and criminal justice systems frequently facilitate violations where restrictions are loosened. This commonly takes the form of broad and vaguely worded offences or exceptions based on emergency or counter-terrorism laws, which are often complemented by limited if not altogether lacking effective judicial oversight and redress. There is a long-standing history of the use of emergency laws; the virtually permanent states of emergency in Egypt and Syria were particularly notorious for turning the exceptional into the rule.[3] Counter-terrorism laws have also been used extensively worldwide. The United Nations (UN) Security Council's resolution 1373 (2001), which made the adoption of counter-terrorism legislation mandatory for UN members, resulted in the proliferation of laws whose compatibility with international standards has often

---

1   See chapter 4.

2   See Human Rights Committee (HRC). 1997. *Concluding Observations: Iraq*. UN Doc. CCPR/C/79/Add.84, para. 12.

3   Until developments in 2011, states of emergency had been in place in Egypt since 1967 (with short interruptions), see UN Special Rapporteur on the promotion and protection of human rights and fundamental freedoms while countering terrorism, Martin Scheinin. 2009. *Mission to Egypt*. UN Doc. A/HRC/13/37/Add.2, paras 4–8; and in Syria since 1962, see Committee against Torture (CAT). 2010. *Concluding observations: Syria*. Advanced Unedited Version, para. 10.

been questionable.[4] Such concerns are long-standing and predate 2001. The practice of Latin American states, particularly from the 1970s to the early 1990s, illustrates the systematic use of the anti-terrorism paradigm against domestic opposition, in which relevant laws vested states with broad powers of arrest and detention, undermined fair trial guarantees (including the infamous 'faceless' judges in Peru), and widened the scope for prosecutions, thereby facilitating practices of torture and disappearances. The International Commission of Jurists' panel of eminent jurists on terrorism, counter-terrorism and human rights highlighted that:

> The experiences in Argentina and other countries of the Southern Cone are a forceful reminder of: the dangers of an existential war against a 'demonised' enemy in which the end justifies the means; the dangers of an approach that gives the military unfettered powers in internal security matters; the dangers of combating an ideology rather than clearly prescribed criminalised behaviour; and, it illustrates; how easily human rights protections can become subordinated to an all encompassing notion of national security.[5]

Many conflicts have been characterized by the use of legal tools of repression as part of the state's armoury. This includes the use of offences against the state against suspected members of opposition groups, particularly rebel forces, as well as the adoption of states of emergencies and anti-terrorism legislation that give virtually free reign to government forces. A case in point is Sri Lanka's Prevention of Terrorism Act No. 48 of 1979, which contains, *inter alia*, broad offences, such as:

> [Any person who] by words either spoken or intended to be read or by signs or by visible representations or otherwise causes or intends to cause commission of acts of violence or religious, racial or communal disharmony or feelings of ill-will or hostility between different communities or racial or religious groups … shall on conviction be liable to imprisonment [for between five to 20 years].[6]

Police officers enjoy broad powers of arrest under the act and the responsible minister can order that a person be held for an aggregate period of up to 18 months without being brought before a judge.[7] Confessions made before police officers are admissible and defendants have the burden of proof that such confessions have

---

4   See reports of the UN Special Rapporteur on the promotion and protection of human rights and fundamental freedoms while countering terrorism, Martin Scheinin. Available at: http://ejp.icj.org/IMG/EJP-Report.pdf [accessed 16 December 2010].

5   Eminent Jurists Panel on Terrorism, Counter-terrorism and Human Rights. 2009. *Assessing Damage, Urging Act.* [Online: International Commission of Jurists] Available at: http://ejp.icj.org/IMG/EJP-Report.pdf [accessed 16 December 2010], 33–4.

6   See section 2(h) of the Prevention of Terrorism Act No. 48 of 1979, Sri Lanka.

7   Sections 6 and 9 Prevention of Terrorism Act, Sri Lanka.

been extracted under torture, even those who had been held *incommunicado*.[8] Prominent observers have commented on the impact of this law in Sri Lanka as follows:

> Sri Lanka's experience with emergency powers, and the Prevention of Terrorism Act (PTA) illuminates the complex interaction between violence and repression by the state, and violence and terror by non-state actors. Many commentators maintain that the draconian measures taken by Sri Lanka have only enhanced the cycle of violence, leading to the destruction of the social and political fabric of a democratic society.[9]

Unsurprisingly, the repeal of broad criminal laws and emergency laws, as well as fundamental reforms of counter-terrorism legislation, have been a frequent demand in transitional contexts and were among the measures addressed to overcome legacies of past violations, especially in Latin American countries.[10]

International standards

There is no single right or obligation under international law that addresses the various aspects of repressive laws. However, international human rights law provides a framework that circumscribes states' freedom to adopt criminal laws and to prescribe any form of punishment. It also sets limits to the use of emergency laws and counter-terrorism legislation.

The principle of legality

Legality is one of the most important fundamental principles governing criminal law. One of its central tenets is expressed in the maxim *nullum crimen sine lege, nulla poena sine lege* (no crime and punishment without a law). The principle of legality is meant to protect against the arbitrary imposition of criminal liability and punishment after an act has occurred, which are also known as *ex post facto* (literally 'after the fact') laws. It finds its rationale in notions of fairness, that is, that

---

8   Section 16 Prevention of Terrorism Act, Sri Lanka. See also *Singarasa v Sri Lanka*, HRC, Communication No. 1033/01. UN Doc. CCPR/C/81/D/1033/2001 (2004), para. 7.4.

9   Coomaraswamy, R. and de los Reyes, C. 2004. Rule by Emergency: Sri Lanka's Post Colonial Constitutional Experience. *International Journal of Constitutional Law* 2(2), 272, quoted in Eminent Jurists Panel Report. 2009, 39.

10   Popkin, M. and Roht-Arriaza, N. 1995. Truth as Justice: Investigatory Commissions in Latin America. *Law & Social Inquiry*, 20(1), 79–116, at 86–7 and 91 on Chile, El Salvador and Honduras, and generally on the relevant practice of Truth Commissions, the country studies in Hayner, P.B. 2010. *Unspeakable Truths: Transitional Justice and the Challenge of Truth Commissions*. Abingdon Oxon and New York: Routledge.

everyone should understand what type of conduct entails criminal liability, so as to be able to act accordingly and only to be held responsible for having (knowingly or negligently) breached the law. This entails that laws are sufficiently precise. The principle is recognized in international human rights law, in particular article 15(1) of the International Covenant on Civil and Political Rights (ICCPR), and is subject to one significant exception; the prohibition of retroactive application does not apply to international crimes as stipulated in article 15(2) of the ICCPR.

Criminal sanctions and the exercise of rights

Legislation prescribing specific offences must itself be compatible with human rights, since the subjection of a certain type of conduct to criminal sanctions can constitute a violation. This applies in particular where the subject matter encroaches on the scope of a right; for example, vague offences of treason against the state that include verbal critique of politicians, or offences that unduly restrict public gatherings may violate freedom of expression, assembly and movement.[11] The exercise of qualified rights, such as freedom of expression, may be subject to criminal liability. However, two conditions must be met to this end: (i) the criminal offence concerns a recognized ground for limiting the exercise of the right, such as the protection of national security or the reputation of others; and (ii) criminal liability (and the punishment prescribed) is a necessary and proportionate response to safeguard the rights of others and/or protected interests.[12] The threat of criminal sanctions is a serious restriction that is only justified where other less restrictive and equally effective measures are not available. It is immaterial in this context whether anyone concerned is actually subjected to criminal sanction since the very threat of punishment can have a prohibitive effect on the exercise of rights.[13] Article 20 of the ICCPR constitutes an explicit exception by obliging states to prohibit certain types of expression, namely those that constitute 'propaganda for war' as well as the 'advocacy of national, racial or religious hatred that constitutes incitement to discrimination, hostility or violence'.[14]

---

11   HRC. 2010. *General Comment 34: Article 19*. UN Doc. CCPR/C/GC/34/CRP.5, para. 31.

12   See for example article 19(2) of the ICCPR. *Jong-Choel v Korea*, HRC, Communication 968/2001, UN Doc. CCPR/C/84/D/968/2001 (2005), para. 8.3; and *Cumpǎnǎ and Mazǎre v Romania*, 41 EHRR 200 (2005), paras 111–19.

13   See for example, *Dudgeon v United Kingdom*, 4 EHRR 149 (1981), para. 41 and *Toonen v Australia*, HRC, Communication No. 488/1992 (1994), UN Doc. CCPR/C/50/D/488/1992, paras 8.1. and 8.2.

14   See UN Office of the High Commissioner for Human Rights. 2008. Papers prepared for the Expert Seminar: Freedom of Expression and Advocacy of Religious Hatred that Constitutes Incitement to Discrimination, Hostility or Violence, in particular Ghanea, G. *Articles 19 and 20*, and Thornberry, P. *Forms of Hate Speech and the Convention on the Elimination of All Forms of Racial Discrimination (ICERD)*. [Online, 2–3 October]

Criminal offences that are overly broad and vague may also make arrests and detentions arbitrary where they permit the same on spurious grounds that are not compatible with international human rights law. This would constitute a violation of the right of liberty and security, and may result in a violation of the right to a fair trial depending on the procedures in place for the prosecution and trial, as well as defence, in relation to such charges.[15]

Punishments and human rights

A state does not have unlimited discretion to impose certain types of punishments; international human rights law prohibits cruel, inhuman or degrading punishment. However, it does not explicitly proscribe particular forms of punishment.[16] The terms 'cruel', 'inhuman' or 'degrading' are value-laden and may give rise to conflicting interpretations. Treaty bodies such as the European Court of Human Rights (ECtHR) have sought to define these terms in their jurisprudence.[17] There is also a growing corpus of jurisprudence according to which corporal punishments fall within the scope of cruel, inhuman and degrading punishment.[18] The death penalty is not prohibited as such under present international law though there is a growing momentum towards its abolition.[19] Even where it is still recognized, the death penalty may only be applied for the most serious crimes following a fair trial

---

Available at: http://www2.ohchr.org/english/issues/opinion/articles1920_iccpr/2008_experts_ papers.htm [accessed 16 December 2010].

15   See Part II, Introduction to II: Arrest, detention and fair trial.

16   Article 7 ICCPR; article 5 AfrCHPR; article 3 ECHR and article 4 ACHR.

17   *Ireland v United Kingdom,* 2 EHRR 25 (1978), para. 162; and *Ilascu and others v Russia and Moldova,* 40 EHRR 46 (2005), paras 425–7.

18   *Osbourne v Jamaica*, HRC, Communication No. 759/1997 (2000), UN Doc. CCPR/ C/68/D/759/1997, para. 9.1; *Dr. Curtis Francis Doebbler v Sudan*, African Commission on Human and Peoples' Rights (ACHPR), Communication 235/2000 (2003), paras 36– 42; *Tyrer v UK* (1978) 2 EHRR 1, paras 28–35; Inter-Am. CtHR. *Caesar v Trinidad and Tobago*. Merits, Reparations and Costs. Judgment, 11 March 2005. Ser. C. No. 123, paras 52–89; CAT. 2002. *Concluding Observations: Saudi Arabia*. UN Doc. CAT/C/CR/28/5, paras 4(b) and 8(b); HRC. 2007. *Concluding observations: Sudan*. UN Doc. CCPR/C/SDN/ CO/3/CRP.1, para. 10.

19   See in particular the Second Optional Protocol to the International Covenant on Civil and Political Rights Aiming at the Abolition of the Death Penalty (1990), the Sixth Protocol to the European Convention on Human Rights concerning the abolition of the death penalty (1983) and the Thirteenth Protocol concerning the abolition of the death penalty in all circumstances (2002).

and in a manner that does not cause unnecessary suffering.[20] Children under the age of 18 and pregnant women must not be subjected to the death penalty.[21]

Emergency legislation

International law recognizes that states may declare an emergency and pass emergency laws as temporary measures of last resort in exceptional circumstances. The rules governing the imposition of states of emergency are characterized by their goal of upholding the rule of law while accommodating security concerns. Most international human rights treaties, with the notable exception of the African Charter on Human and Peoples' Rights,[22] permit resort to this measure.[23] States may declare a state of emergency in situations that 'threaten the life of the nation' and need to notify the relevant treaty body of the proclamation of an emergency.[24] National, regional and international courts and bodies tend to leave states considerable discretion in determining whether there is a threat justifying the declaration of a state of emergency, especially in the context of armed conflict or a terrorism threat, but will exercise close scrutiny regarding the measures taken by states in response.[25] States may not derogate from certain rights, such as the prohibition of torture and the right to *habeas corpus*, and may restrict other rights only in so far as necessary and proportionate in the circumstances.[26] Notably, the ECtHR has frequently held that states must ensure that arrested and detained persons are brought before a judicial body within a few days, and that adequate custodial safeguards are put in place to prevent ill-treatment and torture, as well as other violations, such as unfair trials.[27]

---

20   HRC. 2008. *General Comment 6: Article 6* (30 April 1982). Compilation of General Comments and General Recommendations adopted by Human Rights Treaty Bodies. UN Doc. HRI/GEN/Rev.9 (Vol.1), 176–78, at paras 6 and 7. See on the requirement that the death penalty should only be imposed for the most serious crimes also HRC. 2007, para. 19.

21   Article 6(5) ICCPR.

22   See *Article 19 v Eritrea*, ACHPR, Communication 273/2003 (2007), para. 87.

23   See in particular article 4 ICCPR, article 15 ECHR and article 27 ACHR.

24   HRC. 2001. *General Comment 29: States of Emergency (article 4)*. UN Doc. CCPR/C/21/Rev.1/Add.11, para. 2.

25   See HRC. General Comment 29, para. 4; *Ireland v United Kingdom*, paras 202–24 and the ruling by the House of Lords on the anti-terrorism measures taken by the United Kingdom following the attacks of 9 September 2011, *A (F.C.) and others (F.C.) (Appellants) v Secretary of State for the Home Department (Respondent), X (F.C.) and another (F.C.) (Appellants) v Secretary of State for the Home Department* [2004] UKHL 56.

26   HRC. General Comment 29, in particular paras 5–9, and Inter-Am. CtHR. *Habeas Corpus in Emergency Situations (Arts. 27(2), 25(1) and 7(6) American Convention on Human Rights)*. Advisory Opinion OC-8/87. 30 January 1987. Series A No. 8, as well as *Judicial Guarantees in States of Emergency (Arts. 27(2), 25 and (8) American Convention on Human Rights)*. Advisory Opinion OC-9/87. 6 October 1987. Series A No. 9.

27   See in particular *Aksoy v Turkey*, 23 EHRR 553 (1996), paras 67–87.

Counter-terrorism legislation

Counter-terrorism legislation must comply with international human rights standards, particularly by ensuring that: (i) offences of terrorism are clearly defined and not overly broad; (ii) safeguards are in place against arbitrary arrest and detention as well as ill-treatment and torture (including refoulement, that is, sending individuals to a place where they are likely to be at risk of torture or other forms of ill-treatment); (iii) the rights of the defence and fair trial principles are guaranteed, with particular regard to the type of tribunal mandated to try terrorism offences; (iv) punishments imposed are not cruel, inhuman or degrading and do not violate the right to life (such as the death penalty imposed following an unfair trial); and (v) anyone who alleges that his or her rights have been violated has access to an effective remedy.[28]

---

28 See UN Special Rapporteur on the promotion and protection of human rights and fundamental freedoms while countering terrorism. 2005. *Report*. UN Doc. E/CN.4/2006/98, paras 26–50 on the definition of terrorism, and 2008. *Report*. UN Doc. A/63/223, on fair trial rights.

Chapter 3

A Legacy of Institutionalized Repression: Criminal Law and Justice in Sudan

Amin M. Medani

Introduction

Sudan's legal system is riddled with repressive legislation that has been accumulating since the early nineteenth century. This includes laws that form part of the colonial legacy, the 1983 September laws, public order laws and legislation introduced since 1989. The term 'repressive legislation' used in this context denotes overly broad crimes coupled with a system of harsh punishments and a series of legislative acts that are either ideologically motivated or dictated by security considerations. This includes the national security law, anti-terrorism laws and emergency acts that have created a veritable system of exceptionalism, which vests the authorities with broad powers yet provides limited safeguards against abuse, if any.

This chapter examines the nature of this repressive legislation, its incompatibility with human rights obligations and its propensity to result in violations. This encompasses provisions of the 1991 Criminal Act, the National Security Law and the Combating of Terrorism Act. Other pieces of repressive legislation, in particular laws pertaining to public order and sexual violence, are addressed in chapter 10. In addition, the institutional framework governing criminal justice is examined with a view to identifying areas for substantive and institutional reforms.

Repressive legislation and human rights in Sudan

Background

The National Congress Party (then called the National Islamic Front) came to power in 1989 and confirmed its Islamic orientation with a series of legislative reforms.[1] It replaced the 1983 Criminal Act with the current 1991 Criminal Act while retaining the Islamic philosophy underpinning the former, also known as

---

1   See Human Rights Watch/Africa. 1996. *Behind the Red Line: Political Repression in Sudan*. New York: Human Rights Watch, and Medani, A.M. 2001. *Crimes against International Humanitarian Law in Sudan: 1989–2000*. Cairo: Dar El Mostaqbal El Arabi, 79–94.

the 1983 September laws. The *Shari'a* (Islamic law) crimes and punishments remained essentially unchanged. However, the crime of *ridda* (apostasy) was added to the Criminal Act.[2] The new Act streamlined and consolidated the 1983 Criminal Act, reducing the number of sections from 458 to 185.

Various Public Order Acts promulgated were intended to repress the population under the pretext of protecting religion and public morality, and punishing consumption, possession and dealing in alcohol, late parties, so-called indecent dress and, more recently, the smoking of *shisha* (or 'hubble bubble') in public places.[3] These laws have been excessively enforced: accused persons are promptly arrested, kept in custody overnight to be summarily tried, and are punished the following morning by Public Order Courts that routinely impose flogging as punishment.

Criminal Act of 1991: Offences and criminal responsibility

Homicide and the death penalty
Section 131 of the 1991 Criminal Act expressly provides that culpable homicide does not amount to murder as defined in section 130, in several specific circumstances, namely:

    i.   If the criminal act was not intentional and death was not a 'probable' consequence thereof;

    ii.   If a public servant in good faith exceeds his lawful authority believing that his act was necessary for the performance of his duties;

    iii.   If death is caused by a person by committing an act in excess of his right of private defence;

    iv.   If death is caused by a person threatened by death;

    v.   If death is committed by a person as a necessity to protect himself or others from death;

    vi.   If death is caused on the basis of consent of the deceased;

    vii.   If death is caused under loss of self control as a result of grave and sudden provocation;

    viii.   If the accused exceeded the limits of his lawful act, causing death;

    ix.   If the death is caused by person who suffers acts under such mental or psychological disturbance which seriously affect his ability to appreciate his actions or control them.[4]

---

2   Section 126 of the 1991 Criminal Act. The Islamic Scholar Mohamed Taha was executed for apostasy in 1983, though it was not recognized as an offence in Sudan's criminal law at the time. See chapter 2.

3   See for example the Khartoum Public Order Act of 1998. Available at: http://www. pclrs.org/Khartoum_Public_Order_Act_1998.pdf [accessed 28 December 2010].

4   This is the defence of 'diminished responsibility' introduced in England by the Homicide Act, 1957. In a well-known Sudanese case, *S.G. v Nafisa Dafalla, Sudan Law*

These clear exceptions notwithstanding, judges of the Supreme Court tended to disregard extenuating circumstances and convict persons of murder and sentence them to death, in application of what they considered to be the penalty of *qisas* (retribution) under the laws of *Shari'a*.[5] This practice amounted to a flagrant miscarriage of justice.

The 1998 Constitutional Court Act gave the Constitutional Court powers not only to examine constitutional issues, but also to reconsider judgments of the Supreme Court. This resulted in severe tensions between the two courts, as the Supreme Court was essentially being made subordinate to the Constitutional Court. Advocates and litigants who obtained unfavourable decisions from the Supreme Court naturally sought to have those decisions overruled, even if the question was not essentially over the constitutionality of the decision at issue. As a result, many defence lawyers referred cases to the Constitutional Court in which they contested the constitutionality of such Supreme Court decisions as an infringement of the basic constitutional right to life, in disregard of the express provisions of section 131 of the Criminal Act.

The Constitutional Court largely agreed with this interpretation and intervened in a number of cases to reduce convictions of murder by the Supreme Court to culpable homicide not amounting to murder, by applying the abovementioned exceptions in section 131. However, the later Constitutional Court Act of 2005 omitted the express provision in the old Act, according to which the Constitutional Court could review the decisions of the Supreme Court. This means that it can no longer reverse the death penalty on the basis of an infringement of the constitutional right to life. The new Constitutional Court has not acted as an appellate body in homicide cases, and where it has been called upon to rule on the compatibility of the death penalty with the Bill of Rights, it has invariably upheld previous convictions.[6]

Offences against the state
Part V of the Criminal Act of 1991 contains a series of 'offences against the state'. Criminal offences to protect the state are part of many criminal laws. However, their broad scope in Sudanese law makes these offences susceptible to abuse,

---

Journal and Reports (1961), 199, Justice B. Awadalla introduced this principle to reduce murder to culpable homicide. The re-enacted 1974 Penal Code formally introduced it in its section 149(6). It is now section 131 of the 1991 Criminal Act.

    5   See cases reported in *Journal of the Constitutional Court*. 1999–2003. Khartoum (in Arabic).

    6   See *Paul John Kaw and others v (1) Ministry of Justice; (2) Next of kin of Elreashhed Mudawee*. Case No. MD/QD/51/2008, Constitutional Court, Judgment of 13 October 2009, confirming the death sentence of six men accused of murder committed in the Soba Aradi riots of May 2005, and *Isahq al-Sanusi and others v Successors of deceased Mohamed Taha Mohamed Ahmed*, Case No. MD/QD/121/2008, Constitutional Court Order of 23 March 2009, confirming the death sentence of nine men convicted of the murder of journalist Mohamed Taha.

as evident in a number of apparently politically motivated prosecutions. It is a hallmark of criminal law that the elements of criminal offences should be as clear and precise as possible. This is indispensable as a matter of justice, as required by the principle *nulla poena sine lege* (no punishment without law), so that anyone knows what he or she should be doing in order to conform to the law. The principle also acts as protection against arbitrary law enforcement.

The offence of 'undermining the constitutional system' in section 50 of the Criminal Act provides that 'any act [committed] with the intention of undermining the constitutional system of the country, or exposing to danger the unity and independence thereof, shall be punished with death, life imprisonment or for a lesser period'. The scope of section 50 is extremely broad as it potentially covers peaceful acts, such as calls for an independent state, that are protected by the freedom of expression. Phrases such as 'undermining the constitutional system' or 'exposing to danger the unity' do not indicate with sufficient precision which acts are covered. In conjunction with the fact that such acts may carry the death penalty, the provision is prone to deter peaceful political activities. The offence of 'waging war against the state' in section 51 governs military acts against the state. It also carries a maximum punishment of death or life imprisonment. While the offence specifies military acts, its net is cast widely, including '[abetting] the offender, or support[ing] him in any manner'.

'Espionage against the country' in section 53 is subject to the same punishments and raises similar concerns. It is defined as 'whoever spies against the country, bycommunicating with any foreign state, or the agents thereof, or communicates, or conveys secrets thereto, with intent to assist it in its military operations, against the country, or prejudice the military position thereof'. Significantly, this definition has been expanded beyond the military context to encompass acts 'likely to prejudice the country politically, or economically', which carry a punishment of up to ten years' imprisonment. This element potentially covers any form of criticism because political and economic prejudice are vague terms and subject to broad construction, in particular where the threshold is one of 'likely' prejudice, which implies that there should be an assessment of the expected impact of any act.

Charges of offences against the state have been relied upon frequently in cases targeting journalists, human rights defenders and opposition members. Arrest and detention by security forces are often made without any charges brought. However, where prosecutions have been brought, existing patterns demonstrate the political utility and use of offences against the state for a wide range of acts, many of which appear to fall squarely within the legitimate exercise of the right to freedom of expression and political association. Journalists have been prosecuted for espionage, such as Abu Zar al-Zamin for an article concerning the clandestine building of an Iranian weapons factory in Sudan,[7] and for waging war against

---

7   Al-Amin was sentenced to five years imprisonment in July 2010 for attempting to destabilize the political system, while two other journalists were sentenced to two years' imprisonment each. See 2010. Sudanese court sentences three opposition journalists to jail

the state, such as Al-Haj Ali Warrag for an article supporting calls for an election boycott in early 2010.[8] Human rights defenders such as Dr Mudawi, Director of the Sudan Social Development Organization (SUDO), have been repeatedly charged with espionage, with undermining the constitutional system and with waging war against the state for their work in Darfur.[9] Mohamed al-Sary Ibrahim, a former security officer, was charged, *inter alia*, with espionage and dealing with an enemy country, for allegedly cooperating with the International Criminal Court (ICC).[10] Political opposition members such as Hassan al-Turabi have also been charged with offences against the state.[11] Such charges have been used in particular against suspected Justice and Equality Movement (JEM) members in Darfur who have been routinely arrested, detained and prosecuted for waging war against the state and similar offences.[12]

Rioting

Article 40 of the Bill of Rights in the Interim National Constitution (INC) expressly guarantees the freedom of assembly and association.[13] The former right is confined to peaceful assembly and thus excludes the use of force, rioting, threatening the security and safety of others and their property, all of which would be unlawful and punishable by the Criminal Act. Section 67 of the 1991 Criminal Act defines 'rioting' as the participation 'in an assembly of five or more persons *which shows or uses force, intimidation or violence* and whenever the prevailing intention therein is achieving any of the following objectives: (i) resisting the execution of the provisions of any law or legal process; (ii) committing the offence of criminal

---

time. *Sudan Tribune* [Online, 16 July] Available at: http://www.sudantribune.com/spip. php?article35679 [accessed 6 December 2010].

8   Committee to Protect Journalists. 2010. *Sudanese journalist charged with 'waging war' against the state.* [Online, 14 April] Available at: http://cpj.org/2010/04/sudanese-journalist-charged-with-waging-war-agains.php [accessed 6 December 2010].

9   See Frontline. 2005. *Sudan–Dr. Mudawi Ibrahim Adam.* [Online] Available at: http://www.frontlinedefenders.org/node/420 [accessed 6 December 2010].

10   2008. Sudan tries man accused of spying for the ICC. *Sudan Tribune* [Online, 23 December] Available at: http://www.sudantribune.com/spip.php?article29662 [accessed 6 December 2010].

11   2004. Turabi charged with damaging Sudan's security, Islamist party shut down. *Sudan Tribune* [Online, 1 April] Available at: http://www.sudantribune.com/spip. php?article2297 [accessed 6 December 2010].

12   African Centre for Justice and Peace Studies. 2010. *Special courts in Darfur sentence nine individuals, including four children, to death.* [Online, 28 October] Available at: http://sudantribune.com/spip.php?page=imprimable&id_article=36737 [accessed 6 December 2010].

13   Article 40(1): 'The right to peaceful assembly shall be guaranteed; every person shall have the right to freedom of association with others, including the right to form or join political parties, associations and trade or professional unions for the protection of his/her interests'.

mischief, criminal trespass or other offence; (iii) exercising any existing or alleged right in a manner which is likely to disturb peace; and (iv) compelling any person to do what he is not bound by law to do, or to refrain from doing what he is authorized by law to do' (emphasis added).

Under section 68 such an offence is punishable with up to six months of imprisonment or flogging of up to 20 lashes; if the accused carries arms or a weapon 'the use of which is likely to cause death or grievous hurt', the punishment may be increased to two years imprisonment or fine or both. Under section 69, any persons who disturbs the public or commits an act that may lead to the disturbance of public peace and tranquillity may be liable to up to one month imprisonment, fine or up to twenty lashes.

The foregoing sections must be read in conjunction with the relevant section of the 1991 Criminal Procedure Act. Section 124 of that Act authorizes a police officer or prosecutor to order the dispersal of any assembly that is unlawful or may commit riot or disturb the public peace. If the assembly disobeys the order, force may be used to disperse it, provided that firearms may be used only with the permission of the prosecutor. Section 127 empowers the *Wali* (Governor) of a state or the *Mutamad* (provincial ruler) to issue an order that prevents or restricts any meeting or public assembly that may disturb public order in the streets or public places.[14] Section 127 requires the persons organizing the assembly to 'inform' the authorities of their intention to assemble, the interpretation being that the purpose is for the authorities to make the necessary arrangements, including security, traffic, routing and so on.

All the above provisions are meant to preserve public peace and tranquillity rather than deprive citizens of their constitutional right to peaceful assembly. An intention to disturb the peace cannot be simply inferred or assumed from the mere meeting of a number of people who wish to assemble peaceably. It is perhaps natural in many systems that the authorities are 'informed' of the intention to organize a demonstration or public rally. This may be necessary to enable relevant authorities to help organize the route of the procession to avoid busy areas, regulate the traffic and protect members of the public and of the assembly equally. Such information is a 'matter of course' measure, which must not be equated to a permit that restricts the exercise of the constitutional right to freedom of assembly and freedom of expression. However, this was the apparent ground on which the government of Sudan justified measures taken in the context of pre-election demonstrations in late 2009.

---

14 See on recent amendments in this context: 'On 20 May 2009, the National Assembly passed amendments to the 1991 Criminal Procedures Act. One amendment gives powers to State Governors or Commissioners to issue orders prohibiting or restricting the organisation of public meetings, which the Special Rapporteur notes is not in conformance with the guarantees of freedom of assembly and association enshrined in the CPA, INC, and ICCPR'. UN Special Rapporteur on the situation of human rights in the Sudan, Sima Samar. 2009. *Report.* UN Doc. A/HRC/11/14, para. 24.

Two incidents that occurred in Khartoum in December 2009 illustrate the lack of respect for these constitutional rights in practice, and the limited protection afforded to those exercising such rights. The Sudan People's Liberation Movement (SPLM) and political opposition parties organized a peaceful gathering in front of the Sudanese Parliament to deliver a letter to the Speaker. The letter voiced protests against the National Congress Party (NCP) government's refusal to adopt or amend certain laws (including the National Security Act) that contravened the provisions of the Comprehensive Peace Agreement (CPA) and the INC on public freedoms and transition to democracy.[15] Ironically, the streets were closed and thousands of armed members of the police and the State Security sealed all avenues to Parliament. This was done notwithstanding the fact that the organizers of the assembly had informed the authorities concerned and had warned the public against committing any acts of violence, resistance to the security forces, mischief or destruction of property. Nevertheless the security forces violently attacked members of the public using tear gas, electronic rods and physical violence, leading to the arrest of dozens of citizens (including Members of Parliament and ministers belonging to the SPLM). These acts amounted to a serious violation of the law and the constitutional freedoms of peaceful assembly and expression. A peaceful rally with a previously declared intention simply to deliver a letter to the Speaker of Parliament, with prior notice having been given to the appropriate circles, can by no reasonable account be construed as constituting an unlawful assembly aimed at rioting or disturbing the peace.[16]

Criminal responsibility, with particular reference to the minimum age
Section 9 of the Criminal Act stipulates that 'a minor who has not reached puberty' cannot be held criminally responsible. Further, a child who has reached the age of seven can be transferred by the court for child care and rehabilitation. Evidence of whether a child had attained puberty is determined by the court after hearing medical specialists. However, the procedure is arbitrary, since determining the age of a child by reference to reaching puberty may be approached differently, even by specialists. In practice, judges often make the decision themselves by looking at the child and asking him or her in private to take off his or her clothes to have a look at the breasts, armpits and private parts.

The criterion of puberty, as interpreted in Sudan, restricts the determination of the child's congenital ability to his or her physical rather than mental or psychological ability, and his or her attitude towards what could or could not be a criminal act. It would therefore be preferable to determine a fixed age on the basis of which a child's ability can be determined. The Peking Rules for the

---

15   All Political Parties Conference. 2009. *Juba Declaration on Dialogue and National Consensus.* [Online, 26–30 September] Available at: http://www.splmtoday.com/docs/All%20Sudan%20Political%20Parties%20Conference%20English.pdf, paras 3.2. and 4.ii.

16   Independent Expert on the situation of human rights in the Sudan, Mohammed Chande Othman. 2010. *Report.* UN Doc. A/HRC/14/41, para. 22.

Administration of Juvenile Justice, adopted by the United Nations (UN) General Assembly in 1985, state that the lowest age of criminal responsibility 'shall not be fixed at too low an age level, bearing in mind the facts of emotional, mental and intellectual maturity'.

The 2010 Child Act has responded to some of this criticism. It fixed the age of children at 18 and the age of criminal responsibility at 12 years of age, the latter of which is, however, still rather low in comparison. Younger children should be considered for correction and rehabilitation from the age of 8 years onwards. In this connection, it is worth recalling that section 49 of the 1974 Penal Code absolved from criminal responsibility (i) the acts of a child under the age of 10, and (ii) the act of a child over 10 but under the age of 14 years if he or she had not attained adequate maturity to understand the nature of his or her act and its consequences.

The system of punishments

Huddud and Qisas
The Islamic punishments of *huddud* and *qisas*, first introduced in Sudan by the 1983 re-enactment of the Penal Code, remain in force today. Several countries with Muslim majorities do not recognize the *huddud* punishments of death by stoning, crucifixion, amputation, cross amputation and flogging.[17] This is generally based on the premise that contemporary times have radically changed from Islamic life 14 centuries ago and that punishments such as imprisonment and fines were not available during the early days of Islam. It is also based on the understanding that modern political, economic and social conditions impel governments to adapt to theories of penology, which better suit the present needs and circumstances of the community. The present undeclared moratorium on *huddud* punishments in Sudan, in spite of their continued stipulation in the Code, is a mockery of the law that masks the hypocrisy of Sudan's *Shari'a* law. While it is publicly upheld in order to demonstrate the government's Islamic credentials on the one hand, it is applied selectively on the other when convenient. This selective application concerns flogging in particular. Flogging is used almost indiscriminately as a disciplining punishment to repress a wide range of acts beyond the strict letter of *Shari'a* (see below, *Flogging*). Abolishing *huddud* and *qisas* punishments and replacing them with more appropriate ones based on modern theories of criminology and penology would bring Sudan in line with the insights of contemporary religious scholars, social and political scientists and lawyers and best practices elsewhere.

In light of these considerations, the author proposes that the punishments of *huddud*, which, except in cases of consumption and dealing in alcohol, are presently

---

17 This comprises most North African countries, including Egypt. See for the historical background on the waning influence of Islamic criminal law in the nineteenth- and early twentieth century, Peters, R. 2005. *Crime and Punishment in Islamic Law: Theory and Practice from the Sixteenth to the Twenty-first Century*. Cambridge: Cambridge University Press, 103–5.

under an undeclared moratorium, should be abolished and replaced by those punishments prescribed in the corresponding sections of the 1974 Penal Code. To keep the punishments in the Code, and at the same time not to enforce them, be it for lack of conviction, dissatisfaction with their efficacy or because of adverse political consequences, makes a mockery of the law. If other Islamic countries have exerted their efforts and used the *Ulemma* (Islamic legal scholars) to dispense with those punishments, there is no reason why Sudan cannot do the same. The fact that *Shari'a* punishments were introduced into the law in a mood of political frenzy rather than being based on religious conviction or popular demand and acceptance,[18] adds further weight to the desirability of undertaking the proposed changes.

Sudan, like almost all Islamic countries, is unlikely to abolish *qisas* as a punishment for murder in the near future, hence, it has not ratified the Second Optional Protocol to the International Covenant on Civil and Political Rights (ICCPR) (on the abolition of the death penalty). This does not mean that Sudan cannot abolish or replace the death penalty for less heinous crimes with other less final, alternative punishments, by relying on contemporary concepts of penology. Criminal justice systems have moved beyond the rule of 'an eye for an eye'. At the same time, the principle of *dia*, as compensation for injury caused to the victim, may be retained as an instrument of justice. Islamic penal principles also encourage the concept of forgiveness or pardon by the victim (or his or her next of kin in case of death) in all cases of *qisas*. This would of course be notwithstanding the public policy that the state may impose sentences of imprisonment, fines or otherwise on those who violate the criminal law of the land.

Flogging

Apart from the application of flogging as a *huddud* punishment for rape (which is mistakenly classified as a *huddud* crime, see chapter 10), adultery, sodomy and the consumption of or dealing in alcohol, the punishment of flogging is found in about another 20 sections of the 1991 Criminal Act that deal with common crimes amounting to more than 10 per cent of its entirety.

The 1898 Sudan Penal Code, which was based on the then applicable Indian Penal Code, has been amended and re-enacted several times, but the abhorrent corporal punishment introduced by the British for a number of offences remains one of its enduring legacies and ugliest features. Corporal punishments have been frequently used by military regimes as an oppressive measure, which has also served to reinforce the Islamic nature of the regime, particularly in respect of the consumption of and dealing in alcohol. Corporal punishment is presently an everyday occurrence in almost all trial courts across the country.[19] In this context women are particularly harassed by the Public Order Police, especially over their style of dress, which police officers may arbitrarily determine to be repugnant to

---

18   See chapter 2.

19   The author is not aware of any systematic compilation of case law or statistical evidence made publicly available on the prevalence of flogging in Sudan.

the so-called 'Islamic dress code'.[20] This code stipulates that a woman is decently dressed if she is not unreasonably showing parts of her body in a provocative or indecent manner. However, the practice of declaring a dress to be un-Islamic was developed to provide a source of revenue for police officers, who either receive bribes or detain the (mostly young) women in night custody to await flogging in the morning.

In view of the fact that most Islamic countries have abolished the punishment of flogging on the basis of *fatwas* (edicts) from Islamic scholars, and in view of the fact that the Human Rights Committee of the ICCPR, which Sudan has ratified, described corporal punishment as cruel, inhuman and degrading to human dignity,[21] Sudan is duty-bound to reconsider and change this practice. In this connection it becomes pertinent to recall the explanatory note that the drafters of the 1983 Code prepared. On the question of flogging they had this to say:

> The law has relied a lot on the punishment of flogging due to the inadequacy of the system of imprisonment as a deterrent ...
>
> Sharia flogging is a medium flogging, with a medium instrument. It should not be inflicted on a drunk person, or in extreme cold, or in extreme heat, or in extreme sickness. But flogging in *huddud* cannot be stopped in serious permanent sickness such as diabetes and other diseases, as there are no alternatives for *huddud* punishments or discretion for judges except as mentioned above in deferring infliction of punishment in cases of drunkenness or cases of extreme cold or heat. We recommend for judges to continue inflicting the *huddud* flogging even after the death of the convicted person so that his soul is cleansed before God.[22]

One can hardly add more when calling for the punishment of flogging to be abolished.

National security law, counter-terrorism legislation and emergency laws

The CPA and INC contain numerous provisions to restore peace, democratic transition, the rule of law and promotion of human rights.[23] However, little progress has been made in its implementation. Several arbitrary laws have been kept on the books and a number of new laws have been enacted in direct contradiction to the CPA and INC.

---

20   Government of Sudan. 1983. *Explanatory Memorandum on the 1983 Penal Code*, 6–7.

21   Human Rights Committee (HRC). 2007. *Concluding observations: Sudan*. UN Doc. CCPR/C/SDN/CO/3/CRP.1, para. 10. See also *Curtis Francis Doebbler v Sudan*, African Commission on Human and Peoples' Rights (ACHPR), Communication 236/2000 (2003).

22   Government of Sudan. 1983.

23   See in particular the CPA's Chapeau as well as Preamble, articles 1 and 4 of the INC and the Bill of Rights forming an integral part of the INC.

The National Security Law

Most states enact legislation that establishes an organization or organizations intended to be responsible for the internal and external security of the state. The term 'national security' can, in this context, be understood as protecting the country and its people against invasion, the threat of war, espionage, activities affecting the political and economic security of the country, terrorism, cross-border crimes such as trafficking in persons, drugs or arms, money laundering and other such activities.

In contrast, in totalitarian regimes there is a general conception that the state security organization's main task is to protect the regime in power and to curb any opposition to it by any and all means necessary. The present regime in Sudan, in power since its coup d'etat of 1989, is no exception. It has from the outset been completely dependent on its security apparatus, whose powers and resources have outgrown those of the police. The state security organization, officially known as the National Security Service (NSS), previously the National Intelligence and Security Service (NISS) is not only in uniform and expressly considered part of the regular forces, but is also armed to the teeth, and has thousands of members and 'collaborators'. Given the sensitive nature of the role of the security services, both the CPA and the INC provide for the status of NSS in no uncertain terms. A.2.7.2.4. of the CPA states: 'The National Security Service shall be professional and its mandate shall be *advisory and focused on information gathering and analysis*' (emphasis added). Article 150 of the INC provides: '(1) There shall be at the national level a National Security Council, the composition and functions of which shall be determined by a National Security Act. (2) The National Security Council shall define the national security strategy based on the analysis of all threats to security of the Sudan'. It is apparent from the express wording of the above articles that what is intended is 'the security of the Sudan', not that of the government of the day, nor the regime in power. However, from the day the military regime took over, serious human rights violations, which still continue today, on a lesser scale, have been attributed to the NSS.[24] Following the conclusion of the CPA and the INC, political opposition parties, together with the SPLM, have endeavoured to adopt a new state security law instead of the one that was enacted by the NCP shortly after coming to power whose amended versions have remained in force, comprising most notably the 1999 National Security Forces Act. The security law had been criticized on mainly the following grounds:

---

24   See the number of reports published by the then UN Special Rapporteur on human rights in the Sudan and the current Independent Expert as well as other UN reports, for example, UN High Commissioner for Human Rights. 2008. *Tenth periodic report on the situation of human rights in the Sudan, Arbitrary arrest and detention committed by national security, military and police*. Geneva.

i.   It allows members of the organization and their 'collaborators' to arrest any person without charge or trial and detain him for a period of up to three days;

ii. It allows them to enter and search any place at any time and seize property without a warrant;

iii. It allows the director of the organization to extend the detention period for one month; the suspect may remain in detention for a further similar period if the director is of the opinion that the suspect may have committed an offence against the state, in which case he is only required to inform the prosecutor;

iv. In cases where the director decides that the person may commit an act of terrorizing the community, he may order his detention for three months, renewable for another three months; again, he only needs to 'inform' the prosecutor. The detainee may complain to the magistrate for the first time after a period of six months. However, no instances of a judicial reversal of such detention orders are known;

v.   The law allows the NSS Council to extend the detention period up to three further months at a time. In other words, a person may be detained for nine months, then released for a few hours or days and the process repeated full circle;[25]

vi. The law gives immunity for acts by members of the organization. This may only be removed with the consent of the director. Acts of torture and inhuman treatment have been a normal occurrence. No cases are known in which any members of the security have been prosecuted for any unlawful acts despite a number of allegations to this effect over the years.[26]

Despite the fact that its provisions were in violation of the CPA, the INC and the international instruments which Sudan has ratified, the NCP rejected all calls to change the law to conform to the present 'transition for democracy'. A new National Security Act was passed in late 2009 and signed into law in early 2010, in the face of objections by the SPLM, the main partner in government and of all the opposition parties.[27] The new Act introduces some changes but essentially retains

---

25   The recently adopted National Security Act of 2010 has reduced this overall period to four-and-a-half months, but the process may be repeated full circle, ad infinitum.

26   See for further analysis of the 1999 National Security Forces Act, REDRESS and SORD. 2009. *Security for All: Reforming Sudan's National Security Services.* [Online, September] Available at: http://www.pclrs.org/downloads/Resources/Resources/ Security%20for%20all%20Final.pdf [accessed 7 December 2010].

27   The text of the law is available online at: http://www.pclrs.org/downloads/ bills/Institutional%20Law/National%20Security%20Act%202010%20UNMIS%20 unofficial%20English%20%20Transaltion%20final%20version%202010-02-03%20 single%20space.pdf [accessed 7 December 2010].

broad powers of arrest and detention without adequate safeguards and continues providing immunities for NSS members notwithstanding recommendations by the UN Human Rights Committee and the African Union High-Level Panel on Darfur to the contrary.[28] Its adoption was a retrograde step, coming at a time when the country was facing general elections in April 2010.

The Combating of Terrorism Act 2001

Following the September 11 events in the United States of America and the wave of terror throughout the world, many countries adopted legislative action and other security measures in an effort to curb terrorism. However, in many of these countries, including some in the West, such measures have been criticized as being too rigid and overly detrimental to basic human rights and personal freedoms. Sudan adopted its own anti-terrorism legislation in 2001, known as the Combating of Terrorism Act. The Act defines several unlawful acts within a very wide ranging definition of what constitutes terrorism.[29] The provisions of the Act, in relation to the prosecution and trial of terrorism, give rise to serious concerns regarding its compatibility with principles of the sanctity of the rule of law and the protection of human rights as included in the 2005 INC, which followed the adoption of the Act.

The Act has several features that are of particular concern. Cases of alleged terrorism are not subject to trial before ordinary courts, but are subject to the exclusive jurisdiction of 'Special Courts' established by the Chief Justice. The rules of procedure for these courts are established by the Chief Justice 'in consultation with the Minister of Justice'. The latter is a member of the executive whose participation in the establishment of trial courts is a flagrant violation of the principles of independence of the judiciary and of the separation of powers. In addition, the Act enables the Chief Justice to establish a 'Special Court of Appeal', in flagrant violation of the provisions of the Code of Criminal Procedure, under which there is a standing Court of Appeal. The Special Court of Appeal is authorized to confirm the death penalty and life imprisonment. Again, this constitutes a violation of the Code of Criminal Procedure, which gives such powers exclusively to the Supreme Court.[30] In this connection, reference must be made to the recent case of *Kamal Mohammed Saboon v Sudan Government*.[31] The case concerns a massive raid by the Darfur rebel forces of JEM on the city

---

28   See chapter 5 for an analysis of the changes made.

29   See on the definition of these crimes and an overview of measures taken by Sudan, Permanent Mission of the Sudan to the United Nations. 2005. *Note verbale dated 15 November 2004 addressed to the Chairman of the Counter-Terrorism Committee*. UN Doc. S/2004/953.

30   See Medani, A.M. 2008. *Legal Opinion on the Judgment of the Constitutional Court Concerning the Case of Terrorism* (unpublished, on file with author).

31   *Kamal Mohammed Saboon v Sudan Government*. CS (Constitutional Court) (60) of 2009.

of Omdurman. Several hundred armed rebels in vehicles entered the city causing panic and alarm in the capital. They were eventually overcome by the army and security forces in serious battles resulting in hundreds of casualties on both sides including dozens of civilians. The reaction of the government was excessive. Thousands of suspected Darfurian citizens were arrested, including women and children, simply on the basis of ethnic features, colour, accent or place of living.[32] Several hundred persons were considered suspects and charged to stand trials before six special courts in the three towns of the capital. In accordance with the abovementioned powers under the said terrorism act, the Chief Justice and the Minister of Justice formulated the rules of procedure of trial courts in a flagrant violation of the principle of independence of the judiciary.[33] These rules included the following:

    i.   The rules expressly provided that they should apply, *notwithstanding any provisions of the Code of Criminal Procedure and the Evidence Act* (emphasis added), in effect making the regulations adopted by the Chief Justice and the Minister superior to the applicable laws, and a clear violation of legal and constitutional principles.

    ii.   The period for appealing from decisions of the Special Courts to the Appeals Court was reduced from two weeks to one week only, in violation of the express provisions of the Code of Criminal Procedure.

    iii.   Again, in clear violation of the Code of Criminal Procedure, the regulations restricted the appeal procedure confirmation of sentence from two stages, namely the Court of Appeal and then the Supreme Court, to that of the Special Court of Appeal, thereby depriving convicted persons of their right of appeal (and revision) to the Supreme Court.

    iv.   The rules permitted the trial of persons *in absentia* contrary to the express provisions of the ICCPR, which has been ratified by Sudan and become an integral part of the INC by virtue of its article 27(3).

    v.   The rules provide that the accused should appoint his defence counsel as soon as he is informed of the date of the trial. However, in this case, the accused were held in *incommunicado* detention and as a consequence could not appoint or even meet defence lawyers before trial. Requests by lawyers to meet defendants before the trial were adamantly rejected by the trial courts.[34]

---

32   UN Special Rapporteur on the situation of human rights in the Sudan, Sima Samar. 2008. *Report*. UN Doc. A/HRC/9/13, paras 20–33.

33   Order No. 82. 2008.

34   The author of this paper, together with other defence counsel, withdrew from the first trial after their request to meet with the defendants was rejected. The said court proceeded with the trial, accepting some volunteer lawyers from the Ministry of Justice to represent the defendants in spite of their objections.

vi. In the case of a confession of guilt made during investigations, the law requires the court to take special precautions before convicting a person solely on the basis of such alleged confession, especially when it has been retracted subsequently. The rules empower the courts to convict on the basis of such alleged confessions, without investigating the circumstances under which they have been made, or whether the accused has understood their consequences. Concerns over the scope of this rule were compounded by the fact that allegations raised by some of the accused that their statements had been coerced under torture, were dismissed by the trial courts without serious consideration.[35]

On the basis of the foregoing arguments, a group of leading trial lawyers submitted a petition to the Constitutional Court in the abovementioned case of *Kamal Mohammed Saboon v Sudan Government*, claiming the unconstitutionality of the proceedings relating to the trials of the JEM suspects on the grounds mentioned above. They argued that the accused had been denied a fair trial in accordance with the law, the Constitution and the international human rights instruments ratified by Sudan.

The Constitutional Court dismissed the petition virtually out of hand, and the trial courts proceeded with the case.[36] As of early 2010 about 105 death penalties had been passed by the trial courts. In what the author considers a typical political judgment, the Constitutional Court manipulated the law so as to appease the regime in power, by upholding one of the most unfair civil trials in the history of the country. This, perhaps, cannot be more aptly described than by simply quoting from the opinion given by the president of the Constitutional Court:

> Yes, this Court is not a political one; but it is also not an island isolated from what is happening in the Country. It cannot, in my opinion, in considering the Regulations whose constitutionality is contested, do so without reconciling itself with some departure from usual norms. This is not an innovation. In Nuremberg the serious loss of lives and property, and the cruelty and brutality with which the war was conducted forced those in power to disregard one of the most settled principles of law, that is the retroactivity of laws. It is quite normal in times of disaster, invasion, war and other national crises to suspend some basic rights temporarily, property may be confiscated and persons may be detained in disregard of the normal law. Therefore I refuse to decide against Regulation 25, which requires the application of its provisions, notwithstanding the provisions of the laws of Criminal Procedure and Evidence. This would no doubt be in

---

35 See Medani. 2008.

36 It took the Constitutional Court less than two months to dismiss the petition, although some suits have been pending before it for more than four years.

contradiction of the principles of jurisprudence and judicial precedent, which place constitutional provisions at the top of the pyramid, followed by laws emanating from the legislative authority. Any provision in any law or subsidiary legislation which contradicts the Constitution, and any legislation which contradicts with the law becomes void. Thus I should be impelled to pronounce the illegality of Regulation 25, had it not been for the exceptional circumstances and the exceptional crimes which prompted the adoption of the said Regulations, as I explained in this paragraph.[37]

This opinion is faulty and a regrettable statement in the application of all principles of the law and constitutionalism. The analogy of the JEM attack with Nuremberg trials is staggering. Not even ardent supporters of the regime went that far. Furthermore, the learned judge quoted Nuremberg in the context of the retroactivity of laws, which was certainly not the issue in the JEM trials.

Thirdly and even more drastically, the statement is self-contradicting, stipulating the overriding force of constitutional provisions and legislative enactments over regulations, while at the same time upholding the validity of regulations contrary to the constitution and the law. The effort to justify this decision by reference to exceptional circumstances and terror crimes having been committed during the JEM attack, presumes the existence of a state of emergency under which certain rights are derogated from. However, no such state of emergency had been declared and it should not be the task of the Constitutional Court to justify the derogation from basic rights and freedoms where no such emergency is legally declared by the competent authority – that is, the Executive and/or the Legislature.

Emergency laws

The problematic nature of emergency laws and the broad power with which they vest the authorities are well known; it is for this reason that any emergency measures should be exceptional and temporary, and that any restrictions imposed should be necessary and proportional.[38] However, the use of emergency laws in the course of conflict and as a means of consolidating state power has been a recurring theme in Sudan's legal history. The coup of 1989 that brought President Bashir to power was followed by the adoption of Decree No. 2, which gave the Sudanese authorities sweeping powers to detain anyone 'suspected of being a threat to political or economic security'. This power was granted without the need to provide any reasons for arrest and detention. Anyone detained was not given the right to challenge the legality of such detention; he or she was also made subject to the jurisdiction of special courts. These extraordinary powers were freely used to crack down on anyone seen to be opposed to the regime, and they resulted in

---

37 *Saboon v Sudan*. Author's translation and emphasis.

38 See HRC. 2001. *General Comment 29: States of Emergency (article 4)*. UN Doc. CCPR/C/21/Rev.1/Add.11.

a series of violations, as *inter alia* held by the African Committee on Human and Peoples' Rights (ACHPR) in *Amnesty International and others v Sudan*.[39]

The INC vests the President of the Republic with considerable powers during a state of emergency, which includes suspending the Bill of Rights with the exception of core rights, namely the 'right to life, sanctity from slavery, sanctity from torture, the right of non-discrimination on the basis of race, sex, religious creed, the right in litigation or the right to fair trial'.[40] The Emergency and Protection of Public Safety Act of 1997 (Act Number (1) 1998) provides the statutory legal framework for emergencies. Its article 5 gives the authorities broad powers in relation to searching and entering buildings, surveillance, seizure and confiscation, movement of persons as well as economic transactions and services. It also vests the competent authority with the power to arrest anyone 'suspected of participating in crimes related to the declaration [of emergency made by the President of the Republic]'. This provision is problematic because it does not specify the crimes in question, which are instead subject to the provisions of the declaration. It is, therefore, essentially an executive act, albeit one needing parliamentary approval since 2005.[41] The Act does not provide any safeguards against arbitrary arrest and detention. Instead, if read in conjunction with section 15 of the Emergency and Public Safety Bylaw of 1998, it allows preventive arrest and detention on the basis of broad grounds, such as belief on the part of the authorities that the person concerned has acted or may act in a way that 'affects public security, or public safety, or … participated in any crime related to the declaration'.[42]

The ACHPR has repeatedly held that it is impermissible to detain individuals indefinitely without charge or trial.[43] Section 15 of the Emergency and Public Safety Bylaw stipulates that the order of arrest be made provisionally, thus indicating that any arrest should be of a temporary nature. However, the Emergency and Public Safety Bylaw does not set any time limits. There is no judicial oversight to determine whether the competent authority may have

---

39   *Amnesty International and Others v Sudan*, ACHPR, Communications 48/90, 50/91, 52/91, 89/93 (1999), para. 59.

40   Article 211(a) INC.

41   Article 210 INC.

42   See in this respect also the recommendation of the Group of experts that '[e] mergency laws should not grant security agencies broad powers to arrest and to restrict freedom of movement, assembly and expression'. UN Special Rapporteur on the situation of human rights in the Sudan, Sima Samar. 2008. *Status of implementation of the recommendations compiled by the Group of Experts mandated by the Human Rights Council in resolution 4/8 to the Government of the Sudan for the implementation of Human Rights Council resolution 4/8 pursuant to Human Rights Council resolution 6/34.* UN Doc. A/HRC/9/13/Add.1, 73, Recommendation 1.1.4.

43   See for example, *Achutan and Another (on behalf of Banda and Others) v Malawi*, ACHPR, Communications 64/92, 68/92 and 78/92 (1995), para. 9 and *Constitutional Rights Project and Others v Nigeria*, ACHPR, Communications 140/94, 141/94 and 145/95 (1999), para. 55.

exceeded a time period that could reasonably be called 'provisionally'. In granting the competent authorities the sole authority to determine the length of detention, section 15 of the Emergency and Public Safety Bylaw effectively allows for prolonged and even indefinite detention.

In addition, the Emergency and Protection of Public Safety Act vests the president with the powers to give the authorities any other powers deemed necessary and to set up special prosecution offices and special courts. The president, or any person exercising delegated powers, can also specify the procedures of the special courts, which may issue additional punishments for a range of offences. These laws create a regime of legal exceptionalism that provide the executive with extraordinarily broad powers, which are virtually unrestrained by any safeguards or judicial oversight. Indeed, the use of emergency laws has been of major concern in Darfur. It has led to the disruption of peaceful civil society activities and resulted in arbitrary arrest and prolonged detention without any procedural safeguards or effective oversight, which greatly enhances the risk of torture.[44]

The institutional framework

The role of the prosecution

The system of a separate prosecution is relatively new in Sudan.[45] It has in recent years taken on such an important role that consideration of its function in the criminal justice system and its impact on the basic rights and freedoms of the individual warrants serious consideration. Historically, the role of the prosecutor was fulfilled by the police. The police took cognizance of the First Information Report on the commission of a crime, proceeded with the investigation, executed search and arrest, and after signature of the relevant warrant by the competent magistrate, decided on the charge, summarized the case and finally presented the case to the court for trial. With the establishment of the Public Prosecutor Office and the increasing numbers of lawyers at the Ministry of Justice, work previously done by the police has gradually shifted to prosecutors who at present cover most criminal cases within the country where criminal courts are found. Prosecutors now issue warrants of arrest to be executed by the police, and can order search and detention of a person for up to three days, a task previously in the hands of magistrates. Moreover, they may ask magistrates to extend detention beyond

---

44 See for example the submission in the case of *Mayor Hussein Ishaq Yahia Sayo and Others v Director of North Darfur State Police & Others* lodged before the Sudanese Constitutional Court in 2007 (on file with editor) and Independent Expert on the situation of human rights in the Sudan. 2010, para. 69.

45 The legal framework for the work of Sudan's prosecution services discussed in this section is provided for in the Regulations of the Work of Public Prosecutions, 1998.

the three days for the purposes of continuing the investigation. Furthermore they conduct prosecutions during the trial.

One criticism of the present prosecution system is that the prosecutor is part of the Ministry of Justice, which is comprised of officials of the executive, with the inherent risk of bias in favour of his or her employer, the government. In many systems public prosecution is undertaken by prosecutors working under the public prosecutor or director of public prosecutions, who is responsible to the Attorney General. Under such systems the Attorney General is an independent office, not subordinate to the Minister of Justice, who is part of the political regime in office. Proponents of an independent prosecutor system argue, in particular, that the power of *nolle prosequi* (stopping proceedings in a criminal case at any stage before reaching a verdict by the court) may be abused or influenced by political considerations if the minister is himself the Attorney General, or if the latter is subordinated to him. In Sudan, the Attorney General is, in that capacity and by virtue of that office, also the Minister of Justice.

Another concern regarding the present prosecution system is the complex hierarchy of procedures in criminal litigation. A person aggrieved of a decision to refuse a criminal complaint or to frame a charge relating to restriction of freedom, whose case is refused by a prosecutor, can appeal to the Higher Prosecutor, then to the Chief Prosecutor of the State, then to the Public Prosecutor at the Ministry of Justice and, finally, to the Minister. Such a protracted process may take months or even years, thus seriously jeopardizing basic rights and freedoms. It also underscores the fact that the old system of having independent magistrates in control of such basic matters of justice is much more protective of basic liberties.

Further, the system of 'specialized' prosecutors raises the question of the prosecutor's impartiality towards the public, vis-à-vis the organization to which he is assigned. There are now a number of specialized prosecutors related to state security, the media, banks, the tax department, the house rates department, public funds, the Sudatel Telephone Company and others; more of these specialized prosecutor roles can be expected. The advantages of such specialized prosecutors for banking and telecom companies is that such institutions provide prosecutors with well-equipped offices, transportation, allowances and other privileges that are not readily available at government offices. However, this consideration highlights the difficulty of maintaining the integral character and the independence of such prosecutors vis-à-vis the average member of the public.

The judiciary

It is perhaps trite to state that the independence of the judicial system is a prerequisite to the rule of law, respect for human rights and the administration of justice. The UN has developed guiding principles to assist member states in formulating principles and rules to guarantee the independence of the judiciary, the prosecutors and practicing lawyers,[46] the tripartite pillars for the administration of justice.

Sudan's experience with the independence of the judiciary, especially under the military regimes, which ruled Sudan for 37 out of its 55 years of independence, is far from encouraging. Presently, although the CPA and INC provide for the ambitious principles of preserving an independent judicial system, no concrete steps seem to have been taken over the last five years to put the principle into practice. The very same cadres that were present in 2005 continue to fill all the judicial posts. None of the judges previously arbitrarily dismissed at the time of the military coup d'etat has been reinstated in office. Special courts, where the basic principles for a fair trial are absent, are routinely established to try opposition members for offences against the state. Judges have no powers to oversee the work of the NSS, a branch of the executive, which has extensive powers of arrest, search, confiscation of property and prolonged detention, especially of those opposed to the regime. Moreover, NSS members enjoy impunity by not being accountable for their actions while fulfilling their 'tasks' as a result of the operation of immunity laws, which also apply to the armed forces and the police in their respective laws.

One extremely serious consideration is the guarantee of judicial independence by the institution responsible for overseeing it. In democratic regimes a High Judicial Council, constituted mainly of the Chief Justice, several high court judges and one or two ex-officio members, such as the Minister of Justice and the Dean of the Faculty of Law, tend to fulfil such function. Such was the case under the 1986 Judiciary Act and the 1986 High Judicial Council Act before they were changed in 2005.

Under the present system, however, this consideration seems to have been overlooked by the two partners of the Government of National Unity in their strong power sharing urge. Article 129 of the INC provides for the establishment of a National Judicial Service Commission to undertake 'the overall management of the National Judiciary' whose composition and functions are to be determined by law. The National Judicial Service Commission, adopted under the National Judicial Service Act in 2005, can hardly be described as a body responsible for the independence of the judiciary. First, it is constituted of 14 members: the Chief Justice (Chairperson), the Chairman of the Supreme Court of Southern Sudan, and Deputies of the Chief Justice – all four of whom are appointed by the executive. It is further composed of the National Minister of Justice (NCP), the Minister of Finance (NCP), the Legal Affairs Director of Southern Sudan (SPLM), the Chairperson of the Legal Committee of the National Council (NCP), the Chairman of the Legal Committee of the Council of States (NCP), and the Chairperson of the Legal Committee of South Sudan Legislative Council (SPLM). Additional members are the Dean of the Khartoum University Faculty of Law, two members

---

46 *Basic Principles on Independence of the Judiciary*, UN General Assembly resolution 40/32 (1985); and *Guiding Principles on the Role of Public Prosecutors*, and *Basic Principles on the Role of Lawyers*, 8th UN Conference on the Prevention of Crime (1990).

representing the two Bar Associations in the North and South, and three persons of relevant experience appointed by the president of the country. It is obvious that almost the total membership of the commission are political party members reflecting the power-sharing formula between the two ruling parties, the NCP and SPLM, rather than an independent commission responsible for the establishment and functioning of an independent judicial system.

In addition, the functions of the commission are not defined in such a way so as to oversee the independence of the system. Its task is limited to adopting the budget of the judiciary, making 'recommendations' to the executive on the appointment of judges of the Constitutional Court, the Chief Justice and his deputies, judges of the High Court and other judges. It can also recommend the promotion of judges and can endorse the dismissal of judges by the Chief Justice. In other words, the commission mainly makes 'recommendations' and does not take decisions. It has no effective role in the selection, appointment, promotion, discipline or dismissal of judges. Thus far, the commission has played no active role in enhancing the independence of the judicial system. Although its rules require it to meet regularly, at least once every four months, it is a known fact that it has only met twice since its formation. It is also no secret that the commission has delegated its powers to the Chief Justice in compliance with section 6(c) of its Act.

Conclusion

This chapter has endeavoured to examine several critical aspects of Sudan's criminal law in the context of its practical application. The main ruling party (NCP) has been in almost full control of all aspects of governance since it staged the military coup d'etat in 1989 during which period all the said laws proclaimed in the name of Islam and/or national security were adopted. Full control of power was ensured through the draconian violations of human rights and freedoms. During the state of emergency, which lasted several years, the ruling party succeeded in fully controlling all levels of government: security, the civil service, banking, insurance, construction, commercial companies and others, systematically executed in their declared programme of *Tamkeen* – that is, the empowerment of their cadres to run the state and control and use all sources of revenue for the benefit of the party and its leaders in both the public and private sectors.

The scope of this chapter does not permit going into the personal effect of these oppressive laws and policies, and the serious violations of human rights and humanitarian laws, especially in the context of the armed conflicts, first in the South and currently in Darfur. Neither in the violations in the urban areas nor in those in the armed conflicts have there been any efforts to remedy situations, redress the losses, bring perpetrators to justice, compensate victims or initiate any process of national reconciliation and healing. Needless to say, embarking on such colossal task would first require a genuine determination and political will and, secondly, the creation of a legal framework and institutional infrastructure to deliver those tasks.

When the CPA was signed in 2005, after both fighting parties grew weary of the war, the NCP considered it an opportunity to give itself a new lease of life by entering a partnership with the SPLM to the exclusion of all other political parties. With the world pressure that has been brought to bear on the parties, the CPA became not only a document for a ceasefire and accommodation of the respective forces, but also a comprehensive peace agreement touching upon all aspects of political life. When the INC was adopted a few months later, there were high hopes among all Sudanese that at last the democracy for which they had yearned for more than 15 years had arrived. Indeed the INC seemed to have provided the golden opportunity for the Sudanese people to aspire to democracy, justice, human rights and freedoms.

As highlighted, the outcome has been far from satisfactory. The constitutional requirements to adopt new laws or amend existing ones, and to reconcile them with the INC have not materialized. This is exemplified by new laws such as the National Security Act, with its negative impact on human rights and criminal justice, the existing Combating of Terrorism Act, immunities granted to members of the security, the army and the police, the weakness of the judicial system, the use of special courts, and the partiality of the new Constitutional Court to the regime in almost all its decisions so far. These and other factors make the hoped-for transition to democracy, peace and promotion and protection of human rights appear as empty slogans without effect or meaning. At a time when the country is undergoing momentous changes, including the referendum for the independence of the South in January 2011, and with the war going on unabated in Darfur, the need for urgent reform of laws and institutions is all too evident.

Chapter 4

Challenging the Ugly Face of Criminal Laws in East Africa: Repressive Legislation and Human Rights in Uganda, Kenya and Tanzania

Jamil Ddamulira Mujuzi

Introduction

Repressive legislation in East Africa is of particular importance because of the manner in which governments can and have used it to entrench themselves in power. This has been done through different avenues, from harassing the political opposition by prosecuting its leaders on trumped-up charges such as treason, to taking newspaper editors and media houses to court for publishing seditious publications and 'false' news, and thereby restricting rights to free speech. All East African countries have inherited most of their repressive legislation from their former colonial masters, which the latter had used to suppress local opposition to colonial rule. Because of the archaic nature of these laws, those targeted by them have more recently begun to petition the courts and challenge their constitutionality, especially in Uganda, with the result that courts are increasingly declaring such repressive legislation to be unconstitutional.

This chapter deals with the use of repressive criminal legislation in Uganda, although where possible examples from the other East African countries of Kenya and Tanzania are given. The discussion focuses in particular on the substantive provisions and practice relating to offences against the state, and emergency legislation and public order legislation in Uganda as well as any legislative reform initiatives in relation thereto. The chapter also provides a brief discussion of the law and practice relating to human rights and freedoms in the countries of study in order to situate the discussion of criminal law reform in a human rights arena.

Law and practice relating to human rights in Uganda, Kenya and Tanzania

The discussion of human rights and freedoms in Uganda, Kenya and Tanzania will be limited here to the constitutional provisions that relate to criminal law. The constitutions of the three countries protect different civil and political rights such as the right to freedom from torture and other forms of cruel, inhuman and degrading treatment or punishment,[1] the right to liberty (including freedom of movement),[2] the right to a fair trial,[3] the right to freedom of assembly and association,[4] and freedom of expression.[5] Courts and national human rights commissions in all the three countries are empowered to protect[6] and promote these constitutional rights (this is the domain of the human rights commissions).[7]

The three states are parties to regional and international human rights instruments relating to civil and political rights, such as the African Charter on Human and Peoples' Rights (AfrCHPR)[8] and the International Covenant on Civil and Political Rights (ICCPR).[9] Unlike Tanzania, both Uganda and Kenya have acceded to the United Nations Convention against Torture and other Cruel, Inhuman or Degrading Treatment or Punishment (UNCAT).[10] The failure by state parties to submit their periodic reports to the relevant treaties enforcement bodies in time has made it difficult to know what measures, if any, have been implemented to protect and promote the rights enshrined in the relevant treaties. With regard to the African human rights system, article 62 of the AfrCHPR requires states parties to submit to the African Commission on Human and Peoples' Rights (ACHPR),[11]

---

1   Article 24 Constitution of Uganda (1995), article 29 Constitution of Kenya (2010), and article 13(6)(e) Constitution of Tanzania (1965).

2   Article 29 Constitution of Uganda, article 39 Constitution of Kenya, and article 17 Constitution of Tanzania.

3   Article 28 Constitution of Uganda, article 13(6) Constitution of Tanzania and article 50 Constitution of Kenya. For a detailed discussion of the right to a fair trial in Kenya see Mujuzi, J.D. 2008. The Constitution in practice: An appraisal of the Kenya Case Law on the Right to a Fair Trial. *Malawi Law Journal.* 2(1), 135–57.

4   Article 29 Constitution of Uganda, article 80 Constitution of Kenya, and article 20 Constitution of Tanzania.

5   Article 29 Constitution of Uganda, article 79 Constitution of Kenya, and article 18 Constitution of Tanzania.

6   Article 50 Constitution of Uganda, article 84 Constitution of Kenya, and article 30(3) Constitution of Tanzania.

7   For the functions of the human rights commissions see section 16 of the Kenya National Commission on Human Rights Act, No. 9 of 2002; article 52(1) Constitution of Uganda and section 7 of the Uganda Human Rights Commission Act, 1997; and section 6 of the Commission for Human Rights and Good Governance Act of 2001, Tanzania.

8   Kenya ratified the AfrCHPR on 23 January 1992; Tanzania on 18 February 1984, and Uganda on 10 May 1986. See: http://www.africa-union.org/root/au/Documents/Treaties/List/African%20Charter%20on%20Human%20and%20Peoples%20Rights.pdf [accessed 6 January 2010].

9   Kenya acceded to this treaty on 1 May 1972; Tanzania on 11 June 1976; and Uganda on 21 June 1995.

10   Kenya acceded to this treaty on 21 February 1997 and Uganda on 3 November 1986.

11   The African Commission on Human and Peoples' Rights (ACHPR) was established by Article 30 AfrCHPR. See Ouguergouz, F. 2003. *The African Charter on Human and Peoples' Rights – A Comprehensive Agenda for Human Dignity and Sustainable Democracy*

initial and periodic reports detailing the measures that they have taken to promote, protect and fulfil the rights and duties in the charter. Kenya has so far submitted one report; its initial report was submitted in 2006 and combined all the overdue reports. Uganda has submitted three reports, the latest one, the third periodic report, was submitted in May 2009. Tanzania has submitted two reports, with the latest one, the second period report submitted in May 2008.[12] At the international human rights level, several state party reports on the measures taken to implement the rights and freedoms under the ICCPR and UNCAT were overdue at the time of writing.[13]

Offences against the state

Unlike Kenya and Tanzania, Uganda has witnessed unconstitutional changes of governments[14] since independence.[15] These changes have been characterized by gross human rights violations, especially of civil and political rights such as the right to freedom from torture, freedom of movement, freedom of expression, and the right to a fair trial.[16] Most of these violations have been committed by the respective government(s) in order to 'deal with' those opposed to, or presumed or suspected to be opposed to it. One could argue that, apart from the lawlessness that has always preceded or accompanied unconstitutional changes of governments, several provisions in the Penal Code Act[17] that categorize many acts or omissions as offences against the state have also contributed to blatant

---

in Africa. The Hague: Nijhoff Publishers, and Viljoen, F. 2007. *International Human Rights Law in Africa*. Oxford: Oxford University Press.

12   See Status on Submission of state initial/periodic reports to the ACHPR (updated August 2009) [Online] Available at: http://www.achpr.org/english/_info/statereport_considered_en.html [accessed 2 October 2009].

13   Kenya's third periodic report was due on 1 April 2008, Uganda's second periodic report on 1 April 2008 and Tanzania's fourth periodic report on 1 June 2002. See Human Rights Committee (HRC). 2008. *Report (91st, 92nd and 93rd sessions)*. UN Doc. A/63/40 (Vol.1), Annex III. Uganda's second period report to the Committee against Torture (CAT) was due on 25 June 2008, and Kenya's initial report was considered at the CAT's 852nd and 854th meetings held in Geneva on 13 and 14 November 2008 respectively. See CAT. 2009. *Report (41st and 42nd sessions)*. UN Doc. A/64/44, Annex XI and para. 41(1) respectively.

14   See Kanyeihamba, G.W. 2002. *Constitutional and Political History of Uganda: From 1894 to Present*. Kampala: Centenary Publishing House. The preamble to the Constitution of Uganda expressly recalls Uganda's 'history which has been characterised by political and constitutional instability'. Article 3 of the Constitution expressly prohibits the unlawful change of government and provides for the offence of treason for anyone who unlawfully amends the Constitution or overthrows the democratically elected government.

15   Uganda was a British protectorate until 9 October 1962.

16   See generally Commission of Inquiry. 1994. *The Report of the Commission of Inquiry into Violations of Human Rights: Findings, Conclusions and Recommendations*. Kampala.

17   Penal Code Act, Chapter 20 of the Laws of Uganda.

violations of human rights. This is because governments have used the relevant legislation not to achieve their original intended objective – of protecting the state against its enemies especially people intending to use unlawful means to bring about regime change – but to entrench themselves in power and also to persecute opposition politicians.

Chapter VI of the Penal Code Act of Uganda, like in some cases Chapter VII of the Penal Code of Kenya[18] and Chapter VII of the Penal Code Act of Tanzania,[19] provides for several offences against the state that may be grouped into three categories:

1. Offences against the state that relate to treason: concealment of treason (section 25);[20] the offence of treason (section 23);[21]
2. Offences that relate to war: promoting war on chiefs (section 27);[22] aiding soldiers or policemen in acts of mutiny (section 29);[23] inducing soldiers or policemen to desert (section 30);[24] aiding prisoners of war to escape (section 31);[25] and
3. Offences that relate to publications and other related matters: delivery of prohibited publications (section 36);[26] publication of information prejudicial to security (section 37);[27] seditious offences (section 40);[28] promoting sectarianism (section 41);[29] making or administering an unlawful oath

---

18   Penal Code Act, Chapter 63 of the Laws of Kenya.

19   Penal Code Act, Chapter 16 of the Laws of Tanzania.

20   Section 42 of the Penal Code of Kenya. The Tanzanian Penal Code does not provide for the offence of concealment of treason.

21   Section 40 of the Penal Code of Kenya and section 39 of the Penal Code of Tanzania.

22   Section 43 of the Penal Code of Kenya and section 43 of the Penal Code of Tanzania.

23   Section 48 of the Penal Code of Kenya and section 45 of the Penal Code of Tanzania.

24   Section 49 of the Penal Code of Kenya and section 47 of the Penal Code of Tanzania.

25   Section 50 of the Penal Code of Kenya and section 48 of the Penal Code of Tanzania.

26   The Penal Code of Uganda does not give an exhaustive list of these prohibited publications although section 34 provides that, whenever the Attorney General 'considers it in the public interest so to do, he or she may, in his or her absolute discretion, prohibit by statutory order, the importation of all publications or any of them, periodical or otherwise'; see also sections 52–54 of the Penal Code of Kenya. In Tanzania, provisions relating to the offence of prohibited publications were repealed in 1976.

27   Such a publication is one that is likely to: endanger the safety of military installations, equipment or supplies or of the members of the armed forces of Uganda; assist the enemy in its operations; or disrupt public order and security. See also section 66 of the Penal Code of Kenya. The Penal Code of Tanzania does not provide for such an offence.

28   These offences consist of uttering any words with a seditious intention (which is defined under section 39); printing, publishing, selling, offering for sale, distribution or reproducing any seditious publications; or importing any seditious publication.

29   The penal codes of Kenya and Tanzania do not provide for this offence.

(sections 45 and 46);[30] unlawful drilling (section 48);[31] publication of false news (section 50);[32] incitement of violence (section 51);[33] and incitement to refuse or delay payment of tax (section 52).[34]

The offence of terrorism is provided for under the Anti-Terrorism Act.[35]

Treason
The Constitution of Uganda in article 3(2), like that of Tanzania[36] but unlike that of Kenya, specifically establishes the offence of treason. The article is reinforced by section 23(1) of the Penal Code, which provides and defines the offence of treason. It is to the effect that any person who:

> (a) levies war against the Republic of Uganda; (b) unlawfully causes or attempts to cause the death of the President or, with intent to maim or disfigure or disable, unlawfully wounds or does any harm to the person of the President, or aims at the person of the President any gun, offensive weapon, pistol or any description of firearm, whether it contains any explosive or destructive substance or not; (c) contrives any plot, act or matter and expresses or declares such plot, act or matter by any utterance or by any overt act in order, by force of arms, to overturn the Government as by law established; (d) aids or abets another person in the commission of the foregoing acts, or becomes an accessory before or after the fact to any of the foregoing acts or conceals any of those acts, commits an offence.

The High Court of Uganda held that treason is a 'very serious and grave crime'.[37] Section 23(1) of the Penal Code is broad and, as the discussion below illustrates, there have been recent cases of prosecutions for treason in trials, some of which

---

30   Sections 59–62 of the Penal Code of Kenya and sections 60–61 of the Penal Code of Tanzania.

31   Section 65 of the Penal Code of Kenya and section 62 of the Penal Code of Tanzania.

32   The penal codes of Kenya and Tanzania do not provide for this offence.

33   Section 93 of the Penal Code of Kenya. The Penal Code of Tanzania does not provide for this offence.

34   The penal codes of Tanzania and Kenya do not provide for this offence.

35   The Anti-Terrorism Act, 2002.

36   Article 28(4) of the Constitution of Tanzania. The Court of Appeal of Tanzania held that the offence of treason can only be committed against a sovereign state. See *S.M.Z. v Machano Khamis Ali and others* (Criminal Application No. 8 of 2000) [2000] TZCA 1 (21 November 2000), in which treason charges had been brought against that accused for allegedly attempting to overthrow the government of Zanzibar.

37   *Pascal R. Gakyaro v Civil Aviation Authority* (Civil Suit No. 13 of 2005) [2006] UGHC 16 (12 May 2006), para. 5. The plaintiff was awarded damages for his wrongful arrest and suspension from employment for allegedly committing the offence of treason.

have been preceded or accompanied by human rights violations. Some of these charges bore the characteristics of politically motivated charges, which suggests that they were instituted with the sole or main objective of persecuting opposition politicians.

The human rights violations that have been associated with some of the treason trials can be illustrated by an incident where 21 treason suspects were forcibly removed from a civilian prison and transferred to Uganda Peoples' Defence Forces headquarters, where they were detained and interrogated for several days, leading to the death of one of the suspects.[38] In what appeared to be an attempt to use treason charges to harass, weaken, disorient and disorganize opposition politicians, the government sought to prevent opposition leader, Dr Kizza Besigye of the Forum for Democratic Change, from contesting for presidency on the grounds that he was a treason suspect.[39] In *Kabatsi Joy Kafura v Bangirana Kawooya Anifa and another*,[40] the High Court heard that the Attorney General had advised the government that because Dr Kizza Besigye was a treason suspect he could not contest for a presidential office. However, the Electoral Commission allowed Dr Besigye to contest for presidency on the basis that the constitution did not bar him from doing so.[41] The government appeared to have used treason charges to ensure that Dr Besigye spent as much time and money as possible in courts defending himself.[42] The leader of the opposition in the parliament of Uganda, Professor Morris Ogengo Latigo, reportedly said that 'the government is framing opposition MPs [Members of Parliament] by linking them with rebels so as to intimidate them'.[43]

---

38   In *Norbert Mao v Attorney General of Uganda* (Constitutional Petition No. 9 of 2000) [2003] UGCC 3 (17 March 2003), the Constitutional Court dismissed the applicant's petition on the ground that it raised the same issues as those that had been raised before the High Court.

39   See Human Rights Watch. 2005. *Uganda's Electoral Commission Must Uphold Presumption of Innocence.* [Online, 12 December] Available at: http://www.hrw.org/en/news/2005/12/11/uganda-s-electoral-commission-must-uphold-presumption-innocence [accessed 4 January 2010].

40   *Kabatsi Joy Kafura v Bangirana Kawooya Anifa and another* (Parliamentary Election Petition No. 0001 of 2006) [2007] UGHC 7 (24 January 2007).

41   See Human Rights Watch. 2006. *Uganda: Military Must Bow to Civilian Courts.* [Online, 19 January] Available at: http://www.hrw.org/en/node/69846 [accessed 4 January 2010].

42   In *Uganda Law Society v Attorney General of the Republic of Uganda* (Constitutional Petition No. 8 of 2005) [2006] UGCC 10 (31 January 2006), the Constitutional Court held that the trial of the opposition leader, Dr Kizza Besigye, in the High Court for treason and in the General Court Martial for terrorism when both offences were based on the same facts violated his constitutional right to a fair trial.

43   See Tebajjukira, M. 2009. Government Framing Opposition. *The New Vision* [Online, 6 January] Available at: http://www.newvision.co.ug/D/8/13/667180 [accessed 6 January 2010].

Because of the fact that treason is a serious offence, it has been held that an individual who has been maliciously accused by another of treason is entitled to sue for damages.[44] Unlike in Tanzania,[45] where treason suspects have no right to bail, the Ugandan Constitutional Court held that even treason suspects have the right to bail because:[46]

> While the seriousness of the offence and the possible penalty which could be meted out are considerations to be taken into account in deciding whether or not to grant bail, applicants must be presumed innocent until proved guilty or until that person has pleaded guilty. The court has to be satisfied that the applicant will appear for trial and would not abscond. The applicant should not be deprived of his/her freedom unreasonably and bail should not be refused merely as a punishment as this would conflict with the presumption of innocence. The court must consider and give the applicant the full benefit of his/her constitutional rights and freedoms by exercising its discretion judicially. Bail should not be refused mechanically simply because the state wants such orders. The refusal to grant bail should not be based on mere allegations. The grounds must be substantiated. Remanding a person in custody is a judicial act and as such the court should summon its judicial mind to bear on the matter before depriving the applicant of their liberty.

In *Attorney General v Joseph Tumushabe*,[47] in which 27 persons were detained in a military facility and denied bail while awaiting trial for treason before the General Court Martial, the Supreme Court held, *inter alia*, that:

---

44   In *Silver Cohens Okullu v Santos Okot Lapollo* (Civil Suit No. 26 of 2004) [2008] UGHC 83 (28 March 2009), the High Court awarded damages to the plaintiff for the defendant's insinuation that the former was a rebel. In *Patrick Makumbi v The New Vision Printing and Publishing Corporation and another* (Civil Suit No. 216 of 2003) [2006] UGHC 68 (25 August 2006), the High Court awarded the plaintiff damages when it was held that the material published by the defendant that the plaintiff had committed acts of treason were defamatory. In *Eng. Pascal R. Gakyaro v Civil Aviation Authority* (Civil Appeal No. 60 of 2006) [2007] UGCA 4 (15 November 2007), the appellant was awarded damages for his wrongful arrest and dismissal from his employment on allegations that he had committed treason.

45   See section 150(1) of the Criminal Procedure Act of 2004 (Tanzania). For a brief discussion of this provision see *D.P.P. v Juma* (Criminal Application No. 2 of 2005) [2005] TZCA 81 (13 December 2005).

46   *Uganda (DPP) v Col (Rtd) Dr. Kiiza Besigye* (Constitutional Reference No. 20 of 2005) [2006] UGCC 2 (22 September 2006). Article 49(1) of the Constitution of Kenya provides for the right to bail of any arrested person. For a detailed discussion of the right to a fair trial in Kenya including the right to bail see Mujuzi. 2008.

47   *Attorney General v Joseph Tumushabe* (Constitutional Appeal No. 3 of 2005) [2008] UGSC 9 (9 July 2008).

The detainees were remanded in custody for more than 120 days while awaiting trial for the offence of treason which offence is triable by the General Court Martial, a subordinate court, as well as by the High Court. Under Article 23(6) (b) [of the Constitution] it was mandatory to release them on bail, irrespective of the provisions of the UPDF Act[48] concerning bail. Failure to release them on bail after expiry of the said period was inconsistent with and contravened Article 23(6) (b) of the Constitution.

Although the Ugandan judiciary has developed rich jurisprudence on the right to bail,[49] the government has been very critical of the judiciary, especially in cases where treason suspects have been released on bail. In an unprecedented and widely condemned move, the government even went to the extent of using its security operatives to besiege the High Court in order to ensure that treason suspects who had been released on bail were re-arrested.[50] The Ugandan President reportedly suggested in May 2009 that Ugandan laws should be amended so that terrorism and treason suspects are detained without the right to bail for at least six months.[51] Treason being a serious offence, a magistrate does not have jurisdiction to grant bail to a person arrested for allegedly committing treason.[52]

Until 2005 the death penalty was mandatory for the offence of treason under section 23(1) of the Penal Code Act. The Supreme Court held in *Attorney General v Susan Kigula and 417 others*[53] that a mandatory death sentence for any offence

---

48   Uganda Peoples' Defence Forces Act, Chapter 307 of the Laws of Uganda (1992).

49   In *Foundation for Human Rights Initiatives v Attorney General* (Constitutional Petition No. 20 of 2006) [2008] UGCC 1 (26 March 2008), the Constitutional Court held that section 16 of the Trial on Indictment Act, section 76 of the Magistrates Court Act, sections 219, 231 and 248 of the Uganda People's Defence Act, and section 25(2) of the Police Act were unconstitutional because they infringed the accused's right to bail and personal liberty.

50   See Human Rights Watch. 2007. *Uganda: Government Gunmen Storm High Court Again.* [Online, 5 March] Available at: http://www.hrw.org/en/news/2007/03/04/uganda-government-gunmen-storm-high-court-again [accessed 4 January 2010]. For the judiciary's criticisms of the government's actions in this regard see *Dr. Kizza Besigye and Others v Attorney General* (Constitutional Petition No. 7 of 2007) [2010] UGCC 6 (12 October 2010).

51   Mugisa, A. 2009. Museveni Wants Corruption Suspects Denied Bail. *The New Vision* [Online, 14 May 2009] Available at: http://www.newvision.co.ug/D/8/12/681378 [accessed 6 January 2010].

52   Section 63(2) of the Magistrate Courts Act, Chapter 16 of the Laws of Uganda. In *Uganda v David Ntege* (Criminal Revision No. 10 of 2005) [2006] UGHC 59 (10 November 2006), it was held that the magistrate did not have jurisdiction over the offence of treason.

53   *Attorney General v Susan Kigula and 417 others* (Constitutional Appeal No. 3 of 2006) [2009] UGSC 6 (21 January 2009). For a detailed discussion, see Mujuzi, J.D. 2009a. International Human Rights Law and Foreign Case Law in interpreting constitutional rights: the Supreme Court of Uganda and the Death Penalty question. *African Human Rights Law Journal*, 9(2), 576–89, and Mujuzi, J.D. 2009b. Execution by hanging not torture or cruel

is unconstitutional because it violates the offender's right to a fair trial, in the sense that he or she cannot be heard in mitigation, and also that it violates the doctrine of separation of powers because the judges did not have the discretion to determine which sentence to impose on the offender after considering the mitigating and aggravating circumstances. Byamugisha JA of the Constitutional Court held that:

> Needless to say is the fact that offences like treason that attract the mandatory death sentence were a result of the ancient belief that the King is next to God and therefore to plan his death would be equivalent to wanting ones creator dead. This belief in my view has lost root in society and as such the mandatory death sentence is not tenable in modern society.[54]

The Uganda Constitutional Review Commission wrote in 2003 that, '[a]ccording to the people's views, the death penalty should be restricted to the most heinous crimes. Most people do not recommend the death penalty for treason'.[55] It is against that background that it recommended that '[t]he death penalty should be retained and should remain mandatory only for the crimes of murder, aggravated robbery, kidnapping with intent to murder, and defilement of minors below fifteen years of age'.[56] In its White Paper[57] and in the 'Report of the Legal and Parliamentary Affairs Committee on the Government White Paper on Constitutional Review and Political Transition', the government accepted the Commission's 'recommendation and not[ed] that treason is not included in the list of crimes to which a mandatory death penalty applies'.[58]

Article 72(3) of the old Constitution of Kenya (which was repealed in 2010) provided that a person arrested on suspicion of having committed any offence that did not attract the death penalty, must be released within 24 hours if that person had not been brought to court within that period. However, the same provision provided that a treason suspect can lawfully be detained for 14 days before

---

punishment? Attorney General v Susan Kigula and others. *Malawi Law Journal*, 3(1), 133–46.

54   *Susan Kigula and 416 others v Attorney General* (Constitutional Petition No. 6 of 2003) [2005] UGSC 8 (10 June 2005), in which the Constitutional Court held that the mandatory death sentence for offences such as murder and treason was unconstitutional. This holding was upheld by the Supreme Court in *Attorney General v Susan Kigula and 417 others* (Constitutional Appeal No. 3 of 2006)[2009] UGSC 6 (21 January 2009).

55   See Commission of Inquiry. 2003. *The Report of the Commission of Inquiry (Constitutional Review): Findings and Recommendations*, 13–175.

56   Commission of Inquiry. 2003, para. 13.7(i).

57   Government of Uganda. 2004. *White Paper on the Report of the Commission of Inquiry (Constitutional Review)*, para. 12.3(i).

58   Legal and Parliamentary Affairs Committee. 2004. *Report on the Government White Paper on Constitutional Review and Political Transition*, 49.

appearing before court because of the fact that treason is a capital offence. [59] The Kenyan Court of Appeal held that:

> It is therefore evident that it is not correct to say that the police have no right to arrest a suspect until they are in a position to charge the suspect forthwith. Moreover, with regard to bringing the person so arrested upon suspicion, the obligation to bring such person to court within twenty four hours … is imposed for an offence which does not appear to be of a serious nature. As regards the offence of … treason, it would seem that the requirement to bring the person suspected of such offence within twenty four hours does not apply [that person has to be brought to court within 14 days of his arrest or detention in terms of Article 72(3) of the Constitution]. It would be ideal to bring all persons suspected of having committed an offence to court within twenty four hours but from experience it is well known that it is not practicable to do so. This does not mean that the court approves or condemns the failure of the police to bring such persons to court within twenty four hours. Each case must be looked at from its own circumstances. [60]

In a parallel development, the Kenyan Constitutional Court held in July 2010 that the mandatory death sentence for any offence, including treason, was unconstitutional. [61] In an earlier development, the Kenya National Commission on Human Rights had noted that several Kenyans had been executed for treason and other offences, and urged the government to abolish the death penalty on grounds that it violates the right to life, among others. [62] In August 2009 the Kenyan President commuted all death sentences to life imprisonment and asked the relevant government departments to investigate whether it was still necessary to retain the death penalty for any offence. [63]

---

59   Section 40 of the Penal Code of Kenya provides that '[a]ny person who is guilty of an offence of treason shall be sentenced to death'. In light of the Court of Appeal's decision of *Godfrey Ngotho Mutiso v Republic* (Criminal Appeal No. 17/2008, Court of Appeal judgment of 30 July 2010), in which the court declared as unconstitutional all the Penal Code sections that provided for mandatory death sentences for, *inter alia*, violating the offender's right to a fair trial (in the sense that he could not be heard in mitigation), the death sentence provided for under section 40 is no longer mandatory. Tanzanian law also provides the death penalty for the crime of treason. See sections 39(1)(b), 39(2)(d), 39(3) (c), 39(4), 40 of the Penal Code.

60   *Republic v Hussen* (No. 2) Kenya Law Reports 425, at 434–5.

61   See *Godfrey Ngotho Mutiso v Republic*, Criminal Appeal No. 17/2008, Court of Appeal judgment of 30 July 2010.

62   See Kenya National Commission on Human Rights. Undated. *Position Paper No. 2 on the Abolition of the Death Penalty*. [Online] Available at: http://www.knchr.org/ dmdocuments/PositionPaperonDeath.pdf [accessed 4 January 2010], para. 10.

63   See 2009. Kibaki Commutes Death Sentences to Life Imprisonment. *Kenya Broadcasting Corporation* [Online, 3 August] Available at: http://www.kbc.co.ke/story.

Promoting Sectarianism

Promoting sectarianism is an offence against the state under section 41(1) of the Ugandan Penal Code, which provides that:

> A person who prints, publishes, makes or utters any statement or does any act which is likely to – (a) degrade, revile or expose to hatred or contempt; (b) create alienation or despondency of; (c) raise discontent or disaffection among; or (d) promote, in any other way, feelings of ill will or hostility among or against, any group or body of persons on account of religion, tribe or ethnic or regional origin commits an offence.

Some individuals have been prosecuted for this offence. In 2004 a senior military officer was detained while awaiting trial before the General Court Martial for, *inter alia*, the offence of sectarianism.[64] There has at least been one reported case in which the Penal Code provision prohibiting sectarianism has been blatantly abused not only by the law enforcement officers but also by the magistrate. In the case of *Uganda v David Ntege*, the magistrate convicted the accused, on his plea of guilt, of promoting sectarianism and sentenced him to nine months' imprisonment based on the facts that '[o]n 15th October 2005 at Nakaseke town as His Excellency the President of Uganda addressed a gathering of people, David Ntege ... [the accused] interrupted the President's speech. He commented that the district of Nakaseke had been given to herdsmen'. However, the accused's sentence was set aside by the High Court, which held that the magistrate did not have jurisdiction over the matter. Judge Lugayizi held that:

> The provisions of section 41 of the Penal Code Act (Cap. 120) are a serious affront to the inherent human right of freedom of speech found in Article 29(1) of the Constitution. For that reason, Court greatly doubts their constitutionality and consistency with National objective No. 1 i.e. '... *the establishment and promotion of a just, free and democratic society*' in Uganda (emphasis in original).[65]

Although the matter in this particular case was never pursued to the Constitutional Court, which is empowered under the Constitution to determine the constitutionality or otherwise of any piece of legislation,[66] it is indicative of the willingness of some judges to scrutinize some repressive laws in the light of the Constitution with the purpose of ensuring that they do not conflict with the supreme law of

---

asp?ID=59004 [accessed 4 January 2010].

    64   See *Tumukunde v Attorney General and another* (Constitutional Petition No. 6 of 2005) [2005] UGCC 1 [1 January 2005].

    65   *Uganda v David Ntege*.

    66   Article 37(1) of the Constitution of Uganda provides that '[a]ny question as to the interpretation of this Constitution shall be determined by the Court of Appeal sitting as the Constitutional Court'.

the land. However, when the constitutionality of the offence of sectarianism was challenged in another matter, the Constitutional Court held that the offence was not unconstitutional. In *Andrew Mujuni Mwenda v Attorney General*[67] the petitioners, *inter alia*, challenged the constitutionality of section 41 of the Penal Code, and the court held that:

> This section [41 of the Penal Code] criminalizing sectarianism was made Law on the 7th December 1988 before the 1995 Constitution was promulgated. Article 274 of the Constitution saved existing laws which were in force on coming unto force of the Constitution. It's therefore lawful. After perusing the relevant provisions of the Constitution and considering, submissions of counsel for the petitioners and respondent together with authorities referred to us, we find nothing unconstitutional about it. We decline to grant the declaration on sectarianism as prayed.[68]

It is argued that the basis on which the Constitutional Court found section 41 of the Penal Code to not be unconstitutional is not convincing. The court was correct that article 274 of the Constitution saves existing laws. However, the article also provides in detail that:

> the operation of the existing law after the coming into force of this Constitution shall not be affected by the coming into force of this Constitution but the existing law shall be construed with such modifications, adaptations, qualifications and exceptions as may be necessary to bring it into conformity with this Constitution.

The mere fact that the law was in force before the coming into force of the Constitution does not in itself mean that that law is constitutional. In fact, as it has been illustrated throughout this chapter, there are cases in which the Constitutional Court has found that some legal provisions that were in force at the time of the Constitution were contrary to it.

Promoting sectarianism is an offence in Uganda, and there have been recent instances where the law has been invoked to suppress some rights, such as the right to freedom of expression. In September 2009 the Ugandan government ordered the closure of a Buganda kingdom-owned radio station (Central Broadcasting Corporation) on the grounds, *inter alia*, that it promoted sectarianism.[69] The

---

67 *Andrew Mujuni Mwenda v Attorney General* [2010] UGCC 5 (25 August 2010).

68 *Mwenda v Attorney General*, 13.

69 Olupot, M. and Musoke, C. 2009. Museveni Blames Riot on Opposition. *The New Vision* [Online, 15 September] Available at: http://www.newvision.co.ug/D/8/12/694767 [accessed 4 January 2010].

Ugandan president has also reportedly said that 'those who fish the line of sectarianism were acting against the interests of Ugandans'.[70]

Terrorism

Uganda's 2002 Anti-Terrorism Act provides a comprehensive definition of terrorism (or acts of terrorism)[71] and repeals section 26 of the Penal Code Act, which had hitherto provided for the offence and definition of terrorism. The UN Human Rights Committee expressed concern 'that section 10 of the Act criminalizes a "terrorist organization" without any reference to a particular criminal offence committed by or through such an organization. It is also concerned that section 11 of the Act does not establish objective criteria for determining membership in a "terrorist organization" (arts. 2 and 15)'. The Committee recommended that Uganda 'should review the Anti-Terrorist Act with a view to ensuring that the provisions set out in sections 10 and 11 are in full conformity with the Covenant'.[72] In Kenya, terrorism is defined as one of the threats 'to the security of state' in the National Security Intelligence Service Act.[73] Tanzania has passed specific anti-terrorism legislation to boost its fight against this crime.[74]

All the three countries have been direct or indirect victims of terrorism, leading to the loss of lives and revenue.[75] Uganda has been a victim of terrorist attacks from the Somalia-based Al-Shabab[76] and the notorious Lord's Resistance Army.[77] Kenya and Tanzania were victims of the Al-Qaeda bombings in August 1998. Thus the seriousness of the acts of terrorism cannot be underestimated. However, it is worrying that the governments of Uganda and Kenya failed to resist the misuse of the anti-terrorism legislation to violate human rights, especially the rights to freedom from torture, and the right to personal liberty. In Uganda,

---

70   Kiwanuka, F. 2009. Shun Sectarianism – Museveni. *The New Vision* [Online, 8 September] Available at: http://www.newvision.co.ug/D/8/13/693908 [accessed 4 January 2010].

71   Section 7(2).

72   HRC. 2004. *Concluding Observations: Uganda*. UN Doc. CCPR/CO/80/UG, para. 8.

73   See sections 2 of the National Security Intelligence Service Act, Act 11 of 1998.

74   The Prevention of Terrorism Act, Act No. 21 of 2002 (Tanzania).

75   For example, the government of Uganda noted that the threat of terrorist attacks in East Africa had affected the tourism industry. See *Uganda Revenue Authority v Speke Hotel 1996 Ltd* (Civil Appeal No. 12 of 2008) [2008] UGCommC 54 (22 September 2008).

76   See Mmali, J. 2010. Uganda's World Cup Shattered by Blasts. *BBC News* [Online, 12 July] Available at: http://www.bbc.co.uk/news/10605457 [accessed 3 August 2010], where it was reported that over 70 people were killed in terrorist attacks in the Ugandan capital, Kampala, when they were watching the FIFA World Cup finals.

77   For the atrocities committed by the Lord's Resistance Army, especially in northern Uganda, see Ssenyonjo, M. 2007. The International Criminal Court and the Lord's Resistance Army Leaders: prosecution or amnesty? *Netherlands International Law Review*, 54(1), 51–80.

terrorism suspects have been charged before the General Court Martial, which does not have the jurisdiction over the offence of terrorism.[78] Terrorism charges against the opposition leader Dr Besigye were not only filed in a Court Martial that lacked jurisdiction over the matter, but ostensibly had the objective of crippling his political activities. In addition, those who demonstrate against some of the government's policies have been threatened with terrorism charges and some have actually been charged with terrorism. This was the case, for example, in September 2009 when several people who protested against the government's perceived interference in the affairs of the Buganda Kingdom were arrested and charged with terrorism.[79]

In Uganda[80] terrorism carries the maximum penalty of death and in Tanzania it carries a maximum of 30 years' imprisonment.[81] In Kenya the Court of Appeal notably held in passing that even terrorism suspects are protected by the Constitution, and can only be detained while awaiting trial in accordance with the Constitution.[82] In *Mohammed v Republic*, an application for *habeas corpus* was filed on behalf of the accused, who had been detained by the police on allegations that he was a terrorism suspect. In granting the order the High Court of Kenya held that: '[t]errorism is a heinous crime committed against any country and its peoples. It is for this that those given the authority to prevent or detect terrorist activities operate within the law so that terrorists do not go unpunished on grounds of flawed investigations and breaches of any Constitutional provisions'.[83]

Seditious publications and publication of false news
Section 33(e) of the Ugandan Penal Code Act creates the offence of seditious publication, which refers to 'a publication having a seditious intention'. Section 39 defines 'seditious intention' to mean an intention:

(a) to bring into hatred or contempt or to excite disaffection against the person of the President, the Government as by law established or the Constitution; (b) to excite any person to attempt to procure the alteration, otherwise than by lawful means, of any matter in state as by law established; (c) to bring into hatred or

78   In *Uganda Law Society v the Attorney General of Uganda* (Constitutional Petition No. 18 of 2005) [2006] UGCC 11 (31 January 2006), the Constitutional Court held, *inter alia*, that the trial of the 23 accused, including an opposition leader for terrorism before the General Court Martial, was unconstitutional because the Court lacked jurisdiction over the offence. See also *Dr. Kizza Besigye and 10 others v The Attorney General* (Constitutional Petition No. 7 of 2007) [2009] UGCC 7 (1 September 2009).
79   See Nsambu, H. and Nansubuga, R. 2009. Court to Consider Bail for Terrorism Suspects. *The New Vision* [Online, 7 December] Available at: http://www.newvision.co.ug/D/8/13/703535 [accessed 6 January 2010].
80   Section 7(1)(a) of the Anti-Terrorism Act, Act 14 of 2002.
81   Sections 13–27 of the Prevention of Terrorism Act, Act No. 21 of 2002.
82   *Murunga v Republic* (2008) 1 Kenya Law Reports (Gender and Family) 1223, 1227.
83   *Mohammed v Republic* (2003) Kenya Law Reports 344, at 350.

contempt or to excite disaffection against the administration of justice; (d) to subvert or promote the subversion of the Government or the administration of a district.

Section 50 provides for the offence of publication of false news. It states that '[a] ny person who publishes any false statement, rumour or report which is likely to cause fear and alarm to the public or to disturb the public peace commits a misdemeanour'. The government has used and still uses the prohibition of seditious publication and statements to harass journalists[84] and opposition politicians.[85] In the case *Uganda Journalist Safety Committee and another v Attorney General* the Constitutional Court dismissed the petitioner's constitutional challenge of sections 41 and 50 of the Penal Code that criminalize sedition and the publication of false news respectively, on the grounds that the petitioners had not followed the proper procedure in filing their petition.[86] What is vital to note about this case is that the second petitioner, a practising journalist, had been convicted and sentenced to five months' imprisonment and to one years' imprisonment with the option of a fine in both cases, for sedition and publishing false news respectively.

The constitutionality of the offence of sedition was later successfully challenged before the Constitutional Court in the case of *Andrew Mujuni Mwenda and Another v Attorney General.*[87] The first petitioner, who hosted a radio talk-show, had been charged with sedition before the magistrate's court for questioning the government of Uganda's decision to declare a public holiday to mourn the death of a prominent Southern Sudan politician, Dr John Garang. He had also insinuated that the Ugandan government had a hand in Garang's death. He added that the president, Kaguta Museveni, was a coward, and that that is why he was always accompanied by many security officers and armoured vehicles. The prosecution argued that the petitioner had uttered the above words 'with intention to bring into hatred or contempt or to excite disaffection against the person of the President, the Government as by law established or the Constitution'.[88] The petitioner argued that his prosecution violated his constitutional rights to freedom of expression, freedom of speech and the press guaranteed under article 29(1) of the Constitution, as well as his right to a fair trial while the respondents argued that the limitations

---

84   See Anyoli, E. 2009. Journalist Charged over Sedition. *The New Vision* [Online, 23 September] Available at: http://www.newvision.co.ug/D/8/13/695564 [accessed 6 January 2010].

85   See for example, Ssejjoba, E. 2009. DP's Betty Nambooze Charged with Sedition. *The New Vision* [Online, 10 December] Available at: http://www.newvision.co.ug/D/8/13/703933 [accessed 6 January 2010], and Anyoli, E. Court rejects Lubega Appeal. *The New Vision* [Online, 30 October 2009] Available at: http://www.newvision.co.ug/D/8/13/699609 [accessed 6 January 2010].

86   *Uganda Journalist Safety Committee and another v Attorney General* (Constitutional Petition No. 6 of 1997) [1997] UGCC 8 (16 December 1997).

87   *Mwenda v Attorney General.*

88   *Mwenda v Attorney General,* 2.

imposed on the right to freedom of expression through the offence of sedition were justified in a free and democratic society. The court held that:

> Apart from citing some international conventions, [the] … respondent adduced no evidence that the limitation was justifiably acceptable in a democratic society … [The respondent's submissions do] … not solve the fundamental criticism that the wording creating the offence of sedition is so vague that one may not know the boundary to stop at, while exercising one's right under 29(I) (a). [The petitioners] complained that the section does not define what sedition is. It is so wide and it catches every body to the extent that it incriminates a person in the enjoyment of one's right of expression of thought. Our people express their thoughts differently depending on the environment of their birth, upbringing and education. While a child brought up in an elite and God fearing society may know how to address an elder or leader politely, his counterpart brought up in a slum environment may make annoying and impolite comments, honestly believing that, that is how to express him/herself. All these different categories of people in our society enjoy equal rights under the Constitution and the law. And they have equal political power of one vote each. That explains [the second petitioner's] observation that during elections voters make very annoying and character assassinating remarks and yet in most cases false, and yet no prosecutions are preferred against them. The reason is because they have a right to criticize their leaders rightly or wrongly. That is why [the second petitioner] suggested, rightly so that leaders should grow hard skins to bear. We find that, the way impugned sections were worded have an endless catchment area, to the extent that it infringes one's right enshrined in Article 29(1)(a). We answer issue one in affirmative and in favour of the petitioners.[89]

The effect of the above ruling was that the offence of sedition has ceased to be an offence in Uganda, unless the Supreme Court sets aside the Constitutional Court's ruling should the government appeal against the Constitutional Court's ruling.[90] However, courts have started giving effect to the Constitutional Court's ruling; two months after the Constitutional Court judgment, the Magistrates' Court dismissed a charge of sedition that had been filed against one journalist, on the ground that sedition was no longer an offence under Ugandan law.[91]

---

89   *Mwenda v Attorney General*, 12.

90   The Information Minister, Ms Kabakumba Masiko, reportedly said that the government will appeal against the Constitutional Court's ruling. See Mulondo, E. 2010. RDCs can Vet Radio Talk Show Guests, Says Minister. *The Daily Monitor* [Online, 24 September] Available at: http://www.monitor.co.ug/News/National/-/688334/1017132/-/cnli3ez/-/index.html [accessed 1 December 2010].

91   See Wesaka, A. 2010. Court Drops Sedition Charge Case against Radio Journalist. *The Daily Monitor* [Online, 6 October] Available at: http://www.monitor.co.ug/News/National/-/688334/1026858/-/cn0hy4z/-/index.html [accessed 1 December 2010].

In *Charles Onyango Obbo and another v Attorney General*,[92] the petitioners, who were practising journalists, were jointly charged in the Magistrates' Court on 24 October 1997 on two counts of 'publication of false news', contrary to section 50 of the Penal Code Act. The charges arose out of a story that the petitioners had extracted from a foreign paper called *The Indian Ocean Newsletter*, and had published in the *Sunday Monitor* on 21 September 1997 under the headline: 'Kabila paid Uganda in Gold, says report'. The petitioners submitted before the Supreme Court that section 50 of the Penal Code was unconstitutional because it conflicted with articles 29(1)(a) and (b), 40(2) and 43(2)(c) of the Constitution, which when read together guarantee the right to freedom of expression. The Supreme Court unanimously found in the petitioners' favour and declared section 50 of the Penal Code to be unconstitutional. In his separate concurring opinion, Byamugisha JA held that:

> Uganda chose a path of democratic governance and therefore she has a duty to protect the rights regarding the free flow of information, free debate and open discussion of issues that concern the citizens of this country. In order to exercise these rights there must be an enabling regime for people to freely express their ideas and opinions as long as in enjoying these rights such people do not prejudice the rights and freedoms of others or public interest ... As long as in expressing one's opinion even if it is false, the person doing so does not prejudice the rights and freedoms of others, or the public interest there would be no harm done. In my view, section 50 is inconsistent with Article 29(1)(a) of the Constitution for criminalising every statement that is published even if that statement has not caused any prejudice to the rights of others. Even if there is a violation or prejudice of other people's rights, there is a remedy or remedies that are provided under the existing law where one can seek redress in a civil court. This means that our society must learn to accommodate a wide variety of views, beliefs etc, even if such views or beliefs are repugnant and contrary to our own.

However, in the latest amendments to the Penal Code Act that took place three years after the judgment,[93] section 50 was not repealed. It is noteworthy that, although section 50 is yet to be repealed, the automatic result of the judgment is that it no longer forms part of the Ugandan laws. The above discussion shows that the Ugandan judiciary has ensured that some legal provisions that infringe the right to freedom of expression and speech are held as unconstitutional, unless their use can be justified in a free and democratic society. In May 2009 the government of Uganda notified the ACHPR that sedition laws exist in Uganda and have 'given

---

92   *Charles Onnyango Obbo and another v Attorney General* (Constitutional Appeal No. 2 of 2002) [2004] UGSC 1 (11 February 2004).

93   See the Penal Code (Amendment) Act, 2007.

rise to the emergency and protection of a free and robust press'.[94] In its concluding observations on Uganda's report the African Commission did not express its views on the impact that sedition laws have on the right to freedom of expression and the press in Uganda. That notwithstanding, the African Commission was concerned by Uganda's 'failure to ensure the full enjoyment of the right to freedom of expression by introducing legislative measures that restrict the right to freedom of expression'.[95] It recommended that Uganda '[e]stablish adequate legislation on freedom of expression to fulfil its obligations under the [African] Charter'.[96]

Emergency legislation

Gross human rights violations – sometimes under the cover of emergency legislation – became one of the defining features of a succession of short-lived, undemocratic governments between 1962, when Uganda attained independence, and 1986, when the National Resistance Movement (NRM) government came into power.[97] In 1988 the NRM government started the process of enacting the new constitution. It established the Uganda Constitutional Commission (which was popularly known as the Odoki Commission because it was chaired by Justice Benjamin Odoki) that traversed the whole country gathering the views of Ugandans on what they thought should be included in the new constitution in order, *inter alia*, to bring about political stability in Uganda and to ensure respect for human rights and the rule of law. In its report the Odoki Commission reported that:

> The declaration of a state of emergency in Buganda [central Uganda] from 1962 to 1971 was used to intimidate people into silence and fear and soon led to the ill-considered policy, enshrined in the 1967 Constitution, of detention without trial, an instrument which has continued to be used to silence political opposition and to deal with any critic of government, whether real or imaginary.[98]

The Odoki Commission wrote further that:

> The issues of whether a state of emergency should be permitted, and if so the extent of government powers permitted during an emergency were extensively discussed in people's submissions. The majority view was that there was a need

---

94   See Report by the Government of Uganda to the ACHPR presented at the 44th Ordinary Session Abuja, Federal Republic of Nigeria (10–24 November 2008), 12.

95   See ACHPR. 2009. *Concluding Observations on the 3rd Periodic Report of the Republic of Uganda*, para. 23.

96   ACHPR. 2009. Concluding Observations, Part V, para. c.

97   See generally *Report of the Commission of Inquiry into Violations of Human Rights*. 1994.

98   Uganda Constitutional Commission (UCC). 1992. *Report: Analysis and Recommendations*, para. 7.49(d).

for government to have special powers in real emergencies. On the other hand, an emergency should be clearly and strictly defined by the new Constitution and the powers available in an emergency clearly spelt out. Otherwise there could be no guarantee that fundamental rights and freedoms of individuals would not be arbitrary suppressed by power-hungry governments which might manipulate declarations of emergencies to their own advantage.[99]

The Odoki Commission recommended several inclusions to the new Constitution to prevent governments from violating people's rights during a state of emergency, which were that the Constitution should clearly stipulate: the circumstances under which the state of emergency could be declared, and the rights that can and cannot be suspended or derogated from during a state of emergency; the powers of parliament during the state of emergency; and the rights of people detained under a state of emergency.[100] During the debates of the Odoki Commission Report in the Constituent Assembly, there were intense discussions about the circumstances under which a state of emergency could be declared, and the rights of those detained during a state of emergency.[101] One of the delegates, Mr Tiberio Okeny, argued that the new Constitution should unambiguously protect the rights of Ugandans during a state of emergency because 'the country has had more than enough of its shares of atrocities done to the population of this country, during ... the state of emergency'.[102] It is against that backdrop that the 1995 Constitution contains comprehensive provisions regulating not only the circumstances in which a state of emergency can be declared, but also the safeguards to ensure that people's rights are protected during one.

Under article 110(1) of the Constitution of Uganda:

[t]he President may, in consultation with the Cabinet, by proclamation, declare that a state of emergency exists in Uganda, or any part thereof if the President is satisfied that that circumstances exists in Uganda or that part of Uganda – (a) in which Uganda or that part of it is threatened by war or external aggression; (b) in which the security or the economic life of the country or that part is threatened by internal insurgency or natural disaster; or (c) which render necessary the taking of measures which are required for securing the public safety, the defence of Uganda and the maintenance of public order and supplies and services essential to the life of the community.

A state of emergency is supposed to be maintained for not more than 90 days, but can be extended by Parliament for as long as necessary (with each extension up to

---

99   UCC. 1992, para. 7.109.
100   UCC. 1992, paras 7.110–7.115.
101   See Constituent Assembly. 1994. *Proceedings of the Constituent Assembly (Official Report)*, 2172–6.
102   See Constituent Assembly. 1994, 2172.

90 days)[103] and can be revoked by the President by proclamation if he is satisfied that circumstances that led to the declaration have ceased to exist.[104] During a state of emergency the President is required to submit regular reports at such intervals as prescribed by parliament on the measures being taken during the state of emergency.[105] Parliament is empowered to enact laws that limit the enjoyment of some of the rights during a state of emergency for the purpose of taking measures that are 'reasonably justified in dealing with the state of emergency'.[106] Such laws can provide, for example, for the detention of persons where necessary for the purpose of dealing with the state of emergency.[107] However, the Constitution puts in place measures to ensure that the rights and freedoms of any person detained as a result of the implementation of the law relating to the state of emergency are protected. Article 47 provides that:

> Where a person is restricted or detained under a law made for the purpose of a state of emergency, the following provisions shall apply – (a) he or she shall, within twenty-four hours after the commencement of the restriction or detention, be furnished with a statement in writing specifying the grounds upon which he or she is restricted or detained; (b) the spouse or next-of-kin of or other person named by the person restricted or detained shall be informed of the restriction or detention and allowed access to the person within seventy-two hours after the commencement of the restriction or detention; (c) not more than thirty days after the commencement of his or her restriction or detention, a notification shall be published in the *Gazette* and in the media stating that he or she has been restricted or detained and giving particulars of the provisions of the law under which his or her restriction or detention is authorised and the grounds of his or her restriction or detention.

A person restricted or detained in terms of the law relating to a state of emergency has a right to consult with his/her lawyer. The Uganda Human Rights Commission (UHRC) is also obliged to review that person's case 'not later than twenty-one days after the commencement of the restriction or detention, and after that, at intervals of not more than thirty days'.[108] The UHRC, after reviewing the case, may order the release of that person or uphold the grounds of restriction or detention.[109] The relevant minister is obliged on a monthly basis to notify parliament of the measures taken to implement the recommendations of the UHRC in relation to

---

103 Article 110(2) of the Constitution of Uganda.
104 Article 110(3).
105 Article 110(6).
106 Article 46(1).
107 Article 46(3).
108 Article 48(1).
109 Article 48(3).

the person detained or restricted under emergency legislation.[110] The minister is also obliged to publish in the gazette and in the media the number, names and addresses of the persons restricted or detained, the number of cases reviewed by the UHRC and the acts taken in compliance with the UHRC's findings.[111] Although the Constitution does not specifically provide that a person detained in terms of emergency legislation has the right to challenge the lawfulness of his arrest or detention, such a person or any person or a non-governmental organization can, on behalf of that person, challenge such arrest or detention in terms of article 50(1) and (2) of the Constitution. Redress in terms of article 50 of the Constitution is not limited to compensation awarded by a court. It could also include the release of the detainee. Because of the fact that the UHRC has the powers to constantly monitor the situation of people detained under emergency legislation, such people can also challenge the lawfulness of their detention before the same.

The Emergency Powers Act[112] provides, *inter alia*, for the provisions that should be included in emergency regulations. The detailed and clear provisions in the Constitution relating to the state of emergency mean that the circumstances under which a state of emergency is to be declared are very clear, and that there are mechanisms in place to protect the rights and freedoms of those who might be detained during such a period. It also makes it very difficult for a state of emergency to be declared unjustifiably. In the past emergency regulations have been used to detain people.[113] However, since 1986, when the current government came to power, a state of emergency was only declared in September 2007 when the eastern and northern parts of the country were ravaged by floods to help the government, *inter alia*, to get external support for the flood victims.[114]

Offences against public order

Offences against public order fall under the broad category of 'unlawful assemblies, riots and other offences against public tranquillity' and they include: the formation and management of an unlawful society,[115] unlawful assemblies and riots,[116] and incitement to violence.[117] The Penal Codes of Kenya and Tanzania also contain

---

110   Article 49(1).

111   Article 49(2).

112   Emergency Powers Act, Chapter 297 of the laws of Uganda.

113   See for example, *Opoloti v Attorney General* [1969] E.A. 631, where the Ugandan High Court and later the East African Court of Appeal both held that the applicant's detention under emergency regulations was lawful. See also *Uganda v Commissioner of Prisons, Ex parte Matovu* [1966] E.A.514.

114   See Odyek, J. and Musoke, C. 2007. Museveni Declares State of Emergency. *The New Vision* [Online, 19 September] Available at: http://www.newvision. co.ug/D/8/12/587526 [accessed 4 January 2010].

115   Sections 56(2) of the Penal Code of Uganda.

116   Section 65.

117   Section 83.

110 *Criminal Law Reform and Transitional Justice*

similar provisions.[118] The Penal Code of Uganda provides that 'any person who takes part in a riot commits a misdemeanour'.[119] The punishment for taking part in an unlawful assembly is imprisonment for up to one year[120] and for inciting violence imprisonment for up to three years.[121]

There have been occasions where Ugandans have been prosecuted for committing one or more of the offences against public order. In *Uganda v Tibemanzi Deus*, in acquitting the accused on the charge of the offence against peace, the High Court held that according to the facts:

> the learned trial Magistrate erred in law in convicting the accused of the offence of being idle and disorderly contrary to section 167 (d) of the Penal Code Act … Merely taking a photograph of the President without permission does not constitute an offence under section 167 (d) of the Penal Code Act.[122]

The above decision shows, *inter alia*, that the police are ready to arrest and prosecute people on flimsy grounds because the Penal Code has a wide range of acts that are categorized as offences against public order. It also shows that some magistrates have a long way to go in understanding and correctly interpreting the laws that they are required to apply. The Ugandan police, in the name of enforcing the Penal Code provisions on offences against public order, have been instrumental in especially dispersing people found to be exercising their right to freedom of assembly by holding demonstrations. In *Muwanga Kivumbi v Attorney General*, the Constitutional Court held that section 32 of the Police Act, which gave the Inspector General of Police powers to prohibit the convening of an assembly or forming of the procession, was unconstitutional.[123] In his concurring opinion, Mpagi-Bahigeine JA held that:

> It is the paramount duty of the police to maintain law and order but not to curtail people's enshrined freedoms and liberties on mere anticipatory grounds which might turn out to be false. Lawful assemblies should not be dispersed under any circumstances. Most importantly in such cases the conveners of the assemblies

118 See Chapter IX of the Penal Code of Kenya and Chapter IX of the Penal Code of Tanzania.

119 Section 67 of the Penal Code of Uganda. The punishment for a misdemeanour is provided for under section 22 of the Penal Code which provides that, '[w]here in this Code no punishment is specially provided for any misdemeanour, it shall be punishable with imprisonment not exceeding two years'.

120 Section 66.

121 Section 51.

122 *Uganda v Tibemanzi Deus* (Criminal Revision No. HCT-00-CR-CV-CO-02-2006) [2006] UGHC 47 (2 November 2006).

123 *Muwanga Kivumbi v Attorney General* (Constitutional Petition No. 9 of 2005) [2008] UGCC 4 (4 May 2008).

can be required to give an undertaking for good behavior and in default face the law.[124]

Byamugisha JA held that:

> The justification for freedom of assembly in countries which are considered free and democratically governed in my view is to enable citizens together [sic] and express their views without government restrictions. The government has a duty of maintaining proper channels and structures to ensure that legitimate protest whether political or otherwise can find voice. Maintaining the freedom to assemble and express dissent remains a powerful indicator of the democratic and political health of a country. I, therefore, find that powers give[n] to the Inspector General of Police to prohibit the convening of an assembly or procession [impose] an unjustified limitation on the enjoyment of fundaments right. Such limitation is not demonstrably justified in [a] free and democratic country like ours.[125]

Although the Constitutional Court held that section 32 of the Police Act was unconstitutional, there have been cases where the police have prevented members of opposition parties from holding demonstrations, especially those against government policies, hence violating their right to freedom of assembly. For example, in early January 2010 a demonstration by a coalition of opposition parties was called off at the eleventh hour because the government, instead of guaranteeing the security of demonstrators, 'chose to act in an uncivilized manner by deploying armed Police and soldiers on the streets'.[126] This could be interpreted to mean that the executive is ignoring court rulings.

Punishments held by the Constitutional Court to be unconstitutional

Banishment/exclusion for witchcraft

A person convicted of witchcraft in terms of the Witchcraft Act,[127] which was introduced during the colonial period, is liable to be sentenced to various terms of imprisonment, up to life imprisonment where the person 'directly or indirectly threatens another with death by witchcraft or by any other supernatural means'

---

124   *Mwanga Kivumbi v Attorney General*, 7.

125   *Mwanga Kivumbi v Attorney General*, 16.

126   See Bekunda, C. et al. 2010. Police Blocks Protest March. *The New Vision* [Online, 4 January] Available at: http://www.newvision.co.ug/D/8/12/706126 [accessed 6 January 2010].

127   Witchcraft Act 125 of 1957.

(section 2(1)). Although the Witchcraft Act does not define witchcraft,[128] there are indeed cases where some people have been convicted of witchcraft and sentenced accordingly. In *Salvatori Abuki and another v Attorney-General*,[129] the first petitioner was charged with practising witchcraft contrary to section 3(3) of the Witchcraft Act. The prosecution witnesses testified before the magistrate that 'the petitioner had practiced witchcraft on the complainants with the use of a tortoise, goat horns and other substances contained in a pot and a gourd'.[130] He pleaded guilty to the charge of practising witchcraft and was sentenced by the magistrate to 22 months' imprisonment. In addition, the magistrate ordered that the petitioner was 'to be banned for 10 years from [his] home after serving the sentence'.[131] The exclusion order was based on section 7 of the Witchcraft Act which empowered the court to impose an exclusion order against a person convicted of witchcraft. The petitioner challenged the constitutionality of the Witchcraft Act arguing that it violated his right to a fair trial (because the offence of witchcraft was not defined in the Act), his right to property (because the exclusion order prevented him from using his property) and that the sentence imposed, that is the exclusion order, violated his right to freedom from cruel, inhuman or degrading treatment or punishment. The Constitutional Court, by majority with Justice Manyindo dissenting, held that section 7 of the Witchcraft Act was unconstitutional for its violation of the petitioner's constitutional rights to property, life and the right not to be subjected to cruel, inhuman and degrading treatment or punishment. The Court held that the trying and sentencing of the petitioner under the Witchcraft Act violated his right to a fair trial because the offence of witchcraft was not defined under the Act. Although it has been over three years since the Constitutional Court declared section 7 of the Witchcraft Act to be unconstitutional, the Ugandan government is yet to repeal that section. However, in light of the Constitutional Court ruling, no court can impose on any person the punishment provided for under section 7 of the Witchcraft Act because it no longer forms part of Ugandan law and no person can be charged with the offence of witchcraft under the Witchcraft Act.

---

128   Section 1 of the Act does not define witchcraft. Instead, it provides that for the purposes of the Act '"witchcraft" does not include bona fide spirit worship or the bona fide manufacture, supply or sale of native medicines'. The Constitutional Court held by majority in *Salvatori Abuki and another v Attorney-General*, Constitutional Case No. 2 of 2007 (Constitutional Court decision of 13 June 1997), that the offence of witchcraft was vague and violated article 28(12) of the Constitution, which provides that no person shall be charged with an offence that is not clearly defined in law.

129   *Salvatori Abuki and another v Attorney General*, Constitutional Case No. 2 of 2007.

130   *Abuki v Attorney General*, 9.

131   *Abuki v Attorney General*, 9.

Corporal punishment

The Penal Code of Uganda provided for several offences for which a person could be sentenced to corporal punishment in addition to other sentences.[132] Section 125 provided that a person convicted of rape was liable to imprisonment for life with or without corporal punishment. Sections 128(1) and 147 provided that a person convicted of indecent assault was liable to be sentenced to fourteen years' imprisonment, with or without corporal punishment. Under section 129(2) a person convicted of attempted defilement was liable to imprisonment for eighteen years with or without corporal punishment.[133] In *Simon Kyamanywa v Uganda*,[134] the petitioner had been convicted of robbery and sentenced to imprisonment and to corporal punishment. He challenged the constitutionality of the corporal punishment on the ground that it violated article 24 of the Constitution, which prohibits cruel, inhuman and degrading treatment or punishment. The Constitutional Court found in his favour and declared the relevant provisions of the Penal Code to be unconstitutional. As a result the Penal Code was amended in 2007 to specifically abolish the sentence of corporal punishment.[135] Section 94(9) of the Children Act[136] provides in no uncertain terms that '[n]o child shall be subjected to corporal punishment'.

Conclusion

Practice shows that the Ugandan government has on several occasions used offences against the state and public order legislation to harass members of the opposition, and practising journalists. Ugandan courts have held that some of the repressive laws are unconstitutional, often as a result of litigation brought by human rights lawyers, non-governmental organizations, the media or political opposition. However, in some cases the government has continued to violate people's rights, for example the right to assembly, despite the fact that the Constitution guarantees such a right. One lesson to be learned from the Ugandan experience is that, even

---

132   Section 109 of the Trial on Indictment Act, Chapter 23 of the Law of Uganda, provided in detail the manner in which the sentence of corporal punishment was being administered. It provided, *inter alia*, that the rod or cane to be used had to be determined by the Minister; that the punishment had to be administered in the presence and with the approval of a medical doctor; that the punishment was not to be carried out in instalments; that it was not to be imposed on female offenders; it was not to be imposed on males sentenced to death; and was not to be imposed on males whom the court considered to be above forty-five years old. See also section 57 of the Prisons Act, Chapter 304. Rule 78 of the Prison Rules, Statutory Instrument 304-4.

133   See also sections 205 and 288 of the Penal Code of Uganda.

134   *Simon Kyamanywa v Uganda*, Constitutional Reference No. 10 of 2000.

135   See section 1 of the Penal Code (Amendment) Act, 2007.

136   The Children Act, Cap 59 (1997).

if the legislature does not take the initiative to repeal or amend laws that restrict people's rights, such laws should be challenged before courts on the grounds that the impugned provisions not only violate the constitution but also the country's regional and international human rights obligations. Even in cases where courts are not specifically required or empowered to refer to international law and foreign case law in interpreting the constitution, the petitioners should not fail to indicate which international treaties are being violated by repressive laws and cite relevant examples from other countries. In Uganda, for example, petitioners challenging the constitutionality of repressive laws have cited international law and foreign case law in their submission, and the Constitutional Court and the Supreme Court have referred to international law and foreign case law although the Constitution does not expressly require the judges to do so.[137]

---

137   See generally, Mujuzi. 2009a.

II. Arrest, Detention and Fair Trial

Arrest, detention and trials: Nature, practice and concerns

The rights to liberty, security and a fair trial lie at the heart of criminal justice because they seek to protect those accused of crimes (and others deprived of their liberty for various reasons) from an overbearing state by counterbalancing broad powers with adequate safeguards. Arbitrary arrests and detentions are a common feature of many states' practice, particularly of authoritarian and dictatorial states or during conflicts and counter-terrorism operations.[1] Numerous cases can attest to the arrest and detention, with or without charges, of political opposition figures, human rights defenders, journalists and others on insufficient grounds.[2] Safeguards against arbitrary arrest and detention, such as the right to *habeas corpus*, are often lacking, particularly where emergency legislation is in place or where the legal system allows for preventive or administrative detention.[3] Equally, arrest and detention regimes are often characterized by their lack of safeguards against torture and ill-treatment, such as the right to contact family members, to medical care, and to access a lawyer of one's choice.[4] This applies in particular to the practice of secret detentions, which has become widespread in the context of the 'war on terror'.[5] Arbitrary arrest and detention has often been followed by unfair trials. Such trials frequently raise concerns over the lack of judicial independence (particularly trials of civilians by military or special tribunals[6]), the restriction

---

1   See, for example, Chairperson-Rapporteur of the Working Group on Arbitrary Detention, Leila Zerrougui et al. 2006. *Situation of Detainees at Guantánamo Bay.* UN Doc. E/CN.4/2006/120, paras 17–40.

2   See UN Special Rapporteur on the Promotion and Protection of Human Rights and Fundamental Freedoms while countering Terrorism, Martin Scheinin et al. 2010. *Joint Study on Global Practices in Relation to Secret Detention in the Context of Countering Terrorism.* UN Doc. A/HRC/13/42; UN Special Rapporteur on the situation of human rights defenders, Margaret Sekaggya. 2009. *Report.* Doc. A/HRC/13/22, 30, at para. 34.

3   See UN Special Rapporteur. 2010, para. 285. See on the system of administrative detention, for example in Israel, UN Special Rapporteur on the promotion and protection of human rights and fundamental freedoms while countering terrorism, Martin Scheinin. 2007. *Mission to Israel, including Visit to Occupied Palestinian Territory.* UN Doc. A/HRC/6/17/Add.4, paras 22–9; HRC. 2003. *Concluding Observations: Israel.* UN Doc. CCPR/CO/78/ISR, paras 12–14.

4   Special Rapporteur on torture and other cruel, inhuman or degrading treatment or punishment, Theo van Boven. 2003. *Report.* UN Doc. E/CN.4/2004/56, paras 27–49.

5   UN Special Rapporteur. 2010.

6   See for example *Öcalan v Turkey*, 41 EHRR 45 (2005), paras 112–18.

of defence rights, the admission of evidence alleged to have been obtained as a result of torture, and harsh punishments with limited possibility of appeal.[7] The reform of legislation pertaining to arrest, detention and/or trials, such as in Turkey and Peru, has at times been triggered by the jurisprudence of international human rights courts or bodies.[8] It has also formed part of broader institutional reforms concerning the administration of justice undertaken in the course of transitions, particularly in several Latin American countries and in South Africa following the end of apartheid.[9]

International standards

The right to liberty and security

The right to liberty and security is guaranteed in international and regional human rights treaties.[10] Regional and international standards complement and reinforce the treaty obligations, such as 'The Principles and Guidelines on the Right to a Fair Trial and Legal Assistance in Africa',[11] and the United Nations (UN) standards to protect the rights of detainees and prisoners.[12]

'Liberty' refers to the physical liberty of a person, not a mere restriction of freedom of movement.[13] National, regional and international courts and human rights treaty bodies have developed a series of criteria to determine the circumstances that constitute 'deprivation of liberty'. The assessment depends on the context of the situation and the type, duration, effects and manner of the measure concerned, in short, its degree or intensity.[14] The absence of valid consent

---

7   All these concerns were raised in a recent communication relating to Sudan, UN Working Group on Arbitrary Detentions. 2010. *Opinion No. 38/2008 (The Sudan), Communication addressed to the Government of Sudan on 22 August 2008.* UN Doc. A/HRC/13/30/Add.1, 166–81.

8   *Öcalan v Turkey* and Inter American Court of Human Rights (Inter-Am. CtHR). *Case of the Constitutional Court v Peru.* Merits, Reparations and Costs. Judgment, 31 January 2001. Series C No. 71.

9   See chapter 6.

10   Articles 9 ICCPR; 5 ECHR; 7 ACHR; 6 AfrCHPR.

11   *The Principles and Guidelines on the Right to a Fair Trial and Legal Assistance in Africa*, African Commission on Human and Peoples' Rights (ACHPR), (2001) DOC/OS (xxx) 247.

12   *Body of Principles for the Protection of All Persons under Any Form of Detention or Imprisonment*, UN General Assembly resolution 43/173 (1988), and *Standard Minimum Rules for the Treatment of Prisoners*, UN Economic and Social Council resolutions 663 C (XXIV) (1957) and 2076 (LXII) (1977).

13   *Guzzardi v Italy*, 3 EHRR 333 (1980), paras 92–5.

14   *Guzzardi v Italy*, para. 92.

is another element that is important, particularly in cases involving a detainee's confinement in a psychiatric institution.[15]

The deprivation of liberty must be both lawful according to domestic law and reasonable in the circumstances – that is, not arbitrary. As provided in the Principles and Guidelines on the Right to a Fair Trial and Legal Assistance in Africa:

> States must ensure that no one shall be subject to arbitrary arrest or detention, and that arrest, detention or imprisonment shall only be carried out strictly in accordance with the provisions of the law and by competent officials or persons authorised for that purpose, pursuant to a warrant, on reasonable suspicion or for probable cause.[16]

In the defining case of *Mukong v Cameroon*, the Human Rights Committee specified that the meaning of 'arbitrariness' is:

> not to be equated with 'against the law' but must be interpreted more broadly to include elements of inappropriateness, injustice, lack of predictability and due process of law ... remand in custody pursuant to lawful arrest must not only be lawful but reasonable in the circumstances ....[17]

International standards recognize that arrested and detained persons are especially vulnerable to violations of their rights. Anyone arrested and detained must be informed of the charges against him or her at the earliest opportunity so that they are able to challenge the legality of detention.[18] The right to bring such a challenge before a judicial body, known as *habeas corpus*, provides an important safeguard against arbitrary detention, whether in relation to a criminal offence or in a different context (such as confinement in a psychiatric hospital).[19] Significantly, the right to *habeas corpus* cannot be derogated from.[20]

Anyone detained on suspicion of having committed an offence must be brought before a judge promptly – normally within the first 48 hours – and tried within a

---

15 *Storck v Germany*, 43 EHRR 96 (2005), paras 74–8.

16 M(1)(b) Principles and Guidelines on Fair Trial in Africa.

17 *Mukong v Cameroon*, Human Rights Committee (HRC), Communication 458/1991, UN Doc. CCPR/C/51/D/458/1991 (1994), para. 9.8. See also *Article 19 v Eritrea*, ACHPR, Communication 275/2003 (2007), para. 93.

18 Articles 9(2) ICCPR; 5(2) ECHR and 7(4) ACHR. See also Trechsel, S. 2006. *Human Rights in Criminal Proceedings*. Oxford: Oxford University Press, 456.

19 9(4) ICCPR; 5(4) ECHR; 7(6) ACHR.

20 HRC. 2001. *General Comment 29: States of Emergency (article 4)*. UN Doc. CCPR/C/21/Rev.1/Add.11, para. 16, and Inter-Am. CtHR. 1987, *Habeas Corpus in Emergency Situations (Arts. 27(2), 25(1) and 7(6) American Convention on Human Rights)*. Advisory Opinion OC-8/87. 30 January 1987. Series A No. 8.

reasonable time.[21] Wherever possible, he or she should be released on bail.[22] This general rule is based on the presumption of innocence; no one should be held in detention any longer than necessary, especially where it has not yet been proven that he or she is guilty of an offence that is liable to imprisonment.

Preventive or administrative detention constitutes somewhat of a grey area in the law on arrest and detention. Such detention is not explicitly prohibited in international human rights law,[23] but is generally considered to be problematic since it may be a pretext for or result in arbitrary detention. This is the reason for the strict requirements pertaining to it: namely that it be defined by law, that it be necessary (in relation to the objective pursued, which must be legitimate) and that it be subject to continuous judicial review.[24]

The right to liberty and security is closely intertwined with custodial safeguards against torture. Torture and other forms of ill-treatment are often committed upon arrest, during the first 48 hours of detention. It is for these reasons that no one arrested or detained should be held *incommunicado* (without access to the outside world).[25] Persons should be able to notify a family member of their arrest, to have access to a lawyer of their choice and to be subject to a health check upon entering and leaving any place of detention so as to establish an official record of their health status while in detention (and as a means of ensuring their health).[26] The rights to be promptly brought before a judge and to *habeas corpus* are other important safeguards as they allow judicial bodies to establish whether a detainee has been subjected to torture, and to receive complaints to this effect.[27]

Importantly, international human rights law also recognizes the right of anyone subjected to arbitrary arrest or detention to compensation.[28] Such compensation

---

21   Articles 9(3) ICCPR; 5(3) ECHR; 7(5) ACHR; 7(1)(d) AfrCHPR.

22   Article 9(3) ICCPR; 5(3) ECHR; 7(5) ACHR.

23   Article 5 of the ECHR is an exception as it does not list preventive detention as one of the grounds of legitimate arrest and detention.

24   HRC. 2008. *General Comment 8: Right to liberty and security of persons (Art. 9) (30 June 1982).* Compilation of General Comments and General Recommendations adopted by Human Rights Treaty Bodies, UN Doc. HRI/GEN/Rev.9 (Vol.1), 179, para. 4. See also UN Special Rapporteur. 2007, paras 22–9.

25   *Article 19 v Eritrea*, paras 76, 100, 101, and UN Special Rapporteur on the question of torture, Theo van Boven. 2002. *Report.* UN Doc. E/CN.4/2003/68, para. 26(g).

26   Council of Europe. 2003. *CPT Standards: Substantive sections of the CPT's General Reports.* 12th General Report. CPT/Inf (2002) Rev. 2003, para. 40: 'As from the outset of its activities, the CPT has advocated a trinity of rights for persons detained by the police: the rights of access to a lawyer and to a doctor and the right to have the fact of one's detention notified to a relative or another third party of one's choice'. See also principles 15–19 of the UN General Assembly Body of Principles.

27   See in this regard *Aksoy v Turkey*, 23 EHRR 553 (1997), para. 76, and Trechsel. 2006, 505.

28   See articles 9(5) ICCPR and 5(5) ECHR.

is not only a means to vindicate the rights violated but should also serve as a deterrent for the state by making arbitrary arrest and detention costly.

The right to a fair trial

The right to a fair trial is guaranteed in international treaties[29] and in the statutes of international criminal tribunals.[30] The rights to equality of arms and to a fair hearing before an independent tribunal are the cornerstones of the right to a fair trial.[31] In criminal proceedings, fairness implies that a person is presumed innocent until proved guilty, with the burden of proof on the prosecution. Anyone suspected of a criminal offence must be able to defend him- or herself from the outset with the assistance of a lawyer of his or her choice.[32] In this context the equality of arms requires the provision of 'the same procedural rights ... to all the parties unless distinctions are based on law and can be justified on objective and reasonable grounds, not entailing actual disadvantage or other unfairness to the defendant'.[33]

As a general rule, tribunals hearing criminal and civil cases must be impartial and independent. Judges must be shielded from political interference and 'must appear to a reasonable observer to be impartial'.[34] The operation of military or special tribunals raises particular concerns over their compatibility with fair trial standards, particularly where they have the power to try civilians. Such trials must conform to fair trial standards and must be the exception, where only absolute necessary.[35]

Trials must also be public, and persons charged must be granted the requisite rights to defend themselves. This includes the right of access to a lawyer of one's choice or to defend oneself, the opportunity to adequately prepare the case, the right to examine witnesses,[36] and the right to an interpreter where necessary. Trials

---

29   Article 9 ICCPR, article 6 ECHR, article 8 ACHR and article 7 AfrCHPR.

30   Article 21 ICTY; article 20 ICTR, and articles 66 and 67 ICC Rome Statute.

31   HRC. 2007. *General Comment 32: Article 14: Right to equality before courts and tribunals and to a fair trial.* UN Doc CCPR/C/GC/32.

32   HRC. General Comment 32. See on article 6(3) ECHR in particular Trechsel. 2006, 244–51.

33   HRC. General Comment 32, para. 13, with reference to Communication No. 1347/2005, *Dudko v Australia*, para. 7.4.

34   HRC. General Comment 32, para. 21.

35   HRC. General Comment 32, para. 22. See also Akwanga v Cameroon, HRC, Communication 1813/2008, UN Doc. CCPR/C/101/D/1813/2008 (2011), para.7.5. and Separate Opinion of M. Fabián Omar Salvioli.

36   See for the limits of this right in cases where its exercise may clash with the rights of witnesses, REDRESS. 2009. *A Call to Action: Ending threats and reprisals against victims of torture and related international crimes.* [Online, December] Available at: http://www.redress.org/downloads/publications/Victim%20Protection%20Report%20Final%20 10%20Dec%2009.pdf [accessed 16 December 2010], 28–30. For relevant jurisprudence, see in particular *Doorson v The Netherlands*, 22 EHRR 330 (1996), para. 70.

should be conducted without undue delay, since it is in the interest of justice and the individual to know the outcome as soon as feasible. This principle may, however, conflict with the right of the accused to defend him- or herself adequately. The question of undue delay in proceedings must therefore be answered by an assessment that takes into consideration the complexity of the case and the conduct of both parties.[37] The right to appeal is an important safeguard since it enables a higher tribunal to review the lawfulness of the verdict or decision concerned.[38] Another important principle is embodied in the right not to be tried or punished twice for an offence (except where new facts or evidence emerge that justify a new prosecution). This seeks to avoid repeat prosecutions and the abuse of criminal proceedings.[39]

---

37   HRC. General Comment 32, para. 35.

38   See in particular article 15(5) ICCPR and HRC. General Comment 32, paras 45–51.

39   See articles 14(7) ICCPR; article 4 of the Seventh Protocol to the ECHR, 1984; and article 8(4) ACHR.

Chapter 5

At the State's Mercy: Arrest, Detention and Trials under Sudanese Law

Nabil Adib

Introduction

The exercise of the powers of arrest and detention are critical features of any criminal justice system. The individual's personal freedom is curtailed and he or she may be exposed to the risk of violations. The right to liberty and security is therefore not only fundamental in its own right; it is also an essential prerequisite for a fair trial and the protection of other core rights, in particular the prohibition of torture and other forms of ill-treatment.

The importance of the right to liberty and security is evident in Sudan, where there have been longstanding concerns about arbitrary arrest and detentions, unfair trials, and the use of ill-treatment and torture in detention.[1] This chapter examines the Sudanese legal framework relating to arrest and detention, in particular the Criminal Procedure Act of 1991 (SCPA) and the National Security Act of 2010 (NSA). This is with a view to determining its compatibility with the Bill of Rights and applicable international human rights standards and to developing recommendations to overcome any shortcomings identified.

The right to liberty and security in the Bill of Rights

Several articles in the Bill of Rights, which forms Part II of the Interim National Constitution (INC) of 2005, guarantee the right to liberty and security and related rights. Article 29 provides that '[e]very person has the right to liberty and security of person; no person shall be subjected to arrest, detention, deprivation or restriction of his/her liberty except for reasons and in accordance with procedures prescribed by law'. Article 34 provides for the right to a fair trial and article 35 for the right to litigation.

These fundamental rights have to be read in conjunction with international human rights standards that are applicable pursuant to article 27(3) of the Bill of Rights. This provision makes the International Covenant on Civil and Political

---

1 See, for example, Human Rights Committee (HRC). 2007. *Concluding observations: Sudan*. UN Doc CCPR/C/SDN/CO/3/CRP.1, paras 16, 21, 22, 25.

Rights (ICCPR) and the African Charter on Human and Peoples' Rights (AfrCHPR) an integral part of the Bill of Rights. This includes articles 9 and 14 ICCPR and articles 6 and 7 AfrCHPR, which govern the right to liberty and security as well as the right to a fair trial respectively in the two instruments.

Article 9 ICCPR is more detailed in scope than article 29 of the Bill of Rights. Importantly, it specifies that arrest and detention must not only be lawful according to national law; they must also not be arbitrary. This means that national law itself has to comply with relevant international standards.[2] Article 9 ICCPR also provides for the duty of authorities to inform promptly anyone arrested of the reasons for the arrest and any charges against him or her, and to bring 'anyone arrested or detained on a criminal charge ... promptly before a judge or other officer authorized by law to exercise judicial power'. Anyone arrested or detained 'shall [also] be entitled to trial within a reasonable time or to release'. Moreover, a detained person has the right to *habeas corpus*, namely to bring proceedings before a court to obtain a decision on the lawfulness of detention. Finally, '[a]nyone who has been the victim of unlawful arrest or detention shall have an enforceable right to compensation'.

Arrest and detention under Sudan's Criminal Procedure Act

Lawfulness of arrest and detention

Power of arrest and detention
The SCPA recognizes two types of arrest procedures, namely with or without arrest warrant. An arrest warrant may be issued by a prosecutor or a judge where a crime has been committed in their presence or where an individual has contravened a particular court order (article 67 SCPA). Around half of the crimes of the Criminal Act are subject to arrest without warrant (article 68(2) SCPA). These include crimes punishable by a maximum of three months' imprisonment (such as disturbance of the peace), or by lashing and imprisonment of not more than one month. A police officer or public official may arrest a person caught in the act of committing a crime who refuses to give his or her name and address. They enjoy equal powers where a person is found in suspicious circumstances or in the possession of property that has been stolen or is associated with a crime and is unable to present a reasonable explanation. In addition, a police officer or public official has the power of arrest where the individual obstructs the police officer in his or her duties or escapes or attempts to escape from custody (article 68(2) SCPA).

Article 44(2) of the SCPA stipulates that an arrest without warrant must be based on 'information, or [a] complaint ... about facts indicating the commission of an offence', and article 68(2)(a) provides that a 'person [must be] suspected,

---

2   *Mukong v Cameroon*, HRC, Communication No. 458/1991, UN Doc. CCPR/C/51/D/458/1991 (1994), para. 9.8.

or accused of committing an offence in which arrest without warrant may be made'. This should equate to a reasonable suspicion, which, as interpreted by the European Court of Human Rights (ECtHR), requires the existence of sufficient information that will make an objective observer assume that the concerned person may have committed the crime forming the basis of the arrest.[3] The prosecution has to provide at least some factual grounds capable of convincing a court of the probability that the arrested person may have committed a crime. In the case of *Fox, Campbell and Hartley v the United Kingdom*, the claimants were arrested by officers acting in good faith who suspected that they were involved in a terrorist act as two of them had been previously convicted of similar acts. However, as the standard for reasonable suspicion is an objective one, even though the state cannot be asked to disclose the confidential sources of supporting information, it was required to furnish at least some facts or information capable of satisfying the court that the arrested person was reasonably suspected of having committed the alleged offence.[4]

Under Sudanese law, however, the powers of arrest apply to a broad range of crimes without adequately stipulating what constitutes 'suspicious circumstances' that act as a trigger mechanism. Effectively, this leaves the police with the power to determine the reasons for arrest in a given case and increases the risk of abuse.[5] The current provisions find their roots in English laws stemming from the period of transition from feudalism to capitalism. At that time the laws were used to confine the working class to a specific location, which resulted in criminalizing acts for the purpose of preventing movement within cities. This rationale was subjected to scrutiny by the United States (US) Supreme Court in the case of *Papachristou v City of Jacksonville*, in which it ruled on the vagrancy law of Jacksonville.[6] In that case, two white girls were driving around aimlessly with two black youths in their company. They were arrested and charged with driving a car without an apparent legitimate aim. The Supreme Court ruled that the vagrancy law was unconstitutional. It noted that the loose language of the law leads to vesting the judge or police with the powers of a legislative body contrary to the principle of the rule of law. The Court further noted that the law gives the police the authority to arrest anyone who acts suspiciously; that is effectively requiring people to act in a manner acceptable to the police and courts, which is unconstitutional. This resulted in incriminating persons based on ambiguous and imprecise terms that were open to interpretation by the courts at will. The reasoning of the US Supreme

---

3   *Gusinskiy v Russia*, Application no. 70276/01, Judgment of 19 May 2004, para. 53.

4   *Fox, Campbell and Hartley v The United Kingdom*, 13 EHRR 157 (1990), para. 34.

5   See for concerns that '[t]he police tend to make excessive use of [the] unchecked power [to arrest a criminal suspect without first obtaining an arrest warrant]'. United Nations High Commissioner for Human Rights (UNHCHR). 2008. *Tenth periodic report of the on the situation of human rights in the Sudan, Arbitrary arrest and detention committed by national security, military and police*. Geneva, 26.

6   *Papachristou v City of Jacksonville*. 405 U.S. 156 (1972).

Court illustrates how wide and loosely defined powers can result in abuse, and is often used against those not conforming to a particular lifestyle:

> Those generally implicated by the imprecise terms of the ordinance – poor people, nonconformists, dissenters, idlers – may be required to comport themselves according to the lifestyle deemed appropriate by the Jacksonville police and the courts. Where, as here, there are no standards governing the exercise of the discretion granted by the ordinance, the scheme permits and encourages an arbitrary and discriminatory enforcement of the law. It furnishes a convenient tool for 'harsh and discriminatory enforcement by local prosecuting officials, against particular groups deemed to merit their displeasure'. It results in a regime in which the poor and the unpopular are permitted to 'stand on a public sidewalk ... only at the whim of any police officer' [References omitted].[7]

Arbitrariness

Article 29 of the Bill of Rights does not explicitly recognize the prohibition of arbitrary arrest and detention. However, by virtue of article 27(3) of the Bill of Rights, article 29 is to be interpreted in line with article 9(1) of the ICCPR and article 6 of the AfrCHPR, both of which explicitly prohibit arbitrary arrest and detention. As already noted, arbitrariness has to be interpreted in a wide manner, such that it should include meanings of improper, unfair or unreasonable.[8] This may include arrest on vague grounds and detention that cannot be justified by the seriousness of the offence and/or the available evidence, or that lacks essential safeguards to ensure the continuous lawfulness of detention.

Justification of pre-trial arrest and detention

Article 67(a) of the SCPA authorizes the arrest of any person against whom criminal proceedings are taken (as well as in case of breach of certain procedural conditions). However, the power of arrest does not equate to the power of detention. Sudanese law uses the term arrest to mean restricting the freedom of movement of a person in order to take him or her to a certain place, normally a police station, or before a certain official without requiring his or her consent and possibly against his or her will. Detention is used to keep a person in a certain place, without his consent or against his or her will, and therefore implies deprivation of freedom of movement for a longer period than arrest. Deprivation of liberty is primarily justified as punishment resulting from a finding of guilt. Indeed, article 34(1) of the INC stipulates the principle that an accused is innocent until proven guilty. Pre-trial detention should therefore be the exception, which can be justified on narrow grounds only so as not to turn it into a form of punishment prior to any trial.

---

7   *Papachristou v City of Jacksonville.* Per Justice Dougal, 170.
8   See Introduction to Part II: Arrest, detention and fair trial.

Two grounds are generally recognized as justifying pre-trial arrest and detention: detaining a person for the purpose of preventing him or her from concealing evidence or tampering with evidence; and ensuring his or her presence in front of a court in any future proceedings. Article 79 SCPA, however, is wider in scope as it provides the authorities with broad powers of arrest and detention for the purpose of inquiry although interrogating a suspect and taking his or her testimony does not require such powers.[9] A suspect can simply be summoned. If either of the grounds for pre-trial arrest and detention applies, a suspect may be arrested and detained for a period not extending beyond the time required to achieve the purpose of the detention. It should not be lengthened to the extent that it deprives the suspect of his or her personal liberty without valid grounds. This is reflected in article 6(a) of the Tokyo Rules, adopted by United Nations (UN) General Assembly on 14 December 1990, according to which pre-trial detention shall be used as a means of last resort. Article 6(2) of the same rules calls for restricting detention so that it does not last longer than necessary.

Guarantees

Advising suspects on their right to a lawyer and the right to remain silent
The right of a suspect to be assisted by a lawyer is one of the major prerequisites for the exercise of the right to a fair trial, and constitutes an important component of the latter. It is closely connected with another principle, namely the right against self-incrimination. A lawyer's role is to enable a suspect to exercise his or her defence effectively. This includes advice on the right to silence, which may prevent a suspect from incriminating him- or herself. Modern criminal justice imposes a positive duty on the police to advise suspects of their constitutional rights. In this regard, before questioning a person in custody, he or she must be advised of his or her right to consult a lawyer, and the right to remain silent. Sudanese law, however, does not recognize such a duty. In fact, a person being investigated by the police might face imprisonment for a term of up to one month or a fine for committing an offence under article 98 of the Sudanese Criminal Act, 1991, if he or she chooses to refuse to answer a question posed to him or her by the investigator.

Advice on the right to silence requires clear notification that the person concerned has the right to refrain from giving any testimony and that any testimony given may be used against him or her in a court of law. If the police fail to do so, any evidence given by that person shall be deemed unacceptable as evidence in his or her trial. This right of advice first arose in England and Wales in 1912. It was part of the judicial rules that police officers had to remind suspects of their right to silence when questioning them regarding a crime. The rule became widely known when the US Supreme Court adopted it in the precedent of *Miranda v Arizona*.[10]

---

9   See article 79 SCPA governing detention for inquiry and article 80 SCPA on detention for trial.

10   *Miranda v Arizona*. 384 U.S. 436 (1966).

In 1963, Arnesto Miranda was arrested for abduction and rape and confessed to both counts. However, police had failed to notify him of his right to remain silent and to consult a lawyer, if he wished to do so. His confession formed the sole basis of his conviction in the absence of any other evidence. When the case was appealed to the Supreme Court, it decided that the investigation had created a state of fear in Miranda who had not been made aware of his constitutional right to consult a lawyer. He neither knew of the possibility of having a lawyer present during questioning, and of being entitled to request the assistance of a lawyer, if necessary through the provision of legal aid. The judge ruled that the confession was not valid since Miranda's knowledge of the English language, in which the advice was written, was poor. If the law demands that reasons for an arrest be given, it has to be understood by the person to whom it is addressed.[11] The significance of the Miranda precedent cannot be overstated. It provides arrested persons and detainees with a right to be informed about their constitutional rights. It also secures the right against self-incrimination and due process of law by establishing that any testimony made in violation of the Miranda rule would be invalid. Congress subsequently sought to challenge this rule by passing section 3501 of the Omnibus Crime Control and the Safe Streets Act of 1968, which stipulated that the voluntariness of a confession was the sole factor to be taken into consideration when determining its admissibility as evidence. Subsequently, the Supreme Court reaffirmed its earlier ruling in *Dickerson v US* where it held that section 3501 disregarded the Miranda precedent:

> We hold that Miranda, being a constitutional decision of this Court, may not be in effect overruled by an Act of Congress, and we decline to overrule Miranda ourselves. We therefore hold that Miranda and its progeny in this Court govern the admissibility of statements made during custodial interrogation in both state and federal courts.[12]

The right to consult a lawyer of one's choice

The right to consult a lawyer of one's choice is a key constitutional right, which is part of the right to a fair trial. Article 34(6) of the Bill of Rights states that '[a] ny accused person has the right to defend himself/herself in person or through a lawyer of his/her own choice and to have legal aid assigned to him/her by the state where he/she is unable to defend himself/herself in serious offences'. The right is also granted in article 14(3)(d) ICCPR and article 7(1)(c) AfrCHPR that apply on the basis of article 27(3) of the Bill of Rights. Article 83(3) SCPA stipulates a general right of an arrested person to 'contact his advocate', without, however, specifying this right further. Article 135 SCPA governs the right to be defended by a lawyer in Sudanese statutory law:

---

11   *Miranda v Arizona.* Per Chief Justice Warren.
12   *Dickerson v United States*, No. 99-5525, 530 U.S. 428 (2000).

(1) The accused shall have the right to be defended by an advocate, or pleader. (2) The court may permit any person to plead before it, where it deems him qualified therefor. (3) Where the accused is accused of an offence punishable with imprisonment, for the term of ten years, or more, amputation or death, is insolvent, the Ministry of Justice, upon the request of the accused, shall appoint a person to defend him, and the State shall bear all, or part of the expenses.

This provision suffers from a number of shortcomings. The inclusion of article 135 in Chapter V is systematically out of place. Chapter V relates to prosecution procedures. However, the right of a suspect to consult a lawyer should apply from the commencement of an investigation, irrespective of whether the person subjected to an investigation is arrested or not. The place of article 135 and omission of an explicit right of access to a lawyer at an earlier stage is not accidental; it reflects the legislator's intention to restrict this right to the prosecution stage.

The SCPA goes further as it does not even mention the once well-established right of a person, who is in custody, to meet his or her lawyer but for the rather vague article 83(3) SCPA mentioned above, which does not specify timeline, purpose, frequency or confidentiality of such meetings. The legal protection is manifestly inadequate, falling short of international requirements and constituting a step backward within the Sudanese legal system itself.[13] In the 1960s, the right of access to a lawyer was granted by a decision of the Court of Appeal, the highest court in the judicial system, as it then was. The Court held that the right of the accused to meet his lawyer should always be granted irrespective of the seriousness of the offence the accused is suspected of having committed, and irrespective of whether the police investigation has been completed or not. It further held that the interview should be conducted within the sight, but not the hearing of police.[14]

Lawyers also face obstacles in seeking to ensure their client's rights during the investigation. The previous criminal procedure laws provided for the confidentiality of the case diary, which meant that the defence lawyer was prohibited from reviewing the investigation record. This practice continues today even though the relevant provision is no longer contained in the SCPA. When asking a prosecutor for the legal basis of this practice, he claimed that there is a circular from the Minister of Justice denying both the defence and prosecution lawyers the right to review the case diary.[15] If this is correct, it may constitute some sort of equality in injustice. A further area of concern is the practice in Sudan to exclude lawyers

---

13   See in this context also Working Group on Arbitrary Detentions. 2010. *Opinion No. 38/2008 (The Sudan). Communication addressed to the Government of Sudan on 22 August 2008.* UN Doc. A/HRC/13/30/Add.1, 166–181, at para. 31: 'The legal protections for detainees are very weak in the Sudanese legal system'.

14   *Sudan Government v Dikran Haygouni*, Sudan Court of Appeal, AC CR REV 317/1967, SLJR (1967), 208.

15   Author's correspondence with official belonging to Prosecution Department. April 2000. Khartoum.

from all investigation and interrogation procedures, which can be attributed to the lack of clear guarantees laid down in procedural law. It is clear that restricting the role of a lawyer to trials deprives justice of its content. In many cases lawyers who ask to represent a client at the trial stage find their hands tied as a result of the investigation procedures that prejudice subsequent proceedings. This has been recognized elsewhere. For example, in *Murray v UK*, the ECtHR stated that an accused must have the benefit of legal assistance at the initial stages of police interrogation where the rights of the accused may be irretrievably prejudiced.[16]

In brief, the right to consult a lawyer should be available at all stages of criminal proceedings. This includes being questioned as a witness because the status of an individual may change during the investigations. The right of access to a lawyer in strict confidence must be granted prior to questioning in order to be effective. The presence of a lawyer at this early stage is important to ensure that a person can exercise his or her right to a defence effectively, including his or her right to remain silent, and thus secure a fair trial; it is also an important safeguard to ensure that a person is not mistreated, or evidence is not obtained illegally. In addition, the lawyer can seek to maintain the rights of the suspect at this stage, and guarantee that the suspect is not detained for a period longer than requested by law.

The SCPA needs to be amended so as to give a suspect the right effectively to have access to a lawyer of his or her choice at the very outset of procedures and prior to trial. To this end, the sentence 'at all the stages of criminal procedures' should be added to article 135, which in turn should be moved to the chapter on investigations. In order to make this right effective, the law must require police, upon arresting any person, to inform the arrested person of his or her rights in a simple non-technical language, including the right to see a lawyer of his or her choice. The right to seek the assistance of a lawyer has to be made available from the moment a person is being questioned, particularly where a suspect is arrested or indicted. The lawyer must be allowed to attend the procedures that require the presence of his or her client, especially interrogations. The lawyer must also be allowed to review the investigation daily registry once the indictment has been filed by the prosecution (as considerations of confidentiality should no longer apply at that stage) and well in advance of the trial so as to have sufficient time to prepare his or her defence.

Other custodial safeguards
International human rights law forming part of the Bill of Rights recognizes a number of safeguards to protect persons who are taken into custody from a violation of their rights, in particular ill-treatment and torture. These measures encompass the right of access to a lawyer of one's choice, access to a physician, the right to inform and contact members of his or her family[17] and, in the case of

---

16   *John Murray v The United Kingdom*, 22 EHRR 29 (1996), para. 66.

17   Principle 16(2) of the *Body of Principles for the Protection of All Persons under Any Form of Detention or Imprisonment*, UN General Assembly resolution 43/173 (1988),

foreign nationals, access to consular representatives.[18] Article 83 SCPA guarantees several custodial safeguards. Article 83(1) SCPA provides that the arrested person shall be treated with dignity and receive medical attention. Arrested and detained persons have the right to inform their family, or the professional body to which they belong, about the arrest and contact them thereafter pursuant to article 83(5) SCPA. However, this right is subject to the approval of the Prosecution Attorney's Bureau, which means that respect for it in practice depends heavily on the exercise of the Prosecution Attorney's discretion. Furthermore, the provision states the principle but leaves the details to prison regulations and other such instruments, which has in practice weakened the practical value of the guarantee. Article 83(3) SCPA grants the right to contact one's lawyer but, as demonstrated above, the general right is not supported by sufficiently clear provisions that would ensure its effectiveness in practice.

Right to be brought before a judge promptly and to have a speedy trial
The police may detain a person for 24 hours for the purpose of investigation under the SCPA.[19] The prosecuting attorney may renew the detention for a period not exceeding three days, after which the judge may order detention for a period of one week, which can be extended once. The judge must therefore examine the grounds, that is, the legality of detention, after 96 hours the very latest.[20] If the person concerned has been charged, the judge may order to extend detention every two weeks for a total of six months, after which any further extensions need to be approved by the competent Chief Justice.[21] The SCPA does neither stipulate a time limit for pre-trial detention nor a timeframe for trials. In practice, it is for the Chief Justice to decide on the time limit in any given case, which carries the risk of arbitrary decision-making without the possibility of judicial review.

The law also has other apparent shortcomings. The time limit of 96 hours for bringing a detainee before a judicial authority would not appear to constitute 'promptly' within the meaning of article 9(3) of the ICCPR applicable by virtue of article 27(3) of the Bill of Rights. In addition, the law does not specify the reasons that justify continued detention other than for the purpose of inquiry. This ground is rather broad and should be interpreted narrowly so that the suspect is set free

---

and rule 38 of the *Standard Minimum Rules for the Treatment of Prisoners*, Economic and Social Council Resolutions 663 C (XXIV) (1957) and 2076 (LXII) (1977).

18   The International Court of Justice recognized that article 36(1) of the Vienna Convention on Consular Relations creates individual rights for the national concerned, in *LaGrand* Case (Germany v United States of America), ICJ Reports 2001, 466, 494, at para. 77 and in *Case Concerning Avena and other Mexican Nationals* (Mexico v United States of America), ICJ Reports 2004, 12.

19   The OHCHR noted that '[t]he realities on the ground look very different. Police regularly fail to submit cases for review within the legal deadlines … Even suspects of petty crimes may sometimes languish for weeks in jail'. UNHCHR. 2008, 26–7.

20   Article 79 SCPA.

21   Article 79(4) SCPA.

once the main evidence has been secured and/or there are other ways of keeping him or her under surveillance.

The length of time for which a suspect can be detained for investigation purposes contravenes article 9(3) ICCPR and article 7(1)(d) AfrCHPR. The presumption is that a suspect should be released unless there are overriding reasons to detain him or her. This includes a degree of proportionality between the length of the time in detention and the expected punishment. This principle was affirmed by the Inter-American Court of Human Rights in the case of *Suarez Rosero v Ecuador*,[22] where the applicant had been in detention for three years and nine months for a crime carrying a maximum punishment of two years' imprisonment. This treatment breached both the applicant's right to a fair trial because it amounted to the equivalent of a guilty verdict without trial and his right to be tried within a reasonable period. In another case, the UN Human Rights Committee considered a delay of over three-and-a-half years between indictment and trial for murder to be an undue delay contrary to article 14(3)(c) ICCPR.[23] The Committee stated that in cases involving serious charges, such as murder, and where the accused is denied bail by the court, the accused must be tried in as expeditious a manner as possible.[24]

The SCPA should be amended with a view to safeguarding constitutional rights. To this end, the power of the Prosecution Attorney to order the detention of a suspect for investigation purposes should be limited to a maximum period of 48 hours if necessary to prevent influencing the course of justice. A further extension of a week should be subject to review by a judge, taking the form of a hearing where the suspect can challenge the legality of continued detention. In this case, the prosecution shall submit evidence to demonstrate the necessity of continued detention, which the suspect shall be allowed to refute. The law shall oblige a judge, in the case of renewal of detention for investigation purposes, to set a realistic time limit for the completion of the required investigation measures, taking into consideration the seriousness of the crime, after which the suspect should be released in accordance with any conditions imposed by the judge. In no circumstances may a suspect be kept in detention for investigation purposes for more than six months. Such a provision would strike an appropriate balance between the interest of society to prevent crime and the constitutional right of an individual to liberty and security.

Release on bail
According to Sudanese Law, bail denotes the pledge to pay a certain amount of money to the court by a surety in case he or she fails to ensure his or her appearance

---

22   *Case of Suárez Rosero v Ecuador*. Merits. Inter-American Court of Human Rights, Judgment, 12 November 1997. Series C. No. 35.

23   *Gomez v Panama*, Human Rights Committee (HRC), Communication No. 473/1991, UN Doc. CCPR/C/54/D/473/1991 (1995).

24   *Gomez v Panama*, para. 8.5.

at trial. A detainee should be released on bail unless his or her continued detention is necessary based on specific, circumscribed grounds, such as the preservation of evidence, the risk of failing to appear for trial and/or the danger of committing further crimes. The decision to grant bail reflects a balance between the right of the individual to liberty before conviction on the one hand and the administration of justice as well as the right of other persons to protection from crime on the other. Procedurally, equality of arms requires that there should be an adversarial hearing in deciding whether to grant bail in a given case.

Article 105 SCPA provides the general rule that '[r]elease on bail of the arrested person shall be as follows: (a) by the arrested person personally executing a bond to appear, with, or without an assessed financial security; (b) by another person executing a bail, to bring the arrested person, with, or without an assessed financial security; (c) by deposit, with bond, or bail'. However, in Sudanese law, there is no procedure concerning bail, such as requiring the prosecution to disclose information and documents that may help the lawyer to bail out his or her client. The bias against the evidence provided by the defence routinely results in a refusal to grant bail.

As a general rule dating back to Magna Carta and the English Bill of Rights of 1689 'excessive bail ought not be required'. This principle is by now deeply rooted and internationally recognized. In Sudan, article 107 of the SCPA divides the crimes which require deposit of money into two parts. Article 107(1) stipulates that '[n]o arrested person, in an offence relating to any public property, or dishonoured cheque, shall be released, save upon deposit of an amount of money, not less than the amount subject of the criminal suit, or by presenting a bank draft cheque, or letter of credit'. Article 107(2) applies to offences requiring *dia* (blood money) or compensation, in particular murder and assault, and provides that:

> an arrested person ... shall not be released, where there has arisen against him a reasonable prima facie evidence, save upon the deposit of an amount of money equal to such, as may be adjudged against him by the court, or producing an insurance policy, a bank draft cheque, letter of credit or an estate mortgage, or attachment.

The requirement of prima facie evidence appears superfluous as reasonable suspicion is a general requirement for any continuous detention.

Article 107 SCPA, which dates back to the introduction of *Shari'a* in 1983 during the Nimeiri regime (1969–1985), is problematic because its apparent primary purpose is to propel the detained person to reach a settlement or guarantee the payment of money for the benefit of the creditor(s) rather than to guarantee his or her appearance at trial. This practice frequently makes the amount required for release on bail excessive, not least because it treats the suspect as if he or she has already been convicted. On the whole, the practical application of the provision renders continuous detention unreasonable. It also unduly discriminates against persons who do not have the means to provide the deposit. This point was at issue in the case of *Bandy v United States*,[25] where $5,000 was required to bail the accused. The suspect pleaded poverty to the Supreme Court and said he could not obtain the money. Justice Douglas held that it 'would be unconstitutional to fix excessive bail to assure that a defendant will not gain his freedom ... Yet in the case of an indigent defendant, the fixing of bail in even a modest amount may have the practical effect of denying him release'.[26] In a later ruling on the same case, Justice Douglas found that release should not be denied on the mere grounds of indigence but that the accused was 'entitled to be released on "personal recognizance" where other relevant factors make it reasonable to believe that he will comply with the orders of the court'.[27]

Article 106(2) SCPA provides that '[t]he prosecuting attorney, or the Magistrate, may release the arrested person, upon bail, in retribution offences, where release does not constitute a danger thereto, or contravention of public security and tranquility, and the victim, or his guardians consent, with, or without conditions'. This provision is problematic. Public security and tranquility are broad grounds on which to deny bail that appear to go beyond the grounds recognized in most legal systems internationally. Article 106(2) also effectively provides the victim or his or her guardian the right to veto release on bail. This is contrary to sound criminal policy according to which the decision should be solely made by the competent public authority. It places powers that should be exercised by the state in the hands of private individuals. The provision also raises the risk that extraneous factors, such as revenge, enter the decision-making and may thus arbitrarily deprive the suspected person of his or her liberty.

Article 108 SCPA provides a right to release in case of other offences. However, the provision permits the Prosecution Attorney or a judge to refuse bail where 'the release of the arrested person may lead to his escape, or prejudice the inquiry'. The provision gives broad discretion to the Prosecution Attorney or a judge and does not provide for a hearing that would allow an arrested person to challenge the grounds for the decision. These powers, coupled with a lack of safeguards, may result in continuous detention of suspects for minor crimes and/or crimes that relate to the exercise of public freedoms. It would therefore be more appropriate to adopt alternative procedures, for example, strict surety, and to confine pre-trial detention to exceptional cases where no other means are available.

Sudanese law does not provide for any procedure to review the decision whether to grant bail. Decisions on bail applications are made summarily on the basis of applications and recommendations submitted by the prosecution. The requirement that the detainee or his or her legal representative is present when the decision on the renewal of detention is taken is only stipulated in judicial circulars,

---

25   *Bandy v United States*, 81 S.Ct. 197 (1960) and 82 S.Ct. 11 (1961).

26   *Bandy v United States* (1960), quoted in Lay, L.N. 1966. Comment: pre-trial release of indigents in the United States. *University of Tasmania Law Review*, 3, 300–312, at 307.

27   *Bandy v United States* (1961), 307–8.

not the criminal procedural law itself. In practice, this requirement is frequently not followed, contrary to developments in countries such as the United Kingdom whose laws effectively prohibit renewal of detention in absentia. There are also no clearly established rules on the level of proof and the criteria that should be considered in determining whether there are any grounds that justify rejecting release on bail.

Compensation
The Sudanese Bill of Rights provides for a right to compensation for unlawful arrest or detention pursuant to article 27(3) in conjunction with article 9(5) ICCPR. Statutory Sudanese law in theory recognizes the right to be compensated on account of unlawful arrest but one must hasten to add that this is a very limited recognition only. Though article 138 of the Civil Transaction Act of 1984 establishes the right of an aggrieved person to be compensated by anyone who has committed an act causing him or her injury or damage without having to prove any intention or lack of care on the part of the wrongdoer, article 144 of the same act requires bad faith of the latter if he or she happens to be a public servant. Moreover, due to the wide and undefined powers given to officials to arrest and detain, a number of cases that might be seen as unlawful in other legal systems would not be considered as such under the present Sudanese statutory law. Until the law is brought in line with the constitution, and while it remains the source of wide powers that allows arbitrary arrest and/or detention, Sudanese law does not provide an adequate framework for a right to be compensated in line with article 9(5) ICCPR. In addition, the wide range of immunities that officials enjoy under statutory law makes it practically impossible to pursue such claims, in particular against individual officers.[28]

Sudan's national security law

The 1990 and 1995 National Security Act(s) established the framework for a regime of exceptionalism applying to the National Intelligence and Security Services (NISS). This was marked by extremely broad powers of 'preventive detention' without judicial authorization or review and immunity for NISS members for any acts or omission committed in the course of their work.[29] The 1999 National Security Forces Act (NSFA), instead of remedying the deficiencies of the 1995 Act identified by regional and international human rights treaty bodies and various observers, perpetuated the system of exceptional powers as well as lack of oversight and accountability that has come to define the NISS.

This was highlighted in a recent UN report: '[t]he human rights concerns related to the NISS are longstanding and institutionalized problems that could be

---

28 See chapter 7 on immunity legislation.
29 Articles 37 and 38 National Security Forces Act 1995.

addressed through institutional reform'.[30] The Comprehensive Peace Agreement (CPA) of 2005 explicitly mandates the reform of legislation governing the NISS.[31] In furthering the implementation of the 2005 Agreement, articles 150 and 151 of the INC provide for the establishment of a National Security Service that 'shall be charged with the external and internal security of the country; its mission, mandate, functions, terms and conditions of service shall be prescribed by the National Security Act'. The National Security Service established pursuant to article 151(3) of the INC shall 'focus on information gathering, analysis and advice to the appropriate authorities'. On the basis of articles 150 and 151 of the INC, civil society and political parties argued that the NISS should be transformed into an intelligence-gathering agency whose powers are tailored to that mandate and would exclude the power to arrest and detain individuals.[32]

A bill on a new Security Act was introduced in 2009 and adopted by Parliament in December of that year despite vocal opposition. The Government of Sudan described the new National Security Act (NSA), which came into force in 2010, as an 'important achievement ... in the ongoing process of the legislative reform in the Sudan', stressing that a 'number of safeguards to secure the rights of detainees have been introduced'.[33] However, closer scrutiny of the NSA shows that it still falls short of the right to liberty and security, fair trial standards and adequate safeguards against torture that Sudan is required to guarantee under the Bill of Rights and a series of constitutional rights.

Article 50 of the NSA retains the power to detain any suspected person for a period of up to thirty days. This period may be renewed by the Director of the (renamed) National Security Service (NSS) for another 15 days, amounting to a total of 45 days detention without charge. The Act provides a series of broad grounds that allow the Security Council, upon referral by the Director, to extend the detention period for another three months, to a possible total of four-and-a-half months. The regime of arrest and detention in article 50 of the NSA is arbitrary: it does not specify the elements of reasonable suspicion of having committed an offence and effectively allows detention of up to 45 days if not four-and-a-half months without charge.

Article 51 of the NSA grants some safeguards recognized in international human rights law, such as the duty to inform an arrested or detained person of the reasons of his or her arrest or detention. It also provides for a right of an arrested or detained person to inform his or her family members. However, the

---

30   UNHCHR. 2008, 3.

31   Comprehensive Peace Agreement. 2002. Machakos Protocol, Chapter II, 2.7.

32   REDRESS and SORD. 2009. *Security for All: Reforming Sudan's National Security Services*. [Online, September] Available at: http://www.pclrs.org/downloads/Resources/Resources/Security%20for%20all%20Final.pdf [accessed 12 October 2010].

33   *Statement by H.E. Dr. Abdulmoneim O.M. Taha, Rapporteur of the Advisory Council for Human Rights of the Republic of Sudan and Head of Delegation*, African Commission on Human and Peoples' Rights (ACHPR), 47th Ordinary Session (2010).

right to communicate with family members or a lawyer is conditional upon not prejudicing the investigation. This provision is contrary to international standards that provide for a right of access to a lawyer of one's choice at the earliest stages of an investigation.[34] Access to such a lawyer may be restricted only in closely circumscribed circumstances. The jurisprudence of international bodies does not suggest that this includes considerations of the efficacy of investigations that seemingly fall within the sole discretion of the investigating authority.[35]

The NSA provides for a regime of executive control over any arrested and detained person, which designates a prosecutor to ensure that detainees are treated in accordance with regulations. This is inadequate under applicable standards, namely article 9(3) and 9(4) ICCPR, which require that a detained person is to be brought promptly before a judicial authority and has the right to *habeas corpus*. Article 51(10) of the NSA makes it clear that a detained person has no right to challenge the legality of detention before a judicial body for a period of 45 days or four-and-a-half months respectively as any such challenge can only be brought thereafter. This provision grants the security services an extraordinarily long period in which to decide whether they deem the continuous detention justified under the Act, which is in clear contravention of applicable standards under the ICCPR and the AfrCHPR.[36]

Contrary to a series of recommendations made by UN bodies[37] and the African Union High Level Panel on Darfur,[38] the NSA retained immunities for NSS members in relation to any civil or criminal proceedings against them. The NSS director may lift immunities but is only duty bound to do so under the law 'whenever it appears that the subject of such accountability is not related to NSS official business'. Any proceedings against NSS members that are authorized by the NSS director are not public, reinforcing the lack of transparency surrounding the work of the security services.

The legal framework applying to the NSS under the NSA maintains a system that fosters arbitrariness and impunity. The reform of the National Security law could have marked a symbolic break and offered a measure of emancipation that also constitutes a guarantee of non-repetition of human rights violations; instead,

---

34   HRC. 2007. *General Comment 32. Article 14: Right to equality before courts and tribunals and to a fair trial.* UN Doc. CCPR/C/GC/32, para. 34.

35   See Trechsel, S. 2005. *Human Rights in Criminal Proceedings.* Oxford: Oxford University Press, 282–85.

36   See article 9 ICCPR and *Principles and Guidelines on the Right to a Fair Trial and Legal Assistance in Africa*, ACHPR (2001).

37   HRC. 2007. *Concluding observations: Sudan.* UN Doc. CCPR/C/SDN/CO/3/CRP.1, para. 9(e).

38   African Union High-Level Panel on Darfur (AUPD). 2009. *Darfur: The Quest for Peace, Justice and Reconciliation.* PSC/AHG/2 (CCVII), xix, at para. 25(c) and (d); 56–63, at paras 215–38; and 91–2, at para. 336.

it has perpetuated what continues to be one of the most glaring stains of legalized deprivation of rights in Sudanese laws.

The right to a fair trial

The Bill of Rights sets out the right to equality before the law, the right to a fair trial and the right to litigation in articles 31, 34 and 35 respectively. Article 34 stipulates several principles and guarantees rights contained in articles 14 and 15 ICCPR. However, it lacks specificity in respect of a number of rights[39] and does neither include various aspects of the right to defence[40] nor guarantee the right of appeal.[41] These rights must arguably be read into the Bill of Rights pursuant to its article 27(3).

The SCPA and other statutory law have a number of shortcomings in relation to the right to a fair trial. Article 128 INC guarantees the independence of the judiciary. However, the Judiciary Service Commission responsible for the management of the national judiciary is run along party lines as set out in the CPA. Moreover, Sudan has yet to address the fact that a large number of judges were dismissed following the 1989 coup d'etat, to be replaced with judges who were recruited on the basis of their allegiance to the government rather than on merit.[42]

The question as to whether trials should be heard in public is entirely in the discretion of the court without any qualification, which makes the rule open to abuse.[43] The courts are also given broad powers to allow trial in absentia contrary to international standards, in particular in relation to offences against the state where publicity would seemingly be most needed to ensure public scrutiny.[44]

Limitations on the right to access to a lawyer and lengthy detention without trial have already been mentioned (see *The right to consult a lawyer of one's choice* above). The lack of adequate custodial safeguards is particularly problematic as there is no unequivocal prohibition to use confessions or statements that may have been obtained as a result of torture.[45] In addition, the provision of legal aid is confined to serious offences, which further undermines access to a lawyer and

---

39   For example on the circumstances in which the public may be excluded from trials.

40   Article 14(3)(e) ICCPR: 'To examine, or have examined, the witnesses against him and to obtain the attendance and examination of witnesses on his behalf under the same conditions as witnesses against him; (f) To have the free assistance of an interpreter if he cannot understand or speak the language used in court; (g) Not to be compelled to testify against himself or to confess guilt'.

41   Article 14(5) ICCPR.

42   Medani, A.M. 2005. *Human Rights in the Interim Constitution*. Khartoum: Khartoum University Students Union in Cooperation with Sudan Social Development Organization, 37.

43   Article 133 SCPA.

44   See article 34(5) of the Bill of Rights and article 134 SCPA on trial in absentia.

45   See article 10 of the Evidence Act of 1993.

the right to an adequate defence.[46] These concerns are heightened in special procedures, such as under anti-terrorism laws, which further restrict the right to defence and the right to an appeal.[47] Finally, from the perspective of the rule of law and the aggrieved party's right to litigation, the provision that the Ministry of Justice may stay criminal suits is problematic as it allows for overly broad interference of an executive body in judicial proceedings.[48]

Conclusion

The constitutional rights recognized in the Bill of Rights are yet to be fully translated into statutory law, which retains a number of shortcomings, some of which are plainly incompatible with the rights granted in the Bill of Rights. This applies in particular to the NSA. The 2010 Act has failed to remedy previous deficiencies so as to be in line with the CPA and the INC. In light of the record of the security services, it would have been advisable to remove all arrest and detention powers, as well as immunities, from the law. Failing this, the Act should have at least ensured prompt judicial review and access to a lawyer as well as other safeguards recognized in international human rights law binding on Sudan.

The SCPA has several shortcomings, which should be addressed by way of a comprehensive reform with a view to ensuring its compatibility with the Bill of Rights. This includes specifying what constitutes a reasonable suspicion as a prerequisite for arrests and detention in order to avoid arbitrariness. It also encompasses major safeguards against arbitrary arrests and detention, in particular the right of access to a lawyer of one's choice from the outset and the right to be brought promptly before a judicial authority. Judicial review of arrest and detention, which is crucial to avoid arbitrary law enforcement and reduces the risk of ill-treatment, should be provided within 48 hours in line with international standards, rather than after 96 hours as currently stipulated in Sudanese law. The law should provide a presumption of release awaiting trial. The regime of granting bail should be thoroughly revised so as to ensure that bail is not excessive and that the reasons for refusal of bail are confined to the narrow grounds found in other legal systems and in international standards. In addition, anyone whose rights to liberty and security have been violated should have an explicit right to compensation that is not subject to immunity provisions.

The right to a fair trial is not fully guaranteed in the SCPA and other procedural laws. As a starting point, all aspects pertaining to the appointment and tenure of judges should be subjected to a full review in line with international best practices,

---

46   Ibrahim, N. 2008. The Right to fair trial in the light of the Interim National Constitution of Sudan: theory and practice. *Recht in Afrika*, 83–100, at 90.

47   UNHCHR. 2008, 40. See on this point also chapter 3.

48   See article 58(1) SCPA and Ibrahim. 2008, 87–8.

as identified by the Special Rapporteur on the Independence of the Judiciary.[49] This should include the reinstatement of judges who have been unfairly dismissed so as to ensure that judges serve on the basis of merit and personal integrity. Restrictions on the right to a public trial should be explicitly confined to the ones recognized in the ICCPR and the AfrCHPR; the same applies to trial in absentia, which should not be allowed in cases of offences against the state. The right to an adequate defence should be ensured in line with the detailed provisions of article 14(2) ICCPR, especially with respect to access to a lawyer of one's choice from the outset, which applies in particular to the procedures governing anti-terrorism trials. Finally, the prerogative of the Ministry of Justice to stay criminal prosecutions should be reviewed with a view to ensuring that there is no undue executive interference in judicial proceedings.

---

49   See Special Rapporteur on the independence of judges and lawyers, Leandro Despouy. 2009. *Report*. UN Doc. A/HRC/11/41, paras 14–84.

Chapter 6

Some Reflections on Law Reform Pertaining to Arrested, Detained and Accused Persons in South Africa[1]

P.J. Schwikkard

Introduction

Prior to 27 April 1995, South Africa was a profoundly undemocratic country ruled by a white elite that excluded the majority African population from political participation. People of Indian or mixed-race descent had only limited political rights during certain periods. The ruling ideology of race superiority was enforced by draconian security and emergency legislation, which was used to silence political dissent. At the same time reference to the common law provided a veneer of respectability to a legal system that, *de facto*, gave police the power to detain citizens indefinitely without trial, access to lawyers or protection from torture. It has also been clearly established that the apartheid regime used extra-judicial means of killing political opponents, using death squads to 'permanently remove' people from society.[2]

Although the liberation struggle was a long one, the law itself changed abruptly on 2 February 1990 when the then president announced the unbanning of the African National Congress (ANC) and other prohibited organizations. The state of emergency was lifted in 1990, and the most draconian aspects of the security legislation repealed by 1991; a period of political negotiation then followed. Extra-judicial means continued to be used and there were periods of intense instability – although the apartheid state did not invoke either emergency or security laws – in which the rights of arrested, detained and accused persons were governed by the common law.[3]

Law reform was the product of seismic political change. The opponents of apartheid, among them human rights activists, academics and a few judges,

---

1 Portions of this paper are based on prior publications.
2 See Gobodo-Madikizela, P. 2003. *A Human Being Died that Night*. New York: Mariner Books, and Pauw, J. 1991. *In the Heart of the Whore*. Halfway House: Southern Book Publishers.
3 Van Wyk, D. et al. 1994. *Rights and Constitutionalism: The New South African Legal Order*. Cape Town: Juta.

had been consistently scathing of the state security apparatus and this certainly provided a language and discourse that could be used by various political groupings. However, without fundamental political change it is unlikely that the law would have also changed. It was only once the apartheid state realized that it did not have the means to retain power that it accepted that a negotiated path to democracy would serve the white elite better, and began to shed the most blatant legal phrasing of state power – namely its draconian emergency and security powers.

However, the process of law reform ended in neither 1990 nor 1995; it simply provided a new and exciting platform. The negotiated settlement that saw South Africa's transition to a parliamentary democracy had as a crucial component the adoption of the concept of constitutional supremacy and the formulation of a Bill of Rights. This process, which involved a broad sector of society and accommodated those political protagonists who were prepared to engage in the process (this included all significant political movements), was the product of a social revolution, not law reform. However, the Bill of Rights is a product of that political process, a process in which lawyers and legal academics together with other components of civil society exercised a strong influence, and that provided the springboard for the next phase of law reform. Against this background this chapter considers the major reforms that have taken place in the criminal justice sector since 1995, with a particular focus on the role played by the South African Constitutional Court.

The South African post-apartheid Constitution

International human rights conventions provided a strong source of inspiration for the drafters of the constitution and their provisions resonate throughout the Bill of Rights.[4] The impact of this influence is assured by section 39(1) of the constitution, which makes it imperative for South African courts to consider international law when interpreting the Bill of Rights.

Section 39(2) of the constitution directs that, '[w]hen interpreting any legislation, and when developing the common law or customary law, every court, tribunal or forum must promote the spirit, purport and objects of the Bill of Rights'. This has required all courts to interpret both the Criminal Procedure Act[5] and the common law in line with very specific constitutional rights pertaining to arrested, detained and accused persons. These are set out in section 35 of the constitution. Section 35(1) spells out in great detail the rights of anyone arrested, including the right to remain silent, the right not to be compelled to make any confession,

---

4   In respect of the rights of arrested, accused and detained persons, influential sources included in particular the International Covenant on Civil and Political Rights, which was signed by South Africa in 1994 and ratified in 1998.

5   Criminal Procedure Act 51 of 1977.

the right to be brought promptly before a court, and the right to be released if the interests of justice permit.[6] Section 35(2) sets out a number of rights that also serve as important custodial safeguards, including the right to be informed promptly of the reasons of detention, the right to access to a lawyer of one's choice, the right to *habeas corpus*, the right to conditions of detention that are consistent with human dignity and the right to communicate with a partner, next of kin or others as specified.[7] Section 35(3) provides for a number of fair trial rights, in particular the right of defence, as well as several fundamental principles, such as *nulla poena sine lege* (no punishment without a law) and *ne bis in idem* or double jeopardy (no one shall be punished twice for the same offence).[8]

---

6 '(1) Everyone who is arrested for allegedly committing an offence has the right (a) to remain silent; (b) to be informed promptly (i) of the right to remain silent; and (ii) of the consequences of remaining silent; (c) not to be compelled to make any confession or admission that could be used in evidence against that person; (d) to be brought before a court as soon as reasonably possible, but no later than (i) 48 hours after the arrest; or (ii) the end of the first day after the expiry of the 48 hours, if the 48 hours expire outside ordinary court hours or on a day which is not an ordinary court day; (e) at the first court appearance after being arrested, to be charged or to be informed of the reason for the detention to continue, or to be released; and (f) to be released from detention if the interests of justice permit, subject to reasonable conditions.'

7 '(2) Everyone who is detained, including every sentenced prisoner, has the right (a) to be informed promptly of the reason for being detained; (b) to choose, and to consult with, a legal practitioner, and to be informed of this right promptly; (c) to have a legal practitioner assigned to the detained person by the state and at state expense, if substantial injustice would otherwise result, and to be informed of this right promptly; (d) to challenge the lawfulness of the detention in person before a court and, if the detention is unlawful, to be released; (e) to conditions of detention that are consistent with human dignity, including at least exercise and the provision, at state expense, of adequate accommodation, nutrition, reading material and medical treatment; and (f) to communicate with, and be visited by, that person's (i) spouse or partner; (ii) next of kin; (iii) chosen religious counsellor; and (iv) chosen medical practitioner.'

8 '(3) Every accused person has a right to a fair trial, which includes the right (a) to be informed of the charge with sufficient detail to answer it; (b) to have adequate time and facilities to prepare a defence; (c) to a public trial before an ordinary court; (d) to have their trial begin and conclude without unreasonable delay; (e) to be present when being tried; (f) to choose, and be represented by, a legal practitioner, and to be informed of this right promptly; (g) to have a legal practitioner assigned to the accused person by the state and at state expense, if substantial injustice would otherwise result, and to be informed of this right promptly; (h) to be presumed innocent, to remain silent, and not to testify during the proceedings; (i) to adduce and challenge evidence; (j) not to be compelled to give self-incriminating evidence; (k) to be tried in a language that the accused person understands or, if that is not practicable, to have the proceedings interpreted in that language; (l) not to be convicted for an act or omission that was not an offence under either national or international law at the time it was committed or omitted; (m) not to be tried for an offence in respect of an act or omission for which that person has previously been either acquitted or convicted; (n) to the benefit of the least severe of the prescribed punishments if the

In addition, section 12(1) of the constitution provides the right to liberty and security of the person, including the right not to be arbitrarily arrested or detained and to be free from torture or other cruel, inhuman or degrading treatment or punishment.[9] This right has special application to any child under the age of eighteen years as set out section 28(1)(g) of the constitution,[10] which is reinforced by section 28(2) according to which '[a] child's best interests are of paramount importance in every matter concerning the child'. It is important to note that rights in the South African Bill of Rights may be limited provided the requirements of section 36(1) of the constitution are met.[11]

The impact of the adoption of the principle of constitutional supremacy

The influence of the Bill of Rights on the criminal justice system has been significant. It provides grounds for reviewing both the substantive and procedural content of the intricate web of laws shaping criminal justice, as well as providing remedies for constitutional breach. In doing so it has impacted on the content of the law and influenced the conduct of those who participate in the criminal justice system.

Section 35 applies specifically to arrested, detained and accused persons. However, there are a number of other constitutionally entrenched rights that continue to reshape the content and form of the criminal justice system. These

---

prescribed punishment for the offence has been changed between the time that the offence was committed and the time of sentencing; and (o) of appeal to, or review by, a higher court. (4) Whenever this section requires information to be given to a person, that information must be given in a language that the person understands. (5) Evidence obtained in a manner that violates any right in the Bill of Rights must be excluded if the admission of that evidence would render the trial unfair or otherwise be detrimental to the administration of justice.'

9   'Everyone has the right to freedom and security of the person, which includes the right (a) not to be deprived of freedom arbitrarily or without just cause; (b) not to be detained without trial; (c) to be free from all forms of violence from either public or private sources; (d) not to be tortured in any way; and (e) not to be treated or punished in a cruel, inhuman or degrading way.'

10   'Every child has the right [n]ot to be detained except as a measure of last resort, in which case, in addition to the rights a child enjoys under sections 12 and 35, the child may be detained only for the shortest appropriate period of time, and has the right to be (i) kept separately from detained persons over the age of 18 years; and (ii) treated in a manner, and kept in conditions, that take account of the child's age.'

11   'The rights in the Bill of Rights may be limited only in terms of law of general application to the extent that the limitation is reasonable and justifiable in an open and democratic society based on human dignity, equality and freedom, taking into account all relevant factors, including (a) the nature of the right; (b) the importance of the purpose of the limitation; (c) the nature and extent of the limitation; (d) the relation between the limitation and its purpose; and (e) less restrictive means to achieve the purpose.'

include the rights to equality,[12] dignity,[13] life,[14] freedom and security of person,[15] privacy,[16] freedom of religion,[17] freedom of expression,[18] property,[19] and access to information.[20]

Extra-judicial law reform

Post 1995, the Bill of Rights provided a platform for a number of law reform initiatives. In respect of arrested, detained and accused persons one of the first projects was a review of the Criminal Procedure Act 51 of 1977 by the South African Law Reform Commission[21] for consistency with the Bill of Rights.[22] Once submitted to the Minister of Justice this report disappeared in the halls of

---

12   See for example *S v Ntuli* 1996 (1) SA 1207 (CC); *S v Rens* 1996 (1) SA 1218 (CC); *S v Jordan* 2002 (2) SACR 499 (CC).

13   See for example, *S v Makwanyane* 1995 (3) SA 391 (CC); *S v Williams* 1995 (3) SA 632 (CC).

14   See for example, *S v Makwanyane*.

15   See for example, *Nel v Le Roux* 1996 (3) SA 526 (CC); *S v Makwanyane* 1995; *S v Williams* 1995; *S v Thebus* 2003 (2) SACR 319 (CC).

16   See for example, *Case v Minister of Safety and Security* 1996 (3) SA 165 (CC); *National Coalition of Gay and Lesbian Equality v Minister of Justice* 1999 (1) SA 6 (CC).

17   See for example, *S v Lawrence* 1997 (4) SA 1176 (CC), *Prince v President of the Law Society of the Cape of Good Hope* 2002 (1) SASCR 431 (CC).

18   See for example, *Case v Minister of Safety and Security*; *South African National Defence Force Union v Minister of Defence* 1999 (4) SA 469 (CC); *Phillips v Director of Public Prosecutions, WLD* 2003 (1) SSACR 425 (CC).

19   See for example, *Director of Public Prosecutions: Cape of Good Hope v Bathgate* 2000 (2) SA 535 (C); *National Director of Public Prosecutions v Alexander* 2001 (2) SACR 1 (T); *Mohamed v National Director of Public Prosecutions* 2002 (2) SASCR 93 (W).

20   See for example, *Els v Minister of Safety and Security* 1998 (2) SACR 93 (NC); *Shabalala v Attorney-General of Transvaal & another* 1996 (2) SACR 761 (CC).

21   The objects of the South African Law Reform Commission as reflected on its website 'are to do research with reference to all branches of the law in order to make recommendations to Government for the development, improvement, modernisation or reform of the law. The Commission investigates matters appearing on a programme approved by the Minister of Justice and Constitutional Development. Reports and other documents published by the Commission are made available on the Commission's website for general information'. Available at: http://salawreform.justice.gov.za/ [accessed 12 June 2010]. The Commission is appointed by the Minister of Justice and is financed through an allocation of a budget by the Department of Justice. Apart from one full-time Commissioner, Commissioners are appointed on a part-time basis and are not paid a salary; this ensures a level of independency. The Commission in carrying out its mandate has procedures in place to ensure adequate consultation with civil society.

22   South African Law Commission. 2001. *Report Project 101: Application of the Bill of Rights to Criminal Procedure, Criminal Law, The Law of Evidence and Sentencing.*

bureaucracy. Why? The political discourse had changed. The framers of the Bill of Rights had little difficulty in getting agreement on the protection of accused, arrested and detained persons, since it was in this area that the abuses of the apartheid regime had been most keenly felt. For example, in *Osman v Attorney-General*, Judge Madala noted that the right not to be compelled to make an admission or confession,

> is of particular significance having regard to our recent history, when, during the apartheid era, the fundamental rights of many citizens were violated. It is in that context that the right of arrested persons was progressively eroded. The right was honoured more in the breach than in its observance, and our courts found themselves having to adjudicate an ever increasing number of cases where coerced confessions became the order of the day. Police interrogations were often accompanied by physical brutality and by holding arrested persons in solitary confinement without access to the outside world – all in an effort to extract confessions from them. Our painful history should make us especially sensitive to unacceptable methods of extracting confessions. It is in the context of this history that the principle the State should always prove its case and not rely on statements extracted from the accused by inhuman methods should be adhered to.[23]

However, the years following 1995 saw the criminal justice system failing to cope with an increasing crime rate, and in these circumstances it was not politically viable to promote the protection of rights of suspected criminals. The fact that there is little correlation between levels of crime and due process, if any, was possibly too complex to convey to a society that felt very vulnerable to the ravages of crime. Instead the thrust of law reform was directed at exploring ways to limit the rights of detained, arrested and accused persons so as to bring any constitutional infringements within the parameters of the limitations clause, and in ways to increase the 'efficiency' of the criminal justice system.[24] Amendments to the bail provisions in the Criminal Procedure Act 51 of 1977 that shifted the evidentiary

---

Pretoria, and 1999. Discussion Paper 90 Project 101: *The application of the Bill of Rights to Criminal Procedure, Criminal Law, The Law of Evidence and Sentencing.* Pretoria.

23   *Osman v Attorney-General, Transvaal* 1998 (2) SACR 493 (CC), para. 10.

24   See for example South African Law Commission. 2002. *Report: Project 73 Simplification of Criminal Procedure (A more inquisitorial approach to criminal procedure – police questioning, defence disclosure, the rule of judicial officers and judicial management of trial).* Pretoria.

burden in respect of certain offences to the accused[25] provide a legislative example of this trend.[26] These amendments were upheld by the Constitutional Court.[27]

More successful law reform efforts driven by civil society and the Law Reform Commission were those pertaining to sexual offences, domestic violence and child offenders.[28] The Law Reform Commission was requested by both the government and civil society to investigate these areas of law for reform, consulting widely with all stakeholders and these factors no doubt played a strong role in the enactment of the relevant reforms.[29] These reforms were also compatible with widespread public sentiment, and were consequently politically palatable; they focused on victims and children.

The role of the courts

It is inevitable that courts in South Africa need to balance the public interests of convicting those who contravene the criminal law while ensuring that justice is done.[30] The Constitutional Court has an excellent record of upholding the rights of arrested, detained, accused and convicted persons despite the nation's strong public crime control rhetoric. In the sphere of criminal justice, it is the Constitutional Court, empowered by the principal of constitutional supremacy, which has probably contributed most significantly to law reform.

---

25   See article 60(11)(a) of the Criminal Procedure Act 51 of 1977.

26   See the Criminal Procedure Amendment Act 75 of 1995 and the Criminal Procedure Second Amendment Act 85 of 1997. These changes were criticized by a number of academics see Sarkin, J. et al. 2000. The Constitutional Court's bail decision: individual liberty in crisis? *South African Journal on Human Rights*, 16 (2), 292–312.

27   See *S v Dlamini; S v Dladla; S v Joubert; S v Schietekat* 1999 (2) SACR 51 (CC).

28   See for example, the Criminal Law (Sexual Offences and Related Matters) Amendment Act 32 of 2007 and South African Law Reform Commission. 2002. *Report Project 107: Sexual Offences*. Pretoria. This Act broadens the definition of rape and amends the laws of criminal procedure and evidence so as to reduce barriers to reporting and truth finding, as well as introducing mechanisms to assist victims through the court process. See also the Domestic Violence Act 116 of 1998 (South African Law Reform Commission. 1997. Report Project 70: *Domestic Violence*) and the Child Justice Act 75 of 2008 (South African Law Reform Commission. 2000. Report Project 106: *Juvenile Justice*). The underlying rationale of the Domestic Violence Act is to increase the protection afforded to victim of domestic violence by facilitating access to state protection and ensuring that the courts and police service give effect to the provisions of the Act. The Child Justice Act seeks to protect the rights of children that come in contact with the law by, *inter alia*, raising the age of criminal liability and entrenching the notion of restorative justice.

29   See chapter 12.

30   See *Key v Attorney-General, Cape Provincial Division* 1996 (4) SA 187 (CC), para. 13.

In the very first case to come before the Constitutional Court, *S v Zuma*,[31] it rejected the sterile test of trial fairness employed by the courts under the apartheid regime. Under this approach the enquiry was simply whether there had 'been an irregularity or illegality, that [was] a departure from the formalities, rules and principles of procedure'[32] irrespective of the unfairness that might be inherent in those rules themselves. The court in *S v Zuma* held that the constitutional right to a fair trial embraced 'a concept of substantive fairness ... [that] ... required criminal trials to be conducted in accordance with just those "notions of basic fairness and justice"'.[33] In this case the Constitutional Court struck down the reverse onus provision applicable to the admission of confessions recorded by a magistrate or justice of the peace which required an accused to prove that the confession had not been made voluntarily.

The Constitutional Court shortly thereafter struck down the death penalty as being unconstitutional in *S v Makwanyane*[34] and in doing so noted that the high crime rate could be attributed to a variety of intersecting social, economic and political factors that existed entirely independently of the Bill of Rights.[35] It was also responsible for an amendment to section 49 of the Criminal Procedure Act 1977 that allowed the use of lethal force to effect arrest. Amendments to section 49 had been enacted by parliament in 1998 but not brought into effect due to opposition from the police. In 2002 the Constitutional Court in *Ex parte Minister of Safety and Security: in re S v Walters* 2002[36] struck the unamended section down as being unconstitutional, and eventually in July 2003[37] the amendment was brought into effect. Since then, lethal force in effecting an arrest may only be used to protect the arrestor or a member of the public from death or grievous bodily harm.

The influence of the Bill of Rights is to be seen throughout the court hierarchy and in limited instances it has made an impact on conditions of detention. For example, in *Stanfield v Minister of Correctional Services*[38] the applicant applied to be placed on parole under section 69 of the Correction Service Act 8 of 1959, on the basis that he had contracted lung cancer and his life expectancy had been severely shortened. His application was refused and the matter went on review. The applicant argued, *inter alia*, that section 69 should have been interpreted so as to 'promote, the spirit, purport and the object of the Bill of Rights'[39] and that

---

31 *S v Zuma*, 1995 (1) SACR 568 (CC).

32 *S v Rudman and another; S v Mthwana* 1992 (1) SACR 70 (A).

33 *S v Zuma*, para. 16.

34 *S v Makwanyane*. On the basis, *inter alia*, that it constituted cruel, inhuman and degrading punishment.

35 *S v Makwanyane*, paras 117–20.

36 *Ex parte Minister of Safety and Security: in re S v Walters* 2002 (4) SA 613 (CC).

37 See section 7 of the Judicial Matters Second Amendment Act 122 of 1998.

38 *Stanfield v Minister of Correctional Services* 2003 (12) BCLR 1384 (C).

39 Section 39 of the Constitution.

in terms of the section 10 right to dignity the applicant was entitled to die in a dignified and humane way.[40]

The court found that the third respondent had failed to respect the applicant's inherent right to human dignity by ignoring or downplaying the fact that he was 'suffering from an inoperable and incurable disease' that would cause his death within a few months.[41] This was compounded by the third respondent's failure to recognize the inadequacy of the medical facilities in the prisons.[42] The court also found that the third respondent's insistence that the applicant remain imprisoned until it was physically impossible for him to commit any crime was 'inhuman, degrading and thoroughly undignified'.[43] It also held that the failure to take the applicants individual circumstances into account by 'a lumping together of all prisoners suffering from terminal diseases' also undermined the applicant's right to dignity.[44]

In *B and Others v Minister of Correctional Services and Others*[45] the court had to deal with the question whether the applicants and other HIV-infected prisoners were entitled to receive 'appropriate anti-viral medication'.[46] This required the court to consider what would constitute 'adequate medical treatment' in terms of section 35(2)(e).[47] In rejecting the respondent's argument that the state was under no duty to provide prisoners with a greater degree of medical care than that available at state expense outside of the prison, the court held that the state owed a higher degree of care to prisoners.[48] Brandt J's reasons for this conclusion included the fact that '[u]nlike persons who are free, prisoners have not access to other resources to assist them in gaining access to medical treatment',[49] and that in respect of HIV-positive prisoners the prison environment exposed them more 'to opportunistic viruses than HIV sufferers who are not in prison'.[50] Other examples include prisoners' rights to access to electricity[51] and the right of child prisoners to be protected from maltreatment, neglect, abuse or degradation.[52]

Similarly the courts have used the Bill of Rights to promote trial fairness. The right to legal representation is viewed as a primary prerequisite for this, yet the common law did not recognize a right to legal representation for those unable

---

40   *Stanfield v Minister of Correctional Services*, paras 15 and 68.
41   *Stanfield v Minister of Correctional Services*, para. 124.
42   *Stanfield v Minister of Correctional Services*, para. 125.
43   *Stanfield v Minister of Correctional Services*, para. 126.
44   *Stanfield v Minister of Correctional Services*, para. 127.
45   *B and Others v Minister of Correctional Services and Others* 1997 (6) BCLR 789 (C).
46   *B and Others v Minister of Correctional Services and Others*, para. 2.
47   See also *S v Vanqa* 2000 (2) SACR 371 (Tk).
48   *S v Vanqa*, para. 52.
49   *S v Vanqa*, para. 53.
50   *S v Vanqa*, para. 54.
51   *Strydom v Minister of Correctional Services* 1999 (3) BCLR 342 (W).
52   *S v Z and 23 similar cases* 2004 (4) BCLR 410 (E).

to afford a lawyer.[53] The constitution affords detained and accused persons the right to be provided with legal assistance at state expense 'if substantial injustice would otherwise result'.[54] The reason for imposing a restriction on the substantive right to legal presentation is the concern that the South African state simply does not have the resources to provide legal representation for every indigent accused. As an absolute right, the substantive right to legal representation might paralyze an already-overburdened criminal justice system. Factors that will be taken into account in determining whether substantial injustice would result through the absence of legal representation include the complexity of the case, severity of the potential sentence,[55] and the ignorance and indigence of the accused.[56]

Where an accused is unrepresented it is well established that presiding officers have a duty to ensure that the accused is informed of his or her rights, including the right to legal representation, and that this should be done prior to the commencement of the trial.[57] '[D]epending upon the complexity of the charge, or of the legal rules relating thereto, and the seriousness therefore, an accused should not only be told of his right but he should also be encourage to exercise it.'[58] Where there is the possibility of a lengthy term of imprisonment an accused should be advised of this possibility and encouraged to avail him or herself of the services of a legal representative.[59] A presiding officer must also ensure that the accused is aware of and understands his or her right to legal representation at state expense.[60] If an accused who initially declines legal representation subsequently changes his or her mind, he or she must be given the opportunity to obtain legal representation.[61] The duty to provide an accused with a fair opportunity to obtain legal representation also arises in summary proceedings.[62]

Closely related to the right to legal representation is the right to information, as well as the time and facilities necessary to prepare and present a defence.[63] The

---

53   *S v Rudman & another; S v Mthwana* 1992 (1) SA 343 (A).

54   Section 35(2)(c) and (3)(g) of the Constitution.

55   In *S v Moos* 1998 (1) SACR 372 (C), the court held that substantive injustice would occur if the charge was one which would attract a sentence of imprisonment and the accused did not have legal representation.

56   See generally *Pennington v The Minister of Justice* 1995 (3) BCLR 270 (C); *Msila v Government of the RSA* 1996 (3) BCLR 362 (C); *S v Khanyile* 1988 (3) SA 795 (N).

57   *S v Radebe, S v Mbonani* 1998 (1) SACR 191 (T). See also *S v Van Heerden en ander sake* 2002 (1) SACR 409 (T); *S v Thusi* 2002 (12) BCLR 1274 (N). This duty is equally applicable in bail proceedings, see *S v Nzima* 2001 (2) SACR 345 (C).

58   *S v Radebe, S v Mbonani*, 196. See also *S v Manale* 2000 (2) SACR 666 (NCD); *S v Nkondo* 2000 (1) SACR 358 (W).

59   *S v Ndlovu* 2001 (1) SACR 204 (W); *S v Mbambo* 1999 (2) SACR 421 (W); *S v Dyani* 2004 (2) SACR 365 (E). See also *S v Tshidiso* 2002 (1) SACR 207 (W).

60   *S v Visser* 2001 (1) SASCR 401 (C); *S v Monyane* 2001 (1) SACR (T).

61   *S v Pitso* 2002 (2) SACR 586 (C).

62   *S v Solomons* 2004 (1) SACR 137 (C).

63   See sections 35(3)(b) and (i) of the Constitution.

Constitutional Court in *Shabalala v Attorney-General of Transvaal*[64] abolished 'blanket docket privilege', which gave the accused pre-trial access to the police docket and broadened the accused's access to state witnesses. In *S v Nkabinde*[65] the court found that the state infringed both the right to adequate facilities to prepare a defence and the right to privacy, when it came to light that the accused's only facilities to prepare his defence, namely a telephone and consultation room, had been subject to electronic monitoring.

The examples above constitute an illustration of judicial reform impacting on the rights of arrested, detained and accused persons, though they do not constitute a complete account of judicial activity in this area. The effectiveness of judicial reform through the application of a Bill of Rights is dependent on the constitutional adoption of the principle of constitutional supremacy. The recognition of constitutional supremacy does not in itself guarantee judicial reform, for matters to come before the Constitutional Court in the first place requires a legal profession that has been trained so as to be able to identify and exploit the opportunities for constitutional litigation and civil society organizations that can assist in identifying and funding cases. Although access to justice remains a challenge in South Africa the combination of constitutionally mandated institutions such as the Public Protector, the Commission for Gender Equality and the Human Rights Commission together with a wide range of non-governmental organizations (NGOs)[66] has assured a vibrant constitutional jurisprudence that is not restricted to the interests of the elite. Landmark cases have covered, *inter alia*, criminal law, rights of equality, privacy and religion, political rights and a range of socio-economic rights.[67]

How do we measure success in law reform?

If it can be assumed that the goal of law reform is to repeal bad laws, amend existing laws, or introduce new laws to achieve identified objectives, we could ask two questions to establish the success or failure of law reform: (a) does the content of the law reflect the desired change; and (b) is the reformed law implemented in a way that achieves the desired objective?

In South Africa a number of law reform initiatives have resulted in a change in the law. Those which have been achieved through the legislature have enjoyed the support of both civil society and at least some sectors of government, and

---

64   *Shabalala v Attorney-General of Transvaal.*

65   *S v Nkabinde* 1998 (8) BCLR 996 (N).

66   These NGO's include the Legal Resources Centre, Lawyers for Human Rights, the Woman's Legal Centre, the Aids Law Project, The Black Sash, Childline, the Lesbian and Gay Equality Project, and the Open Democracy Advice Centre.

67   Currie, I. and de Waal, J. 2005. *Bill of Rights Handbook.* Cape Town: Juta, and Woolman, S. et al. 2008. *Constitutional Law of South Africa.* 2nd Edition. Cape Town: Juta.

have been widely consulted. An excellent example of this is the Criminal Law (Sexual Offences and Related Matters) Amendment Act 32 of 2007.[68] The rights of detained, arrested and accused persons have in large part only been preserved due to the terms of the political settlement, which saw a transition to democracy and included the notion of constitutional supremacy and a Bill of Rights. This has allowed the courts to uphold constitutional values in areas where majoritarianism might demand otherwise. This has been essential in a country with an extremely high crime rate, making it very vulnerable to political crime control rhetoric.

However, when it comes to answering (b) regarding implementation any claims of success need to be very tentative. A reading of the relevant provisions of the constitution and the examples of constitutional integrity reflected in the sample of decisions set out above might have created an impression that South Africa is a good example of the gains for law reform. However, the lived experiences of arrested, detained and accused persons would appear to fall far below constitutionally determined standards.

What follows is a selective reflection on the failures of constitutional compliance regarding the treatment of arrested, detained and accused persons. In its 2008/2009 report the Judicial Inspectorate for Correctional Services noted that a substantial number of prisons were 'hopelessly overcrowded' which has 'created intolerable conditions for the inmates, most of them spending up to twenty-three hours per day cooped up in communal cells with limited ablution and toilet facilities'.[69] It notes that in many of the prisons 'the conditions under which inmates are detained are not ... consistent with human dignity and the further requirements set forth in section 35(2)(e) of the Constitution'.[70] The report concludes that in most prisons the conditions are 'well-nigh inhuman and unacceptable'.[71] The report notes that approximately a third of these inmates are prisoners awaiting trial who have been arrested without a warrant on the basis of a reasonable suspicion that they have committed an offence, and that charges are frequently withdrawn after many

---

68   See Artz, L. and Smythe, D. 2008. *Should We Consent?* Cape Town: Juta, for a thorough analysis of the Act and the law reform activism that influenced its promulgation.

69   Judicial Inspectorate for Correctional Services (JICS). 2008/2009. *Annual Report*. South Africa. [Online] Available at: http://judicialinsp.dcs.gov.za/Annualreports/ Annual%20Report%202008%20-%202009.pdf [accessed 10 May 2010], 8. On overcrowding see also the Commission of Inquiry into alleged incident of corruption, maladministration, violence or intimidation in the department of correctional services appointed by order of the President of the Republic of South Africa in terms of Proclamation No. 135 of 2001, as amended. 2005. *Final Report*. Vol. 1. [Online, December] Available at: http://www.info.gov.za/otherdocs/2006/jali/jali_comm_full.pdf [accessed 10 May 2010], 620–41. See also Dankwa, E.V. 2008. Overcrowding in African Prisons, in *Human Rights in African Prisons*, edited by J. Sarkin. Cape Town: Human Sciences Research Council, 83–92; Steinberg, J. 2005. *Prison Overcrowding and the Constitutional Right to Adequate Accommodation in South.* Cape Town: Centre for the Study of Violence and Reconciliation.

70   JICS. 2008/2009, 16.

71   JICS. 2008/2009, 21.

months, sometimes years, due to an absence of evidence.[72] In many instances bail might have been granted but the accused remains incarcerated due to an inability to pay of what often constituted a very small amount of money. The report reflects that the significant increase in overcrowding since 1996 can be partially attributed to the rapid increase of prisoners awaiting trial after that date.[73] In 2008, 66 persons died of unnatural causes in prison,[74] a number of these allegedly caused by assaults by warders.[75] There were over 2,000 complainants against warders for assault in 2008.[76] Meanwhile, law reform has played a role in reducing the number of children imprisoned, and in 2008 they constituted only 1 per cent of the prison population.[77] However, 50 per cent of these are awaiting trial and reports of assault and rape of minors are regularly made.[78]

Why has law reform in respect of prisons failed? The main reasons can be identified as the lack of capacity in both material and human resources to implement reforms, and an equivocal attitude towards the constitutional rights of citizens. The legislature has facilitated significant legal reform in the passing of the Correctional Services Amendment Act,[79] but has then used rhetoric elsewhere that suggests that the Bill of Rights hampers the efficient running of the criminal justice system, undermines the fight against crime and even worse, can be used to highlight government failures.[80]

Despite law reform curtailing the power of police to use lethal force during arrests, 556 suspects were killed by police between April 2008 and March 2009.[81] This figure is considerably lower than that of deaths recorded under the apartheid

---

72 JICS. 2008/2009, 9.

73 JICS. 2008/2009, 19.

74 JICS. 2008/2009, 12.

75 JICS. 2008/2009, 27.

76 JICS. 2008/2009, 36.

77 JICS. 2008/2009, 16.

78 See for example, South African Human Rights Commission. 2004. *Children in Prison* (briefing to the Parliamentary Portfolio Committee on Correctional Service). Pretoria.

79 Correctional Services Amendment Act 32 of 2001.

80 See generally Muntingh, L. 2007. *Prisons in South Africa's Constitutional Democracy*. Cape Town: Centre for the Study of Violence and Reconciliation.

81 Alcock, S.S. 2009. Killing by cops at a 10 year high. *Mail & Guardian*. 16–22 October, 3. The combined number of unnatural deaths in prison and deaths by police shooting 662 is slightly lower than prior years – see Independent Complaints Directorate (ICD). 2007. *Research Report: An investigation into deaths as a result of police action*. Pretoria. See generally Bruce, D. 2005. Interpreting the body count: South African statistics on lethal police violence. *South African Review of Sociology*, 36(2), 141–59. The ICD's 2008/2009 Annual Report recorded (at 47) 912 reports of death as a result of police action – this includes categories of action other than the use of lethal force to effect arrest. This represents an increase from the previous year of 792: see ICD. 2007/8. *Annual Report*, 53.

regime, and the statistics do not tell us whether these killing were justified – that is, if in self defence. Nevertheless the high number is sufficient to give cause for concern.[82] In the area of the use of lethal force the misalignment between the government, the legislature and the constitution is perhaps at its starkest with the legislature passing the amendment, the government urging police to shoot to kill,[83] and the Bill of Rights guaranteeing the right to life. In such conditions the normative role of law must inevitably be undermined.[84]

Despite the constitutional protections afforded arrested, detained and accused persons, incidents of torture continue to be reported. The Independent Complaints Directorate (ICD) in its 2007/2008 report noted that:

> In 1998 South Africa ratified the United Nations Convention against Torture, and Other Cruel, Inhumane or Degrading Treatment of Punishment (CAT). In 2006, South Africa signed the Optional Protocol to CAT (OPCAT), and by signing this convention, the state expresses, in principle, its intention to become a party to the Convention or Protocol referred to above. Our courts may take into cognizance these international legal instruments in instances where they are confronted with allegations of torture and it is against this background that we strongly believe that it is time that our courts demonstrate that torture will not be tolerated in the South African Police Service (SAPS). The number of reported cases of alleged torture is alarming especially when perpetrated by some of the police units that are regarded as the 'cream of the crop' in the SAPS.[85]

The ICD's annual reports also reflect a striking number of suicides in police custody: for example, the 2007/2008 report records 94 such suicides.[86] The failure to meet constitutional standards and apply them to the treatment of arrested, detained and accused persons can only partially be explained by ambiguities in the government's political rhetoric, which is itself a product of an inability to deal with high levels of crime, and a public sentiment that is baying for a crime control approach. In areas where there is consistency between the constitution, government policy and public sentiment, law reform has also failed to achieve its objectives, as seen through the common lack of resources and training.

---

82   See Bruce. 2005.

83   Alcock. 2009.

84   There are also reports of torture by the police. See ICD. 2001. *Report on torture cases investigated by the Independent Complainants Directorate*. Pretoria.

85   ICD. 2007/8, 35.

86   ICD. 2007/8, 45.

Conclusion

Prior to the establishment of democracy in South Africa legal activists sought to revolutionize the law rather than reform it. In doing so they challenged the existing legal order to mobilize communities and to gain both national and international media attention in an environment in which the scope for political debate was restricted. By using the courts as one of the arenas in which to challenge the apartheid state, they ironically used the existing legal order as a weapon against itself. Legal activists also attempted to prefigure a democratic legal order. Consequently, at the time of transition, advocates for social justice were well positioned to shape the new constitutional order.

Lessons from South Africa would indicate that safeguarding the rights of arrested, accused and detained persons through law reform requires active engagement in a political process that is committed to minimum human rights standards. This recognition needs to be gained at the foundation stage at which long term values are paramount since, as the new political dispensation progresses, it will inevitably become vulnerable to the short term demands of political expediency in which crime control rhetoric is frequently invoked to gain popular support. All reform initiatives, if they hope to be successful, need to engage all stakeholders. However, even when stakeholders are won over, law reform may still fail if the requisite attention has not been paid to the allocation of resources and training. Although the existence of legal rules may have a limited normative effect on behaviour, their blatant disregard may substantially undermine attempts to establish a democratic order.

III. Accountability for International Crimes

International crimes: Nature, practice and concerns

Genocide, crimes against humanity, war crimes and torture, as well as certain other offences, constitute international crimes, the commission of which have caused immense suffering, such as recently in the course of conflicts in former Yugoslavia, Rwanda, the Democratic Republic of Congo and Sudan. These are egregious offences that carry individual liability and that states have agreed to prevent and punish, either before national or international tribunals. The primary objective of prevention has given rise to the responsibility to protect populations from international crimes.[1] However, recent experience demonstrates, in former Yugoslavia and Rwanda but also elsewhere, not least Sudan itself, that states and the international community at large have failed to prevent the commission of such crimes, which commonly equally constitute serious violations of human rights (and, where committed in a conflict, of humanitarian law). The lack of accountability for international crimes is increasingly seen as contributing to the perpetuation of serious violations resulting in impunity, which has been defined as:

> the impossibility, de jure or de facto, of bringing the perpetrators of violations to account – whether in criminal, civil, administrative or disciplinary proceedings – since they are not subject to any inquiry that might lead to their being accused, arrested, tried and, if found guilty, sentenced to appropriate penalties, and to making reparations to their victims.[2]

The obligation to investigate and punish international crimes is well established but its application frequently encounters multiple challenges in times of transition. This applies in particular to legacies of long-running dictatorships and/or conflicts, which are often characterized by a large number of perpetrators. Many transitions are fragile, with the need to secure peace and reconciliation seen as paramount, which in turn means that the political environment may not be conducive to accountability mechanisms, especially where the alleged perpetrators still wield

---

1   UN General Assembly. 2005. *World Summit Outcome*. UN Doc. A/60/L.1, paras 138–9.

2   Independent expert to update the Set of principles to combat impunity, Diane Orentlicher. 2005. *Updated Set of Principles for the Protection and Promotion of Human Rights through Action to Combat Impunity*. UN Doc. E/CN.4/2005/102/Add.1, 6.

influence. This has resulted in different responses to the challenge of impunity, ranging from inaction to amnesties and to (some) prosecutions.[3] The South African solution of offering conditional amnesties as part of the political compromise and as a means of promoting truth-telling and reconciliation has been referred to as an important if not paradigmatic model.[4] However, the United Nations (UN), international(ized) tribunals and national courts have opposed amnesties, in particular blanket amnesties, for international crimes because they are viewed as being incompatible with the obligation to investigate and prosecute serious violations.[5] They also run contrary to the policy goal of combating impunity. As a result, explicit resort to amnesty laws has decreased, with governments and concerned parties often seemingly relying on an understanding that there will not be any investigations into serious violations. An example is Sudan's Comprehensive Peace Agreement where amnesties were considered by the parties but ultimately omitted following external advice. This step, however, did not change the parties' unwillingness to investigate and prosecute any international crimes that had been committed in the course of the long-standing North–South conflict.[6]

While there is a continuing debate about the relationship between justice (in particular accountability) and reconciliation, not least in terms of fostering or hindering peace, the UN Security Council, the UN and states have created mechanisms and adopted legislation to hold perpetrators accountable. This includes the setting up of mixed courts (also referred to as hybrid courts), ad hoc tribunals, in particular for the former Yugoslavia and Rwanda, and the establishment of the International Criminal Court (ICC).[7] The last two decades have witnessed a

---

3   See for some pertinent case studies, Roht-Arriaza, N. and Mariezcurrena, J. (eds). 2006. *Transitional Justice in the Twenty-First Century: Beyond Truth versus Justice.* Cambridge: Cambridge University Press.

4   See for example, du Bois-Pedain, A. 2007. *Transitional Amnesty in South Africa.* Cambridge: Cambridge University Press.

5   See Redress Trust (REDRESS), Lawyers' Committee for Human Rights and International Committee of Jurists. 2003. *Amicus Curiae on the Legality of Amnesties in International Law. The Prosecutor v Morris Kallon, Special Court for Sierra Leone.* [Online, October] Available at: http://www.redress.org/downloads/casework/AmicusCuriaeBrief-SCSL1.pdf [accessed 16 December 2010] and, on amnesties more generally, Mallinder, L. 2008. *Amnesty, Human Rights and Political Transitions: Bridging the Peace and Justice Divide.* Oxford: Hart.

6   See Crawford-Browne, S. et al. 2006. Obstacles to Transitional Justice in Sudan, in *Peace in the Balance: The Crisis in Sudan,* edited by B. Raftopoulos and K. Alexander. Cape Town: Institute for Justice and Reconciliation, 139–57, at 141–3.

7   Hybrid or mixed courts have been set up particularly in Sierra Leone, Cambodia and East Timor: see for example Agreement between the United Nations and the Government of Sierra Leone on the Establishment of the Special Court for Sierra Leone, signed on 16 January 2002. See on the ad-hoc tribunals, UN Security Council resolution 827 (1993). Annex: Statute of the International Tribunal for the Prosecution of Persons Responsible for Serious Violations of International Humanitarian Law committed in the territory of the

growing number of cases before these tribunals as well as national courts, which have developed principles and procedures for the prosecution of international crimes.[8] This includes both the rights of the defence[9] and the rights of victims who are increasingly recognized as actors in their own rights.[10] It also encompasses the protection of witnesses, which has become ever more important in the investigation and prosecution of international crimes.[11] The exercise of national and/or universal jurisdiction to prosecute those accused of having committed international crimes complements this development.[12]

International standards

The exercise of jurisdiction over international crimes

The investigation, prosecution and punishment of international crimes are of paramount importance in combating impunity. States retain a prime responsibility to exercise their jurisdiction to this end. This is explicitly recognized in the UN Convention against Torture, the Geneva Conventions with regard to war crimes and the Genocide Convention.[13] It is also reflected in the principle of complementarity

---

former Yugoslavia since 1991 (Report of the Secretary-General pursuant to paragraph 2 of Security Council resolution 808 (1993) Doc S/25704 of 3 May 1993); UN Security Council resolution 955 (1994). Annex: Statute of the International Tribunal for Rwanda; and 1998 Rome Statute of the International Criminal Court (ICC).

    8   See for an overview, Cassese, A. 2008. *International Criminal Law*. 2nd Edition. Oxford: Oxford University Press.

    9   See in particular article 67 ICC Rome Statute and Negri, S. 2007. The right to defence, Guiding Light or Empty Shell, in *International Criminal Justice: A Critical Analysis of Institutions and Procedures*, edited by M. Bohlander. London: Cameron Press, 13–73.

    10   See in particular article 68(3) ICC Rome Statute.

    11   See article 68 ICC Rome Statute and REDRESS. 2009. *A Call to Action: Ending threats and reprisals against victims of torture and related international crimes*. [Online, December] Available at: http://www.redress.org/downloads/publications/Victim%20 Protection%20Report%20Final%2010%20Dec%2009.pdf [Accessed 28 December 2010].

    12   See REDRESS and FIDH. 2010. *Extraterritorial Jurisdiction in the European Union: A Study of the Laws and Practice in the 27 Member States of the European Union.* [Online, December] Available at: http://www.redress.org/downloads/publications/ Extraterritorial%20Jurisdiction%20In%20the%2027%20Member%20States%20of%20 the%20European%20Union%20FINAL.pdf [accessed 28 December 2010].

    13   Articles 4–8 UN Convention against Torture and other Cruel, Inhuman or Degrading Treatment or Punishment, 1984 (UNCAT), and articles V and VI Convention on the Prevention and Punishment of the Crime of Genocide of 1948. For grave breaches, see articles 50(1.GC), 51(2.GC), 130(3.GC), 147(4.GC) of the four Geneva Conventions of 1949 and article 85 of the 1. Additional Protocol to the Geneva Conventions, 1977. According to the International Committee of the Red Cross, the obligation to prosecute war crimes also applies to non-international armed conflicts under customary international law.

according to which the ICC should only investigate and prosecute cases where a state is unable or unwilling to do so.[14] The exercise of national jurisdiction requires a legal framework comprising both substantive and procedural elements that allow states effectively to investigate and prosecute international crimes. This may extend to certain crimes committed abroad (the principle of *aut dedere aut judicare* – extradite or prosecute), such as torture, which requires states to establish jurisdiction over such crimes that effectively takes the form of universal jurisdiction.[15] The national framework must also address the protection of the rights of defendants, that is those accused of having committed international crimes, in particular the right to liberty and security, prohibition of torture, and the right to a fair trial as well as the rights of prisoners of wars and others tried in relation to offences committed in the course of armed conflict.[16]

States' positive obligation to prevent and repress violations and international crimes

In international human rights law, the duty of states to take adequate measures to investigate and prosecute serious violations that may amount to international crimes is known as 'positive obligation'. This notion plays an important role in framing states' policies on criminal law and criminal justice. The 'positive' element of this obligation requires states to adopt measures that seek to prevent, and respond to violations, and are necessary as well for the fulfilment of rights, including protection. These obligations are inherent in states' duty to 'respect and to ensure to all individuals within its territory and subject to its jurisdiction the rights recognized in the present Covenant' (article 2(1) of the International Covenant on Civil and Political Rights, a similar formulation is found in article 1 of the African Charter on Human and Peoples' Rights). States' duty to respond to violations has been articulated and developed by human rights treaty bodies and courts, most notably the Inter-American Court for Human Rights in the landmark case of *Velasquez Rodriguez v Honduras*.[17] The obligation is one of means, not results, and requires states: 'to take appropriate measures or to exercise due diligence to prevent, punish, investigate or redress the harm caused

---

See rule 158 of the List of Customary Rules of International Humanitarian Law. Available at: http://www.icrc.org/customary-ihl/eng/docs/v1_rul_rule158 [accessed 12 December 2010].

14   See article 17 ICC Rome Statute.

15   See as a matter of treaty law in particular articles 5–8 UNCAT and article 9(2) International Convention for the Protection of All Persons from Enforced Disappearance, 2006. For war crimes, see articles 50(1.GC), 51(2.GC), 130(3.GC), 147(4.GC) of the four Geneva Conventions of 1949 and article 85 of the 1. Additional Protocol to the Geneva Conventions, 1977.

16   See in particular articles 9 and 14 of the International Covenant on Civil and Political Rights and article 75 of the 1. Additional Protocol to the Geneva Conventions, 1977.

17   *Velásquez-Rodríguez v Honduras*. Merits. Inter-American Court of Human Rights, Judgment, 29 July 1988. Series C No. 4, paras 155–6.

by such acts by private persons or entities [as well as anyone acting in an official capacity]'.[18]

The duty obligates states to enact criminal legislation that is effective in repressing serious human rights violations, including torture, sexual violence, and other assaults on physical or psychological integrity.[19] The elements of the offence should capture the nature of the violation and not establish undue thresholds, such as limiting psychological torture to 'prolonged mental harm', as is for example the case in relevant United States legislation.[20] Liability for certain crimes, such as international crimes, should extend to those involved in the crime at various stages and/or in various ways, in particularly commanders and superiors.[21] Conversely, following orders in respect of such crimes should not constitute a defence although it may be considered a mitigating circumstance.[22] The punishment for the offence in question needs to be commensurate with the seriousness of the offence.[23] A maximum punishment of two years' imprisonment for torture, for example, would be patently inadequate.[24] The effective repression and prevention of serious violations also entails in principle that they are not subject to amnesties, immunities or statutes of limitations that nullify prosecutions.[25] In the context of armed conflict, this is without prejudice to the rule under article 6(5) of the II. Additional Protocol to the Geneva Conventions of 1977 that '[a]t the end of hostilities, the authorities in power shall endeavour to grant the broadest possible amnesty to persons who have participated in the armed conflict, or those deprived of their liberty for reasons related to the armed conflict, whether they are interned or detained', which seeks to protect rebels from being tried before national courts solely for having taken up arms.

---

18   Human Rights Committee (HRC). 2004. *General Comment 31 on Article 2 of the Covenant: The Nature of the General Legal Obligation Imposed on States Parties to the Covenant.* UN Doc. CCPR/C/74/CRP.4/Rev.6, para. 8.

19   See article 4 UNCAT and *M.C. v Bulgaria*, 40 EHRR 20 (2005), paras 148–87; *Zimbabwe Human Rights NGO Forum v Zimbabwe*, African Commission on Human and Peoples' Rights, Communication 245/2002 (2006), para. 143.

20   Committee against Torture (CAT). 2006. *Concluding observations: United States of America.* UN Doc. CAT/C/USA/CO/2, para. 13.

21   See in this context Badar, M.E. 2011. Participation in crimes in the jurisprudence of the ICTY and ICTR, in *Handbook of International Criminal Law*, edited by W.A. Schabas and N. Bernaz. Abingdon, Oxon: Routledge, 247–69, at 257–62, and article 28 of the ICC Rome Statute.

22   *Prosecutor v Erdemović* (Case No. IT-96-22-Tbis), Trial Chamber, Sentencing Judgment, 5 March 1998, para. 17.

23   CAT. 2008. *General Comment 2: Implementation of article 2 by States parties.* UN Doc. CAT/C/GC/2, para. 11.

24   See Ingelse, C. 2001. *The Committee against Torture: An Assessment*, The Hague etc.: Kluwer Law International, 342.

25   CAT. General Comment 2, para. 5 and HRC. General Comment 31, para. 18.

Criminalizing offences in line with these requirements should be complemented by a system of prompt, impartial and effective investigations capable of establishing the facts and identifying the perpetrators, and prosecutions where warranted.[26] This is both with a view to enhancing the effectiveness of case-specific responses and general prevention. Importantly, victims should be recognized as an independent party and rights-holders in such a system, requiring the state to provide protection and to enable victims to participate in criminal proceedings.[27] States must also ensure that victims can exercise their right to have access to effective remedies and reparation. The components of this right have been elaborated in the landmark UN General Assembly declaration 'Basic Principles and Guidelines on the Right to a Remedy and Reparation for Victims of Gross Violations of International Human Rights Law and Serious Violations of International Humanitarian Law'.[28] According to these Principles, the right to reparation comprises access to judicial remedies and reparation taking the form of restitution, compensation, rehabilitation, satisfaction and guarantees of non-repetition in cases of gross or serious violations.[29]

---

26   HRC. General Comment 31, paras 15 and 18.

27   See *UN Declaration of Basic Principles of Justice for Victims of Crime and Abuse of Power*, UN General Assembly resolution 40/34 (1985), and article 6(1) and (2) of the 2000 Protocol to Prevent, Suppress and Punish Trafficking in Persons, Especially Women and Children, Supplementing the UN Convention against Transnational Organised Crime. (2001) 40 ILM 335. *McKerr v the United Kingdom,* 34 EHRR 20 (2002), para. 115.

28   *Basic Principles and Guidelines on the Right to a Remedy and Reparation for Victims of Gross Violations of International Human Rights Law and Serious Violations of International Humanitarian Law*, UN General Assembly resolution 60/147 (2006).

29   Basic Principles.

Chapter 7

The Prosecution of International Crimes under Sudan's Criminal and Military Laws: Developments, Gaps and Limitations

Mohamed Abdelsalam Babiker

Introduction

Sudan's body of criminal law has long been characterized by the absence of international crimes. The gap has come under growing scrutiny in the context of the Darfur conflict, in which a number of observers, beginning with members of the International Commission of Inquiry on Darfur, have reported both evidence of international crimes, and a domestic system incapable of adequately holding suspects accountable. Sudan has responded with adjustments made within the reform of the Armed Forces Act in 2007, and with amendments to the Criminal Act in 2009. This chapter seeks to determine whether the recent changes have created an adequate legal framework for the prosecution of international crimes in Sudan. To this end, it evaluates to what extent the relevant provisions conform to the definition of the international crimes of genocide, crimes against humanity and war crimes as stipulated in the statutes of international criminal tribunals and interpreted in their jurisprudence. It also examines the Sudanese law in respect of principles such as command responsibility and reparations for victims of crimes whose recognition is essential for the effective prosecution of international crimes and justice for victims. It also considers the scope and applicability of immunities and statutes of limitation, which are recognized in Sudanese laws and have contributed to impunity for international crimes in Sudan.

Repression of international crimes under Sudan's criminal and military laws (1983–2007)

During this period, only few legislative steps, policies or other measures had been adopted in Sudan with a view to implementing or enforcing the Geneva Conventions of 1949 and the Additional Protocols of 1977.[1] Since the resumption of the armed

---

1   Sudan acceded to the four Geneva Conventions of 1949 on 23 September 1957, to Additional Protocol 1 of 1977 to the four Geneva Conventions on 7 March 2006, and

conflict in Sudan in 1983, various military laws regulating the conduct of the national armed forces were introduced and subsequently changed in the period between November 1983 and June 1999. The Nimeiri military regime (1969–85) repealed the Armed Forces Act of 1957 and introduced the People's Armed Forces Act of 1983.[2] The new act dealt with the repression of war-related crimes (section 10 on crimes and punishments) and criminalized acts in the field,[3] including pillaging, looting,[4] inhumane treatment of prisoners of war and the wounded or sick,[5] as well as the protection of humanitarian organizations.[6] This act represented a measure of progress. However, it was repealed by the civilian government that took power after the collapse of the Nimeiri regime, and was replaced by the People's Armed Forces Act of 1986.[7] Although the new codification was introduced during a period of civilian rule (1986–89) and is thus supposed to have been better than its predecessor, it constituted the worst military act in Sudan's recent history as it lacked any humanitarian provisions.[8] Significantly, the few 'humanitarian' articles repressing war-related crimes included in the Military Act of 1983 were omitted from the text of the 1986 Act. The purpose was, apparently, to shield military personnel from prosecution under national laws and to give effect to the policy of summary execution of prisoners adopted by successive governments for more than two decades.[9] The current government (1989–) replaced the 1986 Military Act with the People's Armed Forces Act of 1999 (amendment),[10] without, however, reinstating any of the humanitarian articles mentioned above.

Sudan's national laws, therefore, did not provide for the criminal repression of international humanitarian law (IHL) violations. National courts were *de facto* precluded from prosecuting international crimes, which resulted in a serious gap in repressing the crimes of genocide, crimes against humanity and war crimes. It is pertinent to note here that the International Criminal Court (ICC)'s investigation in respect of the Darfur situation, pursuant to a Security Council referral (Sudan has signed the ICC Rome Statute but is not a state party),

---

to Additional Protocol II of 1977 on 13 July 2006. See ICRC. *2006*. Sudan accedes to the 1977 Protocols additional to the Geneva Conventions. News Release No. 06/103 [Online, 13 September] Available at: http://www.icrc.org/eng/resources/documents/news-release/sudan-news-130906.htm [accessed 24 June 2011].

2   People's Armed Forces Act, 6 November 1983 (1983 Military Act*)*.

3   Article 58(2).

4   Article 60.

5   Article 66.

6   Article 67(b).

7   People's Armed Forces Act, 15 April 1986 (1986 Military Act).

8   For a comprehensive and detailed analysis of the military and Islamic military laws, see Babiker, M.A. 2007. *Application of International Humanitarian and Human Rights Law to the Armed Conflicts of the Sudan: Complementary or Mutually Exclusive Regimes*. Antwerp, Oxford: Intersentia, Chapter VI, 185–205.

9   Babiker. 2007. Chapter II.

10   People's Armed Forces Act, 22 June 1999 (1999 Military Act).

originated and proceeded because existing Sudanese laws did not adequately repress international crimes and lacked genuine legal procedures to hold those involved accountable. No doubt this has affected the ICC's approach with regard to the complementarity regime and the Court's determination of whether it has jurisdiction over the international crimes allegedly committed in Darfur. The ICC Prosecutor stated in this respect that:

> In light of the complementarity regime and article 53(1)(b) of the Statute, I am required to consider whether there could be cases that would be admissible within the situation in Darfur. The Office has studied Sudanese institutions, laws and procedures. We have sought information on any national proceedings that may have been undertaken in relation to crimes in Darfur. We have also analyzed the multiple ad hoc mechanisms that were created by the Sudanese authorities in 2004 in the context of the conflict in Darfur, including the Committees against Rape, the Special Courts and the Specialized Courts that replaced them, the National Commission of Inquiry and other ad hoc judicial committees and non-judicial mechanisms. Following this analysis, I determined that there are cases that would be admissible in relation to the Darfur situation. This decision does not represent a determination on the Sudanese legal system as such, but is essentially a result of the absence of criminal proceedings related to the cases on which I will focus.[11]

Incorporation of international crimes into Sudan's criminal & military laws (2007–)

After the Security Council referred the Darfur situation to the ICC, the Government of the Sudan (GOS) took certain legal measures by enacting the Armed Forces Act 2007 and the Criminal Act 1991 (as amended in 2009) in order to incorporate the international crimes of genocide, crimes against humanity and war crimes. The Armed Forces Act 2007 contains provisions on these crimes within a whole chapter on international humanitarian law. The Criminal Law amendments of 2009 added a new chapter (Chapter 18) with a total of seven articles,[12] which had been drafted by a special committee formed in the Ministry of Justice following the ICC intervention in the Darfur situation.

No doubt the incorporation of the aforementioned crimes as part of the Sudanese criminal justice system is a significant step towards combating impunity and repression of IHL violations. However, the process of incorporation has

---

11   Statement of the Prosecutor of the International Criminal Court, Mr. Luis Moreno Ocampo, to the Security Council on 29 June 2005 pursuant to UN SC Resolution 1593 (2005).

12   The amendments were adopted by the National Assembly on 25 May 2009 and signed into law on 28 June 2009 by the President of the Republic.

been incomplete as many gaps still exist in the body of the new legislation and subsequent amendments. These gaps will be discussed below with respect to the crime of genocide, crimes against humanity and war crimes.

Genocide

The definition of the crime of genocide in the Criminal Act 1991 (as amended in 2009) is not in conformity or harmony with the definition contained in the 1948 Convention on the Prevention and Punishment of the Crime of Genocide, which has been incorporated into the statutes of international criminal tribunals.[13] Genocide is defined in article 6 of the ICC Rome Statute. The provision is essentially a copy of article II of the Genocide Convention. The definition set out therein, although often criticized for being overly restrictive and difficult to apply to many cases of mass killing and atrocity, has stood the test of time. The decision by the Rome conference to maintain a fifty-year-old text is convincing evidence that article 6 of the statute constitutes a codification of customary international norm.[14]

Article 6 of the ICC Rome Statute, and article II of the Genocide Convention include five specific acts 'committed with intent to destroy, in whole or in part, a national, ethnical, racial or religious group'. The five acts are:

> (a) killing members of the group; (b) causing serious bodily or mental harm to members of the group; (c) deliberately inflicting on the group conditions of life calculated to bring about its physical destruction in whole or in part; (d) imposing measures intended to prevent births within the group; (e) forcibly transferring children of the group to another group.

The above definition has been incorporated in the penal codes of many countries. In the Sudan, the definition of genocide in article 187 of the Criminal Act 1991 (as amended in 2009) reads as follows:

> There shall be punished with death penalty, life imprisonment or any other lesser punishment whoever commits, attempts or abets the commitment of a crime or crimes of homicide against members of a national, ethnic, racial or religious group with intent to exterminate or destroy them, in whole or in part, and in the context of a systematic and widespread conduct directed against that group and commits in the same context any of the following acts:

---

13   On the definition of these crimes, see for example article 4 of the Statute of the International Criminal Tribunal for the Former Yugoslavia (ICTY) (1993); article 2 of the Statute of the International Tribunal for Rwanda (ICTR) (1994); and article 6 of the ICC Rome Statute (1998).

14   See Schabas, W. 2006. *An Introduction to the International Criminal Court.* 2nd Edition. Cambridge: Cambridge University Press, 38.

(a) killing a member or more of the group; (b) torture, or causing serious harm or bodily or mental harm to members of the group; (c) deliberately inflicting on a member or more of the group conditions of life calculated to bring about its physical destruction in whole or in part; (d) imposing measures intended to prevent a member or more within the group from births; (e) forcibly transferring a child or more from the group to another group.

The definition of genocide in article 187 is only partially in line with the 1948 Genocide Convention definition and the ICC Rome Statute. Three critical points deserve to be highlighted here. First, whereas the 1948 definition of the crime of genocide stipulates that 'any of the following acts' constitutes genocide, article 187 makes the actual commission of a 'crime' or 'attempting or abetting the commission of a crime or crimes of homicide against members of a national, ethnic, racial or religious group' the essential acts that constitute genocide, if the other elements of the crime are present.[15] The reference to homicide appears to narrow the definition and is bound to create serious confusion.[16]

Secondly, the relationship between homicide and the other five acts listed at the end of article 187 is not clear. A literal interpretation of the definition seems to suggest that they are cumulative – that is, that there needs to be the act of homicide as well as any of the five enumerated acts.[17] In the 1948 definition, the five acts are clearly distinct from homicide because genocide is characterized by the intent to destroy a protected group by the enumerated means. Only one of the five acts concerns homicide; the other four acts do not need to result in the death of the targeted members of the group even though the ultimate intention must be to destroy the protected group, in whole or in part.[18] The 1948 definition thus recognizes that there are a number of means or ways in addition to homicide that can bring about the destruction of a group. Making homicide an essential element of the crime of genocide as provided for in article 187 does not fully capture the nature of this crime.

Thirdly, article 187 introduces new elements to the definition of the crime of genocide that are bound to confuse genocide with crimes against humanity. The article provides that genocide can be committed 'against members of a national, ethnic, racial or religious group with intent to *exterminate* or *destroy* them, in whole or in part, and *in the context of a systematic and widespread conduct* directed against that group' (emphasis added). This definition creates confusion with regard to the elements of the crime of genocide recognized under the Genocide Convention

---

15   See REDRESS and KCHRED. 2008a. *Comments on the Proposed Amendment of the Sudanese Criminal Act.* [Online, September] Available at: http://www.pclrs.org/downloads/Miscellaneous/Penal_Code_Amendment_Position%20Paper%20_2_.pdf [accessed 18 February 2010].
16   REDRESS and KCHRED. 2008a, 5.
17   REDRESS and KCHRED. 2008a, 5.
18   REDRESS and KCHRED. 2008a, 5.

of 1948 and article 6 of the ICC Rome Statute. As a result, article 187 introduces a high threshold for the prosecution of the crime of genocide because two aspects need to be proved: (a) intent to exterminate or destroy members of the group (b) that the crime was committed 'in the context of a systematic and widespread conduct'. No doubt the latter element mixes genocide with crimes against humanity.

What sets genocide apart from crimes against humanity and war crimes is that the act – whether killing or murder, or one of the other four acts defined in article 6 – must be committed with the specific or special intent (*dolus specialis*) to destroy in whole or in part a national, ethnical, racial, or religious group as such. 'Special intent' has several components and the perpetrator's intent must be 'to destroy the group'.[19] However, article 187 requires special intent to 'exterminate' or 'destroy' a group or members of the group in whole or in part. Using the word 'exterminate' introduces terminology that is not known either in the Genocide Convention or jurisprudence of international courts. Furthermore, the definition of genocide in article 187 indicates that the crime can be committed '*in the context of a systematic and widespread conduct directed against that group*' (emphasis added). Again, this definition is not in harmony with the Genocide Convention or article 6 of the ICC Rome Statute. Under both instruments the definition of genocide contains no formal requirement that the punishable acts be part of a widespread or systematic attack or conduct,[20] although the ICC's Elements of Crimes take a slightly different perspective, requiring that an act of genocide 'took place in the context of a manifest pattern of similar conduct directed against the group or was conduct could itself affect such destruction'.[21]

In addition, one of the inherent gaps in the definition of genocide under article 187 is that the five genocidal acts can be committed against '*a member or more of the group*' (emphasis added). This definition does not capture the collective nature and 'quantitative' dimension of the crime of genocide, which is indicated by the words 'in whole or in part' used in its definition. The number contemplated must be significant, and the intent to kill only a few members of a group cannot be genocide.[22] The prevailing view is that where only part of a group is destroyed, it must be a 'substantial' part.[23] Recently, another interpretation has emerged by which genocide is only committed if a 'significant part' of the group is destroyed, including persons of 'special significance' to the group.[24]

---

19   Schabas. 2006, 36–8.

20   Widespread and systematic conduct or attack would seem, however, to be an implicit characteristic of the crime of genocide although in the *Jelesic case* a trial chamber of the ICTY entertained the hypothesis of the lone genocidal maniac. See *Prosecutor v Jelisic* (Case No. IT-95-10-T), Judgment, 14 December 1999, para. 100.

21   See ICC Elements of Crimes. ICC-ASP/1/3, 113-5.

22   See Schabas. 2006, 39.

23   *Prosecutor v Jelisic*, para. 82.

24   *Prosecutor v Sikirica et al* (Case No. IT-95-8-1). Judgment of Defense Motions to Acquit, 3 September 2001, para. 80.

It is evident from the above considerations that those who drafted the definition of genocide in article 187 lacked legal expertise and a minimum understanding of the nature of the crime of genocide. The definition of genocide in the article suffers from serious gaps and is not in harmony with the Genocide Convention of 1948, or article 6 of the ICC Rome Statute. As far as victims are concerned, the main point needing to be emphasized here is that article 187 sets an even higher threshold for the prosecution of the crime of genocide under national criminal law than the one provided under international law. This raises an important question: were the serious gaps in the definition of the crime of genocide under article 187 the result of the legislators' intent to bar the effective incorporation of international crimes within the criminal justice system, or rather due to legal 'recklessness' and a lack of expertise on the part of the drafters or legislators?

Crimes Against Humanity

Article 7 of the ICC Rome Statute begins with an introductory paragraph or chapeau stating: '[f]or the purpose of this Statute, "crime against humanity" means any of the following acts when committed as part of a widespread or systematic attack directed against any civilian population, with knowledge of the attack'. This constitutes an important threshold that must be satisfied for the crime to be committed. Article 186 of the Criminal Act 1991 (as amended in 2009) includes a similar definition. It states: '[t]here shall be punished with capital sentence, imprisonment for life or any lesser punishment whoever commits alone or jointly, encourages or supports any widespread or systematic attack directed against any civilian population with knowledge of the attack, where he/she in the same context commits any of the following acts'.

The definition of the crime against humanity contained in article 7 of the ICC Rome Statute requires that an attack must be carried out 'pursuant to or in furtherance of a State or organizational policy to commit such attack'. In the *Tadić* case, the Yugoslav Tribunal held that, under customary international law, crimes against humanity could also be committed 'on behalf of entities exercising de facto control over a particular territory but without international recognition or formal status of a "de jure" state, or by a terrorist group or organization'.[25] Article 186 does not reflect this definition.

Article 186 classifies certain acts as crimes against humanity. This is a welcome step and in line with the dramatic enlargement of the scope of crimes against humanity found in the very substantial list of 'gender crimes' that include 'rape, sexual slavery, enforced prostitution, forced pregnancy, enforced sterilization, or any other form of sexual violence of comparable gravity'. It is also a step towards compliance by the Sudan with its duty to take effective measures against the aforementioned gender-based crimes as recognized in the ICC Rome Statute and

---

25 *Prosecutor v Tadić* (Case No.IT-94-1-T), Opinion and Judgment, 7 May 1997, para. 654.

a series of declarations by United Nations (UN) bodies, such as the landmark Declaration on the Elimination of Violence against Women, and the practice of international human rights bodies.[26]

However, a close analysis of the definition of gender crimes in the Sudan's criminal laws reveals that such laws, including the 2009 amendments to the Criminal Act 1991, are still not in harmony with the definition recognized in article 7 of the ICC Rome Statute. For example, rape as a crime against humanity in article 186 is defined as:

> [Whoever] uses coercion in a sexual intercourse with a female or sodomy with a male, or commits outrages upon personal dignity of the victim if such is accompanied by penetration in any way, provided that coercion always exists if the above said acts are committed against a person incapable of giving consent.

The above definition neither covers all acts of penetration nor specifies the forms of coercion and lack of consent required. However, being more specific on the types of penetration would make article 186 clearer and would enhance protection. This could be done by drawing on the international jurisprudence on rape with objects, which is not confined to vaginal or anal penetration but also encompasses oral rape and penetration with objects.[27]

Rape is not defined in the ICC Rome Statute, and at the time the drafters may have felt that it was to be left to the judges to develop it in their jurisprudence.[28] The Statute also does not specify the meaning of coercion so as to provide prosecutors and judges with guidance in the interpretation of the elements of the crime, by drawing on jurisprudence that has specified the nature of coercion and the definition of consent.[29] However, within a few months of the adoption of the ICC Rome Statute, judgments of the *ad hoc* tribunals had developed two somewhat different definitions of the crime of rape. The first was proposed by the Rwanda Tribunal in the *Akayesu* case, which warned that 'the central elements of the crime of rape cannot be captured in a mechanical description of objects and body parts'.[30] It defined the crime as 'a physical invasion of a sexual nature, committed on a person under circumstances which are coercive'.[31] The definition

---

26   *Declaration on the Elimination of Violence against Women*, UN General Assembly resolution 48/104 (1993).

27   See REDRESS and KCHRED. 2008. *Time for Change – Reforming Sudan's Legislation on Rape and Sexual Violence*. [Online, October 2008b] Available at: http://www.pclrs.org/downloads/Miscellaneous/Position%20Paper%20Rape.pdf [accessed 28 December 2010], 29–31.

28   Schabas. 2006, 47.

29   REDRESS and KCHRED. 2008a, 6.

30   *Posecutor v Akayesu* (Case No. ICTR-96-4-T), Judgment, 2 September 1998, para. 325.

31   *Prosecutor v Akayesu*, para. 326.

was broad enough to encompass forced penetration by the tongue of the victim's mouth, which most legal systems would not stigmatize as a rape, although it might well be prosecuted as sexual assault.[32] Subsequently, a Trial Chamber of the Yugoslav Tribunal reverted to a more mechanical and technical definition, holding rape to be 'the sexual perpetration, however slight: (a) of the vagina or anus of the victim by the penis of the perpetrator or any other object used by the perpetrator; or (b) of the mouth of the victim by the penis of the perpetrator'.[33]

Apart from article 186, gender-based violence is not adequately criminalized in Sudanese laws. For example, the current definition of rape in article 149 of the Criminal Act (which has not been amended) does not include penetration other than sexual intercourse by way of penile penetration into the vagina or anus. The reference to the criminal offence of adultery in defining sexual intercourse has created ambiguity about the applicable rules of evidence, seemingly requiring four male eye-witnesses to the act of penetration or a confession for a conviction, a threshold that is virtually impossible to meet. Reference to adultery also exposes women to the risk of prosecution for the crime of adultery because any complaint about rape may be treated as an admission of having had (unlawful) sexual intercourse. Accordingly, there have been hardly any successful prosecutions for rape in Sudan and the current offence of rape has failed to provide adequate protection for women. Other provisions in Sudan's criminal law are clearly inadequate in cases of serious sexual assault or harassment that do not amount to rape.[34]

The legal confusion created by article 149 of the Criminal Act 1991 was created anew in the Armed Forces Act 2007. Article 153(2)(d) of the latter mixes the crime of adultery, sodomy and 'sexual perversion' with gender-based violence. It does not only include adultery but also adds other categories of crimes not related to gender-based violence such as 'forceful gestation', 'buggery' and 'sexual abnormality' (the correct Arabic translation is sexual perversion). The article states:

> Subject to the provisions of the Criminal Act, 1991, there shall be punished, with imprisonment, for a term, not exceeding ten years, whoever commits, within the framework of a systematic and widespread attack, directed against civilians, any of the following acts:-(d) rape, or practicing adultery with any person, or sexual slavery, or coercion to prostitution, forceful gestation, buggery or any type of sexual abnormality, or coercing him/her therefore, or sterilizing him/her to prevent him/her from propagation.

---

32 Schabas. 2006, 48.

33 *Prosecutor v Furundžija* (Case No. IT-95-17/1-T), Judgment, 10 December 1998, para. 185.

34 See for a thorough analysis of Sudanese laws on rape and sexual violence, REDRESS and KCHRED. 2008b.

War Crimes

In addition to the criminalization of genocide and crimes against humanity in articles 187 and 186 respectively, article 188 of the Criminal Act 1991 (as amended in 2009) criminalizes 'war crimes against persons'. The offence carries 'capital punishment, life imprisonment or any lesser punishment against 'whoever knowingly commits, in the context of an international or non-international armed conflict certain criminal acts'. The Act further represses four other categories of war crimes, namely: (i) 'war crimes against properties and other rights' in article 189; (ii) 'war crimes against humanitarian operations' in article 190; (iii) 'war crimes related to the prohibited methods of warfare' in article 191; and (iv) 'war crimes related to the use of prohibited weapons' in article 192. The five categories of war crimes do not reflect the structure of article 8 of the ICC Rome Statute, which drew upon the existing sources of war crimes as reflected in the article. Unlike the above war crimes provided under the Criminal Act, article 8 of the ICC Rome Statute consists of four categories of war crimes, two of them addressing international armed conflicts and two non-international armed conflicts.

The Criminal Act deals with five categories of crimes, all of which 'can be committed in the context of an international armed conflict or non-international armed conflicts'. This phrasing is confusing as it makes no distinction between the crimes committed in an international context and those committed in internal armed conflicts. This is problematic because the prosecution of a particular category of crime (as in the case of interpreting the ICC Rome Statute) requires an often complex prior assessment of the type of armed conflict involved. Courts are also required to distinguish between international and non-international armed conflicts, and this is further complicated by the fact that within the sub-set of non-international armed conflicts there are two distinct categories. The judgments of international criminal tribunals have already shown how difficult this task of qualification can be. This applies in equal measure to the Sudan. Thus, for the law not to address war crimes categories separately is likely to cause serious problems of qualification as a pre-condition for the prosecution of war crimes in the Sudan.

The qualification of armed conflicts is further complicated by the fact that a distinction must be made between war crimes and the other two categories of crimes, namely crimes against humanity and genocide, with respect to the applicable thresholds. Crimes against humanity must be 'widespread' and 'systematic', and genocide requires 'specific intent'. War crimes, on the other hand, can be committed 'as part of a plan or policy or as part of a large-scale commission of such crimes'. Although this definition brings war crimes closer to crimes against humanity, both have their own thresholds. For example, the preliminary question that needs to be determined for war crimes charges is the existence of an armed conflict, be it international or non-international, and a nexus must be shown between the acts perpetrated and the conflict. Furthermore, the elements of war crimes clarify that, while the prosecutor must establish these thresholds elements of war crimes, he or she need not prove that the perpetrator had knowledge of whether or not there was an armed conflict, or whether it was international or non-international.[35] According to the ICC Elements of Crimes, there is only a requirement for the perpetrator to be aware of the factual circumstances that establish the existence of an armed conflict, which is implicit in the term 'took place in the context of and was associated with'.[36] The definitional threshold for war crimes under articles 188, 190, 191, 192 of the Criminal Act require knowledge and this makes the threshold for committing war crimes very high. The phrase 'whoever *knowingly* commits, in the context of an international or non-international armed conflict the following criminal Acts' (emphasis added) is problematic because it requires knowledge of the commission of war crimes.

In contrast to the ICC Rome Statute, article 188 on war crimes against persons does not include: (i) sexual slavery; (ii) making improper use of a flag of truce, of the flag or of the military insignia and uniform of the enemy or of the UN, as well as of the distinctive emblems of the Geneva Conventions, resulting in death or serious physical injury; and (iii) the transfer, directly or indirectly, by the Occupying Power of parts of its own civilian population into the territory it occupies, or the deportation or transfer of all parts of the population of the occupied territory within or outside its territory.

The definition of torture as a war crime captures recent developments in the international jurisprudence, which does not require the involvement of an official for the act to constitute torture.[37] Under article 188(1)(b), torture as a war crime is committed when an individual:

> tortures a protected person or more or subjects him to inhumane treatment by inflicting a serious bodily or mental pain upon him with the intent to obtain information or confession from or for the purpose of punishing, intimidating or coercing him for any other reason based on any kind of discrimination.

The Armed Forces Act 2007 also introduced in article 153 war crimes offences committed by combatant personnel against civilians during military operations; article 154 on offences against persons enjoying special protection; article 155 on attacks against civilians; article 162 on threatening and displacing the populace; and offences against prisoners of war. However, such offences are confusing because the definition and elements of the crimes are mixed with the elements of the crime of genocide and crimes against humanity. This applies to crimes such as torture, the forceful transfer of children, and intentionally subjecting groups to conditions of livelihood, with intent to destroy them totally or partially. It also applies to offences of murder of an individual, or individuals of a national, ethnic,

---

35   Schabas. 2006, 51–66.
36   Article 8, ICC Elements of Crimes.
37   See on this development Burchard, C. 2008. Torture in the jurisprudence of the Ad Hoc Tribunals: a critical assessment. *Journal of International Criminal Justice* 6(2), 159–82.

racial or religious group, with intent to partially, or totally exterminate, or destroy, 'within the context of a clear methodical conduct, directed against such group'. Similar confusion concerns war crimes and crimes against humanity in relation to crimes committed against the civilian population such as slavery and unlawful detention 'within the framework of a methodical direct and widespread attack, directed against civilians'.

Lack of adequate criminalization of torture and enforced disappearances

The three international crimes outlined above set a high threshold for elements such as deliberate intent to destroy a group in the case of genocide, the existence of a widespread or systematic attack against civilians in the case of crimes against humanity and the existence of an armed conflict in the case of war crimes. International human rights law imposes specific duties on states to repress and punish serious or gross violations of human rights, irrespective of whether they constitute genocide, crimes against humanity or war crimes, which include extrajudicial, summary or arbitrary executions, torture, enforced disappearances and gender-based violence.[38] The Criminal Act (as amended in 2009) does not adequately incorporate or define a number of serious human rights violations amounting to crimes. The crime of torture, for example, is not defined in line with the definition in article 1 of the UN Convention against Torture and Other Cruel, Inhuman or Degrading Treatment or Punishment. The current Sudanese Criminal Act explicitly criminalizes torture in article 115(2).[39] However, this article falls short of international standards as it does not define the elements of the act of torture. The offence only applies to the use of 'torture' to extract or to prevent someone from giving information but does not cover the other purposes recognized under international law, such as intimidation or coercion. The maximum punishment of torture is three months, which is clearly inadequate in light of the seriousness of the offence of torture. Similar considerations apply to the crime of hurt in article 142 of the Criminal Act, which may apply where an official inflicts physical injuries, and stipulates a maximum punishment of two years.[40]

---

38   Human Rights Committee (HRC). 2004. *General Comment 31: The Nature of the General Legal Obligation Imposed on States Parties to the Covenant.* UN Doc. CCPR/C/74/CRP.4/Rev.6, para. 8.

39   Article 115(2) of the Criminal Act of 1991: 'Every person who, having public authority entices, or threatens, or tortures any witness, or accused, or opponent to give, or refrain from giving any information in any action, shall be punished with imprisonment, for a term not exceeding three months, or with fine, or both'.

40   Article 142(1) of the Criminal Act of 1991: 'There shall be deemed to commit the offence of hurt whoever causes any pain, or diseases to another person, and shall be punished with imprisonment for a term not exceeding six month, or with fine, or with both; (2): Where hurt has occurred by dangerous means, such as poison, or intoxicating drugs, or where hurt is caused with the intention of drawing a confession from another, or compelling

The crime of enforced disappearances is not recognized in the Criminal Act 1991. Article 2 of the International Convention for the Protection of All Persons from Enforced Disappearance defines it with elements similar to those of enforced disappearance as a crime against humanity, as:

> The arrest, detention, abduction or any other form of deprivation of liberty by agents of the State or by persons or groups of persons acting with the authorization, support or acquiescence of the State, followed by a refusal to acknowledge the deprivation of liberty or by concealment of the fate or whereabouts of the disappeared person, which place such a person outside the protection of the law.

The current Criminal Act 1991 contains several offences that may be applied in cases of enforced disappearances, such as kidnapping (article 162), unlawful confinement (article 164) and unlawful detention (article 165). Article 165(2) contains elements of the crime of enforced disappearance, but it does not apply specifically to state officials. Its definition is in part too narrow as it requires a particular purpose for the unlawful detention, and the prescribed maximum punishment of three years' imprisonment does not adequately reflect the seriousness of the offence.

The absence of essential international criminal law principles

Command and Superior Responsibility

The Criminal Act 1991 (as amended in 2009) does not include adequate provisions that govern accountability for the commission of international crimes. It recognizes traditional modes of criminal liability for those who directly commit an offence and for anyone who orders, aids and abets an offence, as well as for those who engage in criminal conspiracy in relation to certain offences.[41] However, the act does not recognize criminal liability on the grounds of command/superior responsibility. Command or superior responsibility is a well-established mode of criminal liability in international criminal law that imposes an obligation on commanders and superiors (which includes formal and informal command and hierarchies) to prevent crimes and does not allow them to abdicate responsibility for serious crimes committed by their subordinates.[42]

---

that other to do an act contrary to the law, the offender shall be punished with imprisonment for a term not exceeding two years, and may also be punished with fine'.

41   See Part II and III of the Criminal Act of 1991.

42   See Article 24(1) ICTY Statute, article 23(1) ICTR Statute, and article 27 ICC Rome Statute.

Article 22 of the Armed Forces Act 1999 shields superior army officers from criminal responsibility in Sudan's civil courts for acts committed by their subordinates. Article 39(7) (Immunities and Privileges) also provides that 'members of the People's Armed Forces have no right to take legal proceedings in front of the civil judiciary during and after the service for any negative effects impacted upon them as a result of executing any lawful orders issued to them by those superiors during their service'.[43] This article contravenes article 28 of the ICC Rome Statute, which provides for criminal responsibility of commanders and other superiors. It also contravenes article 27(1) (Irrelevance of official capacity) and article 33 (Superior orders and prescription of law) of the ICC Rome Statute. Both articles apply equally to all persons (whether civilian or military), including heads of states or governments, members of the government or of parliament, elected representatives or government officials who shall in no case be exempted from criminal responsibility under the ICC Statute.[44] These above-mentioned provisions were not substantially changed in subsequent legislative amendments.

Immunities

One of the important principles of international criminal law not addressed by the recently enacted Armed Forces Act 2007 or the Criminal Act 1991 (as amended in 2009) is the issue of immunities for the commission of international crimes. Criminalizing genocide, crimes against humanity and war crimes without removing immunity legislation for officials is bound to result in partial impunity for which there is no objective justification.[45] Under Sudanese law, police officers, security forces members and collaborators and members of the armed forces are granted substantive and procedural immunity. They can only be subjected to a full investigation, prosecution and trial if the head of the respective forces explicitly lifts their immunity. Many current laws provide legal immunities (criminal and civil immunity) for state agents for acts, including human rights violations, done in the course of their duties, in particular, the Armed Forces Act 2007, the Police Act 2008 and the National Security Act 2010.[46]

Article 34 of the Armed Forces Act 2007 (on the institution of legal proceedings against personnel) provides immunity from criminal prosecution for soldiers and officers during the course of their duty. Article 34(1) stipulates that:

> There shall not be deemed an offence any act, which emanates from any officer, or soldier in good faith, in the course, or by reason of performing the business of

---

43   Author's Arabic translation.

44   See article 27(1) ICC Rome Statute.

45   See article 7(2) ICTY Statute, article 6(2) ICTR Statute and article 27 ICC Rome Statute.

46   Article 42(2) of the Armed Forces Act, 2007; article 45(1) of the Police Act, 2008, and article 52(3) of the National Security Act of 2010.

his/her post, or discharge of any duty imposed thereon, or any act done thereby, under any power delegated, or conferred thereon, under the Criminal Procedure Act, or any other law in force, any regulations or orders made under any one of them.

Furthermore, article 34(2) categorically provides that:

no proceedings shall be taken against any officer, or soldier, who commits an act, which constitutes an offence, which occurs in the course, or by reason of his/ her discharge of his/her duties or carrying out of any lawful order, issued thereto in this capacity thereof, and he/she shall not be tried, save upon permission, issued by the President of the Republic, or whoever he may authorize.

This immunity also extends to civil suits with the proviso that *dia* (blood money) is to be paid to victims on behalf of the armed forces in case their members violate the law.[47] The extension of immunities to the army violates the Bill of Rights of the Interim National Constitution 2005, in particular equality before the law and the right to litigation and international criminal law principles.

The Police Act 2008 also maintains immunities. Article 45 of the Act was taken verbatim from article 46 of the repealed Police Act 1999 and replicated the same immunities for the police in the new Act. Article 45 forbids any 'criminal procedure against a police officer accused of an incident representing a criminal offence committed while performing his official duty or because of his official act' unless approved by the minister or his delegate. Article 45 thus represents one of the immunity clauses protecting the police. It also raises an accountability issue.[48] Accountability to oversight institutions, which may include courts, legislatures, complaint review boards and the media, is an important underpinning of democratic policing. Individual officers at all hierarchical levels must not only be accountable to their supervisors for their own conduct, but their conduct must accord with the national law and with professional codes of ethnics and discipline. In the case of criminal conduct all officers should be accountable to the court. Article 45 not only raises the issue of criminal conduct of police and immunity from prosecution, but also of internal mechanisms of accountability of police

---

47 Article 34(3) provides that, '[w]here the discharge of the duty, or carrying out of any other lawful order entails death, or injury, which requires *diya*, the State shall bear payment of *diya*, or compensation on behalf of the officer, or soldier, who acts in good faith, in accordance with the provisions of this section'. For an extensive analysis of the military and Islamic military laws in Sudan (1983, 1986, 1999). See Babiker, 2007.

48 'Accountability entails "a set of normative prescriptions about who should be required to give accountability, to whom, when, how and about what."' Osse, A.2006. *Understanding Policing: A Resource for Human Right Activists*. London: Amnesty International, 185. See also *UN Code of Conduct for Law Enforcement Officials*, UN General Assembly Resolution 34/ 169 (1979).

superiors and ministers. If superiors turn a blind eye to police criminality or misconduct (that is not giving permission to lift immunity) external measures to address misconduct or criminality will have little effect.

Apart from the legal immunity, the Police Act 2008 also lacks accountability mechanisms. Article 45 does not refer to the duties of the Minister of Interior with regard to the criminal act of the police and no internal mechanisms are in place to ensure that the powers of the ministers or any other bodies will not be arbitrarily used. For an internal system to be effective it needs to be backed up by a competent judicial system and independent oversight bodies.

Article 52(3) of the National Security Act 2010 also retain immunity provisions, notwithstanding repeated calls by regional and international bodies, including the African Union High Level Panel on Darfur,[49] as well as Sudanese civil society to abolish immunities because they foster impunity.[50]

The immunity provisions contained in the Police Act 2008, the Armed Forces Act 2007 and the National Security Act 2010 are not in harmony with international criminal law standards and recognized practices, particularly when such provisions are applied in the context of the multiplicity of armed conflicts that have afflicted the Sudan for decades and witnessed the commission of war crimes and crimes against humanity. To legalize immunities in such a context has serious repercussions. International criminal law does not recognize immunities for international crimes because they are by their very nature so serious that no one should be exempt from prosecution. There is a consistent practice of the UN, international tribunals and national courts of refusing to recognize the validity of any immunity or amnesty that might free a person or a category of persons from legal responsibility for international crimes. This principle is also recognized as a matter of international human rights law according to which states are obliged to remove immunities for serious human rights violations. The Human Rights Committee General Comment 31, states:

> where public officials or State agents have committed violations of the
> Covenant rights referred to in this paragraph, the States Parties concerned

---

49   African Union High-Level Panel on Darfur (AUPD). 2009. *Darfur: The Quest for Peace, Justice and Reconciliation, Report to the African Union*. PSC/AHG/2 (CCVII), xix, at para. 25(c) and (d); 56–63, at paras 215–38; and 91, 92, at para. 336. See also Babiker, M.A. 2010. The International Criminal Court and the Darfur crimes: the dilemma of peace and supra-national criminal justice, *The International Journal of African Renaissance Studies*. 5(1), 82–100.

50   See REDRESS and SORD. 2009. *Security for All: Reforming Sudan's National Security Service*. [Online, September] Available at: http://www.pclrs.org/downloads/ Resources/Resources/Security%20for%20all%20Final.pdf [accessed 28 December 2010] 13–14. See also Amnesty International, 2010. *The Agents of Fear: The National Security Service in Sudan*. [Online, July] Available at: http://www.amnesty.org/en/library/asset/ AFR54/010/2010/en/7b11e50c-3a0b-4699-8b6f-08a27f751c6c/afr540102010en.pdf [accessed 24 June 2011].

may not relieve perpetrators from personal responsibility, as has occurred with certain amnesties (see General Comment 20(44)) and prior legal immunities and indemnities. Furthermore, no official status justifies persons who may be accused of responsibility for such violations being held immune from legal responsibility.[51]

In its practice, the Human Rights Committee has repeatedly found immunity legislation to be incompatible with the right to an effective remedy and the concomitant duty to investigate and prosecute officials for serious violations including in the case of Sudan: '[i]t [the Human Rights Committee] is particularly concerned at the immunity provided for in Sudanese law and untransparent procedure for waiving immunity in the event of criminal proceedings against state agents'.[52] Immunities are also incompatible with Sudan's Bill of Rights, in particular article 27(3), which incorporates international treaties ratified by Sudan, and the fundamental rights of freedom from extrajudicial killings and torture (articles 28 and 33) in conjunction with the right to litigation (article 35).[53]

Recent developments of international law confirm that heads of states and senior officials no longer enjoy immunity for international crimes, at least not before international tribunals, as recognized in article 7(2) of the Statute of the International Criminal Tribunal for former Yugoslavia (ICTY), article 6(2) of the Statute of the International Criminal Tribunal for Rwanda (ICTR) and article 27 of the ICC Rome Statute. In Sudan, the Criminal Procedure Act 1991 (as amended in 2009) introduced immunities related to the prosecution of international crimes by non-Sudanese courts and other international bodies. Its article 3 provides for procedural immunities as it prohibits investigation or proceedings outside Sudan against any Sudanese person accused of committing any violation of international humanitarian laws including crimes against humanity, genocide and war crimes. It also prohibits anyone in Sudan from assisting in the extradition of any Sudanese for the prosecution of the above crimes.[54] These amendments act as legal deterrent for any individual or group contemplating cooperation with the ICC. These provisions run counter to the international trend, and obligations to agree on legal mechanisms to assist and cooperate in the prosecution of international and transnational crimes.

---

51   HRC. 2004, para. 18.

52   HRC. 2007. *Concluding observations: Sudan.* UN Doc. CCPR/C/SDN/CO/3/CRP.1, para. 9.

53   See REDRESS and KCHRED. 2008a, 10.

54   Amendment of the Criminal Procedure Act, adopted in the National Assembly on 20 May 2009 and signed into law by the President of the Republic on 9 July 2009.

Statutes of limitation

The 2009 amendments of the Criminal Act 1991 did not include the procedural changes needed to give effect to the prosecution of the international crimes provided therein. International crimes (added to chapter 18 of the Criminal Act 1991) are subject to a prescription period of ten years pursuant to article 38(a) of the Criminal Procedure Act 1991, since the offences are punishable with death or imprisonment of ten years or more. Several international treaties and statutes of international criminal tribunals provide for the non-applicability of statutes of limitation for international crimes. For example, article 29 of the ICC Rome Statute (non-applicability of statute of limitations) provides 'the crimes within the jurisprudence of the Court shall not be subject to any statute of limitations'. As there is no statutory limitation provided within the Statute itself, it seems that article 29 is directed more at national legislation.[55] The effects of gross violations of human rights are linked to the most serious crimes to which, according to authoritative legal opinion, statutory limitations shall not apply.[56] Recent practices of international jurisprudence recognize the relevance of this doctrine not only for genocide, crimes against humanity and war crimes, but also for gross violations of human rights such as torture.[57] Many countries, such as Ecuador and Paraguay, have introduced legislation that abolishes any statutes of limitation for international crimes.[58] There is also national jurisprudence where courts have upheld the constitutionality of laws that remove statutes of limitation for past violations in countries such as the Czech Republic and Hungary.[59]

Although international opposition to statutory limitation for war crimes, crimes against humanity and genocide has taken the form of UN General Assembly Resolutions, and treaties within the UN system and that of the Council of Europe, such treaties have not been a great success in terms of their signature and ratification. The low rate of adhesion to the UN Convention on the Non-Applicability of Statutory Limitations to War Crimes and Crimes Against Humanity, 1968, has led some academics to contest the suggestion that it reflects a

---

55   Schabas. 2006, 115.

56   See UN Special Rapporteur, Theo van Boven. 1993. *Study Concerning the Right to Restitution, Compensation and Rehabilitation for Victims of Gross Violations of Human Rights and Fundamental Freedoms*. Final Report. UN Doc. E/CN.4/Sub.2/1993/8, para. 135.

57   Independent expert to update the Set of principles to combat impunity, Diane Orentlicher. 2005. *Principles for the Protection and Promotion of Human Rights Through Action to Combat Impunity*. UN Doc. E/CN.4/2005/102/Add.1, para. 47.

58   See article 23(2) of the Constitution of Ecuador of 1998 and article 5 of the Constitution of Paraguay of 1992.

59   See Czech Constitutional Court Pl. US 19/9321 (1993) and Hungarian Constitutional Court, 53/1993 (1993).

customary norm.[60] Many domestic criminal law systems provide for the statutory limitation of crimes, even very serious ones, and the role of article 29 of the ICC Rome Statute would appear to be part of the complex relationship between national and international judicial systems. It acts as a bar to states that might refuse to surrender offenders on the grounds that the offence was time-barred under national legislation. In fact, the recent practice in Sudan testifies to this reality. Judicial practice acknowledges that statute of limitations apply even in serious offences such as torture. In the case of *Farouq Mohamed Ibrahim El Nour v Government of the Sudan and the National Assembly*,[61] the complainant submitted a petition to the Constitutional Court on 28 December 2006 in which he requested the court to rule on the constitutionality of article 38 of the Criminal Procedure Act that stipulates a period of two, three and ten years (depending on the nature of the crime) after which the complainant is barred from instituting legal proceedings. The petitioner alleged that he was tortured by the National Intelligence and Security Services (NISS) when he was detained on 30 November 1989. He argued that his inability to institute criminal proceedings under article 38 of the Criminal Procedures Act is a violation of article 35 of the Interim National Constitution (INC) 2005 (right to litigation) as well as to equality before the law. He also argued that article 33(b) of the NISS Act 1999 that provided for immunities for security forces members during the course of their duties violates article 31 of the INC (equality before the law). The Constitutional Court dismissed the petition, stating that Sudan was not bound by article 29 of the ICC Rome Statute or the UN Convention against Torture. However, it failed to take into consideration the jurisprudence of the UN Human Rights Committee and the African Commission on Human and Peoples' Rights on the duty to investigate and prosecute torture under the ICCPR and the African Charter on Human and Peoples' Rights respectively, to both of which Sudan is a state party.[62]

Reparations for victims of international crimes

The right to reparation for international crimes and gross violations of human rights that may not amount to international crimes is recognized in the statutes

---

60   See Ratner, S. and Abrahams, J. 1997. *Accountability for Human Rights Atrocities in International Law: Beyond the Nuremberg Legacy*. Oxford: Clarendon Press, 126. Nevertheless, in the Barbie case, the French Court de cassation ruled that the prohibition on statutory limitations for crimes against humanity is now part of customary law. See Schabas. 2006, 116.

61   *Farouq Mohamed Ibrahim Al Nour v (1) Government of Sudan; (2) Legislative Body*; Final order by Justice Abdallah Aalmin Albashir, President of the Constitutional Court, 6 November 2008.

62   HRC. 2004. para. 18.

of international criminal tribunals,[63] international human rights treaties binding on Sudan[64] and the landmark resolution of the UN General Assembly: Basic Principles and Guidelines on the Right to a Remedy and Reparation for Victims of Gross Violations of International Human Rights Law and Serious Violations of International Humanitarian Law.[65] Those who have suffered harm through acts or omissions that constitute a violation, are entitled to effective access to judicial and non-judicial procedures and to adequate and effective forms of reparation.[66] This right should include compensation and other measures that are often equally important in the circumstances, such as restitution, rehabilitation, satisfaction and other guarantees of non-repetition.[67]

Sudanese criminal and military laws do not recognize an explicit right to reparation or effective remedy for victims of international crimes or other serious violations for that matter, such as grave breaches of the Geneva Conventions 1949. For example, the Armed Forces Act 2007 does not cover comprehensive state liability to pay compensation for the commission of international crimes and serious violations of human rights. Although it is true that the state assumes responsibility for paying compensation in cases of murder, semi-intentional and negligent homicide and wounds committed by any members of the police or armed forces, such practice does not cover all violations and thus still falls short of establishing a legal framework in line with international standards and the Bill of Rights of the Interim Constitution 2005.

Conclusion

The incorporation of the international crimes of genocide, crimes against humanity and war crimes into the Sudanese criminal justice system constitutes progress, and is a positive and significant step. However, the process of incorporation has been haphazard and is incomplete, with many gaps remaining in the body of the new legislation and its subsequent amendments. This applies in particular to international criminal law principles (that is, command responsibility, immunities, statute of limitations and reparation) as part of the criminal and military laws. In the absence of such principles the effective prosecution of international crimes will face serious legal obstacles at the substantive and procedural levels. The definitions of international crimes need to be reviewed so as to be in harmony

---

63   In particular articles 75 and 79 of the ICC Rome Statute.

64   Article 2(3) of the International Covenant on Civil and Political Rights.

65   *Basic Principles and Guidelines on the Right to a Remedy and Reparation for Victims of Gross Violations of International Human Rights Law and Serious Violations of International Humanitarian Law: Human Rights Resolution,* UN General Assembly Resolution 60/147 (2006).

66   *Basic Principles.*

67   *Basic Principles.*

with the standards of the ICC and the dynamic interpretations recently adopted by international tribunals and courts. Sudan, as a country afflicted by protracted armed conflicts and accused of committing and of being involved in international crimes, needs to continue the process of criminal law reform. For this process to be meaningful, stakeholders must make genuine efforts towards effective prosecutions of international crimes allegedly committed in this country.

Chapter 8

The Implementation of International Criminal Law in Arab States: The Jordanian Experience

Ibrahim Aljazy

Introduction

There is a widely held perception that Arab states have not committed themselves to international criminal justice, a view that has been informed if not reinforced by the limited number of states in the region that have become parties to the Rome Statue of the International Criminal Court (ICC). However, some Arab international lawyers have been at the forefront of the development of international criminal law, and the question of accountability for international crimes is becoming increasingly prominent in the region. In addition, Arab states have collectively worked on making international criminal law relevant in the regional context, an endeavour that has resulted in the Arab model law of the ICC prepared by the Arab Justice Ministers' Council, also with a view of facilitating implementation of pertinent norms. These developments paint a picture of a region where the importance of justice for international crimes is undeniable but where both limited political will and capacity are critical factors that may explain the lack of concrete measures taken to address the issue.

Jordan constitutes a notable exception. It is the first Arab state that has become a party to the ICC Rome Statute and embarked on a process to implement the same in its domestic legal system. These developments are taking place in a country that has made some efforts to strengthen human rights protection and the rule of law within the framework of a well-developed legal system.[1] The close relationship between the concept and principles of human rights and the rules of international humanitarian law with the principles of international criminal law has motivated Jordanian decision makers to pay greater attention to the role played by the ICC.[2]

---

1   Tarawneh, M. 2005. *Al-Mahkamah al-Jina'iyah al-Dawleyah* [International Criminal Court: A study of the provision and application and Jordan's position of its Statute]. 1st Edition. Amman: Amman Human Rights Centre, 200.

2   Abu el-Wafa, A. 2006. *Al-Nathariyah al-'Amah lil Qanoun al-Dawli al-Insani* [General Theory of International Humanitarian Law]. 1st Edition. Cairo: Dar Al-Nahdhah al-Arabiyeh, 138–9.

This chapter examines the Jordanian experience against the background of the position taken by Arab states on the ICC. It focuses on obstacles and objections encountered, but also explores the normative significance of, and developments surrounding the Arab model law. This sets the context in which the chapter charts and analyzes the process aimed at implementing the ICC Rome Statute in Jordan, particularly with a view to determining the factors that have impacted on progress made, or the lack of it, in this regard. The importance of the Jordanian implementation experience as a precedent cannot be overstated in a region that has been experiencing serious armed conflicts for long periods. Jordan's example carries the potential to promote and assist in efforts to raise the acceptance and the legal recognition of the ICC Rome Statute. Its potential benefit for advocacy efforts in the region and for Arab states contemplating ratification and implementation of the ICC Rome Statute is readily apparent. Conversely, a failure to effectively and adequately implement this reform in Jordan may further perpetuate perceptions of the lack of capacity and commitment of Arab states to international criminal law, which would constitute a significant setback.

The genesis of the International Criminal Court

The first proposal to establish an international criminal court dates back to 1872 and has been attributed to Gustave Moynier.[3] Growing demands for an international criminal tribunal gained momentum in the wake of the atrocities committed during the First- and the Second World War.[4] This is evidenced by attempts to prosecute the then German emperor for crimes against the peace and crimes against humanity, as provided for in articles 227–30 of the 1919 Treaty of Versailles.[5] Early attempts to establish a treaty to create an international criminal court, such as by the League of Nations in 1937, failed spectacularly, not gaining a single ratification,[6] but the Nuremberg and Tokyo war crimes tribunals following the

---

3   Hall, C.K. 1998. The first proposal for a Permanent Criminal Court. *International Review of the Red Cross*, 38(322), 57–74.

4   For more details on the early twentieth-century efforts to establish international criminal courts see Bassiouni, M.C. 2002. *Al-Mahkamah al-Jina'iyah al-Dawliyah* [International Criminal Court]. Cairo: Matba'at Rose al-Yousef al-Jadidah, 8–33.

5   This treaty conferred upon individual citizens of the victorious powers the right to submit, to the various mixed arbitral tribunals established for the purpose, claims against the government and nationals of the defeated central powers. See Ghazaleh, K.H.A. 2010. *Al-Mahkamah al-Jina'iyah al-Dawliyeh wa al-Jara'im a;-Dawliyeh* [International Criminal Court and International Crimes]. 1st Edition. Amman, Dar Jalees al-Zaman, 26–7, and Bokah, S.T. *Jaraem Didh alinsaniyeah fi dhou alnidham alasasi lil mahkamah aljiyai'yah aldawliyah* [Crimes against Humanity: In light of the provisions of the ICC]. Beirut: Al-Halabi Legal Publications, 8–12.

6   See on the attempts to establish an international criminal court in 1937 and 2002, Chadwick, E. 2004. A Tale of Two Courts: the creation of a jurisdiction. *Journal of Conflict*

Second World War planted the seeds for a permanent international criminal court, and the idea was taken up again after the end of the Cold War.[7] It was in particular the experience of the ad hoc tribunals, namely the International Criminal Tribunal of Former Yugoslavia (ICTY) and the International Criminal Tribunal of Rwanda (ICTR), which heightened calls for the creation of a permanent international criminal court. On 17 July 1998, the Rome Diplomatic Conference, which had been convened at the initiative of the United Nations (UN) General Assembly, adopted the Rome Statute that created the ICC and entered into force on 1 July 2002. The court was vested with jurisdiction over the international crimes of genocide, crimes against humanity, war crimes and the crime of aggression.[8] It was to exercise its jurisdiction on the basis of 'complementarity' – that is, the ICC would only investigate and prosecute these crimes where the state concerned was unable or unwilling to do this itself.[9] Several states in the Middle East and elsewhere declined to support the establishment of the ICC and refused to sign or ratify the ICC Rome Statute, which they considered, *inter alia*, an infringement of their sovereignty. Djibouti and Comoros Island were the only two members of the League of Arab States, other than Jordan, to have ratified the ICC Rome Statute by May 2011, out of a total of 115 states parties.[10] This situation may change following the political revolutions in the region in late 2010 and early 2011 in the wake of which several governments, such as those of Tunisia and Egypt, expressed their intent to become a party to the ICC Rome Statute.[11]

---

and Security Law, 9(1), 71–101.

7   During the 1950s, the United States proposed the creation of a permanent international criminal court. The UN International Law Commission took up the issue and produced a draft statute for such court in 1994. See Sands, P. 2006. *Lawless World*. London: Penguin, 50.

8   Article 5(2) ICC Rome Statute provides that: '[t]he Court shall exercise jurisdiction over the crime of aggression once a provision is adopted in accordance with articles 121 and 123 defining the crime and setting out the conditions under which the Court shall exercise jurisdiction with respect to this crime'. These provisions were adopted at the Kampala Review Conference in June 2010, and the court may exercise jurisdiction over the crime of aggression pursuant to article 15bis(2) and (3) 'after the ratification or acceptance of the amendments by thirty states parties' and 'subject to a decision to be taken after 1 January 2017 by the same majority of States Parties as is required for the adoption of an amendment to the Statute'.

9   Article 17 ICC Rome Statute.

10   See for the status of ratification the website of the International Criminal Court. Available at: http://www.icc-cpi.int/Menus/ASP/states+parties/ [accessed 6 January 2011]. Jordan deposited its instrument of ratification on 11 April 2002, Djibouti on 5 November 2002, and Comoros on 18 August 2006.

11   See Kersten, M. 2011. The Arab World and the ICC: A New Chapter or Smoke and Mirrors? *Justice in Conflict* [Online, 30 May] Available at: http://justiceinconflict. org/2011/05/30/the-arab-world-and-the-icc-a-new-chapter-or-smoke-and-mirrors/ [accessed 11 June 2011].

The ratification and implementation of the ICC Rome Statute by Arab States: Obstacles and objections

States contemplating the ratification and incorporation of the ICC Rome Statute in their domestic legal system are frequently faced with obstacles that can complicate if not altogether frustrate implementation. Various aspects related to national sovereignty, particularly the modalities of the exercise of jurisdiction over nationals, constitute key factors in this regard. Other factors include constitutional and legislative barriers as well as concerns regarding the politics associated with international instruments. This is particularly true in the Arab world, where many states and observers view international economic, political and legal organizations as tools used by western powers only to serve and further their multifaceted interests.[12]

Implementing the ICC Rome Statute in Islamic or Arab states requires, as in other legal systems or regions, that states bring their constitution and statutory law in conformity with the statute, which may necessitate a string of legislative reforms.[13] This task can pose considerable difficulties, largely due to the complex procedures for amending their constitutions. Such amendments, particularly those related to the immunity conferred to national leaders and officials where such constitutional clauses are inconsistent with the ICC Rome Statute, have formed a major obstacle that prompted many Arab states to refrain from ratifying it in the first place.[14]

Defining international crimes that fall within the ICC's jurisdiction has formed an even greater obstacle for Islamic and Arab states. Article 7 of the ICC Rome Statute, for example, defines the crime against humanity in very broad terms.[15] Most of the various crimes against humanity provided for in article 7 are derived from international human rights treaties and declarations such as the International Covenant on Civil and Political Rights and the Universal Declaration of Human Rights respectively. For these reasons, states with a Muslim majority have expressed the same objections that they had already expressed in relation to these

---

12   Shoamanesh, S. 2009. The ICC and the Middle East: A needed Relationship. *Jurist Legal News & Research.* [Online, 24 September] Available at: http://jurist.law.pitt.edu/ forumy/2009/09/icc-and-middle-east-needed-relationship.php [accessed 12 December 2009].

13   Majid, A. 2001. *Al-Mahkamah al-Jina'ayah al-Dawleyah wa al-Siyadah al-Wattaniyah* [International Criminal Court and National Sovereignty]. Cairo: Al-Ahram Centre for Political and Strategic Studies, 107–9.

14   It is noteworthy that many Arab states have adopted considerable constitutional reforms. Several of the current Arab constitutions were the subject of major amendments in the 1990s (for example Lebanon in 1990, Saudi Arabia in 1992, Yemen in 1994, Oman in 1996 and Morocco in 1996) and at the beginning of the new millennium (Bahrain 2002 and Qatar 2003).

15   Yashwi, L.M. 2005. *The permanent International Criminal Court and the extent of its jurisdiction in adjudicating the violations of the occupying forces in Iraq.* Research Thesis. Muta University, 124 (unpublished, copy on file with author).

international human rights treaties and declarations when considering the scope of the article, claiming that it does not take into consideration the social and cultural characteristics prevailing in their countries.[16] This applies particularly to article 7(1)(k) of the ICC Rome Statute:

(1) For the purpose of this Statute, 'crime against humanity' means any of the following acts when committed as part of a widespread or systematic attack directed against any civilian population.

(k) Other inhumane acts of a similar character intentionally causing great suffering, or serious injury to body or to mental or physical health ....

Some countries that have a Muslim majority, such as Saudi Arabia, retain criminal legislation that provides for the imposition of Islamic punishments such as lashings or amputation of limbs for crimes such as theft.[17] Such laws may be considered to fall within the scope of article 7 of the ICC Rome Statute and states may be concerned that the notion of crimes against humanity may in this context be used against their political and legal regimes.

The initial absence of a clear definition for the crime of aggression has also attracted objections from many countries in the world. The crime has great significance for Arab countries and those Arab states that attended the Rome Conference sought to include it in the list of the crimes falling under the jurisdiction of the court. During the Rome negotiations it was agreed that a definition for the crime of aggression will be determined at a later stage by the ICC Assembly of States Parties.[18] The fact that Arab states did not ratify the ICC Rome Statute halted their efforts to influence the definition of the crime of aggression; the Assembly of States finally agreed on the definition and modalities of the exercise of jurisdiction over the crime of aggression in June 2010.[19]

Another source of contention has been the power of the UN Security Council, by means of article 16 of the ICC Rome Statute, to defer ICC investigations and prosecutions for twelve months on a renewable basis. The potential political interference inherent in this power granted to the UN Security Council prompted

---

16   Yashwi. 2005.

17   See Committee against Torture. 2002. *Concluding Observations: Saudi Arabia.* UN Doc. CAT/C/CR/28/5, para. 4(b).

18   Schabas, W. 2007. *An Introduction to the International Criminal Court.* 3rd Edition. Cambridge: Cambridge University Press, 88 and 133–40.

19   At the Kampala ICC treaty review Conference, the then 112 states parties agreed on 11 June 2010 on the definition of the crime of aggression and on the exercise of the ICC's jurisdiction in this regard. The definition to be included in the statute is that recommended by the Special Working Group on the Crime of Aggression prior to Kampala. See http://www.icc-cpi.int/iccdocs/asp_docs/Resolutions/RC-Res.6-ENG.pdf [accessed 6 January 2011].

a number of states to object to the inclusion of the article in the ICC Rome Statute during the Rome Conference.[20]

A number of additional factors have contributed to the opposition of Arab states to the ICC and help to explain the limited number of ratifications. These include:

- The perception that major powers may use the ICC to put pressure on Arab countries. This issue was at the centre of heated debates in the Arab media following the 2005 UN Security Council resolution that referred the Darfur situation to the ICC prosecutor.[21] A further issue concerned the possible exercise of referral powers by the UN Security Council in relation to acts committed in the course of national resistance against occupying forces, with situations such as in Lebanon providing a case in point.[22]

- The concern of states that the ICC prosecutor may abuse his considerable powers. This concern came to the fore in the context of an application made by the prosecutor on 14 July 2008 for an arrest warrant for President Omar Hassan Ahmed al-Bashir on charges of genocide, crimes against humanity and war crimes. On 4 March 2009, the ICC issued an arrest warrant on charges of crimes against humanity and war crimes,[23] and on appeal, the

---

20   See on the ICC and the UN Security Council, Hassan, S.A. 2004. *Al-Mahkamah al-Jina'iyah al-Dawliyah* [The International Criminal Court]. Cairo: Dar al-Nahdhah al-Arabiyah, 299–305. The Egyptian Government, as expressed by Chief Justice Maraghi during the Rome Conference, sought to limit the role of the UN Security Council to cases concerning the crime of aggression. Justice Maraghi also rejected the proposed power of referral conferred on the UN Security Council. Available at: www.un.org/icc/speeches/615egy4.htm, 4. A similar position was expressed by Qatar, which stressed the need for the court to be impartial and independent from 'the control of any political authority'. Available at: www.un.org/icc/speeches/618qat3.htm, 2. See for other relevant positions, the statements by delegates from Syria, available at: www.un.org/icc/speeches/616syr3.htm, 3; United Arab Emirates, available at: www.un.org/icc/speeches/617uae4.htm, 3; Libya, available at: www.un.org/icc/speeches/617lib3.htm, 3; Kuwait, available at: www.un.org/icc/speeches/616kuw4.htm, 4; Lebanon, available at: www.un.org/icc/speeches/617leb.htm, 1; and the Sudan, available at: www.un.org/icc/speeches/618sud.htm, 2 [all accessed 6 December 2010].

21   UN Security Council Resolution 1593 (31 March 2005) adopted under Chapter VII of the UN Charter.

22   Harb, A.J. 2010. *Al-Qada' al-Jina'i al-Dawli, al-Mahakim al-Jina'iyeh al-Dawliyeh* [International Criminal Judiciary, International Criminal Courts]. 1st Edition. Beirut: Dar al-Manhal al-Lubnani, 598.

23   ICC Pre-Trial Chamber. *Warrant of Arrest for Omar Hassan Ahmad Al Bashir.* ICC-02/05-01/09-1. 04-03-2009. 1/8 SL, PT. Available at: http://www.icc-cpi.int/iccdocs/doc/doc639078.pdf [accessed 6 January 2011]. It is worth noting that the Arab League rejected the issuance of the arrest warrant. See 2009. Sudan's president safe to attend Arab summit in Quatar. Arab League rejects ICC request to arrest Bashir. *Al Arabiya* [Online, 17 March] Available at: http://www.alarabiya.net/articles/2009/03/17/68653.html [accessed 6 January 2011].

arrest warrant was amended in July 2010 to include charges of genocide.[24] In response Arab states, together with African states and bodies called on the UN Security Council to use the very deferral powers they had objected to during the Rome Conference.[25]

- The varying levels of prohibition of surrendering nationals to the ICC, or any other court for that matter, in the constitutions and laws of many Arab states. Article 38 of the Constitution of the United Arab Emirates, for example, explicitly declares that '[t]he extradition of citizens and of political refugees shall be prohibited'.[26]

- Concerns regarding the removal of immunities granted to heads of state in line with article 27 of the ICC Rome Statute, which may expose these highest ranking officials to ICC investigations and prosecutions if the states were to become party to the ICC Rome Statute.[27] Provisions to this effect are particularly common among the constitutions of the Arab monarchies. A case in point is article 30 of the Jordanian Constitution that stipulates that '[t]he King is the Head of State and is immune from any liability and responsibility', which has, however, not prevented Jordan from ratifying the ICC Rome Statute. Article 54 of the Kuwaiti Constitution, article 23 of the Moroccan Constitution, article 20 of the Qatari Constitution and article 41 of the Omani Constitution all follow exactly the same pattern.[28]

The Middle East is an area plagued by conflicts that has witnessed many human rights violations and war crimes. This background makes the adoption and implementation of the international criminal law model of the ICC into the

---

24   ICC Pre-Trial Chamber. *Second Warrant of Arrest for Omar Hassan Ahmad Al Bashir*. ICC-02/05-01/09-1. 12-07-2010. 1/9 SL, PT. Available at: http://www.icc-cpi.int/iccdocs/doc/doc907140.pdf [accessed 6 January 2011].

25   See Oette, L. 2010. Peace and justice, or neither? The repercussions of the al-Bashir case for international criminal justice in Africa and beyond. *Journal of International Criminal Justice* 8(2), 345–64, at 348–9.

26   Article 44 of the Yemeni Constitution followed a similar pattern by stating that '[n]o Yemeni citizen shall be delivered up to a foreign authority'. Similar language can be found in article 22 of the Mauritanian Constitution.

27   Yashwi. 2005, 126–7.

28   The scope of immunity is different in a number of Arab republican regimes. Article 60 of the Lebanese Constitution, for example, grants the President of the Republic immunity during the performance of his functions except for violations of the constitution or cases of high treason. The article adds that the president is liable for ordinary crimes and subject to public laws upon a two-thirds majority decision by the members of the Chamber of Deputies. A.J. Harb argues that the ICC Rome Statute contradicts the Lebanese Constitution because it removes the immunity granted to certain categories of individuals due to the nature of their work. In addition, the Lebanese Constitution assigns to a special tribunal the power to try certain category of individuals (ministers, prime minister and the president of the republic). See Harb. 2010, 586–9.

domestic laws of the Middle East desirable if not imperative. The application of international criminal law in the Middle Eastern legal systems at large, including Israel, would be a great step forward in combating impunity for international crimes, and thereby reduce if not altogether prevent their commission

Arab Model Law for the repression of the crimes under the jurisdiction of the International Criminal Court

The Arab Justice Ministers' Council decided to approve the Arab Model Law for the 'Repression of Crimes under the Jurisdiction of the ICC' in its Decree number 598-21d dated 29 November 2005.[29] The Model Law was drafted with a view to providing guidance to Arab states on legislation pertaining to crimes falling within the ICC Rome Statute. The first chapter of the Model Law includes rules for jurisdiction. Article 2 provides that its provisions shall be enforced irrespective of the place where the criminal acts were committed, if one of the following conditions has been fulfilled:

- The accused is a national of the state.
- The accused was present on the territory of the state after the crime was committed.
- The victim was a national of the state.

Significantly, article 3 stipulates that the official capacity of an accused person is irrelevant and cannot be used as the basis for their exemption from prosecution. Article 3 further adds that the determination of this principle shall be left to the domestic legislature of each Arab country in accordance with its legal system. This is problematic because it provides a loophole that domestic leaders may be expected to exploit by attempting to influence the drafting of laws that exempt them from prosecution. If this were to happen, the Model Law would have failed unequivocally to establish the principle that there should be no immunity for international crimes. Meanwhile, article 6 of the Model Law provides that the crimes recognized therein shall not be subject to any statutes of limitation, and article 7 states that such crimes are not subject to general or special amnesties. With regard to criminal liability, article 8 recognizes the principle of superior command responsibility, and article 9 stipulates that following orders is no defence.

The second chapter of the Model Law is largely consistent with Chapter II of the ICC Rome Statute. Articles 10–13 of the Model Law concern the definition of crimes and jurisdiction broadly in line with articles 5–13 of the ICC Rome Statute. The list of crimes set out in the Model Law includes genocide, crimes

---

29   The text of the Arab Model Law is available at: http://www.iccnow.org/documents/ ArabLeague_ModelImplementationLaw_29Nov05_en.pdf [accessed 6 January 2011]. A meeting to review the Arab model law was held in Rabat, Morocco, in January 2011.

against humanity, war crimes and the crime of aggression. Although the definition of these crimes is largely based on the ICC Rome Statute, there are some notable variances, such as a narrower definition in respect of sexual offences such as rape.[30] Notably, article 13 of the Model Law provides a detailed list of acts that fall within the scope of the crime of aggression. This reflects the strong interest taken by Arab states to develop a clearer understanding and recognition of the crime of aggression, the absence of which, as noted, constituted one of the criticisms levelled against the ICC Rome Statute. In terms of applicable penalties, the Model Law recognizes capital punishment for international crimes, which is at variance with the ICC Rome Statute and developments in international human rights law towards the abolition of the death penalty.

The Model Law constitutes an important first step in developing the understanding of international criminal law in the region with a view to enhancing implementation. However, it mainly concerns questions of jurisdiction, which means that it does not address a number of other important aspects of the ICC Rome Statute, for example the rights of the defence and the rights of victims, including victim protection. With respect to the institutional dimension of prosecuting international crimes, the Model Law makes no mention of the establishment of special courts or courts with the requisite expertise within the legal systems of Arab states, or of the need to guarantee the independence of such courts. This has already become an issue in the course of the drafting of the Jordanian implementing law, as set out in the following section.

The incorporation of the ICC Rome Statute into Jordan's legal system

As established, Jordan is the only Middle Eastern state that has ratified the ICC Rome Statute and has taken steps towards the statute's implementation in its domestic legal system. On 11 April 2002, Jordan enacted the International Criminal Court Ratification Law number 12 of 2002. Article 2 of this law stipulates that the ICC Rome Statute, annexed to the Law, is 'valid and effective' (literal translation) according to the original Arabic draft submitted to the UN Secretary General, which means that it becomes part of Jordanian law. After the ratification of the ICC Rome Statute, the 'Committee for the legal harmonization of Jordanian law with the ICC Rome Statute' was established pursuant to a resolution by the Council of Ministers in August 2002. It is composed of representatives of the Public Security Directorate, the Military Judiciary, the General Intelligence Department, the Ministry of Foreign Affairs, the Ministry of the Interior, the Ministry of Justice, members of the University of Jordan and other legal experts. The main task of the

---

30   See the definition of rape in article 11(7) Model Law: 'Using coercion to have sex with a female, or to sodomize a male, or to rape a victim with penetration of any sort. It is still considered coercion if the aforementioned acts were committed against a person incapable of expressing consent'.

committee was to prepare the requisite legal reforms, namely by reviewing national laws and proposing amendments with a view to adopting legislation in conformity with the ICC Rome Statute. Several laws were reviewed and amended to ensure such harmony. This includes the Penal Military Code, which was amended by means of Penal Military Code number 30 of 2002 and number 58 of 2006.[31] There are also plans to review other legislation such as the public penal law to ensure their conformity with the ICC Rome Statute. The work of the committee has also comprised the drafting of a new law known as the Law of the National Court for International Crimes (draft law). The first draft of the law was completed in 2008,[32] but further revisions were being made at the time of writing in late 2010. The time that it has taken the committee to prepare the draft and the lack of expeditious follow up after 2008 reflect the protracted nature of the process.

The committee used the ICC Rome Statute rather than the Arab Model Law as the main reference point when drafting the law. Article 2 of the draft law provides that international crimes are any of the crimes recognized in the ICC Rome Statute, namely genocide, crimes against humanity and war crimes. It also refers to any other crime included within the ICC's jurisdiction unless the crime was subject to a reservation by the Government of the Hashemite Kingdom of Jordan. This can be understood as an indirect reference to the crime of aggression.

Article 11 of the draft law reproduces *verbatim* the definition of the crime of genocide as stipulated in article 6 of the ICC Rome Statute. Its article 12 reproduces the definition of crimes against humanity found in article 7(1)(a–j) of the ICC Rome Statute but omits the text of article 7(1)(k), namely '[o]ther inhumane acts of a similar character intentionally causing great suffering, or serious injury to body or to mental or physical health'. This reflects concerns that the broad definition contained in article 7(1)(k) of the Rome Statute may prompt national judges to find certain conduct to constitute crimes against humanity contrary to the intention of the legislature. Articles 13–16 of the draft law also provide for a detailed description of war crimes. This includes war crimes against persons, attacks on properties, attacks on humanitarian operations and their emblems, and several crimes relating to the methods of combat, which apply to both international and non-international armed conflict in line with article 8 of the ICC Rome Statute. In addition to the provisions included in the draft law, the Jordanian Penal Military Code number 58 of 2006 also deals with war crimes. This includes article 41 of the Penal Military Code, which was inserted with a view to implementing the ICC Rome Statute, and sets out a list of acts that are considered war crimes if committed during armed conflicts.

In contradistinction to the penalties stipulated in article 77 of the ICC Rome Statute, which envisages a maximum of life imprisonment, the crimes recognized in articles 11–16 of the draft law are subject to the death penalty or 'permanent hard labour' only. Moreover, persons contributing to the commission of the crime,

31   Tarawneh. 2005, 207–9.
32   The draft is on file with the author.

such as by instigating its commission, assisting the main perpetrator or acting as co-perpetrators, are subject to the same penalties as the ones provided for the actual perpetrator. Importantly, the draft law also recognizes that military commanders or superiors are liable on the grounds of command or superior responsibility for the failure to prevent or suppress the commission of crimes falling within its scope, and, if found guilty, are subject to the same penalties as set out above.

The institutional framework vests the public prosecutor with the power to prosecute the crimes set out in articles 11–16 of the draft law[33] and provides for the establishment of a special National Court for International Crimes in the Hashemite Kingdom of Jordan, to be tasked with the hearing of criminal trials pertaining to such crimes.[34] The envisaged court shall be composed of a number of civil and/or military judges, as the case may require, to be nominated by the Minister of Justice and the head of the Joint Chiefs of Staff respectively. The rank of the judge shall be no less than a special rank or its equivalent rank for the military judges. The appointment of military judges in the court's structure gives rise to concerns regarding their impartiality, particularly regarding whether they can remain independent from pressure applied by their military superiors. This point is of particular significance when considering that many of the individuals accused of, or prosecuted for international crimes have been part of the military in the countries concerned, often either as army generals or high ranking army leaders.

Article 8 of the draft law gives the court jurisdiction over: (1) Persons who commit inside the kingdom any of the crimes stipulated in this law; (2) Jordanian nationals who commit outside the kingdom any of the crimes stipulated in this law; (3) Foreign nationals who reside as permanent residents in the kingdom and who commit outside the kingdom any of the crimes stipulated in this law where no extradition has been accepted or requested pursuant to the provisions of the ICC Rome Statute. It therefore recognizes territorial jurisdiction, the active personality principle (the power of a state to exercise its jurisdiction over its nationals irrespective of where the crime was committed) and a limited form of extraterritorial jurisdiction. The latter enables the state to comply with the requirement to prosecute a foreign national suspected of having committed a crime where that individual cannot be extradited. However, the requirement of permanent residence in article 8(3) sets a high threshold that leaves foreseeable gaps in relation to other foreign nationals present in Jordan who may not be extradited to stand trial abroad, in particular where such an extradition would breach the prohibition of refoulement (sending a person to another state where he or she may be at risk of torture or other ill-treatment).

Article 10 contains a general clause that makes the provisions of the ICC Rome Statute and any amendments thereto applicable even if not expressly stipulated in the draft law. This is an important provision that enables Jordanian

---

33   Article 7 Draft Law.
34   Article 3 Draft Law.

prosecutors and judges to refer to the ICC Rome Statute. However, it may have been preferable to incorporate relevant provisions directly into the draft law as the current arrangement leaves prosecutors and judges broad discretion. As a result, the extent to which practice developed in the course of applying this framework draws on and conforms to the ICC Rome Statute will to a large degree depend on the awareness and willingness of judges to use the latter.

The final part of the draft law includes some general provisions that are similar to those included in the Arab Model Law on crimes within the ICC jurisdiction. Importantly, it provides that statutes of limitation shall not apply in relation to the prosecution of crimes, and the execution of punishment for the same, that fall within the scope of the draft law.

Conclusion

Jordan has taken significant steps towards the incorporation of the ICC Rome Statute in its domestic legal system, particularly in form of the draft law. However, as the draft law had not been adopted at the time of writing and the court envisaged therein had not come into existence, it remains to be seen how independent and effective the contemplated institutional set up will prove to be in combating impunity for international crimes. Legislation adopted by late 2010 and measures undertaken to implement the ICC Rome Statute give rise to cautious optimism that Jordan will succeed in putting in place an adequate normative and institutional framework. This may be of interest to other states in the region that are considering the ratification and implementation of the ICC Rome Statute, or the adoption of legislation aimed at effectively prohibiting and prosecuting international crimes more generally. However, the legislative changes undertaken and complemented in Jordan still have some shortcomings in light of international standards, such as omissions relating to crimes against humanity, the provision of the death penalty for international crimes and the role assigned to military courts.

Jordan's implementation efforts, both in terms of the contents of pertinent legislation and its subsequent application, constitute a critical yardstick by which to measure its credibility as a regional leader in the development of international criminal law. Jordan's ability and willingness to adopt and apply effective implementing legislation would in this context complement its efforts at the international stage, which have included promoting the inclusion of a provision in the ICC Rome Statute that recognizes the building of settlements and forced relocation of people as a war crime.[35] However, Jordan has also been the subject of political pressure from the United Stated of America (USA) to grant immunity to US soldiers from being surrendered for prosecution under the ICC Rome Statute. As a result, on 16 December 2004, Jordan and the USA entered into an agreement regarding the surrender of persons to the ICC, under which a US national present

---

35   Yashwi. 2005, 132.

on Jordanian territory shall not be surrendered or transferred by any means to the ICC unless agreed to by the USA.[36] Entering that agreement has been considered a setback for the Jordanian efforts and has cast doubt on its status as a champion for international criminal justice in the region. One shall hope that no further compromises of this nature will be made by Jordan.

---

36   Article 2 of the Agreement between the Government of the Hashemite Kingdom of Jordan and the Government of the United States of America regarding the surrender of persons to the ICC, 2004.

Chapter 9

Lessons from a State of Flux: The International Justice Laboratory of the Great Lakes Pact

Deirdre Clancy[1]

Introduction

The Great Lakes region of Central Africa has been riven apart by contiguous and interlinked conflict for over fifteen years. From Angola to Sudan millions have suffered the consequences of the most heinous of international crimes. It is not surprising therefore that the region has also been the site of a dizzying set of experiments in international justice, becoming a laboratory – to varying degrees of success – for the international justice movement. Through a variety of mechanisms, from hybrid tribunals to truth and reconciliation commissions to traditional processes, and five International Criminal Court (ICC) investigations, some of the most critical questions facing the development of international justice in action are being played out in this region.

These efforts have generally been pursued in isolation, driven by the particular complex politics and experiences of each country and the specific international interests and preoccupations. Increasingly, however, they have been overlaid with, and to some extent spurred by, evolving regional and sub-regional understandings of the role of international justice in transitions from conflict to peace. At the regional level the adoption of the African Union (AU) Constitutive Act in 2000 enshrined the 'condemnation and rejection of impunity' as one of the key principles guiding the functioning of the Union. It was at a sub-regional level, however, that this imperative was most comprehensively seized. In June 2008 the Pact on Security, Stability and Development in the Great Lakes Region (the Pact) came into force. Ultimately signed by eleven states and by January 2011 ratified by ten states – including Sudan – the Pact made the fight against impunity a collective regional priority and an essential component in building peace, security and development.

---

1   The author has drawn on the work of the International Refugee Rights Initiative (IRRI), including that conducted in the course of compiling the report IRRI. 2009. *In the Interests of Justice? Prospects and Challenges for International Justice in Africa*. [Online] Available at: http://www.refugee-rights.org/Publications/2008/In%20the%20Interests%20 of%20Justice.November%202008.pdf [accessed 6 January 2011].

This chapter explores some of the key normative developments relating to the pursuit of accountability for international crimes in the Great Lakes region, focusing on the potential contribution of the Pact to the evolving regional legal framework. In the light of the challenge facing the fight against impunity for international crimes in Sudan it suggests how the Pact might play a role in spurring law reform and as a baseline for negotiations both in Darfur and the new constitutional arrangements in the North and South.

International crimes and institutional and normative developments in the Great Lakes region

The 1994 Rwanda genocide ignited a cycle of conflict in the Great Lakes region that has continued for over fifteen years, at various points drawing in states from across the continent and the international community, whether as warring parties or in an effort to stem the violence.[2] Although the origins of the wars are to be found in deep-rooted contestation over resources and questions of identity, the failure to quickly identify and hold to account those who committed the Rwandan genocide in 1994 was one of the key factors that added new fuel to the conflict cycle. The establishment of the International Criminal Tribunal for Rwanda (ICTR) was one of the more immediate responses to this recognition of the intimate connection between impunity and the generation of conflict in the region. In creating the ICTR the United Nations (UN) Security Council expressed the hope that 'the prosecution of persons responsible for serious violations of international humanitarian law ... would contribute to the process of national reconciliation and to the restoration and maintenance of peace'.[3] Since 1994 pursuing accountability for international crimes has been a key component of policy discussions around preventing atrocities and achieving peace and security in the Great Lakes region. These discussions and the new norms and mechanisms that have evolved in the sub-region have in turn influenced normative and institutional developments in Africa and beyond, from the adoption of the ICC Rome Statute in 1998 to the AU Constitutive Act of 2000 and the International Conference on the Great Lakes region (ICGLR). Built on the recognition that impunity for international crimes played a major role in generating conflict in the region, the ICGLR is the African regional arrangement that has perhaps most strongly embraced – at least at a normative level – the connection between international justice and peace and development.

---

2   See in particular International Panel of Eminent Personalities to Investigate the 1994 Genocide in Rwanda and Surrounding Events. 2000. *Rwanda: The Preventable Genocide. Organization of African Unity.* [Online] Available at: http://www.africa-union.org/Official_documents/reports/Report_rowanda_genocide.pdf [accessed 6 January 2011], in particular para. 20.1.

3   Preamble, UN Security Council Resolution 955 (1994).

The International Conference on the Great Lakes Region (ICGLR)

The ICGLR had its origins in the appointment of Special Envoys in 1996 to lead a joint UN/AU initiative to promote peace, security, democracy and development in the Great Lakes region. By 2000 the International Panel of Eminent Personalities to Investigate the 1994 Genocide in Rwanda and Surrounding Events (Rwanda IPEP) was able to welcome the UN Security Council's endorsement of the creation of 'a special international conference on security, peace and development for the Great Lakes Region'.[4] After a complex and lengthy phase of negotiation that included significant civil society involvement,[5] the Pact on Security, Stability and Development in the Great Lakes Region (the Pact) was finally signed by eleven states in December 2006. The Pact entered into force in June 2008 upon achieving the required number of eight ratifications.[6]

In order to achieve its ambitious vision the Pact creates not just new standards and instruments but a range of new mechanisms and programs. It is a complex instrument, comprising five separate but interlinked elements: the primary instrument of the Pact itself; the Dar es Salaam Declaration (the set of principles upon which the Pact was fashioned); ten Protocols[7] (legally binding instruments); four Programmes of Action; and a set of implementing national and international mechanisms and institutions (the Regional Follow-Up Mechanism).[8] Unusually

---

4   International Panel of Eminent Personalities. 2000. Recommendation 28. For one account of the origins of the process and some of the political dynamics at play within the early years of the process see Heyl, C. 2010. The International Conference on the Great Lakes Region: An Africa CSCE? *Kas International Reports*, (12) [Online] Available at: http://www.kas.de/wf/doc/kas_21242-544-2-30.pdf?101124163347 [accessed 6 January 2011], 87.

5   For a discussion of the historic and potential role of civil society in the development of the Pact, see Danish Refugee Council and IRRI. 2008. *The Great Lakes Pact and the rights of displaced people, A Guide for civil society*. [Online] Available at: http://www. refugee-rights.org/Publications/2008/GLReport.Sep2008.pdf [accessed 6 January 2011].

6   Eleven states in the region are members of the ICGLR: Angola, Burundi, the Central African Republic, the Democratic Republic of Congo, Kenya, the Republic of Congo, Rwanda, Sudan, Tanzania, Uganda and Zambia. Ten states have signed and ratified the Pact; it is understood that Angola intends to ratify imminently.

7   These are the Protocol on the Protection and Assistance of Internally Displaced Persons; the Protocol on the Property Rights of Returning Persons; the Protocol on the Prevention and Suppression of Sexual Violence Against Women and Children; the Protocol on the Prevention and Punishment of the Crimes of Genocide, War Crimes and Crimes Against Humanity; the Protocol on Democracy and Good Governance; the Protocol on Judicial Cooperation; the Protocol on Non-Aggression and Mutual Defence in the Great Lakes Region; the Protocol on Management of Information and Communication; the Protocol Against the Illegal Exploitation of Natural Resources; and the Protocol on the Specific Reconstruction Zone.

8   The full text of the Pact and all the Protocols are available online at the website of the ICGLR Secretariat: http://www.icglr.org [accessed 6 January 2011].

for such a voluminous document, the Pact explicitly identifies all of its components as each constituting an 'integral part' that must be ratified as a whole (article 3(1) of the Pact). Although the precise legal status of those components of the Pact which are not legal instruments as such (such as the programmes of action) is somewhat unclear, the approach taken reflects the extent to which the simultaneous implementation of each of the legal, political and programmatic components was seen by states parties as essential to its success.

The Pact covers a very broad range of areas, from economic integration, to mutual defence, to the use of natural resources. Significantly, at least four of its ten protocols have a direct bearing on how states and other actors are directed to prevent, react to and prosecute international crimes. Indeed all of the protocols are arguably animated by this objective in various ways.[9] In examining the sustaining factors for the cyclical horrors of the region's wars, leaders negotiating the Pact were forced to acknowledge that

> [p]olicies of exclusion ... divisionism [sic] ideologies with ethnic, clannish, religious or regional base have ... limited the range of opportunities for development ... constituted a flagrant violation of human rights and engendered a break-up in the social cohesion by conveying injustice, intolerance, and hatred.[10]

Achieving peace would therefore require the 'eradication of war crimes, genocide, and crimes against humanity and the fight against the use of rape as a weapon of war' through structured regional cooperation around interdependent strategies.[11] Besides combating impunity, therefore, the Pact also commits states to prevention efforts, including dismantling the discriminatory and human rights violating environments that are the seedbeds of violations, promoting democratic governance, and providing for conflict prevention structures and collective intervention in situations of mass atrocity.

---

9   The Protocol on Management of Information and Communication, for example, expresses the determination of States to, *inter alia*, 'safeguard freedom of media from being manipulated as an illegitimate means of inciting propaganda for hatred or hostility, war, violence, discrimination, genocide, ethnic cleansing, and crimes against humanity' (preamble).

10   Para. 1.1, Project No. 2.1.3 of the Regional Initiative for the prevention and the curbing of war crimes, crimes against humanity, genocide and the fight against impunity in the Great Lakes Region. Regional Programme of Action for the Promotion of Democracy and Good Governance. Great Lakes Pact. 2006.

11   Para. 1.3, Project No. 2.1.3 of the Regional Initiative. Great Lakes Pact. 2006.

The 'International Justice' Protocols of the Great Lakes Pact

The International Crimes Protocol

The Protocol on the Prevention and Punishment of the Crime of Genocide, War Crimes and Crimes Against Humanity (International Crimes Protocol or the Protocol) contains a mix of criminal law and human rights law provisions dealing not just with the prosecution of those who commit international crimes but also with the systematic and root causes of such crimes, mandating the creation of early warning mechanisms and measures to combat 'discriminatory ideologies and practices' (article 5). The Protocol's preamble clearly links impunity for international crimes with the challenge of creating peace and security, acknowledging that the region's 'persistent insecurity [is] aggravated by the massive violations of human rights, the policies of exclusion and marginalization [and] impunity'. Addressing directly some of the most egregious aspects of the region's conflicts, the preamble identifies the prevalence of sexual violence, the recruitment of child soldiers and trafficking as among the issues to be particularly tackled by the Protocol. Significant and multiple paragraphs of the Protocol, for example, advert to the suffering of women in conflict situations and the imperative of seeking both criminal and human rights redress for such violations. References are made in the preamble to a range of instruments, from the ICTR Statute to the Protocol to the African Charter on Human and Peoples' Rights (AfrCHPR) on the Rights of Women in Africa, 2003.

The Protocol emphasizes the pre-existing duty of each member State, 'to exercise its criminal jurisdiction over the perpetrators of the crime of genocide, war crimes and crimes against humanity' (the preamble) and ensure 'effective penalties' for such crimes (article 9(1)). States are obliged to assert their jurisdiction where the acts complained of have been committed on their territory as well as where the alleged perpetrator or victim is a national, or where the alleged perpetrator is ordinarily resident on their territory (article 10). This is not the most expansive extraterritorial jurisdiction that could be conceived for such crimes. However, it does reflect the collective and cooperative approach underpinning the construction of member states' responsibilities in the Pact: article 13 provides explicitly that '[s]tates undertake to mutually assist one another through cooperation of their respective institutions with a view to preventing, detecting and punishing the perpetrators of genocide, war crimes, and crimes against humanity'.

The Protocol removes statutes of limitation for the international crimes that it addresses (article 11). It also provides that the official status of an accused shall not 'shield or bar their criminal liability', and, like the ICC Rome Statute, specifically stipulates that the phrase 'official status' encompasses 'a Head of State or Government, or an official member of a Government or Parliament, or an elected representative or agent of a State', although there is no reference to incumbency (article 12).[12] Other aspects of the Protocol facilitate the process of extradition between member states. This includes the provision that the Protocol itself can act as the basis for extradition (article 14(2)) in the absence of a bilateral treaty, and that the political offence exemption shall not apply with respect to crimes that are the subject of the Protocol (article 15(3)). Reflecting the complementary nature of the Pact's undertakings, member states are not obliged to extradite their nationals, which constitutes a significant limitation, although they must 'submit the request to [their] competent authorities with a view to commence prosecution against such a national'. It is further stipulated that the 'requesting State shall be informed of the outcome of any such prosecution' (article 15(3)).

The preventative aspects of the Protocol focus on combating discrimination and societal exclusion. States are required to adopt concrete measures to eliminate incitement to discrimination or acts of discrimination and to 'declare that any circulation of ideas based on the superiority of one group over another' is an offence punishable by law (article 6(2)(a)).[13] Reflecting the complex cross-border tensions that have fuelled conflict in the region the Protocol makes clear that protections against discrimination and the right to a remedy apply not just to citizens or legal residents but to 'anyone' within the jurisdiction of the member states (article 4).

States also commit themselves to 'endeavour to ratify the Statute of the [ICC] in accordance with their constitutional requirements' (article 21). However, the terms of the Protocol equally reflect the reality that not all states had ratified the ICC Rome Statute at the time of negotiations and that there were serious questions beginning to be asked about its reach, in particular as a result of the first UN Security Council referral of the situation in Darfur, Sudan to the Court. Only those member states that had ratified the ICC Rome Statute at the time of the entry into force of the Protocol (article 25), are therefore required to institute ICC cooperation procedures and adhere to a specific set of obligations relating to the operation of the ICC ranging from responses to territory transit requests to execution of prison sentences (articles 22, 23 and 24). At the same time the ICC Rome Statute and the UN Convention on the Prevention and Punishment of the Crime of Genocide are the primary reference points for the Protocol in terms of the definition of international crimes and the general approach to impunity and immunities. War crimes, for example, are described in the Protocol simply as 'any one of the acts set out in article 8 of the Statute of the International Criminal Court' (article 1(i)).

All the protocols of the Pact were designed specifically to address those lacunae in the region's legal framework that had been identified as impeding the achievement of the Pact's objectives.[14] Considering therefore that ten out of

---

12   Article 27 ICC Rome Statute.

13   The breadth of this provision presents questions of compatibility with the right of freedom of thought and expression, including as described in the AfrCHPR.

14   For example, there is a Protocol on Internally Displaced Persons (IDPs) but none on refugees despite the fact that refugee movements, security and rights are recognized as vital issues of concern to the Pact. The reason is that all states in the region are party to the

eleven members had signed the ICC Rome Statute at the time of the negotiations (with all the attendant obligations created by the principle of complementarity), the adoption of the international crimes-related protocols of the Pact must be understood as animated by the desire to create strengthened capacity to do justice in the *region and as a region*: whether in terms of bi-lateral cooperation and/or through the creation of new obligations and mechanisms at a cross-regional level. Although the need to strengthen national capacity to combat regional impunity is emphasized in the Pact, regional action is clearly viewed as essential to support such efforts, whether through cooperation in investigations, harmonization of standards or the creation of collective early warning and prevention strategies.

The International Crimes Protocol creates two new mechanisms to help facilitate this cooperation. The first is the institution of joint commissions of inquiry, envisaged as multi-state membership bodies charged with the determination of jurisdiction and agreement on extradition requests (articles 17–19). The commissions are complemented by processes of more general exchange of information between police forces of member states around investigations, the identity of suspected perpetrators, the conduct of arrests and the collection of evidence (article 20). It does not appear that joint commissions have yet been set up in the region, although there is evidence of increasing police and security cooperation, including through mechanisms created by the East African Community (EAC).[15]

The second mechanism envisaged by the International Crimes Protocol is a Regional Committee for the prevention and punishment of genocide, war crimes and crimes against humanity and all forms of discrimination (article 26). The Committee was established in September 2010 with the adoption of rules of procedure and an action plan that was endorsed by a summit of Heads of State in December 2010:[16] it is the first treaty committee mechanism anywhere in the world to, *inter alia*, monitor the implementation of obligations relating to the prevention of genocide. The functions of the Committee range from early warning ('alerting the summit of the conference in good time in order to take urgent measures to prevent potential crimes'), to 'contributing to raising awareness and education on peace and reconciliation', and recommending compensation measures and monitoring national disarmament, demobilization and reintegration programs (article 38(2)(c), (e), (f) and (g)).[17]

1969 Organization of African Unity (OAU) Convention Governing Specific Challenges of Refugees in the region and the 1951 UN Convention relating to the protection of refugees.

15   See for further information the website of the East African Community. Available at: http://www.eac.int/security/index.php?option=com_content&view=article&id=55&Ite mid=107 [accessed 6 January 2011].

16   See Work Plan for the Regional Committee for the prevention and punishment of genocide, war crimes and crimes against humanity and all forms of discrimination, adopted 23 September 2010 (on file with author).

17   To achieve its goal, the Committee is urged to collaborate with the African Commission on Human and Peoples Rights, civil society organizations and the UN system,

The Protocol on Sexual Violence against Women and Children[18]

The Protocol on the Prevention and Suppression of Sexual Violence against Women and Children (SGBV Protocol, or the Protocol) draws on 'contemporary developments relating to the criminalization of sexual violence and the punishment of the perpetrators of sexual violence under international criminal law' (article 3(1)). It contains a comprehensive set of measures aimed at tackling the phenomenon of sexual violence, ranging from the prosecution of perpetrators to the compensation of victims and treatment of offenders.[19]

The Protocol also strengthens the legal framework for prosecution and punishment of perpetrators by recognizing a broad range of acts of sexual violence that should be subject to criminal sanction;[20] creating new arrangements to facilitate the expeditious surrender of fugitives; and abolishing statutes of limitation.[21] The Protocol particularly takes into account the vulnerabilities of victims of sexual violence in terms of access to justice, requiring the setting up of national institutions both to help provide compensation to victims (article 6(6) and 6(9)) and to facilitate the lodging of complaints. The Protocol also provides for the institution of modified trial procedures that take into consideration 'the emotional state' of survivors of such crimes.[22]

---

and is mandated to resort to any appropriate method of investigation, including interviewing 'any person likely to provide it with useful information' (articles 40 and 41).

18   For an ICGLR perspective on prospects for the impact of the SGBV Protocol in the Region see Mulamula, L. 2008. East Africa: Sex and gender based violence in the Great Lakes region, in *Pambazuka News*: Special Edition Vol. 388: Ending impunity for sexual and gender based violence. [Online, July] Available at: http://www.pambazuka.org/en/issue/388 [Accessed 10 January 2010].

19   Taking a progressive approach to the complexity of sexual violence crimes, and acknowledging that perpetrators of sexual violence are often recidivists, the SGBV Protocol makes provision for the implementation of rehabilitation programs for perpetrators serving their sentences. Thus while article 5 stipulates the need to impose maximum sentences on offenders, it also encourages states to ensure that the perpetrators undergo 'social correction and rehabilitation' and calls for the creation at national level of a 'fund for sensitizing offenders on the wrongfulness of their sexual behaviour' (Article 6(7)).

20   Article 1(5) of the Protocol defines sexual violence as 'any act which violates the sexual autonomy and bodily integrity of women and children under international criminal law' and includes acts such as, for example, 'infection of women and children with sexually transmitted diseases, including HIV/AIDS'. However, there are some internal inconsistencies in the drafting that raise questions about the scope of the Protocol.

21   See article 6. The Protocol clearly states that these procedures should not prejudice the operation of extradition and rendition procedures under the Protocol on Judicial Cooperation (discussed below, *Protocol on Judicial Cooperation*).

22   Article 6(5): 'Victims and survivors shall give evidence in camera, or by video links, and they shall neither be compelled nor required to give evidence in open criminal proceedings, nor shall the casting of aspersions on their character and integrity be permitted as part of the defence of any person charged with a crime of sexual violence'.

The Protocol is sweeping in its approach to the investigation, trial and punishment of SGBV crimes. Unlike the International Crimes Protocol, it appears not to contemplate any restrictions on the capacity of states to establish jurisdiction over crimes that are the subject of the Protocol and their perpetrators – unless limitations can be implied as those pre-existing in international and national law. Neither does it address the question of immunities from prosecution.[23] The extradition provision in the Protocol is also stark: '[m]ember States agree that the requested State *shall* … forthwith comply with the request for the arrest and surrender of an accused person to the jurisdiction of the requesting State' (article 6(3) (emphasis added)). Read at face value, the Protocol raises questions of compatibility with the International Crimes Protocol and the Protocol on Judicial Cooperation (discussed in more detail below, *Protocol on Judicial Cooperation*). The International Crimes Protocol, for example, provides for only a partial form of universal jurisdiction and permits states to refuse to extradite their own nationals (although they must investigate and communicate the outcome of such investigations). The Protocol on Judicial Cooperation also provides that there is no obligation to extradite nationals (article 6). In the light of the simple surrender imperative in article 6(3) of the SGBV Protocol, the fact that the Protocol is intended to provide 'a legal basis for the surrender of persons and fugitives […] *without prejudice* to the Protocol on Judicial Cooperation' [emphasis added] (article 2(3)) presents an interpretative challenge. The apparent choice of the drafters to establish greater capacity and obligation to prosecute SGBV compared to that stipulated for genocide, war crimes and crimes against humanity (where they do not themselves constitute SGBV crimes) is unusual, although the priority accorded to combating SGBV is very much a theme of the Pact. Significantly, the Protocol also provides for the compensation of victims of SGBV, in contrast to the International Crimes Protocol which does not address the matter for any of the range of very serious crimes under its purview.[24]

The Protocol strikingly emphasizes the collective regional nature of the obligations assumed by states with respect to eliminating SGBV. Some of the most sweeping undertakings in the Protocol – including those relating to the requirement for *domestic* harmonization of 'all relevant national laws and criminal procedures' and extradition – are set out in article 6, which is entitled 'regional responses to sexual violence'. Three key features of the Protocol reflect this

---

23   At a minimum, crimes that are the subject of the Protocol but also constitute crimes addressed in the International Crimes Protocol should be considered to be governed by the express immunity provisions in that instrument.

24   These discrepancies might be explained to some extent by the fact that the SGBV Protocol was developed within the humanitarian and social pillar of the ICGLR, a process in which non-governmental and inter-governmental actors with strong concerns about SGBV were very engaged. The Protocol on Judicial Cooperation and the International Crimes Protocol, on the other hand, were drafted as components of the democracy and governance endeavour.

particular insistence on a regional conception of the obligation to combat SGBV. The first is the undertaking to create 'a special regional facility for training and sensitizing judicial officers, police units, social workers, medical officers and other categories of persons who handle cases of sexual violence in the Great Lakes Region' (article 6(9)). The second relates to the responsibility of states to compensate survivors: in addition to provisions that mandate compensation of victims of SGBV by the perpetrators (article 6(6)), the Protocol also contemplates that states 'may' create at the regional level, 'a special facility under the fund for reconstruction and development, the purpose of which shall be to provide social and legal assistance, medical treatment, counselling, training, rehabilitation and reintegration of the survivors and victims of sexual violence, including those who may not be able to identify the perpetrators of sexual violence' (article 6(8)). Finally, model legislation was developed during the drafting process to assist with the Protocol's harmonious regional implementation. Although states ultimately rejected the idea of formally annexing the model legislation to the instrument, it remains an important implementation tool. The legislation contains two interesting innovations: the creation of a Committee for the Protection of Women and Children from Sexual Violence charged with overseeing the protection of women and children in each member state, and a Compensation Commission for Sexual Violence Claims tasked with receiving the assessed claims for compensation from the Committee and deciding on the level of such compensation and the responsible person or organ.

Protocol on Judicial Cooperation

The Protocol on Judicial Cooperation creates a regional framework for handling extradition requests and cooperation in all types of criminal investigations and prosecutions. States recognized that there was a 'particular need for measures to combat impunity at the regional level in order to ensure that all persons against whom there is evidence to show that they have committed offences' were prosecuted. Having identified the legal and institutional gaps preventing the achievement of this objective, the Protocol addresses a range of issues such as: the differential procedures governing the extradition of accused and convicted persons (article 7); the extradition of nationals (article 6); response to concurrent extradition requests (article 12); and the regulation of preventative detention and release (articles 8 and 9). The Protocol also provides for enhanced cooperation in respect of investigations and prosecutions (Chapter III), including the creation of joint investigation commissions (article 17)[25] and exchange of information relating both to the 'prevailing levels of crime and policies and strategies for preventing such crime' and criminal investigations (article 21). Article 21 of the Protocol is the

---

25   Article 18(3) stipulates that the establishment of such Commissions upon request can only be refused if 'the requested State deems it to be a potential threat to its sovereignty or its internal security'.

only provision that specifically addresses international crimes. Echoing the joint commissions of enquiry envisaged in the International Crimes Protocol, police forces of the member states are enjoined ('shall') to both seek and communicate information on: '(a) perpetrators, co-perpetrators and accomplices involved in the preparation or commission of international crimes; (b) any item of evidence related to an international crime actually committed or attempted; (c) materials needed to establish the proof that an international crime has been committed' (article 21(2)).

Other protocols of the Pact

Several other protocols of the Pact address additional dimensions of both preventing and ensuring accountability for international crimes. The Protocol on Non-Aggression and Mutual Defence explicitly acknowledges member states' 'responsibility to protect' populations from the most serious of international crimes.[26] Article 4(8) stipulates that the prohibition on the threat or use of force by a member state 'shall not impair the exercise of their [member states] responsibility to protect populations from genocide, war crimes, ethnic cleansing, crimes against humanity and gross violations of human rights committed by, or within a State'.[27] Any decision to exercise this responsibility, however, is to be 'taken collectively, with due procedural notice to the Peace and Security Council of the African Union and the Security Council of the United Nations'. What type of action might be entailed by this provision is not spelled out but it could include the setting up, or promotion of, an international criminal accountability mechanism. In 2006 the AU Assembly of Heads of State and Governments interpreted similarly worded powers in the AU Constitutive Act, for example, as a basis for the referral of the prosecution of former President Habré of Chad to Senegal 'on behalf of Africa'.[28]

The Protocol on Democracy and Good Governance complements the responsibility to protect by envisaging the convening of an extraordinary session of the heads of state summit in the event of 'threats to democracy and a beginning of its breakdown by whatever process and in the event of massive violations of human rights in a Member State'. Such a summit would facilitate the taking of a series of 'urgent and appropriate measures' in order to 'put an end to the

---

26 For a perspective on the Pact and the responsibility to protect see IRRI. 2009. *Some Reflections on the Legal and Political Mechanisms Bolstering the Responsibility to Protect: The African Union and the Great Lakes, Eastern, Southern and Horn of Africa Sub-Regional Arrangements*. [Online] Available at: http://www.refugee-rights.org/Publications/2008/R2P%20RECs%20Discussion%20paper.102108.pdf [accessed 6 January 2011].

27 The circumstances that may trigger the exercise of the article 4(8) responsibility to protect in the Pact are more expansive than those described in the AU Constitutive Act, as they include situations of 'gross violations of human rights'.

28 See Assembly of the African Union. 2006. *Decision On The Hissène Habré Case And The African Union*. [2 July] Doc. Assembly/AU/3 (Vii). Article 5(1)(d) of the Pact provides that if states fail to comply with the Protocol on Non-Aggression and Mutual Defence an extraordinary summit may be convened to consider appropriate action.

situation' (article 48). Although not explicitly mentioned, measures pertaining to accountability and justice for international crimes and to the implementation of the principle of the responsibility to protect could be envisaged as encompassed within this provision. During the escalation of the crisis in Eastern Democratic Republic of Congo (DRC) in late 2008, for example, the ICGLR initiated a special summit in Nairobi. ICGLR Heads of States warned that they would 'not stand by to witness incessant and destructive acts of violence by any armed groups against innocent people of DRC', and vowed 'if necessary' to send 'peacemaking forces into the Kivu Province of the DRC'.[29] Further to the new round of peace negotiations galvanized by this summit, a Congrès National Pour la Défence du Peuple (CNDP) ceasefire began in early 2009.[30]

Finally, although not a subject matter that might be immediately associated with international crimes, states in the Protocol against the Illegal Exploitation of Natural Resources have recognized that '[the] illegal exploitation of natural resources in the Great Lakes Region is one of the factors causing or aggravating endemic conflicts and persistent insecurity'. Illegal exploitation of natural resources, whether by states or non-state actors (militia or business), is a critical contextual factor at the root of some of the most horrific violence and the commission of international crimes in the region, with parts of Eastern DRC serving as prime examples.[31] States in the Protocol therefore have undertaken 'to end impunity for persons responsible for exploiting natural resources illegally' (article 9). Although the focus is domestic prosecution – each member state 'shall ensure that all acts of illegal exploitation of natural resources are offences under its criminal law' (article 12), the Protocol also contains provisions mandating regional judicial and police cooperation, the easing of extradition procedures, and the creation of a regional certification mechanism and committee.[32] Of all the Pact's protocols dealing with criminal matters this Protocol is the only one requiring that special measures (physical and procedural) are taken by states for the effective protection of 'witnesses, their relatives and other persons close to them' (article 14).

---

29   See Heads of State of the Great Lakes Region. 2008. *Joint statement on the situation in DRC*. Nairobi [7 November], para. (e). (On file with author).

30   See Ambassador Liberata Mulamula, Executive Secretary, ICGLR. 2010. *Consolidating Regional Peace in Africa: The case of the Great Lakes Region*. Paper Presented at the International Peace Institute (IPI). New York [28 April] (On file with author).

31   See for example the work of the non governmental organization (NGO) Global Rights in the Democratic Republic of Congo on human rights and natural resources, available at: http://www.globalrights.org/site/PageServer?pagename=www_africa_drc [accessed 6 January 2011].

32   One of the three stated objectives of the Protocol is '[t]o intensify and revitalize cooperation among Member State with a view to achieving more efficient and sustainable measures against the illegal exploitation of natural resources' (article 1(2)).

Translating norms into action: Implementation and application of the Pact

Taken as a whole the Pact embodies a comprehensive approach to international crimes that sees prosecution and punishment as elements of a continuum of necessary responses, bolstered by the promotion of democracy and good governance, the suppression of 'discriminatory ideologies and practices'[33] and early warning mechanisms. All of this is underpinned by the reaffirmation of member states' 'responsibility to protect' with respect to certain international crimes and gross human rights violations. In terms of substantive law, the Pact extends the range of acts that should be considered the subject of international attention and strengthens the capacity of states to assert such jurisdiction. Some commentators have in fact gone so far as to suggest that the ICGLR represents 'the epitome of a regional organization's commitment to self-organize the prevention of genocidal violence and mass atrocities in an endogenous manner'.[34] The crucial question, however, is to what extent this normative and institutional achievement will be translated into genuine transformation on the ground.

Decades of extreme civil and inter-state conflict and state willingness to use the tools of international justice where political interests align have made the Great Lakes region perhaps the most intense space of transitional and international justice engagement anywhere in the world. In addition to the ICTR in Arusha, special mechanisms to prosecute international crimes have been established in the DRC, Sudan and Uganda and by late 2010 were under active contemplation in Burundi, the DRC, and Kenya.[35] Five of the ICC's open situation investigations were unfolding in neighbouring countries – Central African Republic (CAR), DRC, Kenya, Sudan and Uganda – with eight of the 11 ICGLR states having become states parties to the ICC Rome Statute. As of the beginning of 2011 legislation to implement the ICC Rome Statute had been passed in Uganda and Kenya and was in draft form in Angola, the CAR, the DRC and the Republic of Congo (RoC). It is acknowledged that the pace of adoption of Rome Statute legislation, especially in states that have actively sought out the ICC through self-referrals, is slow. First, the ratification of the Pact should be expected to operate as a spur, particularly as it relates to activating the principle of complementarity

---

33   Article 5, Chapter II, Protocol on the Prevention and Punishment of the Crime of Genocide, War Crimes and Crimes Against Humanity.

34   See Bartoli, A. and Ogata, T. 2010. *Supporting Regional Approaches to Genocide Prevention: The International Conference on the Great Lakes Region (ICGLR)*. [Online] Available at: http://www.gpanet.org/content/supporting-regional-approaches-genocide-prevention-international-conference-great-lakes-regi [accessed 6 January 2011].

35   See, for example, UN Office of the High Commissioner for Human Rights. 2010. *Report of the Mapping Exercise documenting the most serious violations of human rights and international humanitarian law committed within the territory of the Democratic Republic of the Congo between March 1993 and June 2003*. [Online, August] Available at: http://www.ohchr.org/EN/Countries/AfricaRegion/Pages/RDCProjetMapping.aspx [accessed 10 January 2011].

obligations. In addition, even prior to the adoption of the international crimes protocols, universal jurisdiction had been widely accepted throughout the region as a matter of law, particularly *via* the ratification and domestication of the Geneva Conventions. As a matter of practice, however, as of April 2009 '[n]o African state [was] known to have exercised universal jurisdiction effectively'.[36]

The lack of legislative momentum around the implementation of the Rome Statute, and indeed the Pact's international crimes protocols, can to some degree be attributed to legal impediments relating to issues around penalties, immunities and retroactivity. It is the region's ongoing struggle with conflict, delicate political negotiations and fragile democratic processes that presents the stiffest challenge. The existence of amnesties, for example, has been a serious complicating factor. Amnesties are a feature of the post-conflict landscape in many states in the region such as Angola, Burundi, the CAR, the DRC, the RoC, Sudan and Uganda. In Burundi, for example, negotiations around the creation of a Special Chamber alongside a Truth and Reconciliation Commission have been extremely protracted, with the power of the Truth and Reconciliation Commission to grant amnesties constituting a major sticking point.[37] Although the international crimes protocols of the Great Lakes Pact are silent on the issue, amnesties are incompatible with obligations set out in the protocols if they apply to crimes against humanity, war crimes, genocide or the crimes defined in the SGBV Protocol.

It is difficult to discern a clear causal relationship between the imperatives of the Pact itself and recent developments around international justice in the region, such as the expansion of the ICC's reach into the CAR and Kenya, the creation of a war crimes division of Uganda's High Court and discussions about the establishment of mixed tribunals in the DRC. Certainly the new developments can be seen in principle, if not in practice, as contributing to fulfilling the Pact's overall objectives and as having drawn on the philosophical and normative undertakings that it embodies. In practice, however, the particular political exigencies of each context have provided the impetus for measures taken rather than the peer-to-peer regional pressure that was intended to be generated by the ICGLR process. Very rarely, if at all, can references to ICGLR requirements be found in reports of the processes and discussions that led to the establishment of these new mechanisms and initiatives. This applies also where domestic mechanisms are being proffered as alternatives to ICC jurisdiction, such as in Sudan and Kenya. Among the notable exceptions to the peripheral role of the Pact and its protocols in the international

---

36 See AU–EU Technical Ad hoc Expert Group on the Principle of Universal Jurisdiction. 2009. *Report* [Online, April] Available at: http://www.au.int/files/Report_En_AU_EU_Technical_Ad_Hoc_Expert_Group_Jurisdiction_UJ_FINAL_15_04_09_AA.pdf [accessed 6 January 2011], para. 19.

37 See, *inter alia*, the discussion of this issue in Ero, C. and Khadiagla, G.M. 2009. *Expert Report on Impunity, Justice and Reconcilation in Africa: Opportunities and Constraints*. Prepared for the International Peace Institute (IPI) and the AU Panel of the Wise, 27–8.

justice field has been the ICGLR's institutional involvement in the international response to the post election violence in Kenya. A statement by the ICGLR Executive Secretary, Ambassador Liberata Mulamula, spoke early of 'threats of genocide returning to the region' and both the Ambassador and representatives of the Troika (former, current and future Chair of the ICGLR) swiftly arrived in Nairobi in advance of the broader international initiative to halt the violence.[38] It is possible that the engagement of regional leaders through the ICGLR process contributed to accountability becoming a key pillar of the effort to reestablish order after the crisis.

The Pact's international crimes provisions and programmes particularly focus on providing states with new tools to cooperate regionally to combat impunity.[39] There is, however, limited evidence of the actual use of the protocols in the field of bilateral cooperation through joint investigations and more efficient extradition procedures. During 2010 suggestions were made, for example, that General Laurent Nkunda, the former leader of the CNDP, would be transferred under the rubric of the Pact for trial to the DRC, where he has been charged with war crimes. As of late 2010, however, Nkunda remained officially in the custody of the Rwandan authorities. Significantly, the August 2010 UN mapping report on international crimes committed in the DRC between 1993 and 2003 did identify the Pact's Judicial Cooperation and International Crimes Protocols as potential bases for the exercise of jurisdiction over perpetrators by third states. While acknowledging the restrictions created by the Protocols' exceptions regarding the extradition of nationals, the report particularly singled out the Pact's 'interesting provisions' concerning the establishment of joint commissions of enquiry and exchange of information.[40]

It is evident that the promise of the Pact in respect of prevention and combating impunity for international crimes, particularly in terms of regional cooperation, has yet to be fulfilled. This can be attributed both to the slow implementation of the Protocols at the national level, as well as the resource and other constraints facing the ICGLR that appear to have hindered efforts to drive the agenda from the centre. As a matter of practice, the domestication of international treaties relating to criminal law is a complex process. Since its entry into force in 2008, implementation of the Pact has been based on national priorities, tending to follow a sequential and context-specific approach, rather than a comprehensive implementation strategy, although Uganda is considering the passage of omnibus

---

38   See Executive Secretary of the ICGLR. 2008. *Escalating Violence, Loss of Lives and Property in Post Election Kenya*. Press Release [4 January] (On file with author). See also, 2008. Regional body condemns Kenya violence. *The New Times* [Online, 7 January] Available at: http://www.newtimes.co.rw/print.php?issue=14245&print&artic le=3377 [accessed 7 January 2011].

39   See, for example, Project No. 2.1.3, of the Regional Initiative. Great Lakes Pact. 2006.

40   See UN Office of the High Commissioner for Human Rights. 2010, para. 1030. The 544-page report contains only one brief reference to the SGBV Protocol, however.

legislation. Notably, the Pact's International Crimes and Judicial Cooperation Protocols aspects have not been the *express* subject of implementing legislation, although ICC Rome Statute legislation passed in both Kenya and Uganda does partially implement Pact obligations. Implementation of the SGBV Protocol has, however, seen some movement. In Rwanda legislation dealing with SGBV and referencing the Pact was passed in late 2008,[41] and as of the end of 2010, Burundi has a SGBV bill in place. During 2011 it is understood that a special regional summit on SGBV will be held and that a number of member states will carry out compatibility studies to assess national legislation and practice in the light of the Pact's requirements.[42]

At the regional advocacy and technical assistance level the ICGLR's focus has tended to be on other issues such as the fight against the illegal exploitation of natural resources[43] or around specific conflict resolution or disarmament efforts.[44] From an inter-governmental and non-governmental perspective, the protocols in the humanitarian and social pillar, namely those relating to SGBV, the property rights of displaced populations and internally displaced persons, have been given priority. Indeed, the greater involvement of civil society in the drafting of these latter instruments has perhaps resulted in a natural sense of ownership in their operationalization.

Engagement with the international crimes protocols has also been affected by the strong adverse public reaction of African states to the issue of arrest warrants for the Sudanese President al-Bashir. In March 2009 a statement from the ICGLR expressed deep concern at the development although noting that member states, including Sudan, were 'enjoined to implement protocols addressing war crimes, crimes against humanity, fighting impunity as well as protection and assistance to internally displaced persons and refugees'.[45] Nevertheless it was urged that, 'bearing in mind that criminal justice has no time limit', the ICC investigation should be deferred so as to 'enable the AU to find appropriate mechanisms of reconciling the interrelated and equally important notions of justice and peace in Sudan'. Some of the most loudly heard criticisms of the ICC, namely that it constitutes 'outsiders' justice, might have been avoided if recourse had been

---

41   Law No. 009 of 2008 on the Prevention and Punishment of Gender Based Violence, 10 December 2008.

42   Conversations with staff of the ICGLR Secretariat, January 2011.

43   See for example the extraordinary summit of heads of state hosted in December 2010 in Zambia to activate the Protocol on the Fight Against Illegal Exploitation of Natural Resources. 2010. Eleven Heads of State expected at ICGLR summit. *Lusaka Times* [Online, 10 December] Available at: http://www.lusakatimes.com/2010/12/10/eleven-heads-states-expected-icglr-summit/ [accessed 6 January 2011].

44   It is understood, for example, that the Protocol on Non Aggression and Mutual Defence provided the legal basis for cooperation between the DRC, Uganda, Sudan and the CAR in joint operations against the Lord's Resistance Army.

45   See statement, ICGLR. 2009. *Concern about the Implications of Arrest Warrants against President Omar Al Bashir* [6 March] (on file with author).

had more expansively in policy discussions to the undertakings of the ICGLR.[46] Finally, there also appears to be a broader donor fatigue and, some would say, cynicism, about the ICGLR as another regional framework promising much but threatening to deliver little.[47] This may be a dissuasive factor for more active ICGLR engagement in an already crowded international justice field in the region, especially where the ICC appears to be increasingly centre-stage.

It is premature to assess the Pact's capacity to contribute to combating impunity for international crimes in the region barely two years after it came into force. A couple of preliminary conclusions, however, are possible:

- First, the discussion of accountability for international crimes within the ICGLR process over the last ten years has provided the backdrop against which other developments relating to international justice such as state referrals to the ICC and the creation of national level accountability instruments (in Burundi and Uganda for example) have been perhaps more readily encouraged.
- Second, the Pact has been part of a broader normative and ideological process in the region that has firmly and irrevocably confirmed tackling impunity for international crimes as a component of achieving sustainable peace and security. Although this normative acceptance has not yet been translated into effective domestic and regional practice, the region is alive with processes that, despite many inherent weaknesses, should help answer some of the critical questions about what an international justice practice that delivers to communities on the ground should look like in the future. These experiments are turning the region into a space where pursuing accountability for international crimes has become an accepted, albeit controversial, feature.
- Third, by placing SGBV crimes at the forefront of regional priorities (at least normatively and rhetorically) the Pact is helping to generate the fundamental change in cultural, security and political practices in the region that are necessary to put an end to this scourge. The strong advocacy

---

46   In fact in November 2008 the ICGLR Secretariat released a statement that strongly condemned the arrest in Germany of Rwandan official Rose Kabuye, calling it a 'blatant abuse' of universal jurisdiction. See Kagire, E. 2008. Rwanda: ICGLR condemns Kabuye arrest. *The New Times* [Online: all Africa Com, 13 November] Available at: http://allafrica. com/stories/200811130742.html [accessed 10 January 2011].

47   Conversations by author with diplomats from states outside of the region and members of the 'Friends of the ICGLR' grouping, Addis Ababa and Kampala, various dates, 2009 and 2010. The November 2009 donor round table, for example, resulted in few commitments to fund the Programme of Action. At the same time it should be noted that ten out of the eleven member states have themselves provided the expected financial support in the first three years of the ICGLR's operation, reflecting considerable regional buy-in to the process, notwithstanding international reluctance.

engagement by civil society and key UN agencies in relation to the SGBV Protocol testifies to its importance for this project.

- Fourth, although the ICC has dominated regional policy engagement on international justice during the last five years, the growing calls for justice to be done 'in the region' may prompt states to look again at the ICGLR as an alternative, regional framework and baseline for responding to international crimes.
- Finally, the increasing involvement by states in the region in efforts to tackle international crimes, epitomized by the Pact's undertakings, have arguably been an important spur for developments – both positive and retrograde – at the AU level around international justice.[48]

The Great Lakes region and developments at the AU

Developments in the Great Lakes region were in many ways the driver for the AU's re-conception of the role of justice and impunity in the context of conflict and peace. In 2000, African states decided that the protection of human rights would be a defining principle of the new AU and that sovereignty could yield to the principle of protection when exercised collectively through member states. The AU Constitutive Act of 2000 proclaimed that 'respect for the sanctity of human life' and 'condemnation and rejection of impunity' were among the core values that would guide the achievement of the Union's objectives. It asserted that collective interventionist action could be taken 'by the Union' in situations where grievous harm is threatened to individuals and populations. Article 4(h) thus provides for 'the right of the Union to intervene in a Member State ... in respect of grave circumstances, namely war crimes, genocide and crimes against humanity'. The comprehensive peace and security architecture subsequently developed by the AU, from the Panel of the Wise to the Continental Early Warning System, attempts to operationalize these undertakings.

The AU's adoption of the principles of non-impunity and the responsibility to protect marked a clear normative break with the emphasis by post-colonial Africa on the sanctity of traditional concepts of state sovereignty. In making this decision, the AU built upon the steps taken in the previous decades to use humanitarian grounds (among others) as a basis for intervention in situations of mass atrocity in places such as Uganda, Liberia and Sierra Leone. The development of article 4(h) of the AU Constitutive Act was particularly spurred by the recognition of the then

---

48   See discussion below. Although the ICGLR is not one of the eight regional organizations formally recognized by the AU, a memorandum of understanding was finally signed between the AU Commission and the ICGLR in October 2010. See note by the ICGLR. 2010. *ICGLR signs MoU with AUC and COMESA*. [Online, 26 November] Available at: http://www.icglr.org/spip.php?article75 [accessed 14 January 2011].

Organization of African Union's clear past failures to prevent gross human rights violations, especially in the Great Lakes region in CAR, Rwanda and Uganda.[49]

Since the adoption of the Constitutive Act, the pursuit of international justice can be seen as a theme in AU decision-making, whether institutionally, through commitments in the AU Strategic Plan to promote ratification of the ICC Rome Statute, or politically, through decisions of the AU Assembly such as that which mandated Senegal to prosecute former Chadian President Habré.[50] The increasing use of international criminal justice mechanisms to target officials on the continent has, however, shaken this trajectory. There is a growing clamour that the exercise of universal jurisdiction by European judges and the course of the ICC's investigations, such as the issue of arrest warrants against Sudan's President al-Bashir, have become 'abusive'[51] or, as a Rwandan official put it with respect to universal jurisdiction, a 'neo-colonial judicial coup d'etat'.[52] The more extreme potential consequences of the crisis, such as the threatened withdrawal by African state parties from the ICC Rome Statute, appear to have subsided. However, the sense that the region's capacity to deal independently with impunity and chart its own course in terms of ensuring peace and security is under threat from hostile outside forces, appears to be strongly embedded. The stand-off is particularly encapsulated in the AU's repeatedly expressed dismay that the UN Security Council has been ignoring its request for consideration of an article 16 deferral of the al-Bashir investigation.[53] It is in this context not surprising that the AU Assembly, in early 2009, requested the AU Commission, in consultation with the African Commission on Human and Peoples' Rights and the African Court on Human and Peoples' Rights, to examine the implications of the latter Court being empowered to try international crimes.[54] It is presumed that the substantive and procedural law of the Great Lakes Pact around the investigation and prosecution

---

49   See discussion of the evolution of article 4(h) by Kioko, B. 2003. The Right of Intervention under the African Union's Constitutive Act. *International Review of the Red Cross*, 85(852), 807–24, at 812.

50   Assembly of the African Union. 2006.

51   See AU Assembly. 2009. *Decision on the Abuse of the Principle of Universal Jurisdiction*. [July] Doc. Assembly/AU/Dec.243 (XIII).

52   See statement by Rwandan Justice Minister, Tharcisse Karugamara in, 2008. AU ministers condemn foreign indictments. *New Times* [Online, April] Available at: http://www. newtimes.co.rw/print.php?issue=14127&print&article=5743 [accessed 6 January 2011].

53   See AU Assembly. 2010. *Decision on the Progress Report of the Commission on the Implementation of Decision Assembly AU/DEC.270 (XIV) on the Second Ministerial Meeting on the Rome Statute of the International Criminal Court (ICC)*. Doc. Assembly/AU/Dec.296 (XV). [Online, July] Available at: http://www.iccnow.org/documents/AU_Decisions_Declarations_Resolutions__15th_Summit_July_2010_eng.pdf [accessed 10 January 2010].

54   See AU Assembly. 2009. *Decision on the Abuse of the Principle of Universal Jurisdiction*. [February] Doc. Assembly/AU/Dec.213 (XII).

of international crimes will be used as a starting point for any new jurisdiction, considering the extent to which the Pact has been ratified.

This new orientation towards the search for regional solutions to impunity, whether driven by a genuine desire to build local capacity or less principled motivations, may help bring the ICGLR process and the international justice elements of the Pact into greater prominence. The experts appointed jointly by the AU and the EU to examine the use of the principle of universal jurisdiction in 2009 not only endorsed the decision to explore the creation of regional jurisdiction, they also recommended that, in order to make article 4(h) of the Constitutive act effective

> African States should be encouraged to adopt national legislative and other measures aimed at preventing and punishing war crimes, genocide and crimes against humanity. To this end, the AU Commission should consider preparing model legislation for the implementation of measures of prevention and punishment.[55]

The Pact certainly provides a starting point for the creation of model legislation, not least the instrument developed to aid in the implementation of the SGBV Protocol. Discussions on the legislative options generated by the ICGLR process itself could also create momentum for the adoption of new standards and mechanisms across the continent, including consideration of the development of a new African criminal jurisdiction. In what may constitute a significant precedent in this regard, the new region-wide AU Convention on Assistance and Protection of Internally Displaced Persons in 2009 drew extensively on the text of, and the negotiations around, the Great Lakes Pact's Protocol on the Protection and Assistance of Internally Displaced Persons.

Reflections on the Great Lakes experience: Lessons for Sudan?

Over the last six years Sudan has provided a confusing theatre of contestation for the tools and objectives of international justice through interwoven processes of conflict and transition. The complexities of the struggle to do justice in Sudan – particularly embodied in the triggering of an ICC investigation by the UN Security Council – have had global reverberations, sparking perhaps the biggest crisis yet for the norms and mechanisms that have evolved to prevent mass atrocity. As noted in the previous section, the tensions created by the ICC's involvement in Sudan have particularly encouraged African states to explore what 'regional', as opposed to 'international', justice might entail. This has included the adoption of a host of measures from the creation of the AU High Level Panel on Darfur (the

---

55   See Recommendation 2, Conclusions. AU–EU Technical Ad hoc Expert Group on the Principle of Universal Jurisdiction. 2009.

Mbeki Panel) to the proposal to bestow criminal jurisdiction on the prospective African Court of Justice and Human and Peoples' Rights.

The question of impunity is critical to the future of Sudan. The failure in the past to deal effectively with ensuring accountability for mass atrocity in the successive agreements that have purported to end the country's various conflicts has fuelled cycles of conflict.[56] In fact it was the entry of the ICC on to the stage as a result of the Darfur crisis that made international criminal law for the first time both a real object of, and context for, political calculus. In addition, as outlined in the chapter on international crimes in Sudan (see chapter 7), the ICC has clearly had an impact on law reform efforts in relation to the prosecution for international crimes and spurred the establishment of the Special Court on the Events in Darfur in 2005 within days of the ICC Prosecutor being authorized to proceed with his investigation. The results, however, have been mostly cosmetic: no significant prosecutions have been undertaken and no effort has been made to pursue the responsibility of senior officials for the serious and multiple international crimes that are alleged to have been committed both in Darfur and in Sudan more broadly.

At the end of 2009 the Mbeki Panel identified fundamental weaknesses in the Sudanese criminal justice system, finding unequivocally that:

> [t]he perpetrators of the serious crimes in Darfur have overwhelmingly remained unpunished and the needs for healing and reconciliation have remained largely unmet. This situation must be rectified urgently and within the context of achieving a negotiated peace.[57]

At the end of 2010, over a year since the adoption by the AU Peace and Security Council of the conclusions of the Mbeki report, none of the Panel's justice, accountability and reconciliation recommendations – developed explicitly in the context of ongoing political negotiations – have been implemented. The focus of the Panel's efforts have shifted almost wholly to the post Comprehensive Peace Agreement (CPA) transitional arrangements.[58] Against this background, and considering that Sudan has been reaching out to African regional institutions to assist in the solution of its political crises, the role that sub-regional instruments can play in addressing both the current impasse in respect of justice for international crimes committed in Darfur and the need to establish an adequate criminal justice system in the future Sudan(s) – whether for past or future crimes – is likely to

---

56 The Comprehensive Peace Agreement (CPA) embraced the principle of national reconciliation and a bill of rights, but did not include any justice mechanisms to deal with past violations.

57 African Union High-Level Panel on Darfur (AUPD). 2009. *Darfur: The Quest for Peace, Justice and Reconciliation*, Report to the African Union. PSC/AHG/2 (CCVII), xvi, at para. 17.

58 See African Union. 2010. *Report of the Chairperson of the Commission on the Situation in the Sudan and on the Activities of the African Union High Level Implementation Panel on Sudan*. [30 November] PSC/AHG/3 (CCL).

become increasingly relevant. The ratification of the Great Lakes Pact has been one of the most interesting outcomes of Sudan's renewed sub-regional engagement. It is remarkable that Sudan ratified the Pact, containing such significant obligations, at a time when there was so much negative focus by the international community on its human rights record. Whether for reasons of principle, lack of knowledge, or political pragmatics, however, the key regional and international actors have paid little attention to the potential of the ICGLR framework to facilitate engagement on transitional issues in Sudan. The Mbeki Panel report, for example, nowhere mentions the Pact despite the genesis of the Panel in the desire of African states to create a viable regional justice alternative to break the Darfur ICC stalemate.[59] The fact that the Pact contained international instruments with transitional justice components that had arguably[60] been encompassed within Sudanese Interim National Constitution's (INC) Bill of Rights by virtue of article 27(3) did not appear to figure in the Panel's legal or contextual analysis.

As Sudan is in the midst of breaking up into two states that will carry a heavy legacy of impunity for international crimes, the Great Lakes region presents a rich well of experiences in the practice of international justice from which those engaged in Sudanese law and policy reform can draw. The region has employed many of the key mechanisms for the pursuit of international crimes and continues to evolve new approaches. Although the context in Sudan is extremely politically challenging – and it is not clear whether both Sudanese states will remain as parties to and/or accede to the Pact[61] – it is possible that the Pact could provide not just a framework of standards, and for exchange of experiences and regional cooperation but also a regional context for decision making and negotiation in the area of international justice in Sudan:

- First, the Great Lakes Pact itself constitutes a minimum set of legal obligations that can serve as baseline for the current peace and transitional negotiations. Beyond its strictly international criminal law components, the Pact indentifies a range of obligations relating to land restitution, gender equality and SGBV, the principle of non-discrimination, the rights of minorities, protection of the forcibly displaced, and democratic governance

---

59   It had also received submissions on the content of the Pact from the perspective of Sudanese law. See Darfur Consortium. 2010. *Submission to the Mbeki Panel* (confidential, on file with author).

60   In the Pact the combating of international crimes is clearly conceived as a human rights matter: the International Crimes Protocol declares, for example, that States recognize that 'the crimes of genocide, war crimes, and crimes against humanity […] are crimes against people's rights which they undertake to prevent and punish' (Article 8).

61   The Government of Southern Sudan is definitely looking southwards to the sub-regional networks for post-independence membership, including in the East African community and ICGLR. Interviews by the author with officials from the Ministry of Constitutional and Legal Affairs. Juba. July 2010.

that are essential for an effective national programme of transitional justice. The Pact also provides a legal and political foundation stone upon which a regionally mandated mechanism could be constructed or through which regional support could be channeled to a Sudanese special mechanism which adhered to Pact principles and law. Politically, as an international agreement entered into by Sudan at the height of the Darfur crisis, and amid very real tensions around the place of the ICC in Sudan, the Pact is difficult to reject as an inappropriate instrument of reference.

• Second, those aspects of the Pact's framework that can be considered as constitutional norms may provide a source of law for litigation around questions of the right to redress for international crimes – although considering the human rights jurisprudence record of the current constitutional court this potential is perhaps more theoretical than real.[62]

• Third, from the point of view of the law reform *processes* that are expected to unfold in both the South and the North over the next few years, the Pact contains critical standards, monitoring mechanisms (for example the Regional Committee for the prevention and punishment of genocide, war crimes and crimes against humanity and all forms of discrimination), draft legislation and a procedure for civil society involvement in the Pact's implementation and monitoring that can be engaged, either through national or regional fora. Rooting debate on impunity in the Pact's provisions may also create an opportunity for discussion of accountability that is rooted in regional cooperation and less amenable to rejection on the grounds of external or international 'interference'.

---

62   See chapter 3.

IV. Criminal Law and Gender-Based Violence

Gender-based violence: Nature, practice and concerns

Gender-based violence (here used to denote 'violence against women', particularly 'sexual violence') is at its most glaring where used as a 'weapon of war', as recent conflicts in the former Yugoslavia, the Democratic Republic of Congo and Darfur have demonstrated.[1] It is also frequently used as a form of torture and ill-treatment in custodial contexts[2] and committed in the 'private sphere', including in form of domestic violence. These forms of gender-based violence, though perpetrated in seemingly very different contexts, reflect underlying gender relationships and the use of violence to enforce or reinforce power structures. The way in which the state responds to such violence is therefore crucial: does it take measures to prevent and repress sexual violence, including far-reaching reforms, as it did in a number of Southern African countries;[3] or does it fail to take any such measures, thereby perpetuating a situation that facilitates violations?[4] To go even further, does the state entrench a system of gendered justice characterized by discriminatory laws that violate women's rights, as has happened for example in Iran, Pakistan and Sudan?[5] The role of sexual violence and the gender dimensions of conflicts and dictatorship had played a rather marginal role in earlier transitions,[6] but has now become a more prominent feature of 'transitional justice' processes, for example in

---

1 UN Security Council resolution 1820 (2008) refers to the use of sexual violence as 'tactic of war'.

2 UN Special Rapporteur on torture and other cruel, inhuman or degrading treatment or punishment, Manfred Nowak. 2008. *Report*. UN Doc. A/HRC/7/3.

3 See chapter 12 on reforms in Southern Africa.

4 UN Special Rapporteur on Violence against Women, its causes and consequences, Yakin Ertürk. 2006a. *The Due Diligence Standard as a Tool for the Elimination of Violence against Women.* UN Doc. E/CN.4/2006/61.

5 See chapters 10 and 11 on Sudan and Pakistan respectively. On Iran, see UN Special Rapporteur on violence against women, its causes and consequences, Yakin Ertürk. 2006b. *Mission to the Islamic Republic of Iran (29 January to 6 February 2005).* UN Doc. E/CN.4/2006/61/Add.3.

6 Bell, C. and O'Rourke, C. 2007. Does Feminism Need a Theory of Transitional Justice? An Introductory Essay. *The International Journal of Transitional Justice*, 1(1), 23–44.

the recent Truth and Reconciliation Commission in Liberia.[7] Indeed, in a number of states such as Sierra Leone, South Africa and Peru, truth and reconciliation commissions have recommend reparation for victims of sexual violence.[8] This change can be greatly attributed to national and international women's rights movements, and the role of individuals – including judges of international tribunals – who have highlighted the nature of gender-based violence and contributed to the recognition of sexual violence as international crimes.[9]

2. International standards

2.1. Non-discrimination and gender-based violence in international law

The worldwide prevalence of gender-based violence is greatly facilitated by impunity; this is often underpinned by gender bias, the subordination of women, and the lack of political will to effectively repress violations. Women's rights were initially conceived as the right to non-discrimination as reflected in the Convention on the Elimination of Discrimination against Women, with gender-based violence considered primarily a private matter. This prompted sustained critiques of the adequacy of the international legal framework.[10] United Nations (UN) bodies and states slowly began to recognize gender-based violence as a serious human rights violation, significantly with the Declaration on the Elimination of Violence against Women (DEVAW), adopted by the UN General Assembly in 1993.[11] Other bodies, notably the UN Security Council, subsequently condemned rape and sexual violence against women as forms of torture, and as international crimes and violations in their own right.[12] International human rights treaty bodies have also recognized that violence against women may constitute

---

7   See Republic of Liberia, Truth and Reconciliation Commission. 2009. *Report*. Vol. 3, Appendices, Title 1: Women and the Conflict.

8   See for an overview, UN Special Rapporteur on violence against women, its causes and consequences, Ms. Radhika Coomaraswamy. 2003. *International, regional and national developments in the area of violence against women, 1994 to 2003.* UN Doc. E/CN.4/2003/75/Add.3.

9   Halley, J. 2008. Rape at Rome: Feminist Interventions in the Criminalization of Sex-Related Violence in Positive International Criminal Law. *Michigan Journal of International Law* 30(1), 1–123.

10   See Charlesworth, H. and Chinkin, C. 2000. *The Boundaries of International Law: A Feminist Analysis*. Manchester: Manchester University Press.

11   *Declaration on the Elimination of Violence against Women*, UN General Assembly resolution 48/104 (1993).

12   UN Security Council resolutions on Women and Peace and Security 1325 (2000); 1820 (2008), 1888 (2009) and 1889 (2009).

torture or other forms of inhuman, degrading or cruel treatment. This applies in particular to rape committed by or with the acquiescence of state officials.[13]

The adoption of the Protocol to the African Charter on Human and Peoples' Rights (AfrCHPR) on the Rights of Women in Africa in 2003 (of which Sudan is not a state party at the time of writing), is the most significant regional development in recent years, seeking to articulate an approach to women's rights that reflects African realities.[14] Notably, article 1(j) of the Protocol expands the definition of violence against women contained in the DEVAW by stipulating that:

> Violence against women means all acts perpetrated against women which cause or could cause them physical, sexual, psychological, and economic harm, including the threat to take such acts; or to undertake the imposition of arbitrary restrictions on or deprivation of fundamental freedoms in private or public life in peace time and during situations of armed conflicts or of war.

2.2. States' positive obligations to prevent and repress gender-based violence

As specified in the DEVAW, states should 'exercise due diligence to prevent, investigate and, in accordance with national legislation, punish acts of violence against women, whether those acts are perpetrated by the State or by private persons'.[15] The due diligence principle has been applied equally by CEDAW,[16] the Special Rapporteur on the Elimination of All Forms of Violence against Women,[17] and in the jurisprudence of human rights courts and treaty bodies.[18] The principle entails a state duty to enact effective legislation against rape and other forms of

---

13   *Aydin v Turkey*, 25 EHRR 251 (1997), para. 83; *Maslova and Nalbandov v Russia* (Application no. 839/02), European Court of Human Rights, Judgment, 24 January 2008, para. 107; *Raquel Martí de Mejía v Perú*. Case 10.970. Report No. 5/96, Inter-American Commission on Human Rights. OEA/Ser.L/V/II.91 Doc. 7 at 157 (1996); *Miguel Castro-Castro Prison v Peru*. Merits, Reparations and Costs. Inter-American Court of Human Rights (Inter-Am. CtHR), Judgment, 25 November 2006, Series C. No. 160, paras 310–13; *V.L. v Switzerland*, Committee against Torture (CAT), Communication No. 262/2005, UN Doc. CAT/C/37/D/262/2005 (2006), para. 8.10.

14   See Banda, F. 2005. *Women, Law and Human Rights: An African Perspective*. Oxford: Hart.

15   UN General Assembly resolution 48/104 (1993).

16   Committee on the Elimination of Forms of Discrimination against Women (CEDAW). 2008. *General Recommendation No. 19 (11th Session, 1992)*. Compilation of General Comments and Recommendations adopted by Human Rights Treaty Bodies. UN Doc. HRI/GEN/I/Rev.9, 331–6, para. 9.

17   UN Special Rapporteur on Violence against Women. 2006a.

18   *Velasquez Rodriguez v Honduras*. Merits. Inter-Am. CtHR., Judgment, 29 July 1988. Series C No. 4.

sexual violence. In *M.C. v Bulgaria*, the European Court of Human Rights found that Bulgaria's rape laws had failed to provide adequate protection because they fostered impunity and held that: 'states have a positive obligation ... to enact criminal-law provisions effectively punishing rape and to apply them in practice through effective investigation and prosecution'.[19]

This position is echoed in the practice of CEDAW, which issued a number of specific recommendations to states parties, in particular to take:

> Legal and other measures that are necessary to provide effective protection of women against gender-based violence, including, inter alia:

> (i) Effective legal measures, including penal sanctions, civil remedies and compensatory provisions to protect women against all kinds of violence, including inter alia violence and abuse in the family, sexual assault and sexual harassment in the workplace...[20]

This is complemented by the practice of other international human rights treaty bodies, which have repeatedly called on individual states parties to adopt legislation to criminalize and prosecute rape and other forms of sexual violence, including domestic violence.[21]

Acts of sexual violence may also constitute international crimes that entail individual criminal responsibility. The International Criminal Tribunal for Rwanda (ICTR) recognized that rape may constitute genocide even though it is not explicitly mentioned in the definition of genocide;[22] and rape and sexual violence are listed as a crime against humanity in article 5(g) of the Statute of the International Criminal Tribunal for the Former Yugoslavia (ICTY),[23] article

---

19   *M.C. v Bulgaria*, 40 EHRR 20 (2005), para. 153.

20   CEDAW. 2008, para. 24(t)(i). See for the jurisprudence of the Committee on positive obligations, *Ms. A.T. v Hungary*, Communication No. 4/2004, UN Doc. CEDAW/C/36/D/2004 (2006).

21   CEDAW. 2007. *Concluding Observations: India*. UN Doc. CEDAW/C/IND/CO/3, paras 22–3; Human Rights Committee (HRC). 2007. *Concluding observations: Libyan Arab Jamahiriya*. UN Doc. CCPR/C/LBY/CO/4, para. 10; *Concluding observations: Sudan*. UN Doc. CCPR/C/SDN/CO/3/CRP.1, para. 14(b).

22   *Prosecutor v Gacumbitsi* (Case No. ICTR-2001-64-T), Judgment, 14 June 2004, para. 291; *Prosecutor v Musema* (Case No. ICTR-96-13-A), Judgment, 27 January 2000, para. 933; and *Prosecutor v Akayesu* (Case No. ICTR-96-4-T), Judgment, 2 September 1998, para. 508.

23   UN Security Council resolution 827 (1993). Annex: Statute of the International Tribunal for the Prosecution of Persons Responsible for Serious Violations of International Humanitarian Law committed in the territory of the former Yugoslavia since 1991 (Report of the Secretary-General pursuant to paragraph 2 of Security Council resolution 808 (1993) Doc S/25704 of 3 May 1993).

3(g) of the ICTR Statute[24] and article 7(g) of the 1998 Rome Statute of the International Criminal Court (ICC). Both the ICTY and the ICTR found rape to constitute a crime against humanity in several cases, such as *Prosecutor v Furundžija, Prosecutor v Delalic, Prosecutor v Akayesu, Prosecutor v Musema* and *Prosecutor v Semanza.*[25]

Rape is recognized as a war crime if committed in the course of an armed conflict (both international and non-international) as stipulated in article 2 of the ICTY Statute, article 4(e) of the ICTR Statute and article 8(2)(a)(ii), (iii) and 8(2)(b)(xxii) of the ICC Rome Statute. The ICTY held in its jurisprudence in *Prosecutor v Furundžija* that 'rape may amount to a grave breach of the Geneva Conventions [and/or] a violation of the laws or customs of war',[26] and the ICTR ruled that rape is a war crime, such as in *Prosecutor v Akayesu, Prosecutor v Musema* and *Prosecutor v Semanza.*[27]

Rape constitutes a gross violation of international human rights law (if committed by or with the involvement of state agents) and a serious violation of international humanitarian law (if committed in the course of an armed conflict). Victims of rape have the right to an effective remedy and reparation under international law, which can be derived from, *inter alia*, article 2(3) of the International Covenant on Civil and Political Rights (ICCPR)[28] and articles 1 and 5 of the AfrCHPR[29]. Victims of rape and sexual violence must have effective access to judicial remedies that enable them to vindicate their rights. Legislation should spell out the forms of reparation to which rape victims are entitled. In addition to compensation for material and moral damages, this includes rehabilitation services and measures of satisfaction. States should also consider setting up special mechanisms or committees vested with the power to recommend or award reparation to victims of rape and sexual violence, as has happened in a number of instances.[30] As stipulated in the *Nairobi Declaration on Women's and Girls' Right to a Remedy and Reparation*, '[a]ll policies and measures relating to reparation must explicitly be based on the principle of non-discrimination' and should 'be

---

24   UN Security Council resolution 955 (1994). Annex: Statute of the International Tribunal for Rwanda.

25   *Prosecutor v Furundžija* (Case No. IT-95-17/1-T), Judgment, 10 December 1998; and *Prosecutor v Delalic* (Case No. IT-96-21-T), Judgment, 16 November 1998; *Prosecutor v Akayesu* (Case No. ICTR-96-4-T), Judgment, 2 September 1998; *Prosecutor v Musema* (Case No. ICTR-96-13-A), Judgment, 27 January 2000; and *Prosecutor v Semanza* (ICTR-97-20-T), Judgment, 15 May 2003.

26   *Prosecutor v Furundžija*, para. 172.

27   *Prosecutor v Akayesu; Prosecutor v Musema* and *Prosecutor v Semanza.*

28   HRC. 2004. *General Comment 31: The Nature of the General Legal Obligation imposed on States Parties to the Covenant.* UN Doc. CCPR/C/21/Rev.1/Add.13, paras 15–16.

29   See also Basic Principles and Guidelines on the Right to a Remedy and Reparation for Victims of Gross Violations of International Human Rights Law and Serious Violations of International Humanitarian Law, UN General Assembly resolution 60/147 (2006).

30   See UN Special Rapporteur on violence against women. 2003.

sensitive to gender, age, cultural diversity and human rights and must take into account women's and girls' specific circumstances, as well as their dignity, privacy and safety'.[31]

---

31 *Nairobi Declaration on Women's and Girls' Right to a Remedy and Reparation*, issued at the International Meeting on Women's and Girls' Right to a Remedy and Reparation (2007). [Online, 21 March] Available at: http://www.womensrightscoalition.org/site/reparation/signature_en.php [accessed 16 December 2010].

Chapter 10

Gendered Justice: Women and the Application of Penal Laws in the Sudan

Asma Abdel Halim

How are we to understand criminal law reform? The idea seems simple – the criminal law on the books is wrong: it should be changed. But 'wrong' how? By what norms 'wrong'? As soon as one tries to answer those questions, the issue becomes more complex. One kind of answer is that the criminal law is substantively wrong: that is, we assume valid norms of background political morality, and we argue that doctrinally the criminal law on the books does not embody those norms. Another kind of answer is that the criminal law as it stands presupposes certain empirical facts, and yet those facts do not hold. Traditionally, criminal law reform has been informed by both these answers.

Roger A. Shiner[1]

Introduction

This chapter considers why gender disparity in the Sudanese Criminal Act, 1991, and other laws and regulations should be addressed when we theorize or debate the criminal law in the country. I argue that the gendered nature of existing law gravely affects women and their rights, and that gender equality may be achievable through doctrinal reform. The chapter focuses on sexual crimes and the gender-biased laws applied to punish sexual acts.

It is necessary to provide a brief history of the legal status of women in the Sudan and the main challenges women face in seeking the realization of their rights. These challenges emanate from religious conventions and the adoption of a version of *Shari'a* that is often in contradiction with the very international treaties that the Interim National Constitution (INC) of 2005 vows to follow and make part of the law of the land. Given the fact that Sudan's current criminal law is derived from *Shari'a*, one is tempted to examine the doctrinal aspects of it; however, the law presently applied in the Sudan is the result of a political process that is built on the idea of control of the people, especially women, rather than on considerations of a doctrinal nature. As a result, reform is needed, not least because

---

1   Shiner, R.A. 2009. Theorising criminal law reform. *Criminal Law and Philosophy.* 3(2), 167–86, at 167.

current Sudanese laws on gender constitute an international embarrassment for the country and the Islamic world.

The cultural and traditional values of Sudan's people constitute an important aspect of the law and its application. This applies not just to the traditions of Muslims but to all other creeds in the country. If the state had wanted a law to apply to and be accepted by all people within its borders, then choosing a particular interpretation of one religion to rule everyone was the first political mistake. Yet this is not to say that an Islamic legal system cannot be inclusive; at issue is the failure to follow the correct methods, such as adhering to the constitution, avoiding the pitfalls of arbitrary imposition and enforcement of the law (particularly during the Nimeiri era), and paying attention to how Islam is practised in the various parts of the country. This failure resulted in the adoption of a legal philosophy that breached human rights, failed to uphold the rule of law and created a system that did not connect the substantive law to the lives of the people.

The current criminal law embodies gender discrimination that infringes on women's rights by giving women an unfair share of responsibility, a heavy burden in the protection of honour, and a lack of protection against abuse. There is need for a wholesale reform that addresses all aspects of discrimination inherent in the law with a view to ensuring that the state meets its obligation to respect, protect and fulfil women's rights.

The Islamization of all laws that followed the constitutional crisis of 1983, when the judges went on a strike that lasted for three months, ended the plurality of laws that had hitherto been applied in the Sudan.[2] Dina S. Osman summed up the situation when she stated that: '[t]he conflict between *Shar'ia* and other rules has been resolved in favor of the former. One can safely state now that under these laws, *Shar'ia* rules are supreme'.[3] The supremacy of the politically driven version of *Shari'a* defeats any claim of 'giving' women all their rights. The legal situation of women in some areas of the law is actually worse than it was twenty years ago, and closer to norms applied in the *Mahdist* state over a hundred years ago.[4]

Islamic states have applied different versions of Islamic law that have come to be known as *Shari'a*, and as a religious state the Sudan is expected to adopt a version of Islamic law based on the *Qur'an* and the *Sunna* as its main sources. How the *Qur'an* and *Sunna* are interpreted to provide Islamic codes is the basis of law-making in Muslim nations. Sudanese law endorses the gender discrimination found in the early interpretations of Islamic law. This aspect is accentuated in practice because the religious and human rights values are disregarded at the expense of political goals. The Comprehensive Peace Agreement (CPA) of 2005, which ended the war in Southern Sudan, was concluded with an almost total exclusion of women, translating into peace without gender justice. The women

---

2   See chapter 2.

3   Osman, D.S. 1985. The legal status of women in the Sudan. *Journal of East African Research and Development*, 15, 124–42, at 134.

4   See chapter 2.

– whose suffering of sexual violence in their ruined villages or their trafficking to other places, had been one the first issues that attracted international attention – were not active participants in the CPA and it did not contain any mention of women's rights and justice.

The guarantees in Sudan's various successive constitutions have proved to be ineffective in protecting women's rights, since it has kept its reputation of being a place that disregards its own constitutions. The current interim constitution is no exception, notwithstanding the Bill of Rights in the INC, which in its article 27(3) provides that '[a]ll rights and freedoms enshrined in international human rights treaties, covenants and instruments ratified by the Republic of the Sudan, shall be an integral part of this Bill'. The constitution has not resulted in efforts to bring national laws in conformity with the requirements of the International Covenant on Civil and Political Rights (ICCPR) and the African Charter on Human and Peoples' Rights (AfrCHPR) to which the Sudan is a party, virtually ignoring article 27(4), according to which '[l]egislation shall regulate the rights and freedoms enshrined in this Bill and shall not detract from or derogate any of these rights'. In addition, the (selective) recognition of the rights of women in article 32[5] has not been reinforced by the Sudan becoming a state party to the Convention on the Elimination of all Forms of Discrimination against Women or the Protocol to the AfrCHPR on the Rights of Women in Africa. This very fact calls into question Sudan's commitment to respect the rights contained therein.

Issues of gender, class and even ethnicity overshadow the bright Bill of Rights. Gender disparities are readily apparent and the distinction in the Criminal Act of 1991 is clearly an ethnic rather than a religious differentiation.[6] Discrimination on the basis of sex contained in the Criminal Act could make a textbook case for a constitutional challenge. However, as rightly argued by lawyer Taha Ibrahim, the Constitutional Court Act of 2005 has closed the door in the face of any action that challenges court rulings, since its article 15(2) expressly removes the authority of the Constitutional Court to review judgments passed by the judiciary.[7] Therefore judgments will stand even if they were based on a law incompatible with the constitution. To declare a law unconstitutional requires one to a have *locus standi*, a status that is not attainable unless the law has been applied to the

---

5   Article 32(1): 'The State shall guarantee equal right of men and women to the enjoyment of all civil, political, social, cultural and economic rights, including the right to equal pay for equal work and other related benefits. (2) The State shall promote woman rights through affirmative action. (3) The State shall combat harmful customs and traditions which undermine the dignity and the status of women. (4) The State shall provide maternity and child care and medical care for pregnant women. (5) The State shall protect the rights of the child as provided in the international and regional conventions ratified by the Sudan '·

6   The Criminal Act prescribes different punishment for *zina* as well as the consumption and sale of liquor in Southern Sudan.

7   Taha Ibrahim. 2006. *Quaneen ghair dustouria: la dustouriat quaneen al-Inqadh wa dharourat ilgha'iha* [*Unconstitutional laws: the unconstitutionality of the Salvation laws and the necessity for repealing them*]. Cairo: Sudanese Organization of Human Rights.

plaintiff. Fear that such a law may apply in a case is not a sufficient ground to bring a constitutional case, leaving an important gap in the protection of constitutional rights.

Sexual crimes and punishment in Sudanese law

Background

The gender bias that marked the early interpretations of Islamic norms in the eighth and ninth centuries[8] has been carried into the current laws without examination or attention to the constitution. This is evident in the case of sexual offences and applicable punishments. The crime of *zina* (fornication in case of an unmarried partner and adultery in case of a married one) and its punishment have been stipulated in terms that show how womanhood and femininity are seen by the legislature. They serve as instructive examples of how the scale is tipped against women despite the semblance of equality in the law.

At the substantive level Islam has zero tolerance for extra-marital or pre-marital sex. The *hudud* laws mentioned in the *Qur'an*[9] do not attribute any special personality or character deficiency to women that may warrant a different treatment of females. However, women are more likely to be punished for sexual crimes because they are women, and this sexist dimension of the criminal law is particularly evident in the way in which the behavior of women is controlled and criminalized. The presumed equality of the sexes in the *hudud* is defeated by the social construction of femininity as a source of seduction for men, who society, ironically, designates as the stronger sex, assigning them the role of guardians of women. The criminal law is complemented by other laws such as the Public Order Act of the State of Khartoum of 1998[10] whose primary objective is to control and punish women, as discussed in another part of this chapter (see below, *The Public Order Act*).

---

8   See for example the simplified form of the interpretation of the Qur'an by the scholar Ibn Katheer al-Saboony, M.A. (ed.). 1995. *Mukhtasar Tafseer Ibn Katheer*. 8th Edition. Vol. 1. Cairo: Dar al-Saboony, 385.

9   The five crimes agreed upon by all interpreters are those mentioned in the following chapters of the *Qur'an*: *zina* in 24:2; *qadhf* (false accusation of zina) in 24:4; theft in 5:28; *hiraba* (robbery or rebellion) in 5:33 and consumption and dealing in liquor prescribed in *Sunna* by the prophet.

10   Khartoum Public Order Act of 1998. Available at: http://www.pclrs.org/Khartoum_ Public_Order_Act_1998.pdf [accessed 17 September 2010].

Zina

Zina is the act of fornication or adultery in the case of married people.[11] *Shari'a* and the Sudanese criminal law follow an absolute rule of evidence according to which the only acceptable proof of *zina* is the testimony of four well-reputed men (*Udoul*). The witnesses must be in complete agreement on all details concerning the venue of the crime and the actual sexual intercourse. In case of a woman's *zina*, her pregnancy is sufficient evidence if she is not married. Such pregnancy rebuts the legal and constitutional presumption of innocence and immediately shifts the burden to the woman to prove her innocence. Her partner, in contrast, will not be subject to further prosecution if he simply denies *zina*. A woman accused of *zina* may escape punishment by claiming rape, and in an important precedent, Sudan's Supreme Court accepted the rape defence without burdening the woman with proof of that rape.[12] A woman may now claim rape by an unknown person, and in the absence of any proof of her consent to the sexual act, her claim of rape must be accepted as a defence.

A woman has no recourse against a husband who commits adultery unless she produces four witnesses as mentioned above. However, a man may prove his wife's *zina* by taking the oath prescribed in the *Qur'an*[13] and stipulated in section 62(d) of the Evidence Act, 1994.[14] Her only way of avoiding the death penalty in such a case is to take a similar oath denying *zina*.[15] The oath in the *Qur'an* is prescribed according to the socially acceptable behaviour of women in the pre-Islamic era. At that time, women would leave partners or husbands by simply changing the tent door opening. It was for this reason that they were taken to be the ones who were likely to commit *zina*. Notably, the *Qur'an* did not prevent the application of the same procedure of oath and counter-oath in the case of a woman accusing her husband of adultery. In this time of sexually transmitted diseases, reforming the law may involve applying the same procedure for both sexes.

---

11   *Zina* in the Criminal Act, 1991, is defined in section 145(1) as: 'There shall be deemed to commit adultery: (a) every man who has sexual intercourse with a woman without there being a lawful bond between them; (b) every woman who permits a man to have sexual intercourse with her without there being a lawful bond between them. (2) Sexual intercourse takes place by the penetration of the whole glans or its equivalent into the vulva'.

12   See *Sudan Government v al-Hajja al-Hussien Sulieman* SC/84/1406 [*Hijri*] (1985). The principle in this case has been followed in numerous cases.

13   *Surat Alnur*, chapter 24 of the *Qur'an*, verses 6–9, prescribe the oath to be taken by a husband to prove his wife's adultery and the counter-oath to be taken by his wife to refute the evidence and avert capital punishment.

14   The Evidence Act of 1994 (Arabic version). Available at: http://www.pclrs.org/downloads/bills/Miscellaneous/Evidence%20Act%20Arabic.pdf [accessed 17 September 2010].

15   The counter-oath of a woman that spares her punishment for *zina* (capital punishment) is not listed among the reasons for remittance of punishment in section 147 of the Criminal Act, 1991.

Rape and sodomy

The Sudanese law barely views sexual violence as an assault on a woman's body. The first indication of how the law perceives sexual violence is the classification of the crime of rape. Rape does not come under the chapter titled 'Offences Affecting Persons and Human Body'; rather, it is included in the chapter on 'Offences of Honour, Reputation and Public Morality'. Yet the physical and mental harm done to the victim of rape, be it a man or a woman, should be sufficient ground to categorize rape as an offence against the person. Rape is an assault and a violation; it is not just a matter of reputation and a breach of honour as in cases of *Qadhf* (defamation by accusing someone of a sexual crime). Such a classification leaves no doubt that rape is seen as a sexual act that affects honour and reputation, rather than a violent act that has effects on the body and mental state of a person.

The most patent form of gender disparity in the law is found in the wording of section 149(3) of the Criminal Act that punishes rape, and has triggered campaigns by women's and human rights organizations calling for reforms. The section stipulates that: '[w]hoever commits the offence of rape, shall be punished, with whipping a hundred lashes, and with imprisonment, for a term, not exceeding ten years, *unless rape constitutes the offence of adultery, or sodomy*, punishable with death (emphasis added)'. Both rape and *zina* are described as sexual intercourse between a man and a women; the only difference is that *zina* is a consensual intercourse, and rape is defined as non-consensual intercourse.

Article 149 of the Criminal Act creates the strange anomaly that intercourse in the case of rape is subject to the same proof as *zina*. The principle that legislators are supposed to avoid making the law a trap to penalize people appears to have been, and continues to be, ignored by the Sudanese legislature. In a trial of rape the law presumes that a consensual act, *zina*, has been committed whenever a non-consensual act, rape, is alleged. The sheer ability to make such a presumption means that the law starts from the premise that a rape victim is a liar and may not be believed until the prosecution fails to prove that she has committed *zina*. Indeed, the very idea that proof of rape should be the production of four witnesses to the sexual act is a strange one.[16]

Another difficulty for rape victims is that the elements of the crime of rape are similar to those of zina minus consent – that is, there has to be penetration by a man. Other violent acts such as using a bottle neck, a gun or any other object to violate the woman, are not considered rape. This penetration is in line with

---

16   The difference between the instances of a woman initiating criminal proceedings as complainant, and that of the prosecutor initiating proceedings is a technical one. In the first case she must produce four witnesses to prove the rape or suffer the consequences of being prosecuted for *zina*. In the second case the burden of proof is on the prosecution to produce the four witnesses. Failing that the case against the woman will be discontinued.

the classification of rape as a crime against honour and reputation.[17] A woman's honour is not breached, according to the law, unless sexual intercourse takes place. This amounts to saying that attacking the private parts of a woman with any instrument does not breach her honour; it is the organ of the man that determines whether the honour and reputation of a woman is marred. To make the elements of rape the same as a normal sexual act is to give it a benign non-injurious nature, and to suggest that, other than the blemished honour of the victim and her family, there are no further injuries to the woman concerned. This is also evidenced by sections 32 and 62 of the Evidence Act, which rule out the testimony of an expert in proving *zina*. This inadmissibility of expert testimony results from an adherence to the requirement of strict proof by four witnesses prescribed in the *Qur'an*, which was originally aimed at reducing the scope for implicating individuals for a crime that carries a harsh punishment. Also, by declaring rape a crime against honour and reputation, the law does more than hurt a woman's honour; it places her between a rock and a hard place. In Sudanese society the honour of the family supplants that of the victim; she will be pushed to the background if the rape is proven and will be ostracized or even killed if the court decides that rape did not take place. A radical reform is needed here if women's lives count and are to be adequately protected by the state.

Subjecting the crimes of rape and *zina* to the same evidential standard doubles the burden on the woman who files a complaint of rape.[18] The accused man may easily escape any prosecution or conviction by simply denying the woman's claim, and she may have to stand trial for fornication or adultery, depending on her marital status. This is a huge burden that most women would aim to avoid. Yet attempting to avoid possible prosecution may not be the end of a raped woman's ordeal, for if that rape results in pregnancy she also has to face social ostracism. In the case of *Sudan Government v Kalthoum Khalifa Ajabna*,[19] Kalthoum faced prosecution when she gave birth, killed and buried her child in the backyard of her home. Initially she did not contradict the statement by the police that she had committed *zina*, but when the court of first instance decided that she was guilty of a crime punishable by death, she appealed and retracted her confession. Two of the three members of the Supreme Court held that a retracted confession at any stage of the trial, even at the last stage of appeal, is a good reason to remit a *hudud* punishment. In addition, a divorced woman may not be treated as *muhsana* (meaning one in a valid marriage), which is a prerequisite for the application of the *hudud* punishment (that is stoning) for adultery. For those reasons, the Supreme

---

17   Section 145(2) of the Criminal Act, 1991, explains that sexual intercourse that constitutes *zina* is 'the penetration of the whole glans or its equivalent into the vulva'.

18   See for illustration of this, Fricke, A.L. and Khair, A. 2007. *Laws without Justice: An Assessment of Sudanese Laws Affecting Survivors of Rape*. Washington DC: Refugees International.

19   *Sudan Government v Kalthoum Khalifa Ajabna*. HC/48/1992.

Court dismissed the case of *zina* against her. It therefore took the wisdom of the court to avert the consequences of the Criminal Act.

Sodomy[20] is a crime that is treated by Sudanese society and law-makers as an unacceptable act that should be punished. Whether sodomy is between consenting adults, a man and a woman, a man and another man, or is an act of rape, it is punishable under section 148(2) of the Criminal Act. Sodomy is not one of the *hudud* crimes, therefore the punishment is *ta'azir* (crimes punished at the discretion of the ruling authority), with three convictions for sodomy leading to the death penalty. Where a woman is raped through being sodomized the four witnesses rule does not apply, and the court may accept any evidence that is permissible to prove the crime.

Marital rape

While the 1974 Penal Code expressly allowed marital rape, its successor, the Criminal Act, 1991, is silent on the matter. This form of violence against women is closely linked to other *Shari'a* norms, specifically the Personal Status for Muslims Act, 1991 (PSMA). A husband under the PSMA has an unfettered right to his wife's body as long as he does not cause her harm.[21] This amounts to a presumption of the law that a woman consenting to a contract of marriage has also consented to a duty of being sexually available at all times. Although the PSMA quotes the *Qur'an* and *hadith* (words or acts of the Prophet Muhammad constituting a source of Islamic law) regarding cordial and peaceful marital relations, the law is concerned with the technical parts of the contract that makes the *mahr*[22] a consideration for unfettered accessibility. The only instance in which a woman may justifiably deny conjugal services is when her *mahr* is not paid. Lisa Hajjar states that:

> Marital rape is another form of domestic violence for which justification on the basis of shari'a can be found. Although rape is a punishable crime in every

---

20   The translation of the 1991 Criminal Act provided by Brill Publishers translates *liwat* or sodomy as homosexuality. However, sodomy is not necessarily an act committed only by homosexuals: heterosexuals may also engage in it.

21   Sections 75, 91 and 93 of the PSMA regulate the marital relationship by giving the husband control within the marriage as long as he pays *mahr* (see following footnote), provides subsistence and does not harm his wife. A wife is to obey by being confined to the house and not leave it without the permission of the husband. If the husband provides for his wife, she may not work without his permission. The limits to the husband's authority are stipulated in the vague words 'as customarily practiced'. 'Customarily' is subject to the interpretation of the court. If the husband is providing adequately for the subsistence of the wife there are no further obligations on him and he may confine his wife to the house and grant her leave within reason. It is within the authority of the husband to grant permission as he earned the legal right to confine his wife.

22   *Mahr* is a sum of money paid by a husband to the wife as consideration in the contract of marriage.

Muslim society, nowhere is the criminal sanction extended to rape within marriage, because sexual access is deemed elemental to the marriage contract. Under shari'a, there is no harm – and thus no crime – in acts of sex between people who are married. Thus, marital rape is literally 'uncriminalizable' under dominant interpretations of shari'a.[23]

The dominant interpretations of *Shari'a* reflect the assumptions of their time about women and what they 'deserve'. A close reading of the *Qur'anic* verse, 4:34,[24] which stipulates actions to be taken in case of the recalcitrance or disobedience of a wife, reveals that marital rape is illegal in Islam. If we take the most restrictive interpretation it is evident that the beating envisaged in the verse is supposed to bring about consent. It does not allow forcible intercourse. Consent is therefore paramount in Islam and without it a sexual act loses its legitimacy. The *Qur'an* is clear on what follows if the wife continues to refuse to submit to her husband's sexual demands. In the *Qur'an* such a stage of recalcitrance is known as *shiqaq*, which is persistent marital discord. At this stage the panacea is not rape but as verse 35 of the same chapter stipulates, it is arbitration by two people, one from the wife's side and another from the husband's side who may decide whether this marital discord amounts to irreconcilable differences or can still be reconciled between the parties.[25]

Interpretations of verse 34 have varied according to the time and the traditions the interpreter lived in. They have ranged from attributing mental deficiency to such 'recalcitrant' women that may be rectified by the actions prescribed in the verse, to the historical context of the verse that argues that the social circumstances women lived in the pre-Islamic epoch warranted such actions, including 'light beating'.[26] Those who argue with reference to the historical context believe that some of the rules in Islam cease to be valid because of the change of time and circumstances; therefore the rule of hitting a woman to secure her consent may be changed.[27]

The issue we should be concerned with is whether a husband should under the current social circumstances be empowered by law to obtain consent to conjugal

---

23   Hajjar, L. 2004. Religion, state power, and domestic violence in Muslim societies: a framework for comparative analysis. *Law and Social Inquiry*, 29(1), 1–38, at 11.

24   Surat Annis'a (women) verse 34: 'And as for those women whose recalcitrance you have reason to fear, admonish them [first]; then desert them in bed; then beat them; and if they obey, do not seek to harm them. Behold, God is indeed most high, great'.

25   Verse 35: 'And if you have reason to fear that a persistent marital discord might occur between a married couple, appoint an arbiter from among his people and an arbiter from among her people; if they both want to reconcile aright, God may cause their success. Behold, God is indeed all-knowing, aware'.

26   See for early interpretations, Ibn Katheer's and al-Tabari's interpretations and others available at: http://www.altafsir.com/ [accessed 10 February 2010].

27   See Taha, M.M. 1987. *The Second Message of Islam*. Syracuse: Syracuse University Press.

relations by exacting or threatening harm. Even if we adhere to the traditional interpretations, the beating of a wife may qualify her for a divorce, not a rape. Marital rape disrupts the harmony that is the basis of marriage, and it may very well damage the family. In addition, not all marriages are consensual in the Sudan. Rural areas still practise forced marriages, in which lack of consent makes the contract of marriage voidable, and the PSMA allows the marrying of minors as young as ten years old.[28] The inability of the legislator to criminalize marital rape victimizes the minors and adult women who are forced into marriage and causes them to suffer physical and mental harm. The marrying of minors to their guardians is itself an issue that ought to be considered in law reform. It is an oxymoron to accept injustice and discrimination as part of a religious rule that is supposed to be based on peace and tranquility.

Rape in conflict areas

The lack of any important judicial decisions and adequate legal responses to rape cases in Darfur raises the question of whether the legislature views sexual violence during conflict as a normal behavior pattern, unworthy of specific responses such as law reform. Despite the fact that we are well beyond old adages such as 'boys will be boys' and 'women ought to stay out of where men could rape them', accepting the idea that some people should not complain of rape still seems to be prevalent. During my research in 2007–2008,[29] I found a consensus among judges that stems from stereotypes and practices that prevail in parts of Darfur. This is based on deeply entrenched perceptions of Darfur as a place that allows sexual freedom in which it is not unheard of for even married women to have affairs with their husbands' knowledge; pre-marital sex is also known and condoned in some areas. It is suggested, according to this Northern Sudanese scale of morality, that anyone engaging in such activities should treat sexual violence as acceptable too. By not recognizing rape as a violent act against a woman's physical and mental being and only as an act against an abstract or a concept called honour, the law succumbs to stereotypes about women and about the inhabitants of Darfur. Judges therefore find it necessary to combat such stereotypes and resort to their judicial common sense and charge sexual crimes punishable by *hudud* as *ta'azir* crimes.[30]

Justice is extremely difficult to achieve for women suffering sexual violence in Darfur, particularly in cases of perpetration by soldiers and rebel fighters, who all wear military fatigues and look alike and are therefore often difficult to

---

28   Section 40(3) of the PSMA allows a guardian to petition the court to permit him to marry his ward of a discerning age if he can prove a probable benefit to her from such marriage. Section 40(2) specifies a child who is ten years old as a discerning minor.

29   The aim of this research was to examine the record of the Sudanese Judiciary with a view to determining whether claims that it is incapable of trying cases in Darfur correspond to realities on the ground.

30   *Ta'azir* is a punishment other than *hudud* and *quisas* (retaliation).

identify. Women could obtain a degree of justice through the process referred to as transitional justice, which may actually facilitate both reconciliation and the award of compensation. However, this may be the case without the perpetrators ever being held accountable for their acts.

A successful transitional justice process must include women as actors in the process not just as victims. If they are not included as actors, women will fade in the background of a masculine act that manifests itself in men agreeing to reconcile and receive compensation. It remains to be seen whether any type of justice would be included in any peace negotiations. In this context, the precedent of the CPA between the Sudan Peoples' Liberation Movement/Army (SPLM/ SPLA) and the Government of Sudan (GoS) serves a lesson in achieving peace without justice – gender justice in particular. During the war in the South from 1983–2005, Southern women were taken as slaves and often subjected to sexual abuse. Irrespective of whether the culprits belonged to the government or other rebel groups, the result for women was the same.[31] As is the case now in Darfur, the predicament of women has been used to gain international attention but at the negotiation tables they have been totally forgotten. Negotiations between rebels and the government always dwell on power and wealth; crimes committed against Southern women have to date not met with any type of justice.

The sexuality of women and the law

Women in the Sudan are vulnerable to traditional or customary forms of violence like female circumcision (FC), which has existed in the country from time immemorial and has for centuries defied the law. Until recently criminalization of the practice have failed to be adopted due to lack of popular support, however, the past few decades have seen serious campaigns to raise awareness and increase levels of education on and around the issue.[32] Most importantly this has resulted in women themselves increasingly insisting on ending this harmful practice.

The position of the Government of Sudan regarding the practice of FC is unclear; at the local level it supported a symposium on 22 May 2002[33] that praised the very practice, which it later denounced when facing pressure exerted by domestic organizations, the World Health Organization and other international entities. In 2009 domestic advocacy led by Sudanese women's organizations resulted in an agreement with the government to include a section in the Protection of the Child

---

31   See Abdel Halim, A.M. 1998. Attack with a friendly weapon, in *What Women Do in Wartime: Gender and Conflict in Africa*, edited by M. Turshen and C. Twagiramariya. London: Zed Books, 85–100.

32   For the effect of education on FC practice in the Sudan see Islam, M. and Uddin, M. 2001. Female circumcision in Sudan: future prospects and strategies for eradication. *Family Planning Perspectives*, 27(2).

33   A report on the symposium appeared on the front page of the daily newspaper al-Ayyam on Sunday 27 May 2002.

Act that would prohibit FC. The corresponding section 13 was included in the bill, which received the support of all non-governmental organizations (NGOs). However, when the law was enacted the section was dropped, reportedly following an advisory opinion issued by the Islamic Fiqh Academy.[34] This open deception of the activists by the government generated what became known as 'Section 13 Movement'.[35] On 30 October 2009 the Parliamentary Human Rights Committee and the Women's Center of the Federal Ministry of Welfare and Child Affairs held a workshop in the parliament (National Assembly) on FC. In a telling incident, one of the participants disrupted the meeting and snatched the microphone from the President of the Women's Center and accused the other participants of wanting to further the UN's agenda to pass a law against FC.[36]

The fear of women's sexuality and the curbing of their sexual arousal through FC appears to be considered more important than their rights. Such control will continue under the religious norms being implemented at present in the Sudan. By removing section 13, the government has deprived women and human rights activists of any recourse to the court system. Refusal to enact a law is not recognized as an unconstitutional act by a state, even though article 32(3) of the INC provides that: '[t]he State shall combat harmful practices and traditions which undermine the dignity and status of women'.

The Public Order Act

The Public Order Act of the State of Khartoum is a textbook example of gender discrimination.[37] Women have been the main target of the Act; they continue to be arrested for 'indecent dress', which has been neither defined nor otherwise specified in the law.[38] In addition, section 152 of the Criminal Act, which prohibits indecent behaviour and indecent dress, has been used against women. The indecency of behaviour and dress is determined by the religion of the accused or the customs of the place where the act is committed. Unsurprisingly, and tellingly, all arrests and trials so far have been of women.

---

34   See 2009. Sudanese activists slam government position on female genital mutilation. *Sudan Tribune* [Online, 8 February] Available at: http://www.sudantribune.com/Sudanese-activists-slam-government,30099 [accessed 15 June 2010].

35   A group of NGOs in the Sudan drafted a memorandum on the 'missing' section 13 and sent it to the Government of Sudan as well as the international agencies. The text is available at: http://web61388.aiso.net/resources/infoDetail.asp?ID=22955&flag=news [accessed 12 February 2010].

36   Ahmed, A.I. 2009. *A Member of Parliament Disrupts a Workshop on Female Circumcision. Al-Sudani* [in Arabic] [30 October].

37   Khartoum Public Order Act 1998.

38   The law also prohibits certain conduct. For example, section 7(1)(b) of the Khartoum Public Order Act states: 'There shall be no dancing between men and women and women shall not dance in front of men'.

The latest fiasco to be broadcast internationally is what came to be known as the 'trousers case'. The journalist Lubna Hussein and others were tried for wearing an 'indecent dress', having been rounded up from a party in a hotel that they attended wearing trousers. Decency seems to be in the eye of the beholder; when it comes to the Sudan, the beholder is a man with a whip who 'rounds up' women. Women who have internalized gender stereotypes that have been given legal imprimatur have chosen not to defend themselves in the public order courts. The fear factor exerted by public opinion allows the law to be a tool of intimidation of women, which is what happened in respect of the women arrested together with Lubna Hussein. They were summarily tried, flogged and released. The contrastingly defiant stand of the journalist was admired by Sudanese women, many of whom gathered around the court in droves to support her. After her lawyer appealed, her sentence was changed to a fine of the equivalent of $250.00, which she refused to pay. Eventually the Journalists' Association paid the fine on her behalf. When she was released and found her way to France she was even greeted by its prime minister who has his own rigid stand against the way Muslim women dress.[39]

The trousers case clearly shows a fear of sexuality of women that was embedded in regulations such as the local Ordinance of Khartoum State that prohibited women's work at petrol stations and hotels.[40] The protection of women's dignity was cited as the reason for the prohibition, but no explanation was given of how such work may degrade women.

Section 154 of the Criminal Act, which defines and punishes prostitution, is another trap for women and a means to their control.[41] Prostitution is defined as being in a place of prostitution where the person would probably commit sexual acts or financially benefit from such acts. This means that women gathering at

---

39 It is worth mentioning here that the French insistence on forcing women out of the hijab is similar to the Sudanese insistence on forcing them into it, as both reduce women to a piece of clothing that they control and ignore women's freedom to dress as they want.

40 The *wali* (governor) of Khartoum State issued a regulation prohibiting women's work in hotels and petrol stations. For the justification of his decision see, 2001. The Wali of Khartoum defends his decision to prohibit women's work [in Arabic]. *Asharq Al-Awsat* [Online, January 30] Available at: http://www.aawsat.com/details.asp?section=4&article=23894&issueno=8099 [accessed 16 December 2010]. See also United States Department of State. 2001. *Country Reports on Human Rights Practices: Sudan.* [Online] Available at: http://www.state.gov/g/drl/rls/hrrpt/2000/af/822.htm [accessed 16 December 2010].

41 Section 154(1): 'There shall be deemed to commit the offence of practising prostitution whoever is found in a place of prostitution so that it is likely that he may exercise sexual acts or earn there from, and shall be punished with whipping not exceeding 100 lashes or with imprisonment for a term not exceeding three years. (2) Place of prostitution means any place designated for the meeting of men or women or men and women between whom there is no marital relationship or kinship in circumstances in which the exercise of sexual acts is probable to occur'.

home may easily be accused of prostitution since such acts are not defined in the law, and the crime is committed by their sheer presence in a 'place of prostitution', irrespective of whether it actually serves that purpose.

Possibilities for reform

Irrespective of whether the criminal law in the Sudan remains governed by *Shari'a* or another system of law, it is clear that it is in need of radical reform. As indicated by the Supreme Court judgments that reversed capital punishment passed against women for *zina*, the normative content of the law does not match the social perceptions and international perspectives, leaving judges with the duty of interpreting laws to conform to both social and international perspectives. A law that has little or no chance of being implemented hardly deserves its name.

The social construction of gender in the Sudan is not just about the traditional roles assigned to the sexes; it goes further to make the myths about femininity the truth, with the law functioning as the medium to transform these myths into 'realities'. Pregnancy, seeking to prove paternity and being found in a place where it is 'probable' for one to engage in prostitution are not good grounds for criminal proceedings for a serious crime such as *zina*. Crime itself is constructed by law, and acts should not be criminalized only because they were considered to merit criminal sanction a hundred years ago. As we progress in defining roles in society, and work for the equality of the sexes (and equality should not be confused with sameness here), certain paradigms have to be changed. These shifts should include the idea that women's demands of their human rights have nothing to do with 'western ideas'. Demanding rights is not a western idea or act; indeed it is an Islamic ideal that has existed since the early days of Islam.

Gender roles within Muslim Sudanese communities are distributed according to the ways in which those communities perceive sexuality, not just sex. Being a patriarchal society, pressure put on women in the Sudan is more likely to be accepted. Therefore restrictions and their explanations – such as the veiling of women because their sexuality is evil and may destroy the world as men know it – are easily accepted by society and even some women themselves. Whether women's struggle for their rights should be treated as a legitimate cause worth fighting or a mere lustful 'westernized' action seems to have been resolved in the Sudan by a legislature that does not see, or does not want to see any difference in social relations between the twenty-first century and the eighth century.[42]

These are major issues that have direct effect on the reform of criminal law. Issues of guardianship over women, the fear of women's sexuality, the oppression of women as a way of keeping the social fabric intact and other gender-oriented

---

42   For more on this point, see Abdel Halim, A.M. 1999. Reconciling the opposite: equal but subordinate', in *Religious Fundamentalisms and the Rights of Women*, edited by W.H. Courtney. New York: St. Martins Press, 203–13.

attitudes must be discussed with the intent to overcome them. Any effort to reconcile antiquated language or social behavior with the rules of justice will only produce weak and ineffectual laws. For example, when the legislature considers the criminalization and punishment of rape a simple question may put the whole issue into perspective, namely: do we genuinely want to punish rape? Once there is a social attitude that abhors rape as antisocial and immoral, ideas of sexism and racism and other 'isms' will be easier to combat.

Sexism appears even in the writings of progressive Muslims. Contemporary scholars who claim support of women's rights cannot help but set Muslim women apart from other women. Their support comes with a condition attached, that women's rights should not only be a women's affair. Ultimately this translates into a claim to control Muslim women and discourage any of their attempts to step outside the boundaries mapped by the Islamists. Abdelwahab Alaffendi eloquently expresses this Islamist sentiment:

> Islamists must lead the renaissance of women from the swamps of traditionalism and deliver them from the hands of Westernized misguided groups who would love to exploit their predicament. After all, religion requires them to give guidance to humanity and save people from inherited deviations and novel aberrations.[43]

Under existing laws perpetrators of rape escape justice every day and men who commit *zina* are impossible to convict. As a result, sexual offences are on the rise and it is not an exaggeration to expect such crimes to become considered normal behavior with the passage of time. A crime that is out of reach of the law turns the law into an unethical piece of literature. Worse, existing law turns the complainant into the accused and turns the table on a rape victim to rebut a presumption of *zina*.

Bertrand Russell once said: '[l]aw in origin was merely a codification of the power of dominant groups, and did not aim at anything that to a modern man would appear to be justice'.[44] It is about time that law in the Sudan be made with the objective of achieving justice. Admittedly, law may not fully equate with justice; however, justice is attainable through laws that profess equality and seek to serve the well-being of people, rather than those that are a normative expression of dominance. Reform of the criminal law in the Sudan must be done in conformity with international conventions and based on the notion of human rights.

---

43   El-Affendi, A. 1991. *Turabi's Revolution: Islam and Power in Sudan*. London: Grey Seal, 175.

44   Russel, B. 2009. *Bertrand Russel's Best*. New York: Routledge Classics, 117.

Chapter 11

Through the Looking Glass:
The Emergence, Confused Application and
Demise of Pakistan's *Hudood* Rape Laws

Sohail Akbar Warraich

Introduction

The December 2006 amendments of Pakistan's *hudood* laws[1] dealing with sexual offences constituted a major advance for the protection of rape survivors. The amendments, commonly referred to as the Women's Protection Act (WPA), repealed some of the most retrogressive provisions in Pakistan's laws that had been brought in during the controversial 'Islamization' of the country by military ruler Zia-ul-Haq in 1979.[2] The WPA did not meet the demands of Pakistan's women rights groups, which had been campaigning for a total repeal of all the Hudood Ordinances. Nevertheless the changes had major political and legal significance, amending laws that were considered 'divine' and therefore immune to any human intervention. The declared objective of the 1979 Hudood Ordinances had been to bring laws in conformity with the injunctions of Islam as enshrined in the *Qur'an* and *Sunna*; yet the objective of the 2006 Amendment Act is 'to provide relief and protection to women against misuse and abuse of law' and 'to bring in particular the laws relating to zina and qazf in conformity with the stated objectives of the Constitution and the injunctions of Islam'. The reference to Islam reflects the fact that the concept of sexual acts mentioned in the *Qur'an* and laws, which are primarily derived from examples of the lives of the Prophet Mohammad and his close associates, had remained the primary focus of debate since the introduction of these laws and throughout the campaign for their repeal or reform.

This chapter focuses on rape and other sexually violent offences. It also discusses the legal provisions relevant to *zina* (adultery referring to any form of extramarital sexual relations), whose 'Islamization' led to changes in the laws on rape and other forms of sexual violence. The chapter embarks on a journey through

---

1   Two of the five Hudood ordinances, the Zina Ordinance and the Qazaf Ordinance, were amended.

2   The Zina (enforcement of Hudood) Ordinance of 1979 dealt with any form of extra marital sex, rape and some other sexual offences against women. The Qazaf (enforcement of Hadd) Ordinance of 1979 dealt with false allegations of extramarital sex.

the Pakistani experience of these legal reforms. It examines problems inherent in the law and shows how the supposedly Islamic nature of laws related to sexual conduct was used to create stereotypes about sexuality and to promote a particular moral 'code', which violated the bodies and integrity of disadvantaged sections of society. The case law analyzed demonstrates how the ambiguities in these laws were used as a tool of exploitation, and resulted in abuse and discrimination by the public and the state. It is hoped that the experiences related here will help strengthen the analysis of others who campaign for the reform of rape laws in Muslim contexts similar to Pakistan.

Pakistan's legal system

The Constitution of Pakistan[3] declares the state to be an Islamic republic, with Islam as the official state religion.[4] All laws shall be brought in conformity with injunctions of Islam as enshrined in the Qur'an and *Sunna*, and no law shall be enacted that is repugnant to such injunctions.[5] Over the years the Pakistani legal system has become a hybrid of English common law and selective forms of '*Shari'a*-based' laws. This process started during the colonial period when separate laws governing personal status and related matters were enacted for different religious communities. Matters that had not been codified remained subject to customary law unless contrary to concepts of equity, justice and good conscience. The current criminal justice system was introduced by colonial rulers in the second half of the nineteenth century.[6] It was largely based on the British system and remained in place until the end of colonial rule in 1947, after which the domain of family laws, succession and inheritance underwent increased codification and adjudication based on religion. In cases relating to personal status or the conflict of laws, Muslim personal law was accorded overriding effect,[7] and this trend subsequently influenced debates around the position of Islam in the Constitution and its interpretation.[8] However, it was not until February 1979 that Zia-ul-Haq embarked on infusing 'Islam' into criminal laws, which consisted of

---

3   The 1973 Constitution of the Islamic Republic of Pakistan, as amended.

4   Article 2 of the Constitution.

5   Article 227 of the Constitution. An advisory body called the Council of Islamic Ideology was formed under article 228.

6   The main laws were the Penal Code, 1860, Criminal Procedure Code, 1898, Law of Evidence, 1872, and the Police Act, 1861.

7   The landmark case in this respect is *Marina Jatoi v Nuruddin K. Jatoi* PLD 1967 Supreme Court 580.

8   See *Asma Jilani v The Government of Punjab* PLD 1972 SC 139 and *Ziaur Rehman v The State* PLD 1973 SC 49.

hudood laws, covering *zina*, *qazaf* (the false allegation of *zina*), theft, drinking and related offences.[9]

The Zina Ordinance 1979

The Zina Ordinance, in addition to the offence of *zina*, introduced a new definition of rape in the form of *zina bil jabr* (its literal meaning is *zina* through coercion). The two offences carried *hadd* punishments.[10] Prior to this ordinance, *zina* had been an offence only in the form of sex with a married woman[11] and had carried a punishment only for the male accused; the woman was neither made party to the trial nor subject to punishment if adultery was proven.[12] In addition, the ordinance included kidnapping, selling and buying women for prostitution, among other offences related to the coercion of women, all of which were taken from Pakistan's Penal Code (PPC). The content of these offences remained essentially the same, with the exception of the offence of enticement, but saw increased prison sentences and the addition of whipping. Many other provisions relating to sexual violence against women remained part of the PPC, including sodomy and bestiality.[13] The Zina Ordinance mentioned three different statuses of marriage. It also altered the age of adulthood to 18 years of age for a male and to 16 years of age for a female, or the attainment of puberty (whichever was earlier).[14]

Section 6 of the Zina Ordinance defined rape as:

> A person is said to commit zina-bil-jabr if he or she has sexual intercourse with a woman or man [defined as penetration], as the case may be, to whom he or she is not validly married, in any of the following circumstances, namely: (a) against the will of the victim, (b) without the consent of the victim, (c) with the consent of the victim, when the consent has been obtained by putting the victim in fear of death or of hurt, or, (d) with the consent of the victim, when the offender knows that the offender is not validly married to the victim and that the consent is given because the victim believes that the offender is another person to whom the victim is or believes herself or himself to be validly married.

---

9   Five Ordinances called Hudood Ordinances were introduced, four related to the crimes mentioned above and one concerned the punishment of whipping.

10   *Hadd* literally means the limit or boundary. In Islamic criminal law it refers to certain fixed punishments that require a particular mode of evidence.

11   Section 497 Pakistan Penal Code (PPC) that was repealed by the Zina Ordinance.

12   See in this context section 156(4) of the Pakistan Criminal Procedure Code (CrPC) that was repealed by the Zina Ordinance.

13   Neither the PPC nor the Zina Ordinance makes specific mention of male rape. Such an offence is prosecuted under section 377 PPC that deals with unnatural offences.

14   Section 2(a) Zina Ordinance.

A comparison of section 6 of the Zina Ordinance with the offence of rape in section 375 of the PPC that it had replaced shows that *zina bil jabr* fundamentally changed the concept of this crime in the following ways:

1. Rape was no longer a crime committed by a man against a woman. The Zina Ordinance definition used the term 'person' and mentioned the circumstances under which sexual intercourse by a man with a woman or by a woman with a man was rape.
2. It repealed statutory rape by eliminating the age of consent. The earlier definition set the age of consent for woman as fourteen years, with the exception of an underage wife provided that she was not under thirteen years of age. This meant that sexual intercourse with a minor technically could no longer be classified as rape.
3. In addition to the problem of the age of consent, there was no mention of an insane adult or minor. Theoretically sexual intercourse with an insane person did not classify as rape.
4. The provision 'if the man was not lawfully married to the woman' was replaced with 'validly married'. In practice, the issue of status of marriage became relevant mainly in cases of kidnapping. The accused would use the plea of marriage that was challenged by the woman alleging it had been performed fraudulently or through coercion, after her kidnapping or abduction.
5. The Zina Ordinance made rape a form of *zina*, distinguishing *zina bil raza* (*zina* with consent) and *zina bil jabr* (*zina* with force or coercion). The difference was that both parties are guilty in cases of *zina bil raza*, while the woman is exonerated from punishment in cases of *zina bil jabr* because she has been forced to commit *zina* without her consent.

The commission of rape now became liable to *hadd* punishment, which depended on the personal status and the religion of the accused. For unmarried persons the sentence was one hundred stripes in a public place, and for married, divorced or widowed Muslims called *Muhsin*, it was stoning to death in public. A non-Muslim did not qualify as *Muhsin* and would therefore not be subject to stoning. In cases of *zina* where evidence of *hadd* was not available, the sentence was in the second category called *ta'zir*,[15] consisting of imprisonment and whipping.[16] For the crime of rape to fall in the *hadd* category the same degree of evidence was required that made *zina* liable to *hadd*, namely four adult male Muslim witnesses.[17] It was these evidentiary standards that made the concept of rape absurd in the form of *zina bil jabr*. Rape proven through evidence other than that required for *hadd* fell in the

---

15   Section 10(1) Zina Ordinance.

16   Whipping was abolished for *ta'zir* offences through the Abolition of Whipping Act, 1996.

17   Section 6(2) with section 5(1) Zina Ordinance.

second category of *ta'zir* and carried a sentence of death, or a maximum of life imprisonment and whipping.[18]

The application of the Zina Ordinance 1979–2006

As part of the 'Islamization' process, a Federal Shariat Court (FSC) was founded under the Constitution. This became the appellate court for crimes under the Hudood Ordinances and could examine the repugnancy of any law with the injunctions of Islam.[19] One third of the judges of the FSC were *Ulema* (religious scholars) judges and were appointed by the President, who also had the power to appoint serving high court judges. Decisions of the FSC were heard on appeal by a special bench of the Supreme Court.[20]

The age of consent

The definition of a female becoming an adult on reaching puberty raised new complexities, as is evident from the following rape case. Two brothers were tried and convicted by the trial court on charges of kidnapping and raping a 'minor' girl. The FSC as the first appellate court retained the convictions, and the final appeal was heard by a three-member Shariat appellate bench in the Supreme Court,[21] which held that the girl was a minor and that the act constituted rape. However, the judgment was full of contradictions, which demonstrates how the criminalization of sexuality with reference to *zina* created problems. The court agreed with the counsel's contention regarding consent, with some qualification: '[w]e also feel that the conduct of the girl shows that she was a consenting party to the whole affair but the difficulty is that at the time of occurrence she was twelve years and four months old and, being a minor, her consent cannot be taken into account'.[22] The court found that the girl was a minor not on account of her age, but because of the defence's failure to prove that the girl had attained the age of puberty (which, as the court observed, can be attained at the age of nine according to the *Hanifi* jurisprudence). This was not the end of the contradictory findings in this case. The court accepted the appellant's counsel plea that 'she was a grown up girl and this fact should at least be taken as a mitigating circumstance for awarding a lesser

---

18   Section 10(3) Zina Ordinance. Rape by more than one individual called gang rape carried the mandatory death sentence pursuant to section 10(4) inserted in the Zina Ordinance in 1997.

19   See article 203D of the Constitution. Article 203B(c) excludes the Constitution, the Muslim personal law, and any law relating to the procedure of any court or tribunal from examination by the FSC.

20   Article 203F of the Constitution.

21   *Yousaf Masih alias Bagga Masih and another v The State* 1994 SCMR 2102.

22   *Bagga Masih and another v The State*, 2106.

punishment to the appellants'.[23] The contradictory findings of the court spelled out how the legal discourse impacted on and reinforced perceptions of sexuality, especially the sexuality of women.

The case of Jehan Mina: The conversion of zina bil jabr into zina

In Pakistan, societal attitudes towards sexual acts and women's sexuality were already very conservative and harsh.[24] However, the Zina Ordinance created an irresolvable difficulty. A woman had not only to guard herself against any sexual aggression, but also make sure that she had the requisite evidence available if it occurred; otherwise her own body would make her liable to punishment. The *Jehan Mina* case[25] is a classic example of the socially and legally oppressive factors that conspired against minor girls, exposing the injustice caused by removing the age of statutory rape and punishing *zina* by default. Jehan Mina, who was a minor,[26] alleged that she was raped in her aunt's house by one of her uncles and his son, and became pregnant. She felt that she could not complain to anyone, but when another of her uncles asked her why she looked pregnant she told him of the rape; however, he waited for another month before filing a complaint of rape against the alleged perpetrators. By the time that Jehan Mina was medically examined for rape she was six months pregnant.

The rape complaint to the police was converted into a *zina* trial and resulted in the conviction of Jehan Mina and the acquittal of the two male accused. She was convicted because of her pregnancy and sentenced to one hundred stripes. On appeal, her sentence was changed from *hadd* to three years rigorous imprisonment and fifteen lashes under *tazir*. The appellate court agreed with the reasons of the trial court, which had held that the two accused could not be convicted under section 5 of the Zina Ordinance (hadd sentence) merely on the basis of a statement of the co-accused, Jehan Mina, claiming that the violation was *zina bil jabr*. The case is confusing to read because of the frequent mention of *zina bil jabr*, although the court case was for the offence of *zina*. This exposed one of the principal problems of the Zina Ordinance, which created confused conceptions of two offences that were fundamentally different. According to the appellate court, in explaining why Jehan Mina should not benefit from the defence of rape:

---

23 *Bagga Masih and another v The State*, 2108

24 See for a judicial reflection of this attitude, *Begum Tahira Masood v Farid-Ud-Din Masood* PLD 1974 Lahore 500, and *M. Asghar Khan v Fariduddin Masood* PLD 1974 Lahore 1.

25 *Mst. Jehan Mina v The State* PLD 1983 FSC 183.

26 The FSC judgment mentioned that her age was around 15 or 16 years. One of the appeal court judges described her as about 14 years of age in a documentary called *Who shall cast the first stone* (dir. Subiha Sumar, 1988).

in fact the basis of her conviction is her unexplained pregnancy coupled with the fact that she is not a married girl. We also feel that she has not made any statement in respect of number of times that zina was committed with her and at what place and during what hours. She did not take the position that zina had been committed with her at a secluded place in a jungle where she could not cry for help. She has not even explained as to what was the force or threat used against her when she was subjected to zina bil jabr and she has also not explained as to what induced her to keep quiet for such a long time in spite of having had the full and complete opportunity of complaining to her nearest relations namely her grandfather, her uncle and her aunt. In these circumstances we are of the view that Jehan Mina has had an intercourse with someone out of her own free will and she has therefore, committed an offence punishable under section 10 (2) of the Ordinance. Her conviction was altered from *hadd* to *tazir* as evidence of four adult, Muslim eyewitnesses of good repute was not on record of her having committing sexual intercourse.[27]

The court's observations in the judgment show a complete insensitivity to the situation and distress of a pregnant girl. Her not complaining to the grandfather she was living with was taken as her committing sex with someone of her own free will. What would the grandfather have done? According to Jehan Mina's statement before the court, the grandfather, after learning about her pregnancy, wanted to take her away from his son's house so that she could be killed.[28] This case exposed all the potential ills of the Zina Ordinance. For *zina bil jabr* (rape) it showed that an admission of sexual intercourse by a female irrespective of her age may constitute evidence of the commission of consensual sex called *zina* unless the *jabr* (coercive) aspect is proved. In Jehan Mina's situation, consensual sex was presumed on her part despite her tender age, leaving her unprotected and exposing her to punishment on the basis of statements alone.

Pregnancy as evidence for zina and grounds for conviction

In August 1981 Pakistani civil society was shocked by reports of a young woman named Fehmida being sentenced to 100 stripes and her husband Allah Bux's sentence to death by stoning. This case for the first time showed the potential scope of the Zina Ordinance's application. Fehmida, a school girl of 18 years, voluntarily married Allah Bux, who was already married. Her father registered a case of elopement. The trial court acknowledged the marriage, but Fehimda's pregnancy (her daughter had been born before the trial) predated the registered marriage of 28 December 1980. The couple claimed to have contracted *nikah* (marriage) in the previous July, before the date of pregnancy. This was rejected by the trial court, which convicted them of *zina* under *hadd* on account of their statement

---

27 *Mina v The State*, 188.
28 *Mina v The State*, 186.

considered to constitute a confession.[29] On appeal,[30] the couple stated that they would withdraw their statements. The FSC set aside the original judgment and sent the case for retrial because of the retraction of the statements, which formed the sole basis of the conviction.[31]

This case made headlines because of the nature of the sentences, but it also constituted the beginning of conflicting verdicts in cases where couples pleaded that they were married.[32] The FSC remanded the case for retrial on a technicality and refrained from rendering a decision on important points of law such as the mode of confession for the offence of *zina* as a *hadd* crime. In hindsight, the case constituted a missed opportunity; the confused application or abuse of the Zina Ordinance by trial courts caused considerable suffering to those who had been convicted, as well as those lucky to have been acquitted, but subsequently socially humiliated. Though this case was shocking it also set the tone for future campaigns against the Zina Ordinance. A group of concerned women activists in Karachi formed a committee that turned into an action forum called the Women Action Forum (WAF) and campaigned for the repeal of all *hudood* laws.

A licence to abuse

The *zina* law provided a free licence to everyone to prosecute anyone, and this eroded the fundamental rights to privacy and equal protection under the law. The role of the police changed; they became custodians of 'morality', with the mere accusation of *zina* able to strip away any existing legal safeguards. This climate even resulted in the invention of new offences. In one such case the police arrested a man and a woman from a house, accusing them of preparing to commit *zina*. As there was no legal provision to charge them, the police prepared a charge sheet under a section that dealt with sentences for attempting to commit offences under the Zina Ordinance.[33] The trial court sentenced both to five years' imprisonment

---

29   The use of confession for the sentencing of *hadd* was not defined in the Zina Ordinance but its mode and requirements have been explained in many cases, like *Mohammad Sarwar v The State* PLD 1988 FSC 42. Any statement of the accused before the court in response to a charge against him or her that amounted to an admission of guilt did not constitute a confession of *zina* for a *hadd* sentence. A confession required a particular mode of recording, namely four times in four different hearings with the court being satisfied that the person making the confession is aware of its consequences. The admission of an offence amounting to a confession under *hadd* law can be retracted.

30   *Allah Bux v The State* PLD 1982 FSC 101.

31   If the conviction was based upon the confession of the accused which was later retracted, the law required a retrial rather than convicting the accused under *tazir*: see section 9(1) Zina Ordinance.

32   See the contrasting verdict in *Arif Hussain and Azra Parveen v The State* PLD 1982 FSC 42.

33   Section 18 Zina Ordinance.

and ten stripes. They were acquitted on appeal, but it took them seven years to free themselves from prosecution.[34]

The cooperation of police with the public in such cases reached new heights, though the police record for registering complaints and addressing genuine grievances in Pakistan is appalling. However, in most *zina* cases cooperation was extremely cordial and police seemed to be ever ready to register them; an unsigned letter sent through the post was enough to register[35] a *zina* case against a married woman. For example, in one case a brother-in-law of a woman sent an unsigned application to police through the post, alleging that she had become pregnant while her husband was away for four years. The trial court convicted her and sentenced her to five years' rigorous imprisonment, ten stripes and a fine of 1,000 Rupees. She was acquitted on appeal, as there was no direct evidence of *zina* against her.[36] Her husband was living in a nearby village and recognized the child as his, since the couple had had conjugal relations.

One major effect of the *zina* law on the criminal justice system was that the law enforcement agencies, prosecutors and even the courts focused mainly on the body of the woman and eyewitness accounts. The central focus was on any evidence of sexual intercourse, which was considered willful unless a woman could prove it to have been otherwise, and was used to incriminate women because of the perception of crime and pre-existing societal prejudices. A combination of vague laws and these perceptions created anomalies and additional problems in an already poor criminal justice system. The legal introduction of eye witnesses to the act of rape made matters worse.

Distorted investigations in rape and zina *cases: Looking for eyewitnesses*

The Zina Ordinance did not introduce any new procedural mechanism in the investigation and prosecution of rape and *zina* cases under the Criminal Procedure Code (CrPC) and the law of evidence. Eyewitness evidence as requisite proof was technically confined to *hadd* sentences, but it came to dominate prosecutions. There was little emphasis on collecting any other medical or forensic evidence, especially against the alleged male perpetrator in rape cases. At times the higher courts would caution and instruct the police and investigation agencies regarding their mode of gathering evidence, but this seemingly made little difference. In one *zina* case appeal the court remarked that:

> the police investigation in this country is not keeping pace with scientific developments. If facilities for grouping of semen be available, as indeed they are, it is not understandable why the Medical Officers examining the male for

---

34   *Muhammad Saleem and another v The State* 1988 PCr.LJ 2321.

35   A First Information Report (FIR) is registered under section 154 CrPC and requires signing by the complainant or the person giving information about a cognisable offence.

36   *Mst Nemat Bibi v The State* PLD 1984 FSC 17.

potency should not obtain the specimen of semen of the accused so that no doubt be left about the identity of the person committing Zina or zina-bil-jabr. The police officers in their reference to the medical officers should also in such cases invariably request the doctor concerned to take the specimen of semen of the male accused. They should send them for chemical examination and serology along with vaginal swabs and clothes/cloth etc. having seminal stains. The court ordered for the copies of the judgment be sent to the Secretary Interior, Secretary Department of Law, Home Secretaries and the Inspectors-General Police of the Provinces.[37]

In a later rape case where the victim was an 8-year-old girl, an accused was acquitted on account of the benefit of doubt, largely because of the poor investigation methods and non-compliance with the earlier instructions of the courts, with the appellate court repeating instructions for the investigation of rape cases.[38]

The role of women in zina *and rape cases: Prosecutrix, co-accused or sole perpetrator*

The question of a woman's legal status emerged as a key point of law in cases where the woman became pregnant from alleged rape and there was a delay in filing a complaint, such as in the *Safia Bibi* case.[39] Bibi was a blind girl, and was allegedly subjected to rape that resulted in pregnancy. After her medical examination, the police arrested her and made her co-accused in the *zina* case. The male accused was acquitted while Safia Bibi was convicted for being pregnant outside marriage. This was one of the earliest cases to be covered widely in the press outside Pakistan and it became a reference for *zina* law. On appeal, the court considered the positions of different Imams of the Sunni sect and on balance, granted acquittal:

1. Even under Shariah law, if a girl makes such a statement as made in the present case, she cannot be convicted of zina. The principle of Fiqh [Islamic jurisprudence] is that she will be asked about the cause of pregnancy, if she says that she was forced to commit adultery or someone had committed sexual inter-course with her under suspicion about her identity, her statement will be accepted and she will not be convicted. This is based on the tradition of Hazrat Ali that when Shuraha came to him and said, 'I have committed adultery', Hazrat Ali said to her, 'You might have been forced or someone might have committed sexual inter-course with you while you were sleeping' (Kitabul Fiqh alal Mazahibil Arabaa (Urdu translation) Vol. V, page 166, 167).

---

37   *Mst. Ehsan Begum v The State* PLD 1983 FSC 204.
38   *Abid Javed alias Mithu v The State* 1996 P.Cr.LJ (FSC) 1161.
39   *Mst. Safia Bibi v The State* PLD 1985 FSC 120.

2. If an unmarried woman delivering a child pleads that the birth was the result of commission of the offence of rape on her, she cannot be punished …
3. There is little difference between the view of Imam Malik and others on the point of law that rape with a woman absolve her of criminal liability. The only difference is on the point of the evidentiary value of the self-exculpatory statement. Imam Malik places the burden of proving the self-exculpatory evidence on the woman, and this burden can be discharged by her by proving that she raised alarm or complained against it. She can discharge her burden by production of circumstantial evidence.[40]

The introduction of the Zina Ordinance had opened the floodgates for complaints of *zina*. Rape cases in which women were convicted for *zina* added fear and discouraged rape complaints. In addition there was inconsistency in FSC judgments on questions of law. The Safia Bibi case judgment constituted progress in as much as a woman could not be convicted for *zina* on account of her pregnancy outside of marriage if she complained of rape. However, some key questions remained unanswered and it took the courts 17 years to define the nature of the offence of *zina* as 'a joint one, requiring the identification of both a man and a woman "distinctly". Should either of them fail to be so identified, as it had been in the present case, no offence if any of "zina" could be made out by the prosecution'.[41] This judgment observed that the previous decision in Jehan Mina ought to be confined to the annals of legal history and not to be followed.

Despite judgments that sought to limit excesses by providing guidance on the prosecution of *zina* and *zina bil jabr* cases, the cycle of abuse continued.[42] Reading between the lines in these judgments it appears that the courts noticed the abuse and the absurdity of the Zina Ordinance but fell short of making such an outright declaration. While the conviction for *zina* liable to *ta'zir* could be made on circumstantial evidence, the courts increasingly referred to the need for direct evidence – that is, four eyewitnesses. However, the jurisprudence was not consistent on this point and the so-called 'unexplained' pregnancy of woman accused of *zina*, or a rape complainant, continued to be the basis of convictions. The longevity of these kinds of decisions was perhaps the outcome of the basic misperception that, as once expressed by one supporter of this law, 'Zina is Zina, regardless of whether committing it willingly or against one's will'.[43]

---

40 *Bibi v The State*, 124, at para. 20.

41 *Rani v The State* K.L.R 1996 Shariat Cases 150, at 159.

42 See *Zafran Bibi v The State* PLD 2002 FSC 1. Zafran, a married woman, complained of rape but was convicted for *zina* because of her pregnancy. On appeal, the FSC acquitted her.

43 Ghazi, M.A. 1992. *Fikro Nazar*, cited in Government of Pakistan. 2006. *Interim report of Council of Islamic Ideology*. Government of Pakistan, Islamabad.

Crossing boundaries: Criminalizing personal relationships

The criminalization of sex provided another tool with which to harass others, especially women. This was done through challenging the status of their marriage or divorce by launching criminal proceedings rather than through the family court. This resulted in verdicts of the FSC and Supreme Court in criminal cases on the validity of divorce on remarriage by a woman that undermined the personal status laws of Muslims and Christians. Instead of challenging the marriage or divorce or paternity of a child in a civil suit, *zina* law provided a 'statutory' vehicle for prosecution and persecution.

According to the section on definitions in the Zina Ordinance, 'marriage' means marriage that is not 'void' according to the personal law of the parties.[44] However, *zina* was defined as willful sexual intercourse between a man and a woman who are not 'validly' married. For *zina* to be liable to *hadd*, the Zina Ordinance introduced yet another element, namely 'to whom he [she] is not, and does *not suspect himself [herself] to be married* (emphasis added)'.[45] As a result, the various definitions of marriage used brought Muslim laws of personal status in conflict with the Zina Ordinance. Many unclear or irregular marriages came under the scrutiny of *zina*, although doubts about their validity could have been addressed by resorting to plaints before the family courts. This included the remarriage of a woman within the waiting period called *idat* after having obtained a decree of dissolution of the previous marriage from the court, or the situation of an aunt and niece being the wives of the same man simultaneously.[46] A marriage that did not qualify as valid theoretically came within the ambit of *zina* crime and could result in prosecution. A further controversy concerned adequate sentences for sexual intercourse between spouses whose marriage was not valid. The courts rendered conflicting judgments on this issue, finding in some cases that marriages found to be irregular fell within the scope of *zina* liable to *tazir*.[47] It may be noted that under Muslim laws of personal status, as practised in Pakistan, it is a settled position that irregular marriage does not constitute *zina* and that children are legitimate.[48]

The ambiguous legal position and easy registration of *zina* complaints provided a tool for men to harass their former wives once they remarried. Under Pakistani family laws, a Muslim husband can terminate a marriage unilaterally through the

---

44   Section 2(c) Zina Ordinance repealed by the WPA, 2006.

45   Section 5(1) Zina Ordinance.

46   For different statuses of a Muslim marriage as valid, irregular and their effects see Hidayatullah and Hidayatullah (eds). 1990. *Musslah's Mohammadan Law*. 19th Edition. Bombay: N.M Tripathi, paras 252–62.

47   See *Zahida Shaheen v The State* 1994 SCMR 2098 and *Abdul Sattar v Mst. Zahida Parveen* 1991 MLD 403 [Karachi]. For a contrary view on criminal liability of irregular marriages, see *Muhammad Nawaz v the State* PLD 2004 Lahore 265, and *Faiz Batool v Additional Judge* PLD 1997 Lahore 413.

48   See Hidayatullah and Hidayatullah. 1990, para. 267.

talaq form of divorce at any time and does not have to go through any judicial proceedings.[49] However, in many divorces the legal procedures were not properly followed. The Zina ordinance provided a tool to such 'former' husbands, who could register a case of *zina* against the 'former' wife and her new husband, sometimes after several years.[50] The husband would claim that his marriage still subsists and that his wife remarried without legally dissolving her first marriage. A challenge to the legality of a subsequent marriage by a woman should be adjudicated by a family court, but the Zina Ordinance started another trend since the courts started pronouncing verdicts on the legality of divorce and of subsequent marriage in criminal proceedings. This interpretation of Muslim law on divorce eroded the law that women's rights activists were campaigning to save.[51] Such verdicts made women more vulnerable, opening up the prospect of divorce without a record and prosecution of *zina* in case of remarriage.

The application of zina *to Non-Muslims and the erosion of their fundamental rights*

The *zina* law was made a general law applicable to everyone irrespective of religion. However, it ruled out the evidence of a non-Muslim witness for *hadd* cases except if he or she was the accused. Non-Muslim lawyers were also barred from appearing in cases under this law, except to represent a non-Muslim accused. The overriding power of *zina* law[52] intruded upon laws of personal status of the religious minorities and violated constitutional guarantees.[53] In practice, Christian married men would convert to Islam and contract polygamous marriages, thereby evading the application of the laws under which they first married. Christian married women would convert and remarry Muslim men without dissolving their first marriage. Their cases were tried under *zina* law and the application of the benefit of doubt on *mens rea* saw an acquittal in the majority of cases.[54] This

---

49   Section 7 Muslim Family Laws describes the procedure pertaining to notice and reconciliation proceedings in the Arbitration Council.
50   See for an absurd but disturbing example the case of *Noor Khan v Haq Nawaz*. PLD 1982 FSC 265 concerning prosecution of a woman more than ten years after she had left her husband, remarried and had children.
51   See *Noor Khan v Haq Nawaz* PLD 1982 FSC 265, *Mohammad Sarwar v The State* PLD 1988 FSC 42, *Allah Dad v Mukhtar and another* 1992 SCMR 1273. These decisions ran counter to the law of divorce on *talaq*, which provided a period of 90 days for reconciliation after receipt of notice of *talaq* by the chair of the arbitration council and had ended sudden termination of marriage. See also Warraich, S.A. and Balch, C. 1999. Confusion Worse Confounded: A Critique of divorce law and legal Practice in Pakistan, in *Shaping Women Lives*, edited by F. Shaheed. Lahore: Shirkat Gah, 181–225.
52   Section 3 Zina Ordinance.
53   See in this regard article 227(3) of the Constitution.
54   *Sardar Masih v Haider Masih* PLD 1988 FSC 78 and *Mst. Zarina and another v The State* PLD 1988 FSC 105.

practically nullified the application of the personal status laws. At the most, the courts would explain the procedure that the woman should have followed after her conversion to Islam.[55]

The minimal impact of the higher courts

In one appeal[56] against a conviction under the Zina Ordinance the FSC openly acknowledged the abuse of the law and the need to check it. The case of *Abdul Qayum* was registered by police on the report of a stranger who had simply seen a man and a woman in a room and assumed that they would commit *zina*. The court warned against baseless allegations of *zina* against women, stating that:

> Before parting with this case we are constrained to make observation that such reckless allegations are being brought so frequently that something should be done to stop this unhealthy practice. The prosecution agencies before putting people on trial for offences of Zina on flimsy allegations should be mindful of injunctions of the Holy Qur'an and the message conveyed through the decisions from the early period of Pious Caliphs. The charge of Zina carrying a rigorous penalty of rajam [stoning] or stripes should not be casually brought to court nor publicized. It shatters the foundation of a family whose female is accused of such a crime. Human weaknesses should rather be overlooked and ignored unless committed at public places and become a matter of concern from the society's point of view. It is most unbecoming of a stranger to peep into the house of others and show inquisitiveness for detecting the sins of others.[57]

In practice, such rulings made little difference. One key factor for the continued abuse of *zina* law was that complainants did, with few exceptions, not face any repercussions even if a complaint was false although the law provided for *qazaf* (punishment for making false allegation of *zina*). The preconditions for the registration of a case of *zina* set out in the Abdul Qayum case were rarely applied thereafter. The courts fell short of taking effective measures and so continued to endorse an abusive law and condone practices of the authorities that violated rights. *Zina* law also resulted in networks of police informers from the public being able to report baseless cases with impunity. Police officers would themselves invent new ways of registering *zina* cases, not least as a means to first lure women into

---

55 　*Masih v Masih, Mst. Zarina and another v The State*, and *Naziran alias Khalida Parveen v The State* PLD 1988 SC 713. In the last case, the Supreme Court directed the Federal Government to legislate on conflict of laws resulting from conversion to Islam but no such law has been enacted to date.

56 　*Abdul Qayum and another v The State* 1991 PCr.LJ 568 (FSC).

57 　*Qayum and another v The State*, 572, at para. 11.

prostitution and then registering cases against them.[58] Access to the High Court via constitutional petitions provided a degree of safety against police abuse under the Zina Ordinance.[59] A High Court can issue a writ of prohibition or mandamus in appropriate cases to stop any criminal proceedings that amount to abuse of legal process[60] In one case of *zina* where a woman applied for bail, the High Court quashed criminal proceedings.[61] In this case a police informer had reported that a man and a woman were present in a house and would commit *zina*, the police had raided the house, arrested both and registered a case under section 10 of the Zina Ordinance,[62] without any material evidence to implicate them. The court held that 'it is foremost duty of the police to ensure that provisions of the Constitution, especially the fundamental rights, are not violated and transgressed in pursuance of irresponsible complaints made to the police'.[63] Yet the court did not initiate any action against the police for violating fundamental rights. In subsequent cases the higher courts provided relief in broader terms, such as a case[64] in which the court made clear that the police cannot enter a house to make arrests on allegations of *zina*, and that a magistrate has no power to issue any house search warrants under the CrPC for the implementation of *zina* law.[65] Such cases and verdicts provided materials for the ongoing campaign for repeal and reform of this law and examples to demonstrate the injustices caused by it.

Reform of the *hudood* laws

Challenging the law

The rights groups campaigned against the *hudood* laws on the grounds of inherent discrimination on the basis of sex and religion and their unjust application, especially against women and minorities. In addition to regular campaigns for the repeal of these laws on specific days[66] for almost a quarter of a century and

---

58   See *Mst. Hamidan Bibi v The State* 1993 PSC (Crl). The FSC, while acquitting a woman in her appeal against a life sentence, held that the police acted unlawfully and ordered action against the concerned police officer.

59   The High Court and FSC exercised concurrent jurisdiction to hear bail applications for any of the offences covered in the Hudood Ordinances.

60   Article 199 of the Constitution.

61   *Mst. Akhtar Parveen v The State* PLD 1997 Lahore 390.

62   Sub sections of section 10 deal with *zina* and *zina bil jabr* liable to *tazir*. This was a standard practice by the police to just mention section 10 of the Ordinance in the FIR without specifying the sub-clause to identify the exact nature of the charge.

63   *Mst. Akhtar Parveen v The State*, 393, at para. 5.

64   *Riaz v Station House Officer* PLD 1998 Lahore 35.

65   *Riaz v Station House Officer*, 43.

66   This included 8 March, the international women's day, and 12 February, which was named as Pakistani Women's Day by women rights activists after their protest against

protests against emblematic court decisions, the shortcomings of the laws were analyzed in detail.[67] In 2004, the Joint Action Committee for People's Rights and Peace (JAC) and the Women Action Forum (WAF) launched a signature campaign for repeal of these Ordinances and organized many seminars, meetings, protests and press conferences to elaborate on their demands.[68] However, the scope for challenging *hudood* laws was extremely limited during the military rule of Zia-Ul-Haq although the campaign against them started right from the beginning, propelled by individual cases such as *Fehmida, Jehan Mina* and *Safia Bibi* and resulting in strong protests and rallies by women's rights and human rights groups. The proponents of the state-sponsored 'Islamization' process sought to silence any opposition. The opponents of these laws were dismissed as Western elements who wanted to spread immorality and obscenity in Pakistani society, and they were subject to personal attacks in the media and other fora. The state-backed moral campaigns, including official orders for women to cover themselves in educational institutions and related measures of segregation, created an atmosphere of fear. The only option was to challenge the contents of *hudood* laws before the FSC on the grounds of their being repugnant to the injunctions of Islam.

The first such challenge came right at the outset in relation to the punishment of *rajam* (death by stoning), and resulted in two contradictory judgments. In the first verdict the court declared the punishment of *rajam* to be un-Islamic on the grounds that it is not found in the *Qur'anic* injunctions.[69] This created a political uproar and was a serious setback for General Zia's Islamization scheme. He did not accept the verdict and within days made a constitutional amendment that gave the FSC the power to review its decisions.[70] A new bench was constituted, which was headed by the judge who had in the earlier decision held that *rajam* was not a *Qur'anic* punishment but could be given as *tazir*, and included two *alim* (religious scholars) judges.[71] In the review petition the court held that the punishment of stoning was Islamic.[72] Another petition challenged section 3 of the Qazaf Ordinance before the FSC, arguing, unsuccessfully, that the particular verse in the *Qur'an* mentions false allegations against chaste women only but the *qazaf* law includes false allegation against men as also being liable to punishment.[73]

---

the proposed law of evidence on 12 February 1983 in Lahore. This protest rally was baton charged and tear gas was used by the police. Many women rights activists were arrested that day.

67   Jahangir, A. and Jilani, H. 1990. *The Hudood Ordinances, A Divine Sanction? A research study of the Hudood Ordinances and their effect on the disadvantaged sections of Pakistani society.* Lahore: Rohtas Books.

68   See for an example of the booklets distributed as part of the campaign, Shirkat Gah Women's Resource Centre. 2004. *Why The Hudood Ordinances must be repealed?* Lahore.

69   See *Hazoor Bakhsh v Federation of Pakistan* PLD 1981 FSC 145.

70   Constitution (Amendment) Order 1981 (P.O. No. 5 of 1981).

71   Constitution (Second Amendment) Order 1981.

72   *Federation of Pakistan v Hazoor Bakhsh* PLD 1983 FSC 255.

73   *Zaheer Ahmed v Federation of Pakistan* PLD 1982 FSC 244.

In the late 1980s, a senior woman lawyer opposed to the Zina and Qazaf Ordinances from a religious perspective petitioned the FSC, challenging the exclusion of the testimony of women for *hadd* sentences, inclusion of rape as *hadd* crime, and the validity of *tazir* sentences for the crime of *zina*. This case met with a mixed result.[74] The court held that *zina bil jabr* was different from ordinary cases of *zina* and constituted an extreme form of *fasad fil arz* and *haraba* (meaning the causing of disorder or chaos on earth). As such, the court acknowledged that it required a different form of evidence and found that the testimony of two adult male Muslims was sufficient for *hadd* sentences in rape cases and *Tazir* sentences for rape could be based on any other form of evidence. The court recommended an amendment of the law, requesting the President to amend the laws in light of its recommendations by 1 February 1990. The government appealed against this judgment in the Supreme Court and until the enactment of the WPA on 2 December 2006, no verdict had been reached in this case.

Despite acknowledging the abuse of the *zina* law in several cases and proposing measures to prevent it, the FSC remained the custodian of *hudood* laws, as was firmly stated in the appeal of the *Zafran Bibi* case:

> This is an unfortunate case, which received much publicity in the National/ International press ... On account of disinformation, misunderstanding, lack of knowledge of facts and circumstances of the case, some organisations resorted even to take out processions and demand repeal of the hudood laws itself without realising that it was not the laws of Hudood ... but its misapplication which resulted in miscarriage of justice. So, far as Islamic criminal law, including the Hudood laws, are concerned, they are designed, prescribed and promulgated on the basis of clear [Islamic] injunctions ... These time-tested laws mainly aim at preservation and protection of life, honour and property of the citizens of an Islamic state and dispensation of justice without any discrimination.[75]

The path to legal reforms

Background

The *zina* and other *hudood* laws became an ideological battleground. While the actual practice exposed the dilemmas of the law and validated the arguments of its opponents, the *Shari'a* cover served to obstruct any meaningful debate. Orthodox conservative religious political parties (in the form of the MMA, or *Muthida Majlis e Amal*, a six-party religious political alliance from 2002–2007) and their allied clerics wanted the status quo to continue. Any questioning of these laws was denounced as Western conspiracy. These laws were termed divine and

---

74   *Begum Rashida Patel v Federation of Pakistan* PLD 1989 FSC 95.
75   *Zafran Bibi v The State* PLD 2002 FSC 1, at 12.

protectors against Western obscenity.[76] Other proponents agreed on the need for some amendments but declared that these laws are in accordance with Islam and ought to stay on the statue books.

Rights groups campaigning for the repeal of *hudood* faced the challenge of raising awareness about the inherent discrimination and problems of the law at the official and wider public level. Their campaigns began with protests against the judgments and sentencing in *zina* and rape cases. The groups organized public protests, issued press releases and addressed press conferences. The avenues for this campaign were somewhat limited for a variety of reasons. Interest for such legal reforms was mainly driven by those affected, or rights campaigners. The official portrayal of this law as a codification of Islamic injunctions made a broader public debate extremely difficult to have. In addition, patriarchal feudal prejudices and a general lack of understanding of justice prevented any substantive public debate. This response must also be seen against the background of customary practices of dealing with allegations of *zina* or crimes of 'morality'. In these matters the general response tended to be extremely brutal, especially in rural areas. People took matters in their own hands, humiliating and punishing individuals, that is mainly women, even on hearsay. The rights groups concentrated their efforts on exposing the injustices of this law by campaigning around emblematic cases and demanding repeal of discriminatory laws against women. Some comparatively liberal political parties, such as the Pakistan Peoples Party (PPP) and the *Muttahida Qaumi* Movement (MQM) agreed with the demands of the rights groups and even included them in their elections manifestoes, but failed to deliver when in government. Gradually agreement grew as to the flaws in the Zina and Qazaf Ordinances, though the way in which this was expressed and the policy responses pursued differed considerably.

Reports from government-appointed commissions
The Huddod Ordinances were examined by three government-appointed commissions, two of which recommended their repeal. The Commission of Inquiry for Women (1997), headed by a serving judge of the Supreme Court, found in its report that:

> The Commission is convinced that all the Hudood laws were conceived and drafted in haste. They are not in conformity with the injunctions of Islam. Secondly, these laws have come into direct conflict both with the country's Constitution (such as of article 25) and its international commitments (as made at the Fourth World Conference on Women at Beijing and under the UN Convention on the Elimination of All Forms of Discrimination Against Women). Thirdly, in practical terms too, these laws have demonstrably failed to serve their

---

76   Bilqees Said. Member of National assembly, quoted in Council of Islamic Ideology. 2006. *Interim Report 2005, updated July 2006, on Hudood Ordinances 1979.* Islamabad, 36.

purpose. They have not been any deterrent against crimes. And they have only led to proliferation of complaints in the courts, which, as it happens, have mostly been false or unjustified and have caused undue hardship.

It is necessary therefore that:

1. The Hudood laws are repealed.
2. The repealed provisions of the Pakistan Penal Code, 1860, are re-enacted with an amendment to make marital rape a penal offence and to impose a severer punishment for rape on a minor wife.
3. If the Parliament considers it necessary to make any further laws in this area, it should to do so after serious debate and by reaching a consensus that the proposed laws are in accordance with the injunctions of Islam.[77]

The permanent National Commission on the Status of Women (NCSW) was established in 2000. Its mandate included the review of all laws and policies affecting women and to make recommendations to eliminate discrimination. The NCSW constituted an 18-member Special Committee to review the Hudood Ordinances (1979), which included ex-judges of the Supreme Court, High Courts, and Federal Shariat Court, religious scholars, representatives of the religious minorities, lawyers, women's rights activists and the Chairman of the Council of Islamic Ideology. The Committee reviewed each legal provision of the Hudood Ordinances and concluded:

> [It], therefore, wishes to record that [its members] are unanimous in arriving at the conclusion that the Hudood Laws as enforced are full of lacunas and anomalies and the enforcement of these has brought about injustice rather than justice, which is the main purpose of enforcement of Islamic law. Consequently, by a majority [it] recommends that all four Hudood Ordinances, 1979 should be repealed and the original law with regard to offences mentioned in these Ordinances be restored.[78]

The commission came under lot of criticism after the publication of its report.[79] The chair of the commission was subjected to personalized attacks in the press that had been instigated by some religious right lobbies. Government officials did not attend the launch of the report and tried to disassociate themselves from it.

---

77 Commission of Inquiry for Women. 1997. *Towards a Better Tomorrow*. Lahore: Shirkat Gah, 54.

78 National Commission on the Status of Women. 2003. *Report on Hudood ordinances 1979*. Islamabad, 39.

79 The North Western Frontier Province legislative assembly passed a resolution against the NCSW report. See 2003. PA Opposes repeal of Hudood laws. *Dawn* [Online, 10 September] Available at: http://www.dawnnews.tv/2003/09/10/nat9.htm [Accessed 15 January 2011].

The flurry of amendment bills

By 2005 political momentum for debates on the Zina Ordinance had begun to be built by the amendments in the criminal law relating to honour crimes and debates in the parliament on honour killings and *zina* issues. Any change in the *zina* and rape law was a major political decision and the entire debate inside and outside parliament was primarily centred around political negotiations, with a considerable degree of secrecy surrounding the multiple versions of the bills prepared by the government. Several private member bills for amendments were moved in the National Assembly in 2005 and in 2006. The bills acknowledged the flaws in the *hudood* laws but also made unsuccessful attempts to salvage their Islamic nature.[80] Even a female MMA member of the assembly, who otherwise was a staunch defender of *hudood* laws, moved an amendment bill.[81] The government, meanwhile, produced its first draft of the government bill titled Protection of Women (Criminal and Family Laws) (Amendment) Act, 2006, in August 2006. Copies of it were not made publically available and could only be obtained from some members of the parliament, such as the treasury benches. It can be surmised that this draft was floated by the government to test the political waters, as it was not formally introduced in either house of the parliament. The amendments proposed were more comprehensive than the later bills and the amending law itself. Significantly, its statement of objects and reasons acknowledged the problems and sufferings caused by the Zina and Qazaf Ordinances. The bill did not touch criminalization of sex outside marriage and retained the offence of *zina* but attempted to bring in procedural changes to check its abuse. The substantive aspects of the provisions related to *zina* were amended but not repealed. Another significant aspect was the bill's attempt to remove gender and religious discrimination and provisions which barred the testimony of women and non Muslims.[82] In the statement of objectives a specific reference was made to this aspect:

> Punishment, by itself, is not the objective of Quran and Sunnah. The objective is to build a just and crime free society. Restrictions based on gender and faith introduced by the Zina and qazaf ordinances are not mandated by the Quran and Sunnah. These are based on the views of then draftsmen of the two Ordinances. As these restrictions impede the Quranic objectives of justice and social harmony, they are being omitted.[83]

---

80   The bills are on file with the author.

81   National Assembly Bill No. 7 of 2006.

82   These amendments were removed in the subsequent drafts of the bill formally presented in the National Assembly for debate. Another significant amendment concerning the removal of puberty as a factor determining adulthood was also subsequently deleted.

83   The quote is taken from page 18 of the very first draft of the bill which was not published in the official gazette. The author obtained a copy from a member of the Parliament (on file with author).

The government gauged the reaction to the first bill and produced a second draft of the bill, with several different versions of the bill circulating at the time. Even after the formal introduction of the bill in the assembly, many versions on specific clauses kept emerging, causing a great deal of confusion. The texts of changing versions were not available except via the members of the parliament, many of whom themselves complained about not having access to the copies.[84]

Debate in Parliament and the work of the Select Committee
The treasury benches succeeded in having the bill referred to a select committee of the National Assembly for further deliberations.[85] The committee was composed of more than 14 members, including the federal ministers for law, parliamentary affairs, women affairs and religious affairs. Rights activists, while reiterating their demand for a repeal of all *hudood* laws, engaged with the committee by lobbying its members to retain the proposed positive amendments and to propose further amendments. To this end, they provided committee members with legal and jurisprudential materials as well as arguments for debates. There were apprehensions that the committee's work may become overshadowed by the parallel political negotiations between the government and groups wanting to retain the status quo, which became more vociferous in public. However, the debates around the bill on private TV channels and in the print media at this critical time in fact helped the reform campaigners to communicate the discriminations and injustices of the *zina* law to a broader public. The final report of the committee deleted the suggestion of *zina* liable to *tazir* (lewdness), an earlier amendment to grant exception in relation to an underage wife in the definition of rape, and an offence related to the publicity of a case of rape. It also added the definition of confession in the Zina Ordinance as a further safeguard.[86]

Parallel negotiations: Efforts to appease the religious right
The MMA pursued a policy of public onslaught. This alliance consisted of religious political parties from diverse sects of Muslims and schools of thought.[87] Government negotiations with one of these parties and its supporting clerics led to the formation of another committee (called the Ulema Committee). It started working in parallel to the negotiations within the parliament and deliberations in the select committee. Although its members were nominated by the government, the majority of them shared the position of the MMA and other religious lobbies

---

84   For example during a meeting organized by the NCSW in Islamabad on 31 August 2006 more than one version was available with different participants.

85   The committee was formed by the Speaker of the National Assembly, consisting of members from different political parties.

86   Select Committee of the National Assembly. 2006. *Final Report*. Islamabad.

87   It included parties from different Sunni schools of thought like *Brelavi, Deobandi, Ahle Hadith. Jamat i Islami* whose members can be from diverse schools, primarily Sunni, was also a member, as was TNFJ, a Shia party.

who were opposed to any changes in these laws. This parallel committee did not put forward any proposal during the working of the select committee but objected to almost every proposed amendment. A deadlock emerged and the bill worked upon by the select committee was not presented in the National Assembly for debate and voting. An agreement of consensus on principal issues was signed between the Ulema Committee and the government but no progress could be made. The government proposed different drafts but the MMA did not agree to any of them and delayed the passing of amendments by more than two months. In the end the government could not obtain the approval of the orthodox conservative forces, despite bringing a clause relating to fornication into the penal code.[88]

Limitations and resistance from within religion
Only a few religious scholars or personalities opposed the existing *hudood* laws. They based their arguments on *Qur'anic* injunctions, *hadith* (words or acts of the Prophet Muhammad constituting a source of Islamic law) and views of Imams and other jurists. The position of religious scholars can broadly be divided into two categories. There were those who opposed the existing laws as being contrary to the injunctions of Qur'an, which also held a position that the sentences mentioned in the *Qur'an* for offences like *zina* were for special occasions and for a special category of offenders, so not applicable in ordinary circumstances. Their arguments were from within the framework of religion, but there was little acceptance of this position due to the dominant perspective that the laws were divine laws and could not be touched.

The scholars and individuals falling in the other category opposed the existing laws but put forward their own version of *hudood* laws. This meant that they supported reforms but did not join the campaign for a permanent abolition of such laws and harsher punishments. This group agreed that rape is not a form of *zina* and not a *hadd* crime. However, the position of some scholars, such as Dr Tufai Hasmi, who publically opposed the zina and rape laws and whose writings were used in some meetings and seminars demanding their repeal, was controversial as he argued that rape constitutes a form of *haraba* and carries the punishment provided for this offence, including that of crucifixion or stoning.[89]

Changes and remaining gaps in the Women Protection Act

The first and foremost change was the acknowledgement that the Zina and Qazaf Ordinances, which were portrayed as divine, could be amended. To this extent the arguments made from within religion had lost out, with important political implications. The main changes in brief were:

---

88   Section 496B PPC. The difference between *zina* and fornication concerns the number of witnesses to the act of sexual intercourse: *zina* (four male witnesses), fornication (two witnesses).

89   Hashmi, F. 2006. *Hudood Ordinance in light of Quran and Sunnah*. Islamabad: Aurat Foundation, 157.

1. The Zina Ordinance now entails the offence of *zina* liable to *hadd* only. The sentences of one hundred stripes for unmarried offenders and of stoning to death for married Muslim offenders have been retained.
2. The problematic definition of marriage was repealed.
3. The provision that gave the Zina Ordinance overriding effect over all other laws was repealed.
4. All provisions related to sexual violence were moved to the PPC, though without any changes except regarding rape.
5. An offence called fornication was introduced in the PPC for 'wilful sexual intercourse' between a man and a woman not married to each other. A court can take cognizance of the crime if there is evidence of the complainant and at least two eyewitnesses, without any qualifications concerning the sex or the religion of the witness as in *zina* cases. The punishment for fornication is imprisonment of up to five years and a fine. A special procedure to file a complaint of fornication was inserted in the CrPC. This constituted a backdoor entry of *zina* liable to *tazir*.
6. Rape was redefined as: 'sexual intercourse with a woman under circumstances falling under any of the five following descriptions, (i) against her will, (ii) without her consent, (iii) with her consent when the consent has been obtained by putting her in fear of death or hurt, (iv) with her consent, when the man knows that he is not married to her and that the consent is given because she believes that the man is another person to whom she is or believes herself to be married; or (v) with or without her consent when she is under sixteen years of age'.
7. The amended law provided that a complaint of rape could not be converted into a case of *zina* or fornication against the complainant woman and a case of zina could not be converted into one of fornication.
8. A special procedure to lodge a complaint of *zina* or fornication was enacted in the CrPC. The complaint could only be filed before the competent court and not before the police. The procedure required the recording of evidence of the required witnesses before initiating proceedings against a suspect. It also provided protection against false complaints of *zina* and empowered courts to initiate action on their own accord against false complainants and punish them under *qazaf*. The law also provided for punishment for false complaints of fornication.

Some of the key demands made in campaigns for the amendment of rape laws were not included in this new definition of rape, namely those relating to rape in custody, rape using a position of authority and marital rape. The age of consent for sexual intercourse remains an issue. As per the Zina Ordinance, a female having attained puberty is an adult and can be liable for *zina* if the required testimony of four eye witnesses is available, but sexual intercourse with a female under sixteen years of age is considered rape. This conflict has not been tested in the higher courts yet. With these amendments rape is to be tried under the ordinary procedure and law of evidence, however, one controversial clause in the law of evidence has not been repealed, namely that 'when a man is prosecuted for rape or an attempt to ravish, it may be shown that the prosecutrix was of generally immoral character'.[90]

The use of the term 'protection of women' in the title of the amending Act created a general impression that abuse against women would be prosecuted, and seemed to indicate that a new umbrella law providing protection against sexual and physical abuse has been enacted. However, since then there have been many other legal developments in relation to women rights. Bills have been introduced in the parliament on issues that were once considered taboo. Amendments to the PCC that inserted a provision against sexual harassment of women were made in February 2010[91] and a law against the harassment of women in the workplace was enacted in March 2010.[92] Many other bills on issues of discrimination and violence, including on domestic violence, specific forms of violence like acid throwing, the rights of home-based workers, as well as one on the minimum age of marriage were pending in parliament at the time of writing.[93]

Conclusion

The reform of *zina* and rape laws depended entirely upon political will. The 2006 amendment was not the result of new thinking and interpretations of Islam or human rights discourse. Indeed the arguments that were put forward from within the framework of Islam and from a human rights perspective were those that had been advanced for a long time. The process of exposing the discrimination and injustices of the law over a period of 25 years had been conducted solely by women's rights and human rights organizations, rather than by those who took a different perspective from within the framework of religion who had by and large remained a silent opposition over the years. The persistence of this campaign and the creative methods used were instrumental in opening up the political space to change laws that had been widely discredited but still retained a privileged status

---

90   Article 151(4) of Law of Evidence, called Qanun-e-Shadat order 1984. This clause was also present in the Law of Evidence 1872. The FSC declared this provision to be repugnant to the injunctions of Islam in the case of *Captain (retd) Mukhhtar Ahmed Sheikh v The Government of Pakistan* PLD 2009 FSC 65.

91   Section 509 PPC was amended by the Insulting modesty or causing sexual harassment through Criminal Law (Amendment) Act 2010, Act No I of 2010. See Gazette of Pakistan Extraordinary. 2 February 2010, 13–15.

92   Protection Against Harassment of Women at the Workplace Act, 2010, Act No IV of 2010. See Gazette of Pakistan Extraordinary. 11 March 2010, 63–74.

93   See N.A Bill No. 16 of 2010 for the establishment of a Rehabilitation Authority for Victims of Violence and Abuse; N.A Bill No. 37 of 2009, to amend the Child Marriage Restraint Act 1929 and raise the age of marriage for females to 18 years, and the Bill for Domestic Violence (Prevention and Protection) Act, 2009. The latter bill could not be enacted into law and lapsed in the upper house after being passed by the National Assembly.

because of their supposedly 'divine' nature. However, while acknowledging this achievement, implementing the WPA and effectively guaranteeing women's rights will continue to be an ongoing struggle in the volatile environment and easily radicalized atmosphere that is so characteristic of contemporary Pakistan.[94]

---

94   On 22 December 2010, the FSC struck down four provisions of the WPA (ruling in the case of Shariat petitions no. 01/1 (2007), no. 03/1 (2007) and no. 01/1 (2010)). The decision was appealed to the Supreme Court. See Joint Action Committee for People's Rights. 2010. *Shariat Court Decision Anti Women and Undermines Judiciary in Pakistan.* Press Release [29 December] Available at: http://www.sacw.net/article1802.html [accessed 15 January 2011].

Chapter 12

Sexual Violence and the Law: Comparative Legislative Experiences in Selected Southern African Countries

Rashida Manjoo, Gift Kweka and Suzzie Onyeka Ofuani

Introduction

Depending on the context and the political landscape, definitions of sexual violence may be influenced by cultural values, social norms, human rights, gender roles, legal advocacy and criminal offences.[1] The term sexual violence is a gendered phenomenon whose nature and extent reflect pre-existing social, cultural and economic disparities between men and women.[2] While sexual violence during armed conflicts has received considerable international attention, the rising levels of sexual violence against women and girl-children in the domestic sphere, in times of so-called peace, reflects a global phenomenon.

For example, in Namibia, out of 1,500 women between the ages of 15 and 49 years interviewed by the World Health Organization (WHO), 36 per cent reported having been subjected to physical and sexual violence by intimate partners or strangers.[3] In a similar study in Tanzania, 56 per cent of women interviewees reported being subjected to physical and sexual violence.[4] Research in South Africa also suggests that nearly one in four women experiences sexual violence by an intimate partner, while up to one-third of adolescent girls report their first

---

1 National Sexual Violence Resource Centre. 2004. *Global Perspectives on Sexual Violence: Findings from the World Report on Violence and Health*, 4. [Online] Available at: http://www.nsvrc.org/_cms/fileUpload/global_perspectives.pdf [accessed 10 October 2009].

2 Gordon, P. and Crehan, K. 2000. *Dying of Sadness: Gender, Sexual Violence and the HIV Epidemic*. [Online] Available at: http://www.undp.org/hiv/publications/gender/violencee.htm [accessed 12 October 2009].

3 World Health Organization (WHO). 2005. *WHO multi-country study on women's health and domestic violence against women*. [Online] Available at: http://www.who.int/mediacentre/factsheets/fs239/en/ [accessed 4 October 2009].

4 WHO. 2005. Out of 1450 of those interviewed in the Mbeya region, 56 per cent reported to have been subjected to physical and sexual violence.

sexual experience as being forced.[5] The 2003 report of the United Nations (UN) Special Rapporteur on Violence against Women estimates that, in Botswana, over 60 per cent of women have been victims of violence at some time in their lives.[6] A 2006 study relating to Lesotho shows that, of the respondents interviewed, 61 per cent indicated being victims of sexual violence. A 2007 report relating to Zambia indicates a high rate of sexual violence against young children, with 12 girls raped every week.[7] Sexual violence statistics in other countries such as Mozambique reflect rates of approximately 54 per cent of the interviewed women,[8] and in Swaziland, the Sexual Offences and Child Abuse Department investigated over 700 cases of child rape and over 460 cases concerning rape of women in the previous two years.[9] The adverse impact and consequences of violence against women appears to be a significant cause of high rates of morbidity and mortality.[10] Sexual violence against women accounts for as many deaths and cases of ill-health in women aged 15 to 44 years, as those caused by malaria and traffic accidents combined.[11] Yet in spite of its adverse effects, sexual violence against women not only goes unpunished, but it is tolerated in silence by the victims as well as the society as a whole. The factors responsible for this silence usually range from the fear of reprisal, feelings of shame and blame by/of the victim, to the unquestioning acceptance of male domination in most traditions and cultures.[12]

Against this background, this chapter examines regional policies relating to sexual violence and discusses substantive, evidentiary and procedural law reform

---

5   Wood, K. et al. 1998. *He forced me to love him: putting violence on adolescent sexual health agendas*. [Online] Available at: http://www.sciencedirect.com.ezproxy.uct. ac.za/science?_ob=ArticleURL&_udi=B6T [accessed 12 October 2009].

6   UN Special Rapporteur on Violence against Women, Its Causes and Consequences, Ms Radhika Coomaraswamy. 2003. *Integration of the Human Rights of Women and the Gender Perspective: Violence against Women*. UN Doc. E/CN.4/2003/75/Add/1.

7   Mulenga, N. 2006. *Zambia: More than 10 girls raped every week*. [Online] Available at: http://www.wunrn.com/news/12_25_06/123106_zambia_statistics.htm [accessed 7 December 2009].

8   Romao, F. et al. 2009. *Violence Against Women in Mozambique*. [Online, July] Available at: www.gender-budgets.org/component/option,com_docman/task../gid,456/ [accessed 7 December 2009].

9   Amnesty International. 2009. *The State of the World's Human Rights*. [Online] Available at: http://www.thereport.amnesty.org/en/regions/africa/swaziland [accessed 18 December 2009].

10   Venis, S. and Horton, R. 2002. Violence against Women: a global burden. *The Lancet* (9313) [Online] Available at: http://www.thelancet.com [accessed 10 October 2009], 359.

11   WHO. 1997. *Violence Against Women Information Pack: A Priority Health Issue*. [Online] Available at: http://www.met.police.uk/dv/files/violence_ip.pdf [accessed 13 October 2009].

12   Bunch, C. 1997. *The Intolerable Status Quo: Violence against women and girls*, 41–2. [Online] Available at: http://www.unicef.org/pon97/40-49.pdf [accessed 10 October 2009].

efforts in selected countries in the region with a view to assessing the efficacy of legal responses.

Regional instrument: The protocol to the African Charter on Human and Peoples' Rights on the Rights of Women in Africa

This protocol was adopted in 2003 to provide for the recognition of specific rights of women, over and above the rights recognized under the 1981 African Charter on Human Rights and Peoples' Rights (AfrCHPR).[13] The protocol, although modelled after the Convention on the Elimination of all Forms of Discrimination against Women, caters for areas that have not been covered by the Convention or other regional and international instruments.[14] The AfrCHPR includes a number of provisions for the promotion and protection of women's human rights, including the principle of non-discrimination on the grounds of race, ethnic group, colour, sex, language, religion, political or other opinion, national and social origin, fortune, birth or other status; and the prohibition of all forms of exploitation, particularly slavery, slave trade, torture, cruel, inhuman or degrading punishment and treatment. It also stipulates the responsibility of the state to ensure the elimination of discrimination against women and the protection of the rights of women and the girl-child as recognized in international declarations and conventions.

The adoption of the Women's Protocol is an important milestone. It comprehensively addresses the issue of violence against women and girls and also the issue of protection and prevention. Article 1(j) states:

> 'violence against women' means all acts perpetrated against women which cause or could cause them physical, sexual, psychological and economic harm, including the threat to take such acts; or to undertake the imposition of arbitrary restrictions on or deprivation of fundamental freedoms in private or public life in peace time and during situations of armed conflicts or of war.

The protocol reaffirms important obligations and rights applicable in the prohibition of sexual violence, such as the right to dignity (article 3), the rights to life, integrity and security of the person (article 4), the elimination of harmful practices (article 5), and the protection of women and children, particularly girls, in armed conflicts (article 11). Article 11(3) calls upon state parties 'to protect asylum-seeking women, refugees, returnees and internally displaced persons, against all forms of violence, rape and other forms of sexual exploitation, and to ensure that such acts

---

13   Protocol to the African Charter on Human and Peoples' Rights on the Rights of Women in Africa, adopted by the 2nd Ordinary Session of the Assembly of the Union, Maputo. CAB/LEG/66.6. 13 September 2003. Entered into force 25 November 2005.

14   See generally article 22(b) and article 23(b) of the Convention on the Elimination of all Forms of Discrimination against Women respectively.

are considered war crimes, genocide and/or crimes against humanity and that their perpetrators are brought to justice before a competent criminal jurisdiction'.

Sub-regional instruments

Southern African Development Community Declaration on gender and Development[15]

This is a declaration that was signed in 1998 by the heads of states of the Southern African Development Community (SADC). Although it recognized the need for ensuring gender equality through policy and institutional frameworks, it did not deal comprehensively with the issue of violence against women. However, its signatories undertook to fulfil ten commitments, which include among others: repealing and reforming all laws; amending constitutions and changing social practices that still subject women to discrimination, and enacting empowering gender-sensitive laws; protecting and promoting the human rights of women and children; recognizing, protecting and promoting the reproductive and sexual rights of women and children; and taking urgent measures to prevent and deal with the increasing levels of violence against women and children.

Harare Declaration on the Prevention and Eradication of Violence against Women and Children

This declaration is an addendum to the abovementioned declaration and was adopted in 1999 by members of the SADC Women's Parliamentary Network and other SADC parliamentarians during a conference in Harare, Zimbabwe.[16] Under the declaration, the parties recognized the increasing occurrence of sexual violence against women, despite the wide range of international and regional instruments prohibiting such crimes, and also the lack of implementation of such standards by member states. The declaration reiterates a programme of action to curb the problem through legislative measures by addressing sexual violence in the public and private sphere,[17] developing mechanisms under which victims will receive necessary assistance and protection,[18] creating awareness of violence

---

15 As a general principle in international law, declarations are not binding in the strictest sense. The adopted declaration reflects the general view and concern of governments of the SADC region.

16 Harare Declaration on the Prevention and Eradication of Violence against Women and Children. 1999. [Online] Available at: http://www.awepa.org/resources/harare-declaration-on-the-prevention-of-violence-against-sadc-women-and-children_en.html [accessed 7 October 2009].

17 1(a) to (k) Harare Declaration.

18 2(a) to (h) Harare Declaration.

against women, and influencing national budgets to ensure that state resources are allocated to achieving the implementation of this declaration.[19] It is important to point out that these two declarations provided a framework that ultimately paved the way for the adoption of a binding instrument that specifically addresses the area of gender and women's rights.

SADC Protocol on Gender and Development

This protocol is a legally binding sub-regional instrument that was adopted in 2008 by the SADC heads of states. It has clear objectives and sets out twenty-eight targets for the empowerment of women, the elimination of discrimination, and the achievement of gender equality and equity through the development of appropriate gender-sensitive legislation, policies and projects.[20] The protocol imposes obligations on state parties to eliminate all forms of sexual violence and to ensure that the perpetrators are held accountable. It also sets out a deadline of 2015 for member states to, *inter alia*, effect the enactment of laws that address sexual harassment in all spheres[21] as well as gender-based violence with provisions to cater for treatment, testing and caring for victims of sexual violence.[22]

The adoption of regional and sub-regional instruments on gender equality in general and violence against women in particular, reflects a growing trend by states to address the challenges facing African women. The inclusion of provisions regarding law reform in these instruments reflects the political will to tackle impunity, and also the prior lack of sufficient attention to issues of women's human rights. Provisions that require the reform of laws that discriminate against women; and laws, policies and programmes that ensure that all forms of violence against women are eradicated, will have an influence in shaping the response of African states in legislative reforms. The fact that many legislative reform efforts have been undertaken in the SADC region between 1998 and 2008 reflects the influence of among other factors, the commitments made through the adoption of relevant declarations and protocols.

---

19   2(a) to (h) Harare Declaration.

20   Article 3(a) SADC Protocol on Gender and Development.

21   Article 22 SADC Protocol on Gender and Development.

22   Article 20(2) SADC Protocol on Gender and Development. The measures include emergency contraception, access to post-exposure prophylaxis at all hospitals and prevention of the onset of sexually transmitted infections.

Substantive, evidentiary and procedural law reform efforts (1998–2008)

The South African,[23] Lesotho[24] and Namibian[25] laws regulating sexual violence and sexual offences are the most comprehensive pieces of legislation reviewed. They reflect the trend towards gender-neutral definitions and the inclusion of both women and men as potential perpetrators and victims of rape, the addressing of sexual violence crimes committed against children and persons with disabilities, and the recognition and criminalization of marital rape.[26]

In addition, countries such as Lesotho, Malawi, Namibia, South Africa and Zimbabwe have specific legislation dealing with domestic violence. Generally, the term domestic violence has been defined to include numerous forms of violence including the following: physical abuse, sexual abuse, emotional abuse, economic abuse, intimidation, harassment, damage to property, controlling or abusive behaviour, and entering the residence or property of the complainant without the express or implied consent of the complainant, where the persons in question do not share the same residence.[27] Importantly, for any domestic violence claim, the parties thereto must have what has been referred to as a 'domestic relationship'. This covers relationships between persons who are family members and share a household residence or who are dependent on each other financially. In Tanzania the minimal protection for married couples is provided under the Law of Marriage Act with no specific law to protect unmarried women from domestic violence from their partners. Botswana, Mozambique, Swaziland and Zambia have not passed any laws addressing the issue of domestic violence.

Rape and sexual assault

The definition of rape
Definitions of rape have moved from the common law definition, which entailed vaginal penetration by a penis, to the embracing of definitions and the acknowledgement of the different forms of rape as developed by international

---

23　Criminal Law (Sexual Offences and Related Matters) Amendment Act No. 32 of 2007.

24　Sexual Offences Act No. 29 of 2003.

25　Combating of Rape Act No. 8 of 2000.

26　The situation is similar in Botswana where the law has specifically catered for rape by including penetration with any sort of instrument as stipulated under section 141 Penal Code (Amendment) Act No. 5 of 1998.

27　Prevention of Domestic Violence Act No. 5 of 2006 (Malawi); Combating of Domestic Violence Act No. 4 of 2003 (Namibia); Domestic Violence Act of Zimbabwe, Act No. 14 of 2006; Domestic Violence Act No. 116 of 1998 (South Africa).

jurisprudence (most notably of the ad hoc tribunals[28] and special courts[29] as well as the ultimate codification of the elements of the crime of rape under the Rome Statute governing the International Criminal Court (ICC)).[30]

The current laws in South Africa, Namibia and Botswana[31] define rape to cover situations where the perpetrator intentionally effects penetration, however slight; using the penis or any other body parts of the perpetrator, or other objects, into the vagina, mouth or anal cavity of the victim, under coercive circumstances that negate the consent of the victim. The law in Lesotho provides for the crime of an 'unlawful sexual act',[32] rather than using the term rape, but the content is similar to that found in legislation of the abovementioned countries.[33] The Namibian, Lesotho and South African laws also include in the rape and unlawful sexual act definitions, similar acts committed with the aid of an animal as the object of penetration. They also contain another category of rape known as 'compelled rape'[34] and 'compelled sexual acts',[35] which covers a situation where a third party is forced by the accused to perform sexual intercourse or effect penetration to the victim without her consent. Zimbabwean, Zambian and Tanzanian laws do not recognize the category of compelled rape.

The laws on rape in South Africa, Namibia and Botswana reflect the current legal and judicial developments at national and international levels. In contrast, the Tanzanian, Zambian and Zimbabwean laws on sexual violence continue to reflect the old common law definition of what acts constitute rape. These countries still require penetration of the penis in the natural (vaginal) or unnatural (anal) body parts for the constituting of penetration, which is a necessary element for the proving of rape.[36] In Zimbabwe, for example, the category of unconventional acts other than rape constitutes the crime of aggravated indecent assault or indecent

---

28 *Prosecutor v Akayesu* (ICTR-96-4-T). Trial Judgment, 2 September 1998, para. 598; *Prosecutor v Anto Furundžija* (IT-95-17/1-T). Trial Judgment, 10 December 1998, paras 174 and 185.

29 *Prosecutor v Brima et al (*SCSL-04-16-AFRC), Sierra Leone Special Court, Trial Judgment, 20 June 2007, para. 693.

30 Article 7(1)(g) International Criminal Court Elements of Crimes. 2002. ICC-ASP/1/3.

31 Sections 1 and 3 Criminal Law (Sexual Offences and Related Matters) Amendment Act (South Africa); section 2(1) Combating of Rape Act (Namibia); section 141 Penal Code (Amendment) Act (Botswana).

32 Section 3 Sexual Offences Act (Lesotho).

33 Section 2 Sexual Offences Act (Lesotho).

34 See section 2(1)(b) Combating of Rape Act (Namibia) and sections 1 and 4 Criminal Law (Sexual Offences and Related Matters) Amendment Act (South Africa).

35 Section 4 Sexual Offences Act (Lesotho).

36 Section 5 Tanzanian Sexual Offences Special Provisions Act; section 65 Zimbabwean Criminal Law Act No. 23 of 2004; section 132 of the Zambian Penal Code Act [Chapter 87].

assault, which attracts a lesser punishment than punishment for rape.[37] For the crime of rape to be committed, penetration must be effected without the consent of the victim. Different laws within the SADC region have included a list of circumstances that vitiate consent of the victim. These include the use of force or intimidation, the presence of abuse of power or authority to the extent that it affects the victim's ability to give consent, sexual intercourse by false pretence, or committing sexual intercourse against a person who is asleep, unconscious, intoxicated or a child below the age of 12 years.[38]

Sexual assault

The crime of sexual assault addresses other forms of sexual violence that in the strictest sense do not fall under the category of the crime of rape. These are serious forms of sexual violence for which accountability is imperative, in the broader mission of eliminating violence against women. The term 'sexual assault' is found in the current sexual violence legislation of South Africa and Tanzania, although the contents are different. Under the South African law, it includes any act amounting to fellatio or cunnilingus (oral sex), masturbation, kissing in all its forms and any other form of sexual stimulation in any part of the victim's body using an object resembling the genitals of a person or an animal.[39] These acts may be directly perpetrated by the perpetrator or done through compelled forms of sexual violence[40] or self-sexual assault.[41] The Tanzanian law uses the term to cover situations where the perpetrator utters words, sounds, makes any gesture or exhibits any word or object intending them to be heard or seen, with the intent to cause sexual annoyance.[42] A similar provision is found in the Zambian law under the crime of 'indecent assault'.[43] The Tanzanian and Zimbabwean laws have included acts almost similar to the ones amounting to sexual assault in South Africa, under the heading of 'grave sexual abuses' in Tanzania, and 'aggravated indecent assault and indecent assault' in Zimbabwe.[44] The Namibian, Lesotho and

---

37   Sections 66 and 67 Zimbabwean Criminal Law Act.

38   See generally sections 1 and 3 Criminal Law (Sexual Offences and Related Matters) Amendment Act (South Africa); section 2(1) Combating of Rape Act (Namibia); section 141 Penal Code (Amendment) Act of 1998 (Botswana); section 69 Zimbabwean Criminal Law Act; and section 5 Tanzanian Sexual Offences Special Provisions Act.

39   Sections 1 and 5 Criminal Law (Sexual Offences and Related Matters) Amendment Act (South Africa).

40   Section 6 Criminal Law (Sexual Offences and Related Matters) Amendment Act (South Africa).

41   Section 7 Criminal Law (Sexual Offences and Related Matters) Amendment Act (South Africa). This covers instances where the perpetrator compels the victim to perform on herself any act amounting to sexual assault such as masturbation.

42   Section 9 Sexual Offences Special Provisions Act (Tanzania).

43   Section 137 Zambian Penal Code Act.

44   Section 12 Zambian Penal Code Act. See also sections 66 and 67 Zimbabwean Criminal Law Act.

Botswana laws have no category of sexual assault although the acts constitute an offence under the crime of rape or unlawful sexual act while the Zambian law lists the crime of indecent assault without providing for its elements.

Sexual harassment
Sexual harassment is increasingly becoming a problem that requires legal intervention in many African countries. This has led to the adoption of specific laws and amendments to existing laws to provide for a remedy. For example Botswana, South Africa, Namibia, Tanzania, Lesotho and Zimbabwe have laws or provisions addressing sexual harassment in public or private places of work. In Botswana, the Public Services Act (1999) makes sexual harassment in the public services a criminal offence. The Act was amended in 2000 to provide for sexual harassment that is defined as 'unwanted, unsolicited or repeated verbal or sexual advance, sexually derogatory statement or sexually discriminatory remark made by a public officer to another or by a person in authority over another in the public service'.[45] The shortcoming of this provision is that it excludes sexual harassment in the private sector. In Tanzania, sexual harassment is prohibited and is punishable by imprisonment and or the payment of a fine, and the offender may also be ordered to pay compensation to the complainant.[46] Unwelcome sexual advances by words or action used by a person in authority in the work place, whether in the public or private sector, constitutes the offence of sexual harassment.[47]

In Namibia, the Labour Act 6 of 1992 prohibits discrimination in any aspect of employment, on the basis of sex, marital status, family responsibilities and sexual orientation (among other factors), and forbids harassment on the same grounds. The Lesotho Code Order and the Zimbabwean Labour Act have sections that provide for sexual harassment.[48] The South African Code of Good Practice on the Handling of Sexual Harassment Cases, which is only applicable to the workplace, provides for the definition of sexual harassment. It identifies potential victims and perpetrators, as well as various forms of sexual harassment, and sets out the informal and formal mechanisms to deal with claims of sexual harassment (including identifying, among other procedures, the right of the victim to institute

45   Kakooza & Kawuma Advocates. 2006. *Women in Policy Making and the Legislative Process: Assessment of Implementation of the Beijing Platform for Action by Commonwealth Parliaments in the Africa Region* (Final Report), 7. [Online, December] Available at: http://dev.cpahq.org/uploadedFiles/Information_Services/Publications/CPA_ Electronic_Publications/Women%20in%20Policy%20Making%20and%20the%20 Legislative%20Process.pdf [accessed 6 October 2009].

46   Section 138(D)(1) of the Penal Code, added on the basis of section 12 of the Sexual Offences Special Provision Act (Tanzania).

47   Section 138(D)(3) Penal Code (Tanzania).

48   Section 200 Lesotho: Order No. 24 of 1992; section 8(g) Zimbabwe Labour Act, [Chapter 28:1] 1985.

a civil or criminal case).[49] Malawi, Swaziland and Mozambique have no legal provisions addressing sexual harassment.

Female genital mutilation
Female genital mutilation refers to 'all procedures involving partial or total removal of the external female genitalia or other injury to the female genital organs for non-medical purposes'.[50] The existence of female genital mutilation in Africa is generally acknowledged, but the rate of prevalence is unclear, including in the Southern African region.[51] Seen from a human rights perspective, the practice reflects deep-rooted inequality between the sexes, and constitutes an extreme form of discrimination against girls and women.[52] However, there is very little specific legislation addressing this issue in most of the countries reviewed. The Tanzanian and South African laws provide for the offence of cruelty against children where the person who, having the custody, charge or care of any person under eighteen years of age, causes the child to undergo female genital mutilation.[53] In Tanzania, such an act attracts a term of imprisonment of between five and 15 years with or without a fine, and the perpetrator is under a mandatory obligation to pay compensation to the victim, as determined by a court.[54] However, only South African law contains a definition of female genital mutilation, namely 'the partial or complete removal of any part of the genitals, and includes circumcision of female children'.[55] South African law also recognizes the right of every female child under the age of 16 not to be subjected to genital mutilation[56] and deems a violation of this right an offence.[57]

Marital rape and domestic violence
Many women are subjected to different forms of domestic violence in their homes by intimate partners and/or spouses. The treatment of marital rape as a punishable offence reflects a fairly recent development in the protection of women's human rights. With the demise of the ideology that sustained a public/private divide, it is now unacceptable in some geographical contexts for rape in marriage to be treated

49   Employment Equity Act, 1998, Amendments To The Code Of Good Practice On the Handling of Sexual Harassment Cases in the Workplace (South Africa).
50   WHO. 2008. *Eliminating Female Genital Mutilation: An Interagency Statement*, 1. [Online] Available at: http://whqlibdoc.who.int/publications/2008/9789241596442_eng.pdf [accessed 10 October 2009].
51   Tanzania for example had a prevalence rate of 14 per cent in 2004. See WHO. Undated. *Female Genital Mutilation and Other Harmful Practices*. [Online] http://www.who.int/reproductivehealth/topics/fgm/prevalence/en/index.html [accessed 6 August 2010].
52   WHO. 2008.
53   Section 21 Sexual Offences Special Provisions Act (Tanzania), which incorporates section 169(A)(1) of the Penal Code.
54   Section 169(A)(2) Penal Code (Tanzania).
55   Section 1 Children's Act No. 38, 2005 (South Africa).
56   Section 12(3) Children's Act (South Africa).
57   Section 305(a) Children's Act (South Africa).

differently from rape outside of marriage. As a result, the fact that the parties are in a marriage should not be a bar to prosecution.

In Malawi, domestic violence is regulated by the Prevention of Domestic Violence Act.[58] Section 2 defines domestic violence to include physical, sexual, emotional or psychological or financial abuse committed by a person against a spouse, child, or any other person who is a member of the household, or a dependant or parent of a child of that household. These acts have been legislated as criminal offences. However, the offence of marital rape is not recognized under the Malawian criminal law.[59] This effectively means that acts of sexual violence within a marital relationship can only amount to the lesser crime of prohibited sexual violence, as defined under the domestic violence law; and cannot amount to rape. This lacuna in the law is a major issue, as it is estimated that up to 75 per cent of Malawian wives have been forced to have sex with their husbands.[60] In contrast, Namibian law addresses both domestic violence and marital rape. The Combating of Rape Act of 2000 rejects marriage as a defence to a charge of rape.[61] In addition, the Combating of Domestic Violence Act of 2003 prohibits any form of physical abuse, sexual abuse, economic abuse, intimidation, and harassment, emotional, verbal or psychological abuse.[62]

South Africa passed the Domestic Violence Act in 1998, which is viewed as one of the most progressive laws of its kind worldwide.[63] The Act broadens the definition of domestic violence to include physical, sexual, emotional, verbal, psychological, and economic abuse, intimidation, harassment, stalking, property damage, entering the complainant's residence without consent and any other controlling or abusive behaviour towards the complainant.[64] It also recognizes marital rape and allows abused wives to seek redress against their abusive husbands.[65] A husband may be convicted of rape under the Sexual Offences and Related Matters Amendment Act.

In Zimbabwe the Domestic Violence Act covers emotional, psychological and verbal abuse.[66] In addition, section 8 of the Sexual Offences Act recognizes marital rape as an offence. However, no prosecution may be instituted against a husband

---

58   Prevention of Domestic Violence Act 5 of 2006 (Malawi).

59   Aids and Human Rights Research Unit of Pretoria. 2007. *Human Rights Protected? Nine Southern African Country Reports on HIV, AIDS and the Law.* Pretoria: Pretoria University Law Press.

60   UN Special Rapporteur on Violence against Women. 2003, 81, at para. 409.

61   See section 2(3) Combating of Rape Act (Namibia).

62   Section 2(1) Combating of Domestic Violence Act (Namibia).

63   Jewkes, R. et al. 2002. *Risk Factors for Domestic Violence: Findings from a South African Cross-Sectional Study.* [Online] Available at: http://www.sciencedirect.com. ezproxy.uct.ac.za/science?_ob=ArticleURL&_udi=B6T [accessed 1 October 2009].

64   Domestic Violence Act No. 116 of 1998 (South Africa).

65   See also section 5 Prevention of Family Violence Act 133 of 1993 (South Africa).

66   See generally Domestic Violence Act of Zimbabwe Act No. 14 of 2006.

accused of raping his wife, save with the permission of the Attorney General.[67] Botswana, Tanzania and Zambia have no laws specifically prohibiting domestic violence against women, and victims rely on general criminal laws regulating rape, battery and assault. In Zambia the criminal law remedies available to victims are limited to proceedings for assault occasioning actual bodily harm under section 248 of chapter 87 of the Penal Code. In addition, women who have suffered physical injury as a result of domestic violence may also sue their husbands or partners for damages in civil courts, and physical violence is acceptable as a motive for divorce under both customary and statutory law.[68] There are also no specific laws regulating marital rape in these countries, which is premised on the common-law position that a woman is understood to have given her consent to sexual intercourse upon marriage.

Sexual violence and HIV/AIDS
The Zimbabwean, Tanzanian and Botswana laws address deliberate transmission of HIV that amounts to a crime where the victim has no knowledge of the accused's status.[69] In Botswana,[70] Namibia, Lesotho[71] and South Africa, the HIV status of the perpetrator is also taken into consideration when deciding the sentence to be imposed. Furthermore, Lesotho and South African laws provide for the compulsory HIV testing of an accused.[72] Such provisions are not found in the Namibian, Botswana, Zambian and Zimbabwean laws. In Tanzania, the law generally provides for the prohibition of compulsory HIV testing, but this prohibition does not apply to sex offenders, when the process is court initiated.[73]

---

67 Section 68(a) Zimbabwean Criminal Law Act.

68 Aids and Human Rights Research Unit of Pretoria. 2007, 338.

69 Section 79 and 80 Criminal Law (Codification and Reform) Act (Zimbabwe); section 184 Penal Code (Amendment) Act (Botswana); section 47 Tanzanian HIV and AIDS (Prevention and Control) Act No. 28 of 2008.

70 Section 142 Penal Code (Amendment) Act (Botswana). As it stands, once the accused is found guilty of the crime, such (a) convicted person(s) must be tested for HIV. Once the convict tests HIV-negative, the minimum sentence would be ten years and a maximum of life imprisonment. However, if severe violence was used during the commission of the crime, then a higher sentence could be served. On the other hand, if the convict is HIV-positive and was unaware of his or her HIV status as at the time of the rape, the minimum sentence served is 15 years.

71 Section 32(7) Sexual Offences Act of 2003 (Lesotho). Where the convicted person is infected with HIV at the time of the commission of the offence but had no knowledge or reasonable suspicion of the infection, he would be liable to imprisonment for a period of not less than 10 years.

72 Section 30 Sexual Offences Act (Lesotho); Part 2 of chapter 5, Criminal Law (Sexual Offences and Related Matters) Amendment Act (South Africa); Combating of Rape Act (Namibia).

73 Section 15(4)(c) HIV and AIDS (Prevention and Control) Act (Tanzania).

Summary
Many countries in the region have undertaken law reform efforts at the substantive, evidentiary and procedural level. The laws reflect recognition of different forms of violence against women generally and also a more sensitive understanding of the crime of rape in particular. The definition of the crime of rape has evolved to a more comprehensive inclusion of the many forms the crime may take and also the recognition of marital rape. Furthermore, there is a general recognition of sexual harassment in places of work, and also the connection between sexual violence and HIV/AIDS. However, developments are far from uniform throughout the region. There are countries that have more comprehensive pieces of legislation such as South Africa, Namibia and Botswana, while others still need further law reform efforts.

Evidentiary exceptions in sexual violence trials

Evidence of prior sexual conduct
To guard against possible prejudice and further victimization, the Namibian and South African laws do not allow evidence of previous sexual experience or conduct of the complainant or victim to be adduced in a sexual violence trial.[74] However, courts have been given the discretion to grant leave for such evidence to be adduced upon application, provided the conditions for the admissibility of such evidence are met.[75] In South Africa, such evidence is also admissible in the alternative where the prosecutor[76] introduces it.[77] In Lesotho, the law prohibits evidence of previous sexual conduct of the complainant with other persons,[78] but permits evidence of previous sexual experience with the accused.[79] However, evidence

---

74   Section 18 Combating of Rape Act (Namibia), inserting section 227(A)(1) of the Criminal Procedure Act No. 51 of 1977; section 227(1), Schedule to the Criminal Law (Sexual Offences and Related Matters) Amendment Act (South Africa), 2007, which substituted section 227(2) of the Criminal Procedure Act No. 51 of 1977.

75   Section 227(A)(1) Criminal Procedure Act No. 51 of 1977, as amended by section 18 Combating of Rape Act (Namibia) and section 227(2)(a) Criminal Procedure Act No. 51 of 1977 as amended, 2007 (South Africa).

76   Section 227(2)(b) Criminal Procedure Act No. 51 of 1977 as amended, 2007.

77   Centre for Applied Legal Studies University of Witwatersrand. 2006. *Submission on Sexual Offences Bill to the Parliamentary Portfolio Committee on Justice.* [Online, June] Available at: http://www.web.wits.ac.za/NR/rdonlyres/../ParliamentSubmissionSOBill.pdf [accessed 2 October 2009]. In their submission during the reform process, they opposed the judges' discretion on the matter due to fear that defence lawyers will use the opportunity and ultimately be able to use such evidence that has disadvantaged the victim in many prior trials where such evidence was admissible without restriction.

78   Section 26(1) Sexual Offences Act (Lesotho).

79   Section 26(1) Sexual Offences Act (Lesotho). This is inferred from the wording of the provisions of the law that specifically excludes previous sexual experience with the accused as among the prohibited evidence to be adduced.

of previous sexual conduct with other persons is permissible under specific listed circumstances that include situations where 'the identity of the accused is in issue, the complainant is concealing the identity of the real perpetrator, for the proving of presence of semen or vaginal fluid, and for establishing that the complainant was not a virgin before the sexual act'.[80] The Tanzanian, Zambian, Botswana[81] and Zimbabwean laws are silent on the aspect of prior sexual conduct.

Cautionary rule
The 'cautionary rule' is closely related to the requirement of corroboration in cases before the court, but operates differently in sexual violence cases. Under this rule the court is required to 'exercise additional care when assessing the credibility of uncorroborated testimony/evidence from the rape survivor'.[82] The Namibian and Lesotho laws expressly provide a mandatory obligation on judges not to exercise caution in relation to sexual violence cases.[83] The South African law leaves the discretion to the court by using the word 'may' and not 'shall'.[84] The position under Tanzanian law is different. It mirrors the position in the Rules of Procedure and Evidence of the International Criminal Tribunal for Rwanda (ICTR) in relation to the non-requirement of corroboration in cases of sexual violence.[85] The judges, after assessing the credibility of such evidence, can enter a conviction on the basis of uncorroborated evidence, provided the victim-witness's testimony is credible, even in cases where a child is involved.[86] This is a very progressive development and is not reflected in other countries under review.

Procedural protection
Many rape survivors are unwilling to report rape cases because of the adversarial and traumatizing nature of sexual violence case proceedings before the courts. In order to make the court environment more responsive to the victim-witnesses of

---

80   Section 26(1)(a) to (d) Sexual Offences Act (Lesotho).

81   The Criminal Procedure And Evidence Chapter 08:02 part XIV (K) (Botswana) provides for special rules of evidence in particular criminal cases without any reference to particular rules to be observed in rape and other sexual violence proceedings.

82   Nowrojee, B. and Manby, B. 1995. *Violence against women in South Africa: The state response to domestic violence and rape.* New York: Human Rights Watch.

83   Section 5 Combating of Rape Act (Namibia). See also section 18 of the Sexual Offences Act (Lesotho).

84   See section 60 Criminal Law (Sexual Offences and Related Matters) Amendment Act (South Africa). See also the judicial development in relation to the rule *S v Jackson* 1998 1 SACR 470; *Venghani v the State* 2007 SCA 76; Schwikkard, P.J. et al. 2009. *Principles of evidence.* 3rd Edition. Cape Town: Juta, 552–3.

85   Rule 96(i) of the ICTR Rules of Procedure and Evidence. UN Doc. ITR/3/REV.1 (1995).

86   Section 27 of Sexual Offences Special Provisions Act (Tanzania), which amends section 127 of the Evidence Act 1967.

rape and other sexual violence offences, laws have provided for exceptions to the general rules governing criminal proceedings.

A public trial is a right guaranteed to the accused subject to certain exceptions.[87] Several countries have reformed their laws pertaining to the public nature of trials, when witnesses are giving evidence in cases involving rape or sexual offence charges. The most notable is the Malawian (as applicable in domestic violence cases), and the Namibian and Lesotho laws, which provide for a restriction on the number of people who can participate in a rape trial, subject to the discretion of the judge upon the necessary application.[88] The laws further limit the right of the accused to a public trial.[89] In addition, such laws provide for a mandatory obligation not to publish any information that might reveal the identity of the complainant, with a penalty provided for any person who contravenes such a provision.[90]

The Tanzanian law provides for a mandatory requirement of in-camera proceedings for offences where a child is a witness, with this being optional for adult victim-witnesses, as well as for the non-publishing of information of the evidence and the identification of witnesses.[91] The South African law provides for a close-circuit television option during the process of giving evidence, which is granted upon application, or by the court on its own motion.[92] The laws in Zimbabwe, Botswana and Zambia do not have evidential or procedural provisions specifically enacted to govern proceedings of sexual violence trials.

Emergency medical treatment
The South African law is unique in respect of specific provisions for medical assistance to rape victims, and provides for free medical services at a public hospital to the victims who report the offence within 72 hours.[93] This includes

---

87   This is so provided in many constitutions around the world. See also article 14(1) of the International Covenant on Civil and Political Rights.

88   Section 15 Combating of Rape Act (Namibia), which amends section 154 of the Criminal Procedure Act 51 of 1977; section 23 Sexual Offences Act (Lesotho); section 47 Prevention of Domestic Violence Act (Malawi).

89   See the acts mentioned in preceding footnote and section 153(7) of the Criminal Procedure Act 51 of 1977, as amended by section 14 of the Combating of Rape Act (Namibia).

90   Section 154 Criminal Procedure Act 51 of 1977, as amended by section 14 of the Combating of Rape Act (Namibia); section 25 Sexual Offences Act (Lesotho). The penalty for publishing information about the complainant's identity without proper permission is a stiff fine or imprisonment for up to one year, or both.

91   Section 24 Sexual Offences Special Provisions Act (Tanzania), which amends section 186 of the Criminal Procedure Act of 1985; section 25 Sexual Offences Act (Lesotho).

92   Section 158 Criminal Procedure Act (South Africa).

93   Section 28(1) Criminal Law (Sexual Offences and Related Matters) Amendment Act (South Africa).

medication such as Post-Exposure Prophylaxis (PEP) for the prevention of HIV infections.[94] As mentioned above, section 43 of the Malawian Domestic Violence law imposes a general obligation, where necessary, for medical treatment for victims of domestic violence.

Sentencing provisions
All the laws under review provide for penalties that include imprisonment for the offence of rape. The Namibian, Lesotho and South African laws have differentiated the term of imprisonment between first, second and subsequent convictions. For the first conviction in Namibia the imprisonment term ranges from five to 15 years depending on the circumstances of the offence, the age of the victim and whether the offender is infected with serious sexually transmitted diseases,[95] and from ten to 45 years for subsequent convictions.[96] The South African law provides for a minimum sentence of ten to 25 years imprisonment depending on whether the conviction was for the first time or for a subsequent conviction.[97] The law provides for life imprisonment for rape that meets the requirements of aggravated circumstances, including, gang rape, multiple rape, and a perpetrator with HIV/AIDS.[98] Part VII of the Lesotho law provides for the penalties to be imposed upon conviction of different forms of sexual violence.[99]

In Tanzania, the sentence for rape is not less than 30 years imprisonment accompanied by corporal punishment and a fine.[100] In cases of gang rape, each person convicted is sentenced to imprisonment for life, regardless of the role played.[101] In assessing the sentence to be imposed on a child offender, the judge also takes into consideration whether or not they are first time offenders.[102] The Zimbabwean and Zambian laws provide for life imprisonment for any act of rape; in Zambia this includes the crime of attempted rape.[103]

---

94   Section 28(2) Criminal Law Amendment Act (South Africa).

95   Section 3(a) Combating of Rape Act (Namibia).

96   Section 3(b) Combating of Rape Act (Namibia). Examples are where the rape in question or any other rape of which such person has previously been convicted was committed under any of the coercive circumstances to imprisonment for a period of not less than twenty years; where the rape in question or any other rape of which such person has previously been convicted was committed under to a victim younger than 13 years to imprisonment for a period of not less than forty-five years.

97   Section 1 of the Criminal Law (Sentencing) Amendment Act 38 of 2007 (South Africa).

98   Section 1 of the Criminal Law Amendment Act 38 (South Africa).

99   Sexual Offences Act (Lesotho).

100   Section 6 Sexual Offences Special Provisions Act (Tanzania), which amends section 131 of the Penal Code.

101   Section 7 Sexual Offences Special Provisions Act (Tanzania).

102   Section 6(2) Sexual Offences Special Provisions Act (Tanzania).

103   Section 65 Criminal Law (Codification and Reform) Act (Zimbabwe); sections 133 and 134 Penal Code Act (Zambia).

The evidentiary and procedural rules applicable to rape cases reflect attempts to avoid re-traumatization, victimization and even stigmatization in the course of trial or upon its completion. The criminal justice system has been provided with mechanisms to protect the victims of rape and other forms of sexual violence, which are applicable during court proceedings in many Southern African countries. South Africa and Namibia have gone further, and have developed one-stop centres that provide both pre-trial and trial protection measures including the provision of anti-retroviral medication, psychological help and specialized investigative and prosecutorial services. South Africa also provides for witness protection programmes for rape victims. The provision of effective pre-, during-, and post-trial protective measures remains a challenge in the majority of countries.

Proposed law reform in Namibia and Swaziland

Namibia

The Combating of Rape Act was under review by the Law Reform and Development Commission at the time of writing as a result of reform proposals submitted by a public interest non-governmental organization (NGO) that identified the gaps in the newly enacted law when compared to legislation in countries including Lesotho and Kenya.[104] The NGO submission envisions a comprehensive piece of legislation and proposes the following reforms:

- Including the crime of rape of persons with physical or mental disabilities, and the imposition of the highest category of minimum sentence for such crimes.
- Making attempts to commit a rape in terms of the statute subject to the same minimum penalties.
- Placing limits on what portion of a minimum sentence must be served before an offender is eligible for parole.
- Specifically requiring that the prosecutor shall ensure that the complainant receives orientation to the court and court procedures prior to the trial.
- Including, in the definition of 'coercive circumstances' in section 2 of the Act 'abuse of power or authority to the extent that the person in respect of whom an act is committed is inhibited from indicating his or her resistance to such acts or his or her unwillingness to participate in such an act'.

---

104 Namibian Law Reform and Development Commission. 2009. *Discussion Paper No. 1, Project No. 17: Reforming the Rape Act*. Proposals for reform were submitted by the Legal Assistance Centre.

Swaziland

The laws relevant to the prosecution of crimes of domestic and sexual violence date back to 1889.[105] The Sexual Offences and Domestic Violence Bill has been pending since 2006.[106] The bill has provisions addressing marital rape, the indecent treatment of children that does not include penetration, sexual harassment, and trafficking. There is little progress in the country in relation to gender-based violence legislation despite the advocacy efforts of both state and non-state actors (including the Government Gender Unit, CANGO (Coordinating Assembly of NGOs), the Gender Consortium and a UN Gender Theme group). The group drafted an action plan outlining the intended plan to mobilize all sectors of society in the fight against gender violence.[107] Some reasons advanced for the lack of progress include poor coordination and the lack of funding.[108]

The law reform process followed in South Africa, Tanzania and Namibia

South Africa

The law reform process in respect of the new Sexual Offences and Related Matters Amendment Act can be traced back as far as 1998. It was triggered by a LLM (Master of Laws) thesis and proposal submitted to the Law Reform Commission[109] by a student.[110] The Commission concluded that there was a need to address laws on sexual violence against children and adults, including the definition of the crime of rape.[111] Extensive public consultations were held with civil society broadly. The reform bill was tabled in parliament in 2003 but there was very little or no follow-up for almost two years.[112] It was revived in 2006 following the efforts of the National Working Group on Sexual Offences, coupled with pressure from

---

105   The Crimes Act 1889 and the Girls' and Women's Protection Act 1920 (Swaziland); The Criminal Procedure and Evidence Act No. 67 of 1938 (Swaziland).

106   Amnesty International. 2009.

107   Aphane, D. and Mkhatshwa, N. 2009. *SADC Gender Protocol Barometer Baseline Study Swaziland*. [Online] Available at: http://www.genderlinks.org.za/item.php?i_id=217 [accessed 7 October 2009].

108   Aphane and Mkhatshwa. 2009.

109   The South African Law Reform Commission (SALRC) was established by the South African Law Reform Commission Act 19 of 1973 (the Act). Information about the SALRC is available at: http://www.justice.gov.za/salrc [accessed 10 July 2010].

110   Artz, L. and Smythe, D. 2008. Introduction: Should we consent?, in *Should We Consent? Rape Law Reform in South Africa*, edited by L. Artz and D. Smythe. Cape Town: Juta, 1–21, at 4.

111   Artz and Smythe. 2008, 5.

112   Combrinck, H. 2006. Well worth the wait? The sexual offences bill 2006. *South Africa Crime Quarterly*, 17(1), 1–6.

other civil societies including the Western Cape Consortium on Violence against Women. The goal of such advocates was the prioritization of the law reform process and the inclusion of specific crucial provisions.[113] Submissions were also made by the Centre for Applied Legal Studies University of Witwatersrand,[114] the National Association of Democratic Lawyers' and Women's Legal Centre,[115] Rape Crisis[116] and the Transformative Human Rights Unit/Southern African Media and Gender Institute.[117] These efforts shaped and influenced different sections of the law including protective measures for victims.

Challenges

The South African law reform process faced many delays and challenges. This included in particular the lack of a clear consensus between the Law Reform Commission and parliament. In 2003, following a briefing by the Commission, parliament did not approve and adopt some of the contents of the Sexual Offences Bill. The Commission was tasked with evaluating the cost effectiveness of several measures, and ultimately they were not included in the final law. The reform process was also challenged by a lack of information dissemination about the status of reform process to civil society generally, and to the advocates mentioned above, in particular. For two years parliament was silent as regards the draft law and this created tension and anxieties among civil society advocates.[118] Factors such as these resulted in the law reform process lasting ten years.

The outcome of the legislative reform process has brought significant changes to the laws regulating sexual violence in South Africa.[119] In spite of the achievements, the law has not embraced a victim-oriented approach that meets international best practices standards. It has not incorporated significant witness protection measures,[120] such as trauma crisis and counselling support, availability of the morning-after pill to prevent unwanted pregnancies, legal representation

---

113   Artz and Smythe. 2008, 7.

114   Centre for Applied Legal Studies University of Witwatersrand. 2006.

115   Chisala, S. 2008. Rape and HIV/AIDS: Who's protecting whom? in *Artz and Smythe*. 2008, 52–71, at 60.

116   Rape Crisis. IDASA. 2003. *Submission to the National Assembly*. [Online] Available at: http://www.pmg.org.za [accessed 10 October 2009].

117   Transformative Human Rights Unit/Southern African Media and Gender Institute. 2003. *Submission to the National Assembly*. [Online] Available at: http://www.pmg.org.za [accessed 10 October 2009].

118   Combrinck. 2006, 1.

119   Sexual Offences Act 23 of 1957 (South Africa); Correctional Services Act 8 of 1959; Criminal Procedure Act 51 of 1977; Prevention of Organized Crimes Act 121 of 1998.

120   Artz and Smythe. 2008, 6.

for victims,[121] and other rights pertaining to the judicial process.[122] All these were excluded on the basis of limited resources,[123] despite the fact that victims of sexual violence are subjected to acts that have a significant psychological impact.[124]

Successes

The South African law reform process has succeeded in changing the traditional definition of rape, and now encompasses the current developments in international and regional contexts. It has moved away from the usual vagina–penis sexual intercourse definition to include penetration effected by objects, other body parts and even animals.[125] The new law also shifts attention from the absence of consent to an emphasis on the presence of coercive circumstances in rape cases.[126] In addition, it caters for sexual offences against children and those who are mentally ill.[127]

The reform process also included some of the victims' interests. The most notable development in this regard is the availability of state-sponsored medical services.[128] For example, the police official to whom the charge is made or a medical practitioner or a nurse to whom the incident is reported has a duty to inform the victim of the importance of obtaining PEP to prevent HIV infection, within 72 hours after the alleged sexual offence took place, and the need to obtain medical advice and assistance regarding the possibility of other sexually transmitted infections.[129] Considering the current world pandemic of HIV/AIDS and the risks of infection that acts of sexual violence, particularly rape, carry with them, the law reform process has also addressed other aspects of the problem, such as the mandatory testing of sexual offenders if requested by the victim[130] or by the investigating officer.[131]

---

121   Combrinck, H. 2008. Claims and Entitlements or Smoke and Mirrors? Victims' Rights in the Sexual Offences Act, in *Artz and Smythe*. 2008, 262–82, at 271.

122   This includes victims' right to express their opinion and have such opinion taken seriously in all issues affecting them and to be informed of all decisions.

123   Combrinck. 2008, 272. See also Artz and Smythe. 2008, 6.

124   Dennis, M.F. et al. 2009. Evaluation of lifetime trauma, exposure and physical health in women with Posttraumatic Stress Disorder or Major Depressive Disorder. *Violence Against Women*, 15(5), 618–27, at 619.

125   Section 2 Criminal Law (Sexual Offences and Related Matters) Amendment Act (South Africa).

126   Section 3 Criminal Law Amendment Act (South Africa).

127   Chapter 3 and 4 Criminal Law Amendment Act (South Africa).

128   Chapter 5 Criminal Law Amendment Act (South Africa). See sections 28(2)(a) and (b) for the requirements to be met, that is laying a charge with the police and reporting an incident, for a victim to be entitled to PEP.

129   Section 28(3) Criminal Law Amendment Act (South Africa).

130   Section 30 Criminal Law Amendment Act (South Africa).

131   Section 32 Criminal Law Amendment Act (South Africa).

The reform process has limited the application of the cautionary rule. The common law provisions dealing with prior sexual conduct have been changed and the new law does not allow evidence of previous sexual conduct to be adduced.[132] The law also provides for the exclusion of questions to any witness before the court, pertaining to the prior sexual conduct of the victim, unless leave is granted.[133] Significantly, in its preamble, the law has recognized the vulnerability of children in becoming the victims of sexual violence, and a separate section dealing with sexual violence against children in its various forms,[134] including provisions relating to statutory rape, is included herein.[135]

Another development in South Africa has been the setting up of multi-sectoral specialized prosecution units. The Thuthuzela Care Centres (TCCs) were designed and implemented by the National Prosecuting Authority (NPA), together with the departments of Health, Social Development and Justice and Constitutional Development, as well as the South African Police Services. Services offered involve the following:

- An explanation of how the medical examination will be conducted and what clothing might be taken for evidence.
- A consent form to sign, which allows the doctor to conduct the medical examination.
- Facilities to have a bath or shower at the centre after the medical examination.
- An investigation officer to interview the survivor and take his/her statement.
- A social worker or nurse to offer counselling. A nurse to arrange for follow-up visits, treatment and medication for Sexually Transmitted Infections (STIs) such as HIV and AIDS.
- A referral letter or appointment to be made for long-term counselling.
- Transportation home for the survivor by an ambulance or the investigating officer.
- Arrangements are made for the survivor to go to a place of safety, if necessary.
- Consultations with a specialist prosecutor, before the case goes to court.

It has been argued that the TCC's have enabled a 'dramatic drop in the time spent to investigate, prosecute and convict perpetrators', and that offender conviction rates are increasing as a result.[136]

---

132 Amendment article 11 of schedule to the Criminal Law Amendment Act (South Africa).

133 Amendment article 11.

134 Chapter 3 Criminal Law Amendment Act (South Africa).

135 Section 15 Criminal Law Amendment Act (South Africa).

136 UNICEF. Undated. *Thuthuzela Care Centres.* [Online] Information available at: http://www.unicef.org/southafrica/hiv_aids_998.html [accessed 20 October 2009].

Tanzania

The Law Reform Commission of Tanzania initiated a project titled 'Criminal law as a vehicle for the protection of the right to personal integrity, dignity and liberty of women', which ultimately led to the reform of relevant laws governing sexual violence against women following a seven year research and public consultation process between 1991 and 1998.[137] It included consultation with the population in the twenty regions of Tanzania, the courts, relevant NGOs and the Legal Aid Committee of the faculty of law of the University of Dar es Salaam.[138] The reform process focused on relevant areas that included evidentiary issues, sentencing, mandatory compensation, sexual harassment and female genital mutilation.[139] Unlike the South African and Namibian reform process, the Tanzanian process did not make the redefinition of the crime of rape a priority. In fact the definition section of the relevant law on rape is focused mostly on identifying the factors that indicate the absence of consent for sexual intercourse. A likely explanation for this may be that the reform took place in 1998, when legal developments in the region were not as gender responsive.

Challenges
The law reform process in Tanzania failed to define the crime of rape in a broader and more encompassing manner, to reflect the developments in international and regional arenas. In addition, there is no provision prohibiting the adducing of evidence of prior sexual conduct of the victim. The law also fails to articulate the link between HIV/AIDS and sexual violence, and hence there are no provisions in respect of provision of medication or testing of the victim and accused. The Commission proposed that compensation claims could be made and also that the death penalty would be applicable, where a victim contracts HIV/AIDS but these provisions were not included in the law that was subsequently passed.[140] The Tanzanian reform process also failed to provide victims with support services, including trauma and counselling support. Although the reform proposal report had one clause providing that costs for such services 'be borne by the government and to be recovered the same from the convict',[141] this was not incorporated in the final Act.

---

137 Law Reform Commission of Tanzania. 1998. *Report on Criminal Law as a Vehicle for the Protection of the Right to Personal Integrity, Dignity and Liberty of Women.* Presented to the Ministry of Justice and Constitutional Affairs.
138 Law Reform Commission of Tanzania. 1998, 10 and 11.
139 Law Reform Commission of Tanzania. 1998.
140 Law Reform Commission of Tanzania. 1998, 14.
141 Law Reform Commission of Tanzania. 1998, 14.

Successes

The law reform process succeeded in reforming certain sexual violence laws
including the Tanzanian Penal Code, the Criminal Procedure Act,[142] the Tanzanian
Evidence Act,[143] the Children and Young Persons Ordinance[144] and the Minimum
Sentences Act.[145] These amendments have led to the inclusion of other forms of
sexual violence against women and children, including the express prohibition and
criminalization of female genital mutilation.

Overall the reforms address the gaps in the law and provide the possibility of
ensuring women's right to personal integrity, dignity and liberty. It is important
to acknowledge also the important role played by NGOs such as TAMWA, the
Tanzania Law Society, the Tanzania Women's Lawyers Association, the Media
Women's Association of Tanzania, the Women's Association Research and
Documentation Project of the University of Dar es Salaam, SUWATA, Zanzibar
Legal Aid Body and others. Their submissions included crucial information on
discriminatory practices against women and how these needed to be remedied.[146]

Namibia

The major law reform process in Namibia led to the enactment of the Combating
of Rape Act[147] and the Combating of Domestic Violence Act.[148] Other areas of law
such as the Combating of Immoral Practices Amendment Act,[149] and the Labour
Act[150] have been amended to address the growing problem of sexual harassment.
The Criminal Procedure Act has also been amended to provide protection for
vulnerable witnesses, particularly child victims of sexual violence.[151]

---

142   Part III Sexual Offences Special Provisions Act No. 4 1998 (Tanzania), which has
amended the proceedings involving sexual violence charges to give an option for witness
protection measure and requiring mandatory compensation in cases of sexual violence.

143   Part IV Sexual Offences Special Provisions Act (Tanzania) has limited the
requirement of corroboration in cases of sexual violence.

144   Part V Sexual Offences Special Provisions Act (Tanzania) has provided for a
mandatory requirement of in camera proceedings where the victim-witness of sexual
violence is a child.

145   Part VI Sexual Offences Special Provisions Act (Tanzania) provides for the
requirement of adhering to the new sentences provided in the SOSPA which has increased
the term of imprisonment for sexual offences with or without fine and an addition to
mandatory compensation.

146   Law Reform Commission of Tanzania. 1998, 28–9.

147   Combating of Rape Act (Namibia).

148   Combating of Domestic Violence Act (Namibia).

149   The Combating of Immoral Practices Act Amendment Act 7 of 2000 (Namibia).

150   Labour Act 6 of 1992 (Namibia).

151   Criminal Procedure Amendment Act 24 of 2004 (Namibia).

The reform of laws governing rape in Namibia was as a result of advocacy efforts by different NGOs[152] and activists, including the Legal Assistance Centre and the Law Society of Namibia.[153] The process began in 1996 through the Project on Violence Against and Abuse of Women and Children launched by the Women and Law Committee of the Law Reform and Development Commission.[154] It was solidified by a public demonstration organized by the Multi-Media Campaign on Violence against Women and Children in 1997 following the rape of a young girl.[155] Discussions and debates ensued in parliament and the law governing rape was passed in 2000. As indicated above, the current law is undergoing a process of reform.

The reform process of the Combating of Domestic Violence Act followed a more consultative process. It involved country visits, study of laws governing domestic violence, regional hearings and consultation of materials governing domestic violence, including model legislative approaches prepared by the UN Special Rapporteur on Violence against Women.[156] Advocacy efforts came from different groups including the Namibian women's movement,[157] the Legal Assistance Centre,[158] Women's Action for Development, Namibia Women's Voice, the Women's Political Manifesto Network[159] and the initiative from the Multi-

152   Legal Assistance Centre. 2006. *Rape in Namibia: An Assessment of the Operation of the Combating of Rape Act.* [Online] Available at: http://www.lac.org.na/projects/grap/Pdf/rapefull.pdf [accessed 7 October 2009], 68. In 1993 '[a] petition which included specific requests for the reform of the law on rape was signed by ten different NGOs and presented to the Minister of Justice as part of the commemoration of International Women's Day in March 1993'. Another proposal was tendered in 1994 signed by representatives from five government ministries and 10 NGOs. In 1995 following an attempted rape of a woman journalist in Windhoek, the Namibia Media Women's Association presented a petition to the Law Reform & Development Commission for reforming laws governing rape.

153   Legal Assistance Centre. 2006.

154   Legal Assistance Centre. 2006, 69. The reform comprised of 'research by legal and social science researchers, regional workshops coordinated by the Namibia National Women's Organization (NANAWO) in conjunction with NGOs, churches, traditional leaders and regional and local councils, a nation-wide public hearing and a national conference'.

155   Legal Assistance Centre. 2006.

156   Legal Assistance Centre. *Combating of Domestic Violence Act* (forthcoming. Draft on file with authors).

157   Legal Assistance Centre. Forthcoming. The group 'employed intensive lobbying to raise public awareness of the problem of domestic violence, and to move the draft legislation forward'.

158   Legal Assistance Centre. Forthcoming. The centre 'hosted a successful national conference for men against violence against women, ran a public awareness campaign on domestic violence during 2001–2002 and provided a half-day workshop on the Bill in January 2003 for members of the Multi-Media Campaign to explain the Bill in detail so that different groups could lobby from a more thoroughly-informed position'.

159   Legal Assistance Centre. Forthcoming.

Media Campaign.[160] Following heated discussions and debates in parliament (by mostly male members of parliament), the law was passed.[161] It comprehensively addresses different forms of domestic violence against women, including economic, physical and sexual abuse, harassment (including stalking) and emotional, verbal or psychological abuse.[162]

Challenges
The Namibian law fails to provide for HIV testing of the accused despite suggestions from some parliamentarians,[163] and is silent on the provision of medical services and HIV/AIDS preventative drugs. According to the Minster of Health & Social Services, 'PEP is available at all district hospitals in Namibia. PEP works only if it is taken immediately after the rape and continued regularly for 1 month. The course of medicine MUST begin within 72 hours of the rape (the sooner the better), or it will not work'.[164] This seems to imply that access to medication is a right for victims of sexual violence.

Successes
The law has widened the definition of rape,[165] and abolished the cautionary rule, and the practice of using evidence or asking questions relating to prior sexual behaviour of the complainant.[166] Limitations have also been imposed on public trials and the publication of information that reveals the victim's identity.[167] The Namibian law on rape has also addressed the link between HIV and rape by providing that HIV-positive status be regarded as an aggravated circumstance to be considered in sentencing.[168]

A further significant feature is the fact that the Namibian rape law specifically allows for expert evidence of the psychological effects of rape to be adduced. This provision is often found in the general criminal procedure laws of other countries and affirms the general findings of jurisprudence from international

---

160   Legal Assistance Centre. Forthcoming.
161   Legal Assistance Centre. Forthcoming.
162   Section 2(1) Combating of Domestic Violence Act (Namibia).
163   Legal Assistance Centre. Forthcoming.
164   Combrinck. 2006, 310.
165   Section 1 of Combating of Rape Act (Namibia) defines sexual act to include: '(a) the insertion (to even the slightest degree) of the penis of a person into the vagina or anus or mouth of another person; or (b) the insertion of any other part of the body of a person or of any part of the body of an animal or of any object into the vagina or anus of another person, except where such insertion of any part of the body (other than the penis) of a person or of any object into the vagina or anus of another person is, consistent with sound medical practices, carried out for proper medical purposes; or (c) cunnilingus or any other form of genital stimulation'.
166   Section 18 Combating of Rape Act (Namibia).
167   Section 15 Combating of Rape Act (Namibia).
168   Section 3(1)(a)(iii)(dd) Combating of Rape Act (Namibia).

tribunals. In the *Akayesu* case, the court stated, *inter alia*, that gender-based crimes are the worst ways of inflicting bodily and mental harm on the victim.[169] This statement buttresses the degree of mental harm suffered by the victim and helps in determining the appropriate sentence.[170] Protective measures relating to victims were addressed in the subsequent reform of the Criminal Procedure Act. The amendments provided for different measures including testifying behind a one-way screen or by means of closed-circuit television and specific measures for child witnesses.[171] It also takes into account the victims' right to participate in trial proceedings[172] and receive reparation.[173] This is a provision that has been advocated in the international arena since the formation of the ad hoc tribunals, and that finally became a reality under the ICC.[174] The Namibian law requires the victim or the victim's legal practitioner, or the prosecutor acting on the instructions of the victim, to lodge the request for compensation.[175]

Conclusion

All states have an obligation to protect, promote and fulfil rights, whether derived from national, regional or international instruments.[176] In the past decade within the Southern African region, sexual violence laws have undergone a considerable degree of change, both in terms of substance and procedure. Some of the reasons for such developments include: the increase in crimes of a sexual nature committed against both women and girls; the inadequacy of content and procedural aspects

---

169   *Prosecutor v Akayesu*, para. 731.

170   Combrinck. 2006, 110.

171   Section 158(A)(2)(d) and (6), Criminal Procedure Amendment Act No. 24 of 2004 (Namibia). The trial can be held in an alternative venue and support person can accompany witnesses while they are testifying.

172   Section 18 Criminal Procedure Amendment Act (Namibia) provides that a victim of any offence against person or property may appoint a private legal practitioner (at the victim's own expense) to represent the victim's interests at the criminal trial of the offence which caused the injury, damage or loss to the victim.

173   Section 326 Criminal Procedure Amendment Act (Namibia).

174   See in particular article 68 of the ICC Rome Statute.

175   Section 326 Criminal Procedure Amendment Act (Namibia).

176   Committee on the Elimination of Discrimination against Women. 2008. *General Recommendation No. 19 (11th Session, 1992)*. Compilation of General Comments and Recommendations adopted by Human Rights Treaty Bodies. UN Doc. HRI/GEN/I/Rev.9, 331–6. Human Rights Committee. 2004. *General Comment 31: Nature of the general legal obligation on states parties to the Covenant*. UN Doc. CCPR/C/21/Rev.1/Add.13 (2004), para. 8, provides that states must 'exercise due diligence to prevent, punish, investigate or redress the harm caused by acts by private persons or entities which amount to a violation of fundamental human rights'.

of existing legislation; and the positive developments in international criminal law generally, but in respect of sexual violence in particular.

The process of law reform in the countries considered above has been triggered by different motivations and actors. In some countries it was as a result of the external efforts of different interest groups and individuals, to address the high rate of crimes of sexual violence both in the public and domestic spheres. In other countries more formal initiatives were taken by the relevant law reform commissions in efforts to develop the area of sexual violence laws and procedures. The law reform process in the Southern African region involved different actors such as NGOs, civil societies, law reform commissions and the general population who played an important role in bringing about legislative changes. The role of regional and sub-regional bodies was also a significant contributory factor. This brought about shared goals on the need to reform laws governing violence against women as reflected in the declarations and protocol.

Some of the countries have provided more detailed provisions in the law governing sexual violence, yet other aspects still need review and amendment or addition. Notable examples of these are the provisions governing victims' participation, the registering of sexual offenders, female genital mutilation, HIV-related crimes, definition of rape, compensation and victim protection measures, medical and psychological support, evidence of psychological impacts of the crime of rape and laws governing domestic violence.

The success of law reform in the Southern African region has not been all smooth sailing. The process in the different countries has taken a long time – almost a decade in some instances. In other cases the end result has been a compromise between the adoption of particular provisions, and the use of excuses about a 'lack of resources'. Another important factor in the law reform process has been the persistence of activists and advocates that laws be reformed, that regional and international best practices be followed, and that accountability for sexual violence crimes be the norm. The many efforts at law reform in the sexual violence sector are a reflection of the broader goal to address the promotion and protection of women's human rights, by both state- and non-state actors.

Chapter 13

Future Perspectives: Debating Criminal Law Reform and Human Rights in Sudan

Lutz Oette

This chapter reflects on the main themes discussed during a seminar held in Kampala, Uganda, from 1 to 3 March 2010,[1] and highlights suggestions made on how best to address the challenges identified, particularly the need to:

(i)   'demystify' *Shari'a*, including by tackling the legacy of its use for political purposes, and by emphasizing both the fact that it is open to multiple interpretations and the need to move beyond *Shari'a* as currently propagated and applied in Sudan;

(ii) recognize the important role of international human rights standards, both as a yardstick for existing laws and as guide for reforms (with a particular focus on article 27(3) of the Bill of Rights);

(iii) 're-imagine' criminal law by restoring the integrity of the Sudanese legal system that has become an executive tool and subject to arbitrary abuse without sufficient judicial checks, necessitating both legal and institutional reforms;

(iv) develop a culture of accountability based on nationally generated solutions that build on regional and international efforts – such as the Mbeki Panel, commissions of inquiry and the International Criminal Court (ICC) – without overly depending on them;

(v)   adopt a holistic approach to gender-based violence that deconstructs the underlying views and stereotypes used to justify violence and discrimination, while making use of existing openings (such as debates regarding the reform of rape legislation) to influence public debates and change perceptions;

(vi) understand law reform as an ongoing process, and one that, in the absence of the rule of law – characterized by the separation of powers, functioning institutions and an independent judiciary – requires legal and political strategies aimed at generating public awareness and

---

1   The seminar was organized by REDRESS and co-hosted by the Strategic Initiative for Women in the Horn of Africa (SIHA). The occasion provided a forum for Sudanese and international participants to consider the legal and political challenges posed by the reform of criminal laws in Sudan in-depth, and from a human rights perspective.

debates that may provide the impetus for substantive reforms once circumstances become conducive.

Since its politically motivated introduction by the Nimeiri regime in 1983, *Shari'a* has served as a tool to justify repressive legislation. The association with *Shari'a* has made it more difficult to discuss these laws openly due to the risk of being accused of opposing Islam, even though there may be different interpretations of the nature and meaning of *Shari'a* in a given context. Even laws that are *ta'azir* (state-made), such as the punishment of whipping for a range of offences in the Criminal Act of 1991 and public order laws, have been portrayed as forming, or are perceived to form part of an order mandated by a particular understanding of religion. This background may explain why *Shari'a* has not figured prominently in reform debates during the Comprehensive Peace Agreement (CPA) interim period, with the exception of its application to Southern Sudanese, which indirectly served to reinforce its status in the North of the country. There is a growing recognition among those engaged in law reform that the subject of *Shari'a* needs to be addressed squarely. Such development would add an important dimension, namely situating *Shari'a* as being part of Sudan's plurality of laws whose interpretation and use is open to critical scrutiny and change. This has the potential to foster debates that may call into question the legitimacy of *Shari'a* as currently propagated and applied in Sudan, and thereby encourage a broader spectrum of views about the nature, content and form of Sudanese laws to emerge.

The Interim National Constitution (INC) provided an ideal opportunity for an increased reference to international human rights standards, which, by virtue of article 27(3) of the Bill of Rights contained therein, became an officially recognized yardstick for state conduct and Sudanese laws that have a bearing on human rights. However, the lack of subsequent substantial reforms to give effect to the Bill of Rights has been well documented. Several factors, particularly the dominance of the executive and the lack of an independent judiciary, combined with the limited capacity of various actors and the political dynamics leading up to the separation of the South, contributed to this development. Yet importantly, the prominence given to international human rights, at least on paper and in theory before the Constitutional Court, has provided the impetus that has opened Sudanese laws to scrutiny and challenges. The resulting debates questioned the law-making process and the legitimacy of laws falling short of requisite standards. Political protestations, objections raised by civil society and public demonstrations against the National Security Act of 2010, which failed to address long-standing human rights concerns and to guarantee applicable minimum standards, are cases in point. The constitutional review underway in both the North and South in early 2011 in anticipation of Southern Sudan's independence presented a vital test as to whether international human rights can retain its officially sanctioned constitutional status beyond the political arrangement embodied in the CPA. Irrespective of the outcome of constitutional rearrangements, relevant standards look set to remain an integral part of public debates surrounding Sudan's legal identity and future legal make-up.

Law, particularly in Sudan's criminal justice system, has frequently been used as an executive tool, and as a result is widely perceived to serve as an instrument of repression rather than one to provide security and justice. This includes emergency laws, counter-terrorism laws, public order legislation and the use of flogging as a punishment. Such laws have been complemented by criminal procedural laws and national security legislation that facilitate arbitrary arrest and detention, and fail to guarantee fair trials in the absence of a genuinely independent judiciary. This development poses the challenge of how to restore the integrity of law in a system that has eroded its basic tenets and undermined key institutions, notably the judiciary. The Sudanese Constitutional Court, which was set up as an integral part of the INC, has proved unable to fulfil the task of countering repressive legislation and fostering a substantive rule of law because it ultimately remained rooted in existing power structures. This is in marked contrast to countries such as Uganda and South Africa where constitutional courts have acted as guardians of constitutional rights in relation to repressive laws, and to the right to liberty, security and a fair trial respectively. Tensions between these courts and political realities are evident in both these countries, however it is arguably the very ability to develop a stance that is both principled and authoritative that gives constitutional courts legitimacy in such circumstances. The failure of Sudan's Constitutional Court to act likewise points to the need for a more fundamental rethink and reform of existing structures, which at its core concerns the question of the role of law and the effective protection of rights in society.

Justice and accountability for international crimes and other human rights violations in Sudan has been a recurring demand over the last twenty years. However, the absence of national avenues, limited international desire to act, and its omission in the CPA all contributed to suppressing the issue. This has changed dramatically following the United Nations (UN) Security Council referral of the Darfur situation to the ICC, which provided the impetus for Sudan to embark on several reforms. The apparent aim of these measures was to demonstrate that Sudan was capable of investigating and prosecuting those responsible for international crimes in line with the principle of complementarity. Yet a close analysis of the Armed Forces Act of 2007 and the amended Criminal Act of 2009, which for the first time incorporated international crimes into Sudanese laws, reveals a number of shortcomings and inconsistencies in light of relevant international standards. The nature of the reforms, including the absence of concomitant changes to enhance accountability, such as the abolition of immunity laws, appears ill-suited to combat the prevailing impunity effectively. The establishment of the African Union High-Level Panel on Darfur (Mbeki Panel) represented in this context an important regional effort to address the question of justice and accountability, including its relationship with peace and reconciliation, by taking into consideration the views of a range of Sudanese actors. The Mbeki panel report of 2009 appeared to provide an opportunity for Sudanese lawyers and activists to effectively advocate Sudanese approaches to deal with the issues raised. However, by early 2011 frustration had mounted over the lack of progress in implementing the justice component of the recommendations made. Other regional factors and developments are instructive in this context. The role of Arab states and their position towards international criminal law, including the ICC, has been ambivalent. Even where a state is party to the ICC Rome Statute, implementing an effective national legal framework has proved difficult, as the Jordanian experience demonstrates. The Great Lakes Pact, in contrast, seemingly evinces political commitment that resulted in an impressive normative framework aimed at ensuring justice and accountability for international crimes. However, actors have made little use of it in national reform debates, and the institutional weakness of the mechanism risks undermining its potency. While these developments highlight the challenges facing international criminal law in the region, it is equally clear that the question of justice and accountability plays an increasingly prominent role, as has been evident in the course of the political revolutions sweeping North Africa and the Middle East. Measures taken in the Sudanese situation have failed to provide an adequate response; however, the recurring demands made in the context of the various conflicts and transitional justice debates in Sudan underline the fact that the question of justice and accountability has become a reality that the actors concerned ignore at their peril.

'Gendered justice' is deeply embedded in Sudan's legal system. This applies particularly to statutory laws that have enshrined discrimination, as well as customary laws. Legislation is marked by a combination of a lack of protection against gender-based violence, and various types of direct and indirect discrimination that have resulted in the oppression of girls and women. Laws on rape and sexual violence are a stark illustration of this reality. The confusion between zina (adultery/fornication) and rape, the lack of prohibition of marital rape, and prevailing views that see rape as a crime against honour rather than a crime of violence have undermined strategies to effectively combat gender-based violence. Women's rights groups have become increasingly vocal in challenging gender-based discrimination and injustices in Sudan. One element of this mobilization has been dialogue with women's rights groups in the region and beyond. Pakistan's experience is instructive here, in which laws on rape that had some similarity with Sudan's current legislation were changed as a result of sustained campaigns. It also illustrates the fact that legislative changes are but one component, although one of particular importance, in the broader struggle for women's rights. In this context, debates surrounding gender and the law in Uganda can serve as a reminder that dislodging the prevailing mindsets that may stifle reforms, including the recognition of women's rights as rights, frequently constitute an essential prerequisite for making progress in this struggle.

Law reform is a complex process, informed by the political and societal dynamics and the legal system of a country, and frequently influenced by a series of internal and external actors and factors. Experience shows that it is more than a linear, 'rational' process in which a body specifically tasked with law reform generates or takes up proposals for particular reforms that are subsequently adopted. It may therefore appear misplaced to put too much emphasis on such bodies. However, law reform commissions can, and often do have important roles in initiating or framing processes of law reform, as the Ugandan and South African experiences demonstrate. The South African Law Commission, for example, changed its stance from a rule by law, black-letter position during apartheid to recourse to innovative approaches such as in the field of gender-based violence thereafter, reflecting broader societal changes. Law reform commissions can be a useful resource and can contribute to the public debate in a stable political state. They may have a lesser role to play in situations such as in Sudan, where substantial reforms are hampered by the political circumstances. Nevertheless, a strengthening of the institutional framework for the process of law reform would have the advantage of, or at least the potential for greater transparency, co-ordination and quality of law-making. Beyond institutional considerations, and taking a broader perspective, law is a useful site for struggle that can create space for debate, with law reform efforts being part of a broader civil society mobilization and set of political strategies. The South African experience during Apartheid suggests that the campaigns and debates about law reform, though seemingly futile at the time, created an important parallel discourse. They contributed to undermining the legitimacy of an unjust system and paved the way for later changes to be based on a firm commitment to human rights. This experience is significant for Sudan at a time when the North and the South of the country are poised to become separate states, albeit ones with a common legacy and a common challenge of how to develop or reform their respective legal systems in the face of changed circumstances. This carries the potential for joint efforts and a constructive exchange of experiences if the political will can be generated to build on positive legacies, individual expertise and collective experiences to address the myriad challenges identified throughout this book.

Index

investigations 251–2
Jehan Mina case 248–9, 258
licence to abuse 250–51
non-Muslims 255–6
pregnancy as evidence 249–50
role of women 252–3